T0213646

Lecture Notes
in Business Information Processing   **289**

Series Editors

Wil M.P. van der Aalst
  Eindhoven Technical University, Eindhoven, The Netherlands
John Mylopoulos
  University of Trento, Trento, Italy
Michael Rosemann
  Queensland University of Technology, Brisbane, QLD, Australia
Michael J. Shaw
  University of Illinois, Urbana-Champaign, IL, USA
Clemens Szyperski
  Microsoft Research, Redmond, WA, USA

More information about this series at http://www.springer.com/series/7911

Esma Aïmeur · Umar Ruhi
Michael Weiss (Eds.)

E-Technologies: Embracing the Internet of Things

7th International Conference, MCETECH 2017
Ottawa, ON, Canada, May 17–19, 2017
Proceedings

 Springer

Editors
Esma Aïmeur
Université de Montréal
Montreal, QC
Canada

Michael Weiss
Carleton University
Ottawa, ON
Canada

Umar Ruhi
University of Ottawa
Ottawa, ON
Canada

ISSN 1865-1348   ISSN 1865-1356 (electronic)
Lecture Notes in Business Information Processing
ISBN 978-3-319-59040-0   ISBN 978-3-319-59041-7 (eBook)
DOI 10.1007/978-3-319-59041-7

Library of Congress Control Number: 2017940249

Printed on acid-free paper

This Springer imprint is published by Springer Nature
The registered company is Springer International Publishing AG
The registered company address is: Gewerbestrasse 11, 6330 Cham, Switzerland

Preface

The successful implementation, deployment, and exploitation of Internet applications, ranging from omni-channel e-commerce, to e-health, e-learning, e-government, social media, smart logistics, and smart infrastructures, requires a multidisciplinary approach to explore the range of technological, managerial, economic, cognitive, social, ethical, and legal issues.

The seventh edition of the International MCETECH Conference on e-Technologies aimed to bring together researchers and practitioners interested in exploring the many facets of Internet applications and technologies – with a primary focus on technological and managerial issues, but also a keen interest in social, ethical, and legal issues. Original and interdisciplinary approaches were actively sought and highly encouraged.

The seventh edition of MCETECH was held in Ottawa, Canada, during May 17–19, 2017. This year's conference drew special attention to the ever-increasing role of the Internet of Things (IoT) in the service of individuals, organizations, and businesses. In response to our call, we received several papers directly tied to the theme of pervasive computing and smart applications. Additionally, this year's conference also featured contributions related to security, privacy and trust, process modeling and adaptation, and data analytics and machine learning. The conference papers spanned a variety of application domains such as e-Commerce, e-Health, e-Learning, and e-Justice, and they comprised a diverse scope of research ranging from models and architectures, methodology proposals, prototype implementations, and empirical validation of theoretical models.

We received a total of 48 submissions. Each paper was reviewed by three members of the Program Committee following a double-blind review process. The papers were judged based on relevance, originality, soundness, and presentation. Following the review process, 19 high-quality contributions were selected for presentation at the conference and for publication in this volume.

As in previous years, the main scientific conference program of MCETECH 2017 was accompanied by a rich tutorial program that offered an interactive exploration of various topics such as IoT applications, business analytics dashboards, agile business rules development, and context-aware systems in healthcare.

We would like to thank all the authors who submitted papers, the members of the Steering Committee and the Program Committee as well as the external reviewers. We also express our sincere gratitude to the Steering Committee Chair, Hafedh Mili, for his enthusiasm and his invaluable help in organizing this conference. Furthermore, the conference program would not be complete without the help of our Conference Workshops and Tutorials Chair, Hamid Mcheick. We are also very grateful to Daniel Amyot, who helped us with the conference management system and acted as our industrial liaison. Finally, we thank the local organizers, including the many students who volunteered on the organization team. Together, all of them played a key role in making this year's MCETECH conference another successful event.

May 2017   Esma Aïmeur
                                                                                    Umar Ruhi
                                                                              Michael Weiss

Organization

The 7th International MCETECH Conference on e-Technologies (MCETECH 2017) received support from the following sponsors: Université du Québec à Montréal (UQÀM), Carleton University, and the Research Laboratory on e-Commerce Technologies (LATECE).

Conference Chair

Michael Weiss	Carleton University, Canada

Steering Committee

Esma Aïmeur	Université de Montréal, Canada
Daniel Amyot	University of Ottawa, Canada
Gilbert Babin	HEC Montréal, Canada
Ygal Bendavid	Université du Québec à Montréal, Canada
Morad Benyoucef	University of Ottawa, Canada
Jean Bezivin	Université de Nantes, France
Yasmine Charif	Xerox, USA
Peter Kropf	Université de Neuchatel, Switzerland
Lamia Labed	Tunis University, Tunisia
Luigi Logrippo	Université du Québec en Outaouais, Canada
Hamid Mcheick	Université du Québec à Chicoutimi, Canada
Hafedh Mili	Université du Québec à Montréal, Canada (Chair)
Rokia Missaoui	Université du Québec en Outaouais, Canada
Naouel Moha	Université du Québec à Montréal, Canada
Liam Peyton	University of Ottawa, Canada

Program Committee Co-chairs

Esma Aïmeur	Université de Montréal, Canada
Umar Ruhi	University of Ottawa, Canada

Program Committee

Carlisle Adams	University of Ottawa, Canada
Isaac Agudo	University of Malaga, Spain
Imran Ahmad	Cloudanum Inc., Canada
Esma Aïmeur	Université de Montréal, Canada
Harith Alani	The Open University, UK
Daniel Amyot	University of Ottawa, Canada

Gilbert Babin	HEC Montréal, Canada
Nadjib Badache	Centre de recherche sur l'information scientifique et technique, Algeria
Michael Baron	Charles Sturt University, Australia
Ygal Bendavid	Université du Québec à Montréal, Canada
Djamal Benslimane	Institut universitaire de technologie de Lyon, France
Claudio Bettini	University of Milan, Italy
Jean Bezivin	Université de Nantes, France
Fabrizio Biondi	Inria, France
Cédric Bouhours	Université d'Auvergne, France
Amel Bouzeghoub	Institut Mines-Télécom, France
Sonia Camacho	Universidad de los Andes, Colombia
Dalila Chiadmi	Med V University Rabat, Morocco
Ritesh Chugh	Central Queensland University, Australia
Nora Cuppens	Télécom Bretagne, France
Kimiz Dalkir	McGill University, Canada
Ralph Deters	University of Saskatchewan, Canada
Albert Dipanda	Université de Bourgogne, France
Josep Ferrer Domingo	Universitat Rovira i Virgili, Catalonia, Spain
Aidan Duane	Waterford Institute of Technology, Ireland
Benjamin Fung	McGill University, Canada
Sébastien Gambs	Université du Québec à Montréal, Canada
Malek Ghenima	Université de la Manouba, Tunisia
Mahbub Sheikh Habib	Technische Universität Darmstadt, Germany
Hanane Houmani	Université Hassan II de Casablanca, Morocco
Ernesto Ruiz Jimenez	University of Oxford, UK
Laeeq Khan	Ohio University, USA
Peter Kropf	Université de Neuchatel, Switzerland
Lamia Labed	Tunis University, Tunisia
Louis Jean Lanet	Inria, France
Luigi Logrippo	Université du Québec en Outaouais, Canada
Zakaria Maamar	Zayed University, UAE
Hamid Mcheick	Université du Québec à Chicoutimi, Canada
Ali Miri	Ryerson University, Canada
Rokia Missaoui	Université du Québec en Outaouais, Canada
Bamshad Mobasher	DePaul University, USA
Iqbal Mohomed	Samsung Research America, USA
Liam Peyton	University of Ottawa, Canada
Brena Felipe Ramón Pinero	Tecnológico de Monterrey, Mexico
Makan Pourzandi	Ericsson, Canada
Hamed Saremi Qahri	DePaul University, USA
Umar Ruhi	University of Ottawa, Canada
Imad Saleh	Université de Paris 8, France
Indra Seher	Central Queensland University, Australia
Farid Shirazi	Ryerson University, Canada
Sahbi Sidhom	Université de Lorraine, France

Vicenç Torra	University of Skövde, Sweden
Theo Tryfonas	University of Bristol, UK
Julita Vassileva	University of Saskatchewan, Canada
Quan Huy Vu	Victoria University, Australia
Edgar Weippl	Technische Universität Wien, Austria
Michael Weiss	Carleton University, Canada
Osmar Zaiane	University of Alberta, Canada
Justin Zhan	University of Nevada, USA
Ali Zolait	University of Bahrain, Bahrain

Workshops and Tutorials Chair

Hamid Mcheick   Université du Québec à Chicoutimi, Canada

Local Arrangements and Registration Chair

Michael Weiss   Carleton University, Canada

Additional Reviewers

Asan Agibetov	Mike Enescu	Abderrahmane Khiat
Olivier Decourbe	Tesleem Fagade	Abdelkrim Meziane

Contents

Data Analytics and Machine Learning

E-Health and E-Commerce

Pervasive Computing and Smart Applications

Acting as a Trustee for Internet of Agents in the Absence of Explicit Feedback

Abdullah Aref$^{(\boxtimes)}$ and Thomas Tran

School of Electrical Engineering and Computer Science,
Faculty of Engineering, University of Ottawa, Ottawa, ON, Canada
a.m.aref@ieee.org

Abstract. The Internet of Agents (IoA) is an emerging field of research that aims to combine the advantages of multi-agent systems and Internet of Things (IoT), by adding autonomy and smartness to, traditionally, naive things used in IoT. IoA can be used to interconnect agents of different multi-agent systems through web-like technologies or using Internet-like architecture. Trust management can be considered an essential component of successful interactions between autonomous agents in IoA, especially when agents cannot assure that potential interaction partners share the same core beliefs, or make accurate statements regarding their competencies and abilities. To date, most research in trust modeling has focused on mechanisms for agents to model the trustworthiness of potential interaction partners, to decide about which of them to interact with. However, slight consideration has been paid for going beyond trust evaluation to outline actions for directing trustees, instead of trustors, to build a higher level of trust and have a greater impact on the results of interactions. Reaching a higher degree of trust can be challenging, especially when explicit feedback is not available. This paper presents a trust establishment model that uses implicit feedback from trustors to modify the behavior of trustees to build a higher level of trust and have a greater impact on the results of interactions. The proposed model is evaluated through simulation, and results indicate that trustees empowered with our proposal have higher chances to be selected as interaction partners when such selection is based on trust.

Keywords: Trust management · Trust establishment · Multiagent systems · Internet of agents

1 Introduction

Recently, considerable research in the field of artificial intelligence has been conducted for designing intelligent software entities, capable of independent actions [1]. These agents are assumed to be self-interested, goal-driven, and with bounded abilities, which constrains them to work with other agents for accomplishing complex tasks [2]. Such collaboration leads to systems of multi-agents. Multi-agent systems (MASs), which are increasingly popular for modeling systems that are common in virtual contexts, such as e-commerce, smart building

© Springer International Publishing AG 2017
E. Aïmeur et al. (Eds.): MCETECH 2017, LNBIP 289, pp. 3–23, 2017.
DOI: 10.1007/978-3-319-59041-7_1

systems, and intelligent transportation systems [3]. Interconnecting agents of different MASs through web-like technologies or using Internet-like architecture can be referred to as Internet of Agents (IoA). By interconnecting those MASs, agents are not restricted to interact with others in the same subsystem; eventually, they well can interact with others in different subsystems.

In IoA, when agents cannot assure that potential interaction partners share the same core beliefs about the system, or make accurate statements regarding their competencies and abilities, trust is considered essential for making interactions effective. It is argued that when interaction are based on trust, trusted agents have better chances of being chosen as interaction partners and can raise the minimum reward they can obtain for their transactions [4]. However, trust often has to be acquired at a cost, which may be compensated if improved trustworthiness leads to further profitable interactions [5]. Therefore, trustees need to be equipped with a rational reasoning that can trade off the cost of building and keeping trust in the environment with the future anticipated gains from holding the trust acquired. Existing trust establishment models allow trustees to adjust their behavior based on explicit feedback, such as such as [6] or based on implicit feedback such as [7], but they do not address scenarios where services are multidimensional, and trustors can assign different weights for each dimension. In this work, we aim to help honest trustees become more trustworthy to attract more interactions with trustors for situations where services are multidimensional and explicit feedback is not possible or not desirable.

We would like to highlight that the term "trust establishment" is used in different ways in the literature of trust management. Many researchers in the domain of ad-hoc networks, such as the work of Saini and Gautam [8], use the term to refer to trustworthiness evaluation of potential interaction partners. Others in the domain of service-oriented computing, such as the work of Malik and Bouguettaya [9], use it to refer to the bootstrapping or the cold start problem. With this in mind, few works in the literature address trust "establishment" to mean directing trustees to become more trustworthy. Furthermore, in the literature, IoA also referred to as Internet of Smart Things [10], Web of Things [11], Web of Agents [12], Agents of Things [13] as well as IoA [14].

The paper is organized as follows: an overview of most relevant related work is presented in the following section followed by a general overview of the IoA system used assumptions in Sect. 3. We present the details of the proposed model in Sect. 4. Performance analysis, including performance measures, simulation environment, and parameters is described in Sect. 5. The last section presents conclusions and future work.

2   Related Work

As an emerging field of interest, most related work to trust management of IoA lies in the field of trust managements for IoT, as well as trust management for MASs. Though previous research has suggested and analyzed several mechanisms for trustworthiness evaluation, slight consideration has been paid to trust establishment. Recent surveys such as [15–18] provide more insight on existing work in the field of trust modeling for MASa and IoT from the perspective of trustors, which is not directly related to this work.

Modeling buying agents' needs in e-marketplace described in the work of Tran and Cohen [19] and the use of trust-gain as an incentive mechanism for honesty in e-marketplace environments as in the work of Zhang and Cohen [20] are considered initial works for the novel direction of developing models for trustees to establish trust.

The Reputational Incentive (RI) model described in [21] depends on accumulated reputation, represented as real numbers, as the single-criterion to adjust the performance of trustees. Trustees build their models of trustors. To maintain an effective operation, it continuously monitors the trustee's reputation and adopts learning techniques using handcrafted formulas with the purpose of adjusting respective parameters tailored to the current situation. It is a decentralized, generic model that can be instantiated and applied in a wide range of applications. The model can deal with the dynamic characteristics of IoA, such as changeability in trustors' behaviors. When interacting for the first time, trustors are assumed to be neutral. Even though the model allows environments with multiple contexts, context diversity checking, and mapping are not available. Furthermore, the model does not use any defence mechanism against potential attacks on reputation; rather the model assumes that trustees can get an accurate evaluation of their reputation in the community.

The decentralized trust establishment model described in the work of Tran et al. [6], targets selling agents (trustees) for the e-commerce application, in a single context environment. It aims to help selling agents better understand the needs of buying agents (trustors) based on direct Boolean feedback from buyers to indicate whether or not they are satisfied with results of interactions. Each seller builds and maintains its models of buyers. Sellers use reinforcement learning to categorize buyers based on two criteria; namely price and quality. First-time buyers assumed to be neutral. When buyers change their behavior, the model responds by updating their categories. Buyers assumed to be corporative and provide accurate feedbacks. Even though the model has no explicit defense against misleading information, third party information sources are not used, and buyers have no incentive to lie.

The general purpose, decentralized trust establishment model presented in [22] takes advantage of multiple-criteria direct feedback from interaction partners and the general community of trustors to tune the performance of trustees dynamically. Trustors provide their level of satisfaction in a particular aspect of interaction, as well as, the importance of that aspect as a percentage, such that the sum of the importance of all criteria equals one. Each trustee dynamically calculates and updates its predictions for interaction partners using handcrafted equations. The applicability of the model is not restricted to a particular application. Even though context handling in not explicitly addresses in the model, we believe that the dynamic use of different weights for multiple criteria enables context handling. Trustees attempt to attract the attention of trustors by providing high performance in response to the first few interaction requests of a particular trustor. To defend against possible misleading information from a particular interaction partner, the model considers the general needs of all interaction partners, without implying any reliability check. Unfortunately, this model can be attacked by a group of trustor that agree together to provide misleading feedback in an attempt to get an extra performance of trustors. Furthermore, the bootstrapping used in this model make it susceptible to whitewash attack.

Reinforcement Learning based Trust Establishment (RLTE) is a decentralized trust establishment model based on reinforcement learning described in [7]. The model depends on implicit feedback from interaction partners to address the situation where explicit feedback in not possible or not desirable. A trustee y models the retention of all trustors in the system interacted with itself using function $ret_x^y : X \rightarrow [0,1]$, which is called the retention function of y. Initially, y sets the retention rating $ret_x^y = 0$ for every trustor x. After responding to a collaboration request with a trustor x, y will update (increase or decrease) ret_x^y depending on whether or not this response results in an actual transaction. RLTE depends on both the behavior of a particular trustor and the general trend among all interaction partners of y. If the retention rate of a trustor x is less than the average retention rate by all others interacted with y, x assumed to be not so happy with the Utility Gain (UG) provided by y. In response, y attempts to put in some effort to encourage x to interact with it later. When the retention of x is way above the average, then y increases its profit. However, if the retention rate is around the average, then y retains its level of performance, generally, unchanged. Furthermore, when the average retention rate is decreasing, this indicates a general disappointment among the $y's$ partners, which encourages y to increase its rate of enhancement and reduce profit-making. Otherwise, y attempts to increase its profits. The model uses retention as a single criterion represented as a real number and implicitly assumes that trustors are neither cooperative nor liars. The model assumes one-dimensional services, and context handling in not addressed in the model neither explicitly not implicitly.

As with RLTE, other decentralized trust establishment models described in [23] and [24] use retention of trustors as and implicitly assumes that trustors are uncooperative. Those models, generally, differ in the computation engine used. While the Fuzzy-logic-based Trust Establishment model (FTE) [24] uses fuzzy logic, [23] uses a set of handcrafted equations. FTE uses fuzzy logic where retention of a trustor ret_x^y and the general retention of interaction partners are represented by fuzzy sets. Membership functions describe in what degree a parameter belongs to each set, and fuzzy rules are used to predict the necessary improvements in response to requests from trustors. As with RLTE, trustees dynamically update their prediction of interaction partners' behaviors and attempt to attract the attention of trustors by providing high performance in response to the first few interaction requests of a particular trustor, which makes the models susceptible to whitewash attack. Trustors can maximize their gains by choosing different partners each time. Also, context handling is not addressed in those models neither explicitly nor implicitly as services assumed to be one-dimensional, and the use of many parameters and thresholds can limit the applicability of those models, which we aim to avoid in this work.

3 System Overview

In this section, we will present some common notation, and outline the necessary components and assumptions we make about the underlying trust establishment model, which will be referred to in the remainder of the this work.

3.1 Agent Architecture

Based on agent's architecture described in [5], we assume that each agent has a trust management module, which stores models of other agents and interfaces with the communication module and the decision selection mechanism. The trust management module includes an evaluation sub-components, which is responsible for evaluating the trustworthiness of other agents, and an establish sub-components, which is responsible for determining the proper actions to establish the agent to be trustworthy to others.

3.2 Agents and Tasks

We assume an IoA system consisting of multiple interconnected MASs. The IoA consists of a set of m, possibly heterogeneous, agents $A = \{a_1, a_2, ..., a_m\}$, interconnected through an Internet-like structure. Communication protocols used for implementing IoA is outside the scope of this work. Agents are independent, mobile, if needed, autonomous enough to identify specific actions to take, and sufficiently intelligent to reason about their environments and to interact directly with other agents in the IoA system. Also, we assume a set of possible tasks $S = \{s_1, ..., s_k\}$, a set of trustors $X = \{x_1, ..., x_n\}$ and a set of trustees $Y = \{y_1, ..., y_q\}$ such that $X \cup Y \subseteq A$. The trustors and trustees are not mutually exclusive sets, and an agent can play the two roles. Each task $s \in S$ has a set of dimensions, also referred to as features or criteria. The set of features is denoted as $C = \{c_1; c_2; ... c_p\}$. Individual trustors may have different levels of demand for each criterion, such as response time or transaction cost. Furthermore, individual criterion of a service may be of different importance or weight such that $W = \{w_1, ..., w_p\}$ where $0 \leq w_i \leq 1$. This allows a trustor to have a mixed configuration of demand and importance. For example, a trustor may be highly demanding on a criterion, such as response time should be within one seconds, but this criterion is not so important compared to other criteria such as stability or environmental impact. The nature of tasks in S is application dependent, and individual trustees may be able to perform zero or more tasks. Also, individual trustors may be interested in zero or more tasks, any number of times.

A trustor $x \in X$ that desires to see a task $s \in S$ accomplished, considers depending on a trustee $y \in Y$ to perform the task on its behalf. In response to the request req made by trustor x to do task s at time instance t, trustee y proposes to deliver a utility gain for x by a transaction as follows

$$UG_x^y(s, req) = \sum_{i=1}^{p} Imprv_x^y(s_{c_i}, req) + MinUG^y(s_{c_i}) \qquad (1)$$

- $UG_x^y(s, req)$ is the proposed aggregated utility gain by trustee y in response to the request req made by trustor x at time instance t, to do task s.
- $MinUG^y(s_{c_i})$ and $MaxUG^y(s_{c_i})$ are the minimum and maximum possible proposed utility gain that y may deliver to criterion c_i of task s.
- $Imprv_x^y(s_{c_i}, req)$ is the calculated improvement by y for criterion c_i of task s in response to the request req made by x at time instance t. Where

$$0 \leq Imprv_x^y(s_{c_i}, req) \leq (MaxUG^y(s_{c_i}) - MinUG^y(s_{c_i})) \quad (2)$$

After interacting with a trustee y, trustor x then gains some benefits from the interaction requested at time instance t. The outcomes of each task is a real number in [0,1] representing the percentage of satisfaction After interacting with a trustee y, trustor x then gains some benefits from the interaction requested at time instance t such that

$$SAT_x^y(s, tra) = \sum_{i=1}^{p} \frac{w_x(s_{c_i}) * ug_x^y(s_{c_i}, tra)}{d_x(s_{c_i})} \qquad (3)$$

where

- $SAT_x^y(s, tra)$ is the satisfaction of trustor x as a result of interaction tra with y for task s.
- $w_x(s_{c_i})$ is the weight of criterion c_i of task s as determined by trustor x. We assume it is not time or interaction dependent.
- $ug_x^y(s_{c_i}, tra)$ is the utility gain provided by y to x for criterion c_i of task s in the interaction tra. This may vary for different interactions.
- $d_x(s_{c_i})$ is the demand level of criterion c_i of task s as determined by trustor x. We assume that the demand level is not time dependent.

Satisfaction represent the fulfillment of trustor's requirements through interacting with a particular trustee. The aggregation of satisfaction over various interactions represents the direct trustworthiness evaluation of a trustee. The use of demand and weight in Eq. (3) allows for different interpretation of UG between trustors and trustees. In the literature, various approaches were used to model the trustworthiness of trustees, based on the fulfillment of trustor's requirements such as [25,26]. Because of the distributed nature of IoA, no central entity or authority exists to facilitate trust-related communications.

Any trustor x can make a request to collaborate in order to achieve a task $s \in S$. Trustors x may request any task s zero or more times. Agents can communicate with each other in a distributed manner. No service level agreement or contract exists between agents. We assume that trustors are not able or not willing to provide satisfaction feedback for trustees after each transaction.

3.3   Trust Evaluations

As our focus in this work is on trust establishment, we do not discuss how trust evaluations are formed or how they are used. Instead, we assume the existence of a trust evaluation model and a decision-making model based on trust. Each trustor x models the trustworthiness of potential interaction partners in the system using its own trust function of $trust_x^y(t) : Y \rightarrow [minTrust, maxTrust]$, where $minTrust$ and $maxTrust$ are minimum and maximum trust values respectively. Trustors build these models based on direct experience, also referred to as direct trust, of the performance of trustees in different tasks and indirect experience, also referred to as indirect trust, if necessary.

After bootstrapping, trustors select partners to interact with based on the utility gain expected to be gained from the transaction. Such value is calculated as

$$EV_y^x(t) = trust_y^x(t) * UG_x^y(t) \tag{4}$$

- $EV(y)$ is the expected value of the a transaction between x and y as calculated by x a for request at time instance t.
- $UG_x^y(t)$ is the proposed utility gain by y, in response to a request by x at time instance t.
- $trust_y^x(t)$ is trust evaluation of x for y at time instance t.

4   Acting as a Trustee Using Implicit Feedback (ATeIF)

4.1   Fundamental of ATeIF

When trustee y proposes to deliver utility gain for trustor x by a transaction, the proposed utility gain is calculated by Eq. (1) in Sect. 3. The case when trustors are willing to provide detailed and accurate feedback, including the level of satisfaction, and the importance or weight per criterion is, generally, straightforward. Using the proposed value of each criterion (by the trustee) and the satisfaction level (of the trustor) of the same criterion, trustees can determine the appropriate performance improvement as described in [22]. When explicit feedback is not available, trustees can determine the necessary performance enhancement as described in [7,23,24]. However, for multicriteria services, both the proper value per criteria and its importance need to be predicted.

The proposed trust establishment model uses the retention of trustors to adjust the behavior of trustee(s), such that, if the retention rate of x is less than the average retention rate of trustors in the society, this indicates that x is not so happy with previous interaction(s). In response, by ATeIF, y should put some more effort to encourage x to interact with itself later, especially on important criteria. On the other hand, when the retention of x is above the average, then the performance of its interaction partner y can be, carefully, reduced, especially with respect to nonimportant criteria.

Let us define the relative weight (rw) of a criterion as the actual weight $w_x(s_{c_i})$ of the criterion, divided by the level of demand for that particular one $d_x(s_{c_i})$. i.e.

$$rw_x(s_{c_i}) = \frac{w_x(s_{c_i})}{d_x(s_{c_i})} \tag{5}$$

It is this number that represents the relative weight of a criterion and needs to be predicted by trustees. It the absence of explicit feedback, trustees can use the change of trustors' retention to help predicting $rw_x(s_{c_i})$. Initially, values for relative weight are set to random numbers in the range of $[0, 1]$. These values are updated during the life time of agents.

Upon each transaction, information related to this interaction or request will be stored in the trustee's local database. Such information will be retrieved when needed for responding to service requests. Since agents have limited resource (i.e. memory), storing all information about interactions is not necessarily an option. Therefore, each agent will only store information related to interactions and service requests for a maximum of H time interval. Here H is referred to the history size. This parameter is adjustable according to a particular agent's situation.

If the environment of IoA is dynamic, old interactions usually become less important due to changes in the environment [26]. Reducing the influence of old interactions is used in many trust evaluation models such as [26,27]. In the proposed trust establishment model, trustees scale the impact of old transactions using a decaying factor, to reduce the influence of old interactions adaptively.

Let us denote the retention of trustor x as $R_x^y(t)$ such that

$$R_x^y(t) = \sum_{j=1}^{N_x} e^{(-\rho \, \Delta t_{xj})} \tag{6}$$

where

- N_x is the number of transaction between x and y during the last H time unit.
- ρ is the degree of decay. Trustees can specify the degree of decay ρ ($0 \le \rho \le 1$) based on their policies.
- t_{xj} is the time elapsed since the interaction j took place with x.
- t is the time instance of processing the request.

Assuming that rational trustors do not frequently interact with untrustworthy partners, we propose the use of, what we call, Private Retention Index (PRI) to model the satisfaction of trustors. (PRI) combines both:

- The average retention of x relative to the average retention per trustor among those having interacted with y previously
- The average retention of x relative to the maximum retention per trustor among those having interacted with y previously.

$$PRI_y^x(s,t) = \begin{cases} \dfrac{R_x}{\max_{i \in X'}(R_i)} + \dfrac{R_x}{\operatorname{avg}_{i \in X'}(R_i)}, & R_x > 0 \\ \operatorname{avg}_{i \in X'}(R_i), & \text{otherwise} \end{cases} \tag{7}$$

where

- X' is the set of trustors $\in X$ having interacted with the y so far within the last H time units.
- $max(R_i)$ is the maximum retention of an individual trustor in the set X'.
  $i \in X'$
-

$$avg(R_i) = \begin{cases} \frac{\sum_{j=1}^{|X'|} R_j}{|X'|}, & |X'| > 0 \\ 1, & \text{otherwise} \end{cases} \qquad (8)$$
$i \in X'$

- $|X'|$ is the size of the set X'.

$PRI_x^y(s,t)$ is meant to indicate the willingness of x to interact with y at time t for task s. We agree that the $PRI_x^y(s,t)$ says nothing about the relation of x with other trustees, i.e. competitors, as well as other trustors in the community. However, such information might not always be available due to selfishness, privacy, or lack of authorized providers, among other possible reasons.

4.2 Improvement Calculation

When y proposes to deliver UG for x in response to a service request at time t, the proposed UG is calculated by Eq. 1, and the improvement efforts calculated by y in response to the request req made by trustor x to do task s based on implicit feedback depends on:

- The Private Retention Index $(PRI_x^y(s,t))$
- The relative weight of the criterion under consideration $rw_x(s_{c_i})$

Let $Imprv_y^x(s_{c_i}, req)$ be the improvement factor of y for criterion c_i in response to request req by x to perform task s at time t such that

$$Imprv_y^x(s_{c_i}, req) = \begin{cases} rw_x(s_{c_i}) * e^{-PRI_y^x} * MI^y(s_{c_i}), & rw_x(s_{c_i}) * e^{-PRI_y^x} \leq 1 \\ MI^y(s_{c_i}), & \text{otherwise} \end{cases} \quad (9)$$

where maximum possible improvement (MI) for a service criterion (s_{c_i}) by trustee y is $MI^y(s_{c_i}) = MaxUG^y(s_{c_i}) - MinUG^y(s_{c_i})$

4.3 Update Relative Weights

When the change in PRI is greater than or equal to the corresponding proportional change in utility gain for a particular criterion, this indicates that x highly values this criterion, and therefore the predicted relative weight of the criterion needs to be increased. On the other hand, when the relative change in PRI is less than the corresponding proportional change in utility gain for the criteria, this indicates that x does not highly appreciate this criterion. Therefore, the predicted relative weight of the criterion needs to be decreased. The following equations detail the changes.

Let us define PRI change as

$$\Delta PRI_y^x(s,t) = PRI_y^x(s,t') - PRI_y^x(s,t'') \tag{10}$$

Where $PRI_y^x(s,t')$ and $PRI_y^x(s,t'')$ are the most recent PRI of x (at time t') and the one before it (at time t''), respectively

Let us define the proportional utility gain change per criterion as

$$pug_y^x(s_{c_i}) = rw_x(s_{c_i}) * (ug_y^x(s_{c_i},t') - ug_y^x(s_{c_i},t'')) \tag{11}$$

If the utility gain change per criterion changes between time instant t' and the one before it t'', then $rw_x(s_{c_i})$ is updated as follows:

$$rw_x(s_{c_i}) = \begin{cases} (1+\lambda) * rw_x(s_{c_i}), & \Delta PRI_y^x(s,t) \geq pug_x^y(s_{c_i}) \\ (1-\kappa) * rw_x(s_{c_i}), & \Delta PRI_y^x(s,t) < pug_x^y(s_{c_i}) \end{cases} \tag{12}$$

where

– We refer to λ and κ as the relative weights updating factors. It is clear that values of these factors are application dependent. We recommend that their values be in $[0,1]$. Also, we recommend that the value of λ be greater than κ to reduce chances of accidentally underestimating an important criterion.

Note that the relative weight in Eq. (12) is a prediction calculated by y rather than the actual value used by x.

5   Performance Analysis

The effectiveness of various models needs to be assessed under different environmental conditions, research that present performance analysis of trust establishment models evaluate them in a proprietary manner based on simulation, as it is challenging to obtain suitable real world data sets for the comprehensive evaluation. Simulation experiments differ among various works, not only in the simulation parameters but also in nature. Generally, there is no agreed on benchmarks to enable comparing different results.

The effectiveness of various models needs to be assessed under different environmental condition. However, it is challenging to obtain suitable real world data sets for the comprehensive evaluation, and there is no agreed on assessment framework or benchmarks to enable comparing different models. Therefore, existing researches that analyze the performance of trust establishment models use proprietary simulation. With the absence of agreed on benchmarks, simulation experiments differ among various works, not only in the simulation parameters but also in nature.

We compare the performance ATeIF with RI [21], as it is the one mostly used for comparisons in related literature such as [7,23,24].

5.1 Performance Measures

In such situations, building a high trust may be an advantage for rational trustees. Rational trustees need to trade off the cost of building and keeping trust in the community with the future gains from holding the trust acquired. Therefore, to study the performance of the proposed model, we use the following measures:

- Trustworthiness estimation: This metric is calculated as the average direct trustworthiness estimation for all trustees that use a particular model. We agree that precise trustworthiness estimation is highly dependent on the adapted trust evaluation model used by trustors. However, we include this metric in this study as an indicator in situations where trustors use a general purpose, probabilistic evaluation model.
- Average delivered utility gain: This measure indicates the efforts needed to achieve the enhancement in the percentage of overall transactions. It is arguable that an honest trustee y can achieve a higher percentage of over-all transactions if it is committed to delivering the highest possible utility gain transaction. However, providing greater utility gain usually incurs extra cost. Therefore, a rational trustee will attempt to achieve a higher number of transactions while keeping the provided utility gain as low as possible. In this work, the average of delivered utility gain per transaction is defined as the summation of all delivered utility gain values in all transactions be the group of trustees empowered with a particular model divided by the number of those transactions.

$$AverageUG_l(s) = \frac{\sum_{y\in}^{q} \sum_{x\in X} \sum_{k=1}^{NTR_y^x} UG_x^y(k)}{\sum_{y\in Y} \sum_{x\in X} NTR_y^x} \tag{13}$$

Where
  - l is the model used by trustees.
  - NTR_y^x is the number of transactions between x and y.
- Total number of good transactions in the system: When comparing different trust establishment models, the higher the number of good transactions, the more successful the model in predicting the needs of trustors. This metric is calculated as the summation of all transactions took place in the system where the demands of trustors fulfilled completely. Other metrics like percentage of good transactions and the average number of good transactions per trustee, can be seen as derived metric from this one, or just a different presentations based on this metric.
- Total number of bad transactions in the system: When comparing different trust establishment models, the lower the number of bad transactions, the more successful the model in predicting the needs of trustors. This metric is calculated as the summation of all transactions took place in the system where the demands of trustors are not fulfilled completely, i.e. either fulfilled partially or not fulfilled at all. Other metrics like percentage of bad transactions and the average number of bad transactions per trustee, can be seen as derived metric from this one, or just a different presentations based on this metric.

– Number of transactions in a competitive environment: A primary objective of y planning to enhance its trustworthiness estimation value, is to become selected by trustors for future transactions. The larger the number of transactions y performs within the system, the closer it is to achieving this objective. This metric indicates the relative benefits that trustees may achieve by adopting the proposed model.

5.2   Simulation Environment

We use a scenario-simulator approach [28] to compare the performance of different models. Scenarios are pre-generated and not modified during the simulation phase. The generation of scenario files encodes different parameters, such as the number of trustees, the number of trustors, the profile of each agent and so on. These scenarios are then given to the simulator. Thus, multiple simulations, implementing different models, can be run from the same scenario. By fixing every aspect of a scenario run, the only differences between runs will be trust establishment specific.

Generally speaking, a scenario is a sequence of "request for interactions" followed by interactions. Each request specifies a service name and the agent seeking that service. The choice of a trustee to interact with will be made at simulation runtime by trust evaluation model. The value for different dimensions of the selected trustee's response is determined by the trust establishment model at simulation time.

For the general simulation, each scenario is simulated, separately, with all trustees use the same trust establishment model. However, for comparing the number of transactions, we repeat the same experiments with an equal number of trustees using each model, where trustees are randomly set to either use ATeIF or the RI model [21] at creation time, and they do not change that.

For simulation, we use the discrete-event MAS simulation toolkit MASON [29] with trustees providing services, and trustors consuming services. We assume that the performance of an individual trustee in a particular service is independent of that in other services. Therefore, without loss of generality, to reduce the complexity of the simulation environment, it is assumed that there is only one type of services in the simulated system. All trustees offer the same service with, possibly, different performances. Network communication effects are not considered in this simulation. Each agent can reach each other agent. The simulation step is used as the time value of interactions. Transactions that take place in the same simulation step are considered simultaneous. Locating trustees and other agents are not part of the proposed model, as agents locate each other through the system. Trusters can request any number of trustees to bid. No trust certification mechanism exists, and third party witnesses are assumed to be honest.

For trust evaluation, as the evaluation is not the part of our model, trustors use a simple probabilistic trust evaluation

$$trust = 0.5 * directTrust + 0.5 * indirectTrust \tag{14}$$

- Direct trust, or direct experience, is the aggregated percentage of satisfaction from transactions performed so far with the trustee.
- Indirect trust, or indirect experience, represents the reputation of the trustee in the community and is calculated as the average direct trust value of those who previously interacted with the trustee.

Initially, trustors use neutral trust rating for every trustee. Therefore initial trust is set to

$$trust_x^y = \frac{minTrust + maxTrust}{2} \qquad (15)$$

Having selected an interaction partner y, agent x then interacts with y and gains utility. A trustee can serve many users at a time. A truster does not always use the service in every round. The probability a truster requests a service is referred to as activity level. After a transaction, x updates the trustworthiness estimation of its interaction partner. At the end of each simulation step, trustees update the average retention rates of trustors if necessary. Charted values calculated as the averaged value for ten different randomly generated scenarios with the same base configuration.

As we aim to compare the performance of trustees equipped with the proposed model and those equipped with the RI [21], all trustees are assumed to be honest and the only difference among them is the trust establishment model. This way we can relate the difference in performance to the model of trust establishment used.

Table 1 presents the base values for the number of agents and other parameters used in the proposed model and those employed in the environment. When testing the effect of a particular parameter, others are set to those base values.

5.3   Experimental Results

Effects of Trustors' Demand Level. The level of service required to satisfy needs of trustors can vary within the same environment, as well as in different environments. For example, in the context of the smart grid, different electrical vehicles may require dissimilar service levels of charging stations depending on factors like distance to destination, urgency of the trip and so on. To study the effects of trustors' levels of demand on the behavior of the proposed model, we analyze three extreme cases where all trustors belong to the same demand category: all with high demand, all with low demand or all intermediate (normal) demand such that highly demanding trustors requires at least 65% of the maximum possible UG for each criterion, low demanding trustors requires no more than 35% of the maximum possible UG for each criterion and regular demanding trustors requires something in between.

Figure 1 presents the performance of ATeIF, compared to RI model, under different levels of demands. The figure shows that trustees empowered with ATeIF have higher average trust with highly demanding trustors and intermediate demanding trustors (Fig. 1a and b). For regular demanding trustors, trustees can easily satisfy part of them but need more effort to satisfy the others. In this

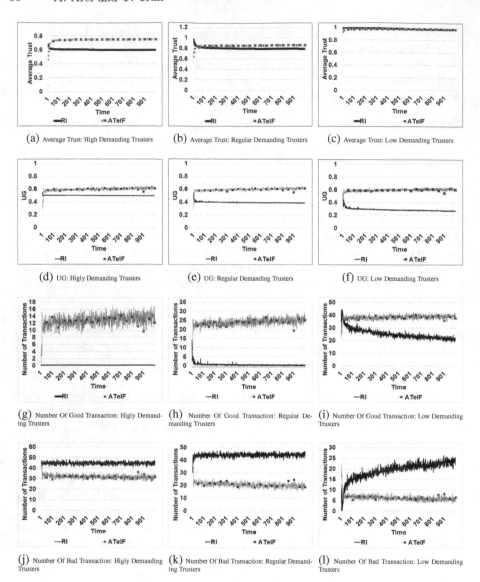

Fig. 1. Effect of trusters' demand

case, nonloyal trustors can cause the provided UG of ATeIF based trustees to increase slightly, and so the average trust of trustees. For easy going trustors, both models cause trustees to provide lower UG and stay trustworthy (Fig. 1c). The higher level of trust is due to higher UG provided in general as indicated in (Fig. 1d–f) and especially for the important criterion.

Figure 2 shows that when the two models coexist in the environment, ATeIF empowered trustees can achieve a higher number of transactions, compared to those using RI model. At the beginning of the simulation, when all trustees have neutral reputation, RI model provides higher UG than ATeIF. The proposed model adjust the provided UG per criterion and gains more transactions as seen in (Fig. 2a–c). The difference in the performance of the two models in much noticeable with highly demanding trustors and the difference declines as the demand of trustors gets lower, where many trustees can fulfill them.

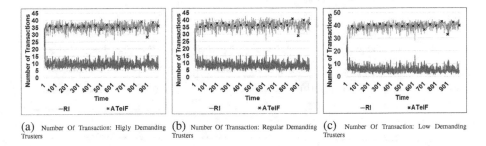

(a) Number Of Transaction: Higly Demanding Trusters   (b) Number Of Transaction: Regular Demanding Trusters   (c) Number Of Transaction: Low Demanding Trusters

Fig. 2. Effect of trusters' demands on number of transactions

Table 1. Values of used parameters

Parameter	Value
Number of agents	100
Number of trustees	10
Number of trusters	90
Percentage of high demand trusters	30%
Percentage of low demand trusters	40%
Percentage of normal demand trusters	30%
Percentage of highly active trusters	30%
Percentage of regular active trusters	40%
Percentage of low active trusters	30%
Number of simulation steps	1000
ρ	1
λ	0.002
κ	0.001
Histroy size (H)	1000
Initial value of trust	0.5
MinUG	3
MaxUG	12

The Effects of Trusters' Activity Level. It is possible that trustors do not always use the service in every round. While some trustors can be highly active, some others can have a low or intermediate level of activity. To study the effects of trustors' activity level on the behavior of the proposed model, we analyze three extreme cases where all trustors belong to the same demand category: all with high activity level, all with intermediate (normal) activity level, or all with low activity level. In each round, highly active trustors request the service with

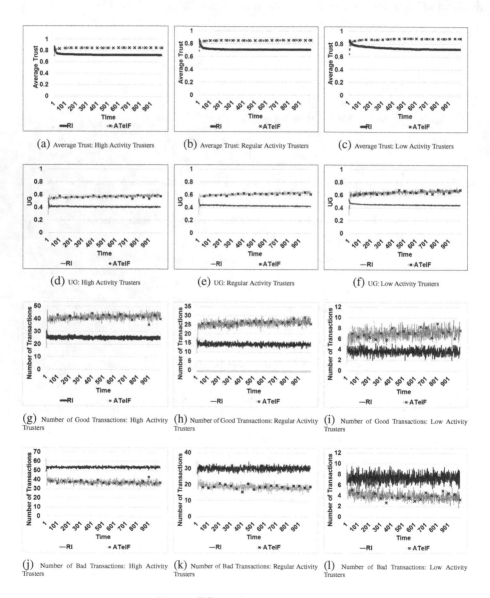

(a) Average Trust: High Activity Trusters   (b) Average Trust: Regular Activity Trusters   (c) Average Trust: Low Activity Trusters

(d) UG: High Activity Trusters   (e) UG: Regular Activity Trusters   (f) UG: Low Activity Trusters

(g) Number of Good Transactions: High Activity Trusters   (h) Number of Good Transactions: Regular Activity Trusters   (i) Number of Good Transactions: Low Activity Trusters

(j) Number of Bad Transactions: High Activity Trusters   (k) Number of Bad Transactions: Regular Activity Trusters   (l) Number of Bad Transactions: Low Activity Trusters

Fig. 3. Effect of trusters' activity

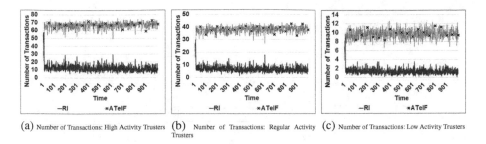

(a) Number of Transactions: High Activity Trusters   (b) Number of Transactions: Regular Activity Trusters   (c) Number of Transactions: Low Activity Trusters

Fig. 4. Effect of trusters' activity on number of transactions

a probability of at least 65%, low active ones request the service with a probability of at most 35%, while trusters with a regular level of activity request the service with a probability in between. Figure 3 presents the performance of ATeIF, compared to the RI model, under different levels of trusters' activity. The figure shows no significant performance variation of the two models under different activity levels. Generally, the proposed model outperforms RI, and as the activity level of trusters increases, the performance of proposed model gets better due to the incremental learning mechanism ATeIF uses. Figure 4 shows that when the two models coexist in the environment, ATeIF empowered trustees can achieve a higher number of transactions, compared to those using RI model. At the beginning of the simulation, when all trustees have a neutral reputation, RI model provides higher UG than ATeIF. The proposed model adjust the provided UG per criterion and gains more transactions as seen in (Fig. 4a–c). The difference in the performance of the two models in much visible with highly active trustors and the difference declines as the activity level of trusters gets lower, where the speed of learning of ATeIF decreases.

The Effects of the Size of Agents' Society. We want to extract conclusions that are unrelated to the number of agents in the system (population size). Therefore, we experiment on different population sizes so we can extrapolate the results. To determine the impact of population size on the performance of the proposed model we considered three different sets of scenarios, one with 100 agents, the other with 500 agents and the last one with 900 agents. For consistency among different scenarios, we use 10% of the population size as trustees.

Figures 5 and 6 presents the performance of ATeIF, compared to the RI model, for three different sizes of the system. The figure shows that using the proposed model, trustees can achieve a higher number of transactions, compared to those using RI model when the size of the system gets larger. As the size of the system gets larger, the number of trustors increases and so the number of transactions.

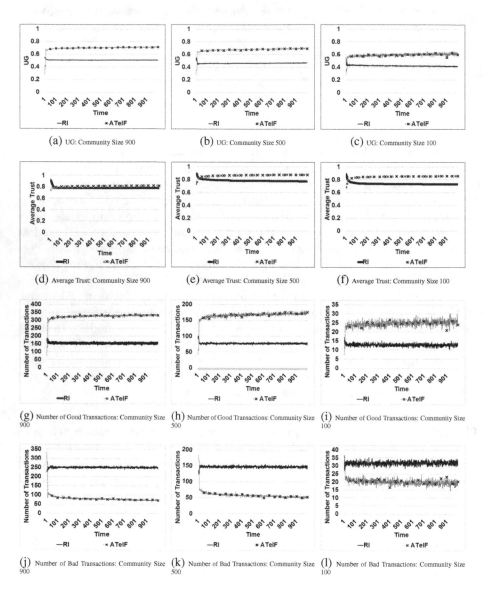

Fig. 5. Effect of society size

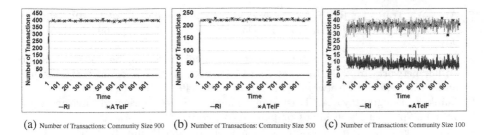

(a) Number of Transactions: Community Size 900   (b) Number of Transactions: Community Size 500   (c) Number of Transactions: Community Size 100

Fig. 6. Effect of society size on number of transactions

6   Conclusions and Future Work

In this work, we presented a trust establishment model for IoA that allows trustees to alter their behavior based on implicit feedback from trustors. The aim of trustees is to enhance their trustworthiness with the hope to be selected for future interactions. Simulation results indicate that, in a competitive environment, trustees can improve their portion of transactions if they use ATeIF to adjust their proposed UG.

We would like to extend the proposed model to address the case when both explicit and implicit feedback available. Furthermore, we would like to study the effects of other parameters such as the type of trust evaluation model used by trustors, partner selection mechanisms, the capacity of trustees, and the percentage of trustees in the community. Moreover, we want to explore the potentials of social relations between trustors and how trustees can use such relations to engender trust. Additionally, we would like to investigate the effects of detecting patterns of trustors behaviors on trust establishment. Also, further performance comparison with other related work is left as future work.

References

1. Wooldridge, M.: An Introduction to MultiAgent Systems, 2nd edn. Wiley, Chichester (2009)
2. Khosravifar, B., Bentahar, J., Gomrokchi, M., Alam, R.: CRM: An efficient trust and reputation model for agent computing. Knowl.-Based Syst. **30**, 1–16 (2012)
3. Ramchurn, S.D., Huynh, T.D., Jennings, N.R.: Trust in multi-agent systems. Knowl. Eng. Rev. **19**(1), 1–25 (2004)
4. Castelfranchi, C., Falcone, R., Marzo, F.: Being trusted in a social network: trust as relational capital. In: Stølen, K., Winsborough, W.H., Martinelli, F., Massacci, F. (eds.) iTrust 2006. LNCS, vol. 3986, pp. 19–32. Springer, Heidelberg (2006). doi:10.1007/11755593_3
5. Sen, S.: A comprehensive approach to trust management. In: Proceedings of the 12th International Conference on Autonomous Agents and Multiagent Systems (AAMAS 2013) (2013)
6. Tran, T., Cohen, R., Langlois, E.: Establishing trust in multiagent environments: realizing the comprehensive trust management dream. In: Proceedings of the 17th International Workshop on Trust in Agent Societies (2014)

7. Aref, A., Tran, T.: RLTE: A reinforcement learning based trust establishment model. In: 2015 IEEE Trustcom/BigDataSE/ISPA, vol. 1, pp. 694–701, August 2015

8. Saini, R., Gautam, R.K.: Establishment of dynamic trust among nodes in mobile ad-hoc network. In: 2011 International Conference on Computational Intelligence and Communication Networks (CICN), pp. 346–349. IEEE (2011)

9. Malik, Z., Bouguettaya, A.: Trust Management for Service-Oriented Environments, 1st edn. Springer Publishing Company Incorporated, New York (2009)

10. van Moergestel, L., van den Berg, M., Knol, M., van der Paauw, R., van Voorst, K., Puik, E., Telgen, D., Meyer, J.J.: Internet of smart things - a study on embedding agents and information in a device. In: Proceedings of the 8th International Conference on Agents and Artificial Intelligence ICAART, vol. 1, pp. 102–109 (2016)

11. Cirani, S., Picone, M.: Effective authorization for the web of things. In: 2015 IEEE 2nd World Forum on Internet of Things (WF-IoT), pp. 316–320. IEEE (2015)

12. Verborgh, R., Mannens, E., Van de Walle, R.: The rise of the web for agents. In: Proceedings of the First International Conference on Building and Exploring Web Based Environments, pp. 69–74, January 2013

13. Mzahm, A.M., Ahmad, M.S., Tang, A.Y.C.: Agents of things (AoT): An intelligent operational concept of the internet of things (IoT). In: 2013 13th International Conference on Intellient Systems Design and Applications, pp. 159–164, December 2013

14. Yu, H., Shen, Z., Leung, C.: From internet of things to internet of agents. In: Green Computing and Communications (GreenCom), 2013 IEEE and Internet of Things (iThings/CPSCom), IEEE International Conference on and IEEE Cyber, Physical and Social Computing, pp. 1054–1057. IEEE (2013)

15. Yu, H., Shen, Z., Leung, C., Miao, C., Lesser, V.: A survey of multi-agent trust management systems. IEEE Access 1, 35–50 (2013)

16. Pinyol, I., Sabater-Mir, J.: Computational trust and reputation models for open multi-agent systems: a review. Artif. Intell. Rev. 40(1), 1–25 (2013)

17. Granatyr, J., Botelho, V., Lessing, O.R., Scalabrin, E.E., Barthès, J.P., Enembreck, F.: Trust and reputation models for multiagent systems. ACM Comput. Surv. 48(2), 27:1–27:42 (2015)

18. Yan, Z., Zhang, P., Vasilakos, A.V.: A survey on trust management for internet of things. J. Netw. Comput. Appl. 42, 120–134 (2014)

19. Tran, T., Cohen, R.: Improving user satisfaction in agent-based electronic marketplaces by reputation modelling and adjustable product quality. In: AAMAS, pp. 828–835 (2004)

20. Zhang, J., Cohen, R.: Design of a mechanism for promoting honesty in E-marketplaces. In: Proceedings of the Twenty-Second AAAI Conference on Artificial Intelligence, Vancouver, British Columbia, Canada, 22–26 July 2007, pp. 1495–1500 (2007)

21. Burnett, C., Norman, T.J., Sycara, K.P.: Trust decision-making in multi-agent systems. In: IJCAI, pp. 115–120 (2011)

22. Aref, A., Tran, T.: A trust establishment model in multi-agent systems. In: Workshops at the Twenty-Ninth AAAI Conference on Artificial Intelligence (2015)

23. Aref, A., Tran, T.: Modeling trust evaluating agents: towards a comprehensive trust management for multi-agent systems. In: Incentives and Trust in Electronic Communities, Papers from the 2016 AAAI Workshop, Phoenix, Arizona, USA, 12 February 2016 (2016)

24. Aref, A., Tran, T.: FTE: A fuzzy logic based trust establishment model for intelligent agents. In: IEEE/WIC/ACM International Conference on Web Intelligence and Intelligent Agent Technology, WI-IAT 2015, Singapore, 6–9 December 2015, vol. II, pp. 133–138 (2015)
25. Jsang, A., Ismail, R.: The beta reputation system. In: Proceedings of the 15th Bled Electronic Commerce Conference, pp. 41–55 (2002)
26. Huynh, T.D., Jennings, N.R., Shadbolt, N.R.: An integrated trust and reputation model for open multi-agent systems. Auton. Agent. Multi-Agent Syst. 13(2), 119–154 (2006)
27. Aref, A., Tran, T.: A decentralized trustworthiness estimation model for open, multiagent systems (DTMAS). J. Trust Manage. 2(1), 3 (2015)
28. West, A.G., Kannan, S., Lee, I., Sokolsky, O.: An evaluation framework for reputation management systems. In: Trust Modeling and Management in Digital Environments: From Social Concept to System Development, pp. 282–308 (2010)
29. Luke, S., Cioffi-Revilla, C., Panait, L., Sullivan, K., Balan, G.: MASON: a multi-agent simulation environment. Simulation 81(7), 517–527 (2005)

Integrating Access Control Obligations in the Session Initiation Protocol for Pervasive Computing Environments

Hassan Sharghi[✉] and Ramiro Liscano

Department of Electrical, Computer and Software Engineering,
University of Ontario Institute of Technology, Oshawa, ON L1H 7K4, Canada
{Mohammadhassan.Sharghigoorabi,Ramiro.Liscano}@uoit.ca

Abstract. The widely use of advanced technologies in the sensor network and computing has facilitated the development of convenient pervasive applications in order to access information at anytime and anywhere. The traditional access control mechanisms cannot appropriately protect the access and usage of digital resources in the highly distributed and heterogeneous computing environment. In such an environment, enforcing continuously the access control policies during the access period is a challenge because traditional authorization decisions are generally made at the time of access requests but do not consider ongoing controls. Obligations are the vital part of many access control policies and they specify mandatory behavior that should be conducted by a user of the access control system in sensitive domains. Therefore, utilizing a mechanism to approve the fulfillment of the obligation is required for continuing or revoking the access decision. We leveraged the capability of Session Initiation Protocol (SIP) to manage the communication between entities in order to provide a mechanism to handle the continuous enforcement of the obligation. Meanwhile, we present several scenarios which indicate our proposed model can manage the obligatory behavior that affects the continuity of access to resources in pervasive computing environment.

Keywords: Access control · Obligation · Behavior · Session initiation protocol · Pervasive computing

1 Introduction

Pervasive computing provides an environment where computing systems can be utilized everywhere in order to allow users to access any time to data and services. The continuous development of mobile devices, sophisticated sensor networks, and the mature communication technologies enable the pervasive computing paradigm to access a variety of resources in order to process the collected data from interconnected objects to provide different services. Satisfying the various needs of users to obtain different services at anytime and anywhere in such a heterogeneous environment generates challenges for security and privacy protection.

© Springer International Publishing AG 2017
E. Aïmeur et al. (Eds.): MCETECH 2017, LNBIP 289, pp. 24–40, 2017.
DOI: 10.1007/978-3-319-59041-7_2

Access control mechanism is an acceptable approach in security domain to allow legitimate users to access different resources in the secure manner. Typically, access control deals only with authorization decision on users request to access the target resources. The objective of access control is to prevent from unauthorized disclosure (confidentiality), avoid improper malicious modifications (integrity), and ensure the access for authorized entities (availability).

Predefined policies are often used to manage the access control system. A policy includes a set of rules to specify the permission of a subject for performing some actions on resources if particular conditions are satisfied. Separating the policy from the implementation of a system helps to modify adaptively the policy. The modification of policies enables the administrator to handle the changes in the strategy for managing the system and controlling the behavior of users without changing the implementation of the underlying components.

Access control is concerned with the problem of granting access to resources and services, but controlling the activities of authenticated and authorized users is not in charge of the traditional access control systems after granting permission. Furthermore, traditional access control models such as Mandatory Access Control (MAC), Discretionary Access Control (DAC), and Role-Based Access Control (RBAC) do not work properly in pervasive computing environment because such an environment is dynamic and sensitive to contextual information as well as pervasive computing applications usually do not have well-defined security perimeter [22].

Context information should be involved in access control system for pervasive computing applications because the effective attributes of entities may change based on the context over time. For example, a subject in the role of data provider, equipped with a mobile device, may send geolocation data to a network operator who has the role of data consumer. However, the role of data consumer for network operator may change to data provider when a location-based service provider requests for this specific data. Context data can come from various sources such as location sensors, calendars, clocks, and many other sensors. The level of granularity is an important characteristic of context data. For instance, a user's location can be represented in exact coordinates, or only the name of country. Consequently, the granularity of provided context data affects the precision of access control system.

Different kinds of policies are required to protect sensitive resources in pervasive computing application domain. Authorization policies representing by a set of rules protect resources through making appropriate access decisions. However, such authorization rules cannot control the activities of the user after granting the access. Integrating obligations into access control policies can dictate the mandatory operation that must be performed by the user before, after, and during the access [7].

We define the obligation as an obligatory behavior that should be conducted by an entity. Obligation is classified in two perspectives: functional and structural [6]. Functional obligation represents what a subject is obliged to perform with respect to change or maintain the state of affairs. In this view, obligation is a commitment that represents a promise to do something or to behave in a particular manner. Structural obligation represents what a subject is obliged to perform in order to fulfill a responsibility such as directing, supervising and monitoring. In this view, obligation is a duty that a subject must perform and it is not specifically part of the access control purpose.

Using obligations to handle the usage of resources raises the question of how the enforcement will be managed. Since traditional access control is performed only once before the resource is accessed by the subject, the access control system is not able to control the fulfillment of obligation while the access is in progress. Therefore, the lack of capability to check the obligations for the continuity of access purpose may lead to the security breach in sensitive environments. To resolve this issue, we proposed to utilize Session Initiation Protocol (SIP) in order to handle the enforcement of obligations. SIP is an application-layer control protocol for creating, modifying, and terminating sessions with one or more participants [8].

In this paper, we propose an approach to integrate obligations into access control system in order to control the behavior of the user. Overall, this paper presents the following contributions: (i) modeling the obligation based on subject's behavior and using a behavior based language to express the obligation, and (ii) applying session initiation protocol to approve the fulfillment of the obligation for the purpose of continuing or revoking the access decision.

The remaining of this paper is organized as follows: Sect. 2 provides an overview of related works. Our proposed approach for modeling and enforcing the obligation is presented in Sect. 3, followed by two application scenarios in Sect. 4 in order to illustrate some of our approach's functionalities. Finally, Sect. 5 provides some concluding remarks and outlines the direction for future research.

2 Related Work

Access control has been intensively explored in recent years and several access control models have been proposed. The dynamic nature of context information makes trouble to develop a fine-grained access control in the pervasive computing application domain. Therefore, there are several attempts such as [18,21] to improve the existing access control models using contextual information for pervasive computing applications. In [12], authors developed a context-aware role based access control model for pervasive computing applications through creating a new model for role. They defined roles as part of an application's design so that roles come into existence only during the application's lifetime instead of giving a long lifetime to a role.

Access control model based on a particular context such as location [2,24], time and spatial information [17] were also suggested. Toahchoodee et al. [23] proposed trust based access control for ubiquitous computing application where users are not known in advance. The access privilege of a user relies on his trust level which in turn depends on the contextual information.

Our research is different because we do not rely on an access control model based on a particular attribute or context. Our approach can be applied for any models that possess extensible capability to express the obligations. However, attribute based access control provides sufficient opportunity to apply our approach for a specific domain.

Damiani et al. [4] proposed a method to solve the problem of how to introduce continuous enforcement in location-based access control. They considered user movement as a parameter for the validity of access request and used the usage control process for the continuous enforcement of a request.

However, existing usage control models [16] are general purpose and do not address the specific aspects of contexts. Meanwhile, the lack of comprehensive ongoing enforcement mechanism and post decision checking limit the application of usage control and its practical utilization. Katt et al. [11] proposed an extension to the usage control model in order to enhance the continuity of enforcement model by configuring a meta-model. This model consists of two sub-modules: attribute decision function and obligation decision function. The first is responsible for authorizing a subject to do some actions and the second checks the obligation that the subject must fulfill.

Using state machines to model obligation enforcement was widely explored in literature so that authors in [11,25] applied formally state machine to model the obligation. Li et al. [13] modeled an obligation as a state machine interacting with PEP (Policy Enforcement Point) and the outside world through events. Meanwhile, using logic rules is another usual method to formalize obligation enforcement [5]. Our proposed enforcement model is different in terms of considering the duration of time for obligation enforcement. We propose that a SIP session be used to constrain the enforcement duration of an obligation.

Liscano et al. [14] leveraged Session Initiation Protocol (SIP) to manage the service discovery process in order to extend access to particular local services to remote participants. Karopoulos et al. [9] applied SIP architecture to handle the continuity of authorization based on usage control model. They proposed an authorization support for SIP by integrating the whole aspects of usage control along with the obligation in SIP system [10].

We also leveraged the SIP protocol to propose an architecture to approve the obligation fulfillment. However, our work is different in terms of modeling and expressing the access control obligation. We modeled the obligation based on the behavior of the subject who is responsible to perform the obligation. To express such a model of obligation, we utilized a behavior pattern language that enables the policy administrator to define a variety of subject's behavior.

3 SIP_Based Enforcement of Obligation

The traditional access control is unable to deal with the changes of attribute values of subject, object and environment after the access has been granted. However, values of attributes, that already participated in making an authorization decision, usually changes in dynamic environment. Condition and obligation are two factors that play significant role in making authorization decision in modern access control systems. Conditions are related to the stateless features of attributes whereas obligations are concerned with commitments of the involved entities. Fulfillment or violation of an obligation often affects the stateful features of attributes.

In terms of approving the fulfillment of an obligation, a predicate represents the obligation in order to verify whether a certain activity has been fulfilled or not. The evaluation of obligation's fulfillment is applied to the access request before, during, and after usage decision. Pre obligation is a predicate that checks if specific activities have been executed or not before usage exercise based on the recorded activities of system's entities. Ongoing is a predicate that should be satisfied periodically during the usage of granted access. If the evaluation of the predicate is postponed after making decision for the current request and used for future usage decision, it is called post obligation. From the continuity perspective, the fulfillment of ongoing obligation has the main effect on the continuity of the granted access. Therefore, we present a mechanism for checking the adherence to the agreed commitments in functional and ongoing obligations that are expressed by access control policy language.

We need to manage an obligation session that allows the system to monitor the behavior of a user to comply the defined obligation for accessing a particular resource or when the access is in progress. We chose SIP from different session control protocols because of its capabilities for event notification, presence and instant messaging service as well as mature features such as:

- SIP allows two or more participants to establish a session without relying on the content of the media streams. The media streams can be audio, video or any other Internet based communication mechanism such as distributed games, shared applications, and shared text editors [19].
- The protocol was standardized by the Internet Engineering Task Force (IETF) and was implemented by a number of vendors. SIP allows the endpoints to create, modify, and terminate any kind of media sessions, such as VoIP calls, multimedia conferences, or data communications in distributed systems.
- The SIP protocol supports an intermediate network element called the Back-to-Back User Agent (B2BUA) which operates between two communicating User Agents (UAs). The main advantage of using B2BUA is that it can provide a session management and full control over the session.
- SIP uses the Session Description Protocol (SDP) to help end users to negotiate the characteristics of the session. After session establishment, the protocol behaves as a Peer-to-Peer (P2P) one and allows users send messages directly to each other.
- Utilizing SDP inside of SIP provides a powerful capability to extend new services such as acquiring information about end-points, identifying the originator of a session, and identifying the content-type of a message in a session initiation request.

Increasing the processing load for parsing SIP messages is the main draw-back of using standard SIP protocol. Particularly, in constrained environments, processing the large size of text-based SIP messages makes trouble in terms of memory and power consumption. However, recent researches [3, 15] to introduce a lightweight SIP targeted to constrained environments encourage us to utilize the capabilities of it for session management in our approach.

3.1   A Behavior-Based Model for Obligation

We define a behavior as a sequence of events that are issued by a subject. An event is represented by a tuple of attributes that describe the characteristics of the interaction between a subject and an object. We assume that events possess the same type in terms of the number of attributes and the domain values of attributes. A behavior consists of two parts "static" and "dynamic".

The static part defines the structure of the behavior and includes the number of events and the event type. In fact, it represents the common characteristics between the events. The dynamic part defines the semantics of the behavior by making a correlation between the events in the behavior. Such correlations are described by a set of constraints that must be satisfied while conducting the behavior. These constraints manage the sequence and association among the events. In other words, the semantics of the behavior is represented by a set of constraints that provide association among the events or specify particular conditions for the behavior.

In access control perspective, the obligation is an operation that should be performed before, after, or during the access. We consider the following features that can specify different aspects of the obligation:

Type: obligations are categorized into three types based on when they become effective. (i) Pre-obligation specifies actions that should be fulfilled before the access of resources is allowed; (ii) ongoing-obligation specifies actions need to be fulfilled during enforcing the access (the usage of resources); and (iii) post-obligation specifies actions required to be performed after accessing to resources.

Subject: the subject of an obligation is a person (in the case of user obligation) or a component of the system (in the case of system obligation) that fulfills the obligation. PEP is responsible to approve the fulfillment of the obligation.

Object: the obligation object presents to whom the obligation must be applied. The obligation object may not be the same object of the access request. The object is a finite set of resources or state of circumstances.

Operation: the subject must perform a mandatory operation. Practically, the operation is relevant to access the resources or its execution affects the state of circumstances. The word "operation" comes from the definition of obligation in XACML standard [1] and we define it as a set of planned actions to achieve a particular purpose. Performing the operation by the subject generates a sequence of events that we call it as the behavior of the subject. Actually, the concept of the obligation dictates the behavior of the subject in a particular situation.

Violation: obligations may include requirements to specify that the fulfillment of the obligation should satisfy particular stateful constraints such as durability, deadline, location, etc.

According to the aforementioned features, we consider formally the obligation as the behavior of the subject who is in charge of performing the obligatory actions and present it as a tuple *obl(w, s, b, o, v)*. *w* represents the obligation fulfillment time and PEP handles when the obligation should be fulfilled. The subject *s* should conduct the behavior *b* on the object *o* in order to satisfy the stateful conditions *v*. The defined model for obligation helps to express the complex obligation specifications in terms of defining a sequence of actions and corresponding conditions.

Specifying precisely the behavior of a user is a challenge. A user should issue a particular behavior to fulfill the obligation so that the characteristics of such a behavior can be represented by a Behavior Pattern Language (BPL) introduced in [20]. The BPL code consists of several parts to represent a typical behavior pattern. The declaration is used to describe different entities existing in the behavior. These entities include: attributes, events, sequence of events and some parameters that specify the structure of the behavior. In other words, the skeleton of a behavior will be defined in the declaration section, then the pertinent operations and constraints will be called to establish the meaning of the behavior. The methods in the operation section are used to define the relation between events. The relation can be defined through applying different statements and operators to manipulate attributes and attribute values. If someone intends to define particular restrictions for the operation, the relevant assertions will be defined in the constraint section.

Such a language allows the access control policy administrator to illustrate primitive events and their attributes, semantics, constraints, and behavior patterns in a detailed and precise manner. The elements of the defined tuple for the obligation can be specified by BPL. However, the obligation specified by BPL should be interpreted and converted to the XML (Extensible Markup Language) format to be compatible with XACML.

3.2   Obligation Handling in XACML

XACML is a standard developed by the OASIS organization [1] for expressing syntax and semantics of access control policies. It provides a language, a reference architecture and the processing model to describe how to evaluate an access request. Briefly, the XACML promises to be an expressive and flexible policy language and architecture for heterogeneous and dynamic environment.

The XACML Technical Committee provides a Policy Schema for the XACML policies so that at the root of all XACML policies there are tags <Policy> or <PolicySet>. A policy set can contain other policies or policy sets. A policy consists of a target, which denotes the target of the policy, a set of rules elements which represent the authorization rules, and a rule combining algorithm. The target specifies the subjects, resources, actions and environments on which a policy can be applied. A rule includes three main components: the Target, the Condition, and the Effect of the rule which can be either Permit or Deny. The Target specifies for which kind of access requests the rule can be applied. The Condition elements denotes predicates in order to evaluate the attributes. A rule can include optionally an ObligationExpression element to specify action that should be performed after enforcing the authorization decision. A rule is applicable to an access request if the target of the access request matches the target of the rule and if all the conditions included in the rule are satisfied. Meanwhile, the predefined combining algorithms are used to resolve the conflict among applicable rules during the decision making.

XACML allows to express fine-grained access control policies, but it is not expressive enough to define different kinds of obligation particularly ongoing obligation that can be used to control the continuity of a granted access. In general, XACML does not possess specific constructs to address the continuity of policy enforcement. Specifying obligations using a behavior-based language and leveraging SIP protocol are our approach to enhance the expressiveness and capability of the XACML.

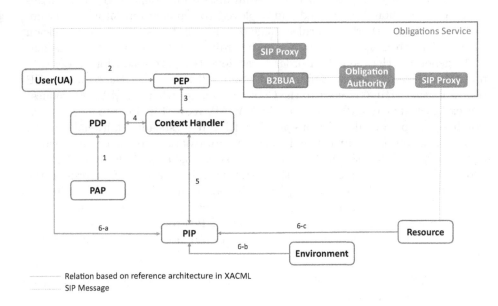

Fig. 1. Extending the obligation service in XACML reference architecture to handle the pre and ongoing obligations

3.3   Wrapping up Obligations in SIP Message

Session Initiation Protocol (SIP) is an application layer protocol that is used to set up a media session and help end users to exchange data. To establish a session, the requester sends the INVITE request that contains a number of header fields. Header fields are named attributes that provide additional information about a message. The body of a SIP message contains a description of the session that is encoded by a protocol called Session Description Protocol (SDP). The TRYING response indicates that the INVITE has been received and the proxy is working on her behalf to route the INVITE to the destination. If the destination decides to answer the request, it will send OK response to the requester. Any of the two users can send a BYE message directly to the other in order to terminate the session.

SIP protocol provides a logical entity called Back-to-Back User Agent (B2BUA) that operates between two communicating User Agents (UAs) and controls all signaling exchanged between them. In other words, it is a concatenation of a User Agent Client (UAC) and User Agent Server (UAS). It receives request from the calling SIP user agent (client), and forwards them to the called SIP (server). Therefore, B2BUA as an intermediary prevents the end points from direct exchanging of messages. Applying the B2BUA provides a facility for communication management for the whole duration and full control over the connection.

As can be seen in Fig. 1, a Policy Administration Point (PAP) determines which policies should be defined and deployed to a policy repository. Later on, such predefined authorization rules inside policies can be used by Policy Decision Point (PDP) to make a decision for an incoming access request. A User Agent (UA) generates the request in order to achieve the permission for access to a particular resource. Policy Enforcement Point (PEP) receives the request. PEP transmits the original request to the Context Handler where an XACML request context is constructed. PDP receives the XACML request in order to make a decision based on policy rules. For this purpose, PDP requests any additional subject, resource, action, environment and other categories attributes from the context handler. Policy Information Point (PIP) is responsible to provide values for such additional attributes and returns the attribute values to the PDP through the Context Handler. PDP evaluates policies based on provided attribute values to make the decision for granting or denying the request. The authorization decision along with obligations will be sent to the PEP through the Context Handler for enforcement. In summary, the procedure to evaluate an access request based on policy rules is as follows:

1. Flow 1: PAP writes policies and corresponding obligations and make them available to the PDP
2. Flow 2: The access requester sends a request for access to the PEP
3. Flow 3: The PEP sends the request in its native format to the context handler
4. Flow 4: The context handler constructs an XACML request context and sends to PDP
5. Flow 4: The PDP requests attribute values and any additional attributes from the context handler
6. Flow 5: The context handler communicates with PIP to obtain the attribute values
7. Flow 6-a, 6-b, 6-c: The PIP obtains attributes of the subject, resource, action, and environment

8. Flow 5: PIP returns attributes to the PDP through the context handler
9. Flow 4: The PDP evaluates the policy
10. Flow 3: The PDP returns the authorization decision along with applicable obligation to the PEP via context handler

In the XACML workflow, there is no information for obligation enforcement and the role of obligation for the continuity of granted access. We leveraged SIP to provide a communication paradigm between entities in a distributed access control system in order to handle the obligation. For this purpose, we add SIP components such as SIP proxy, B2BUA as well as an Obligation Authority (OA) inside of "Obligations Service" provided by XACML architecture. We consider the OA as a third party (or resource owner) that obliges the user to follow a behavior before access to resources or when the access is still in progress. We describe the interactions between SIP and access control components to handle pre-obligation and ongoing obligation as follows:

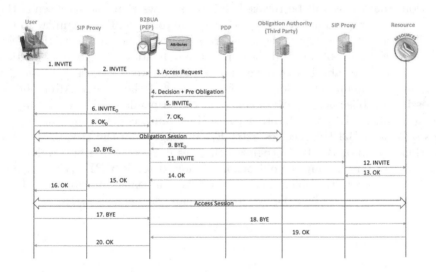

Fig. 2. Applying a SIP session to handle the pre-obligation

Pre-obligation: In some situations, the fulfillment of an obligation is a prerequisite to allow the user to access a resource. Figure 2 shows the sequence diagram in the case of pre-obligation so that the complete execution of an obligation is needed before permitting the user request. We use a B2BUA to achieve a full control over the SIP session. We got the idea from [10] to integrate the B2BUA with the PEP for decreasing the complexity of implementation. Meanwhile, handling obligation outside the PEP will greatly complicate the interface between them and decrease the performance. B2BUA is a logical SIP entity that provides a proper opportunity to implement the logics inside of the PEP for managing the obligation life-cycle. When a user sends a request to access a particular resource, the request will be wrapped up with SIP message called INVITE and will be sent to B2BUA through SIP proxy. PEP extracts the request and sends to PDP to make decision for authorization based on predefined policies and obligations. PDP sends the final decision along with the applicable obligation to the PEP. In this case, we assume that the obligation is a pre-obligation that should be enforced before granting the permission to the requester. Therefore, the B2BUA suspends the request and sends a SIP invite message ($INVITE_O$) to both Obligation Authority(OA) and requester (User) to start an obligation session. When the user performs the obligation, the OA approves the fulfillment by sending a BYE message (BYE_O) to B2BUA. Then, B2BUA resumes the user's access request and sends it to the resource for establishment an access session.

Ongoing Obligation: Ongoing-obligations need to be fulfilled in parallel with the requested access. It means that ongoing-obligations should be executed when the user performs actions on a granted resource. The user may be permitted to access the resource in the beginning, but if the user fails to fulfill the ongoing-obligation, the access will be revoked. Figure 3 shows that the user sends the access request wrapped up by SIP invite message to the B2BUA. Similar to the pre-obligation, PDP evaluates the access request to provide authorization decision plus applicable obligation. However, if the obligation is ongoing-obligation then the B2BUA establishes an obligation session between the user and the OA which should remain active for the whole period of the access. After obligation session establishment, B2BUA conducts the suspended INVITE message to resource through SIP proxy in order to establish an access session. During the access session, if B2BUA receives a BYE_O message from the user to stop the obligation session or B2BUA recognizes changes in specific attribute values for the purpose of terminating the obligation session, it sends a BYE_O message to the OA to terminate the obligation session. Then, it sends immediately a BYE message to the resource and the user to terminate the access session.

4   Case Studies

We describe two application scenarios based on examples presented in [16] in order to illustrate the functionality of our proposed approach. Similar situations to each of these scenarios were applied in literature to focus on particular aspect of the access control. For example, the situation in Scenario 1 was also used in [12] to present the need for extending role-based access control model to support context-based access control requirements for pervasive computing systems. Scenario 2 was widely used as a reference example to apply obligation for handling the usage control [10,13]. Each of such scenarios can be realized by using different aspect of access control such as authorization, obligation, or condition predicates. We look at the obligation perspective of such scenarios to propose a solution that ensures a continuous access control while the subject's behavior changes.

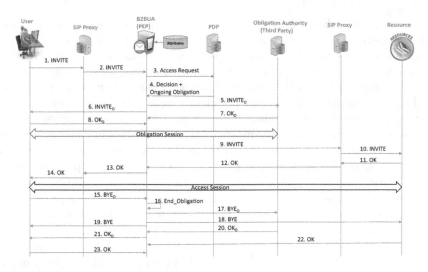

Fig. 3. Applying a SIP session to handle the ongoing obligation

In this paper, we concentrate on the ongoing obligation because the fulfillment of this kind of obligation should be continuously checked after access permission. The continuity of access to a service or resource is a challenge due to the dynamic nature of pervasive environments. In access control, continuity means that a control policy should be enforced not only before an access, but also during the period of the access. The dynamic nature of context information in pervasive environment requires the capability of access control model for revocation or continuity of a granted access when certain context conditions fail to hold. Pre-obligation and post-obligation cannot affect on the continuity of access, although our proposed approach can be used for enforcement of such obligations.

Scenario 1: We focus on combining the smart devices and hospital information system deployed in healthcare centers. Such systems can be accessed remotely or locally by nurses and doctors. The system is able to assign doctors in the capacity of a doctor-on-duty role to a ward during specific time periods. In this role the system allows access to the health records of only those patients who are assigned to the doctor. The system also allows interns to attend in a ward for training purpose. The access permission will be valid until the doctor keeps the role of doctor-on-duty. This role is revoked when the doctor leaves the location, or after the end of her duty time. Doctors allow to create different kinds of diagnostic reports about patients so that an intern can access such reports only if the doctor is present in the ward. We consider a situation where an intern begins to access a report and during the access, the doctor leaves the ward. In such a case, the system needs a mechanism to ensure that the ongoing accessing should be revoked due to the absence of the doctor.

We now illustrate how the access control obligation for the scenario 1 can be modeled and enforced by using our approach. We assume that all doctors, nurses, interns and patients should register to the HIS system. Meanwhile, entrance doors of important places such as ward, operation room, and conference room have been equipped by RFID readers. Therefore, the system is able to track the individuals, because all personnels have to wear a badge embedded by an RFID tag. The requests of all registered users in different roles to access various resources are evaluated based on authorization rules defined in the policy repository. However, we utilize our approach to resolve some issues existing around fulfilling the obligations such as: how policy administrator can express the detail of the obligation and how policy engine enforces the obligation during access.

The obligation specifies that an intern can access diagnostic reports in the presence of a doctor. We use the BPL to express the behavior of the intern who is responsible to perform the obligation. In this case, there is a strong association between the behavior of intern and doctor based on the attribute of location. Code 1.1 illustrates the BPL code to represent the dependency of intern's behavior and doctor's behavior. We assume that the behavior of doctor and intern includes one event (line 6 and 7). The structure of the event is defined in line 4 so that it has six attributes. Line 8 defines the domain values for each attribute. We call two methods in line 9 and 10 to assign values to attributes of each event. In line 11, we emphasize that the occurrence of events should be in the same location.

When an intern sends a request, policy engine evaluates the request by applying policy rules and stateless conditions that are based on the information provided in the access request. The request will be allowed or denied based on the result of the evaluation. However, the authorization system must consider the location of doctor in the role of doctor-on-duty during the execution of the granted access. In this case, the location of the doctor-on-duty is a mutable attribute that presents stateful condition binding to the resource state. Therefore, continuous obligation enforcement is required by the authorization system.

According to Fig. 3, before starting the access session, B2BUA commences an obligation session between the intern and obligation authority (in this case electronic health record system). After establishment of the obligation session, B2BUA transmits the intern's request to the resource manager in order to create an access session. The values of mutable attributes of involved entities will be periodically collected by Policy Information Point (PIP). Once the location of the doctor changes, an "End_Obligation" message will be generated. Then, B2BUA sends a "Bye" message to both obligation authority and resource manager to terminate the obligation session and access session respectively.

Code 1.1. The BPL description of the obligatory behavior of the intern in scenario 1

```
1  PATTERN  Intern_Behavior;
2  TYPE  ongoing−obligation;
3  BEGIN
4    DEFINE  Event = <User, Role, Action, Resource, Location, Time>
5    E[] = new Event(2);
6    set1 = {E[1]};
7    set2 = {E[1]};
8    attVal = {<Role,{"intern", "doctor"}>,<Action,{"read","
         write"}>,<Location,{"ward","operating room" }>,<
         Resource,{"diagnostic report"}>};
9    CALL Op1(set1, attVal);
10   CALL Op2(set2, attVal);
11   ASSERT EQUALITY(set1, set2, Location);
12 END
13
14 /* define operation 1−Behavior of intern*/
15    DEF Op1 (set, attVal)
16    Set[E1].Role=attVal[Role].value[0];
17      Set[E1].Action=attVal[Action].value[0];
18      Set[E1].Resource=attVal[Resource].value[0];
19      Set[E1].Resource=attVal[Location].value[0];
20    END
21 /* define operation 2−Behavior of doctor*/
22    DEF Op2 (set, attVal)
23      Set[E1].Role=attVal[Role].value[1];
24      Set[E1].Resource=attVal[Resource].value[0];
25    END
```

Scenario 2: We consider the case of two individuals, say Bob and Alice, who make a video conversation using free softphone applications. When the caller initiates a conversation, the application requires that an advertisement window is displayed on the caller's device while the call is in progress. The caller have to keep the advertisement window active during the conversation. Consequently, if the caller closes this window while the call is still in progress, the application policy term is violated and caller's access should be revoked.

Obligation in scenario 2 represents the typical example of a usage control that obliges the user to open and watch an advertisement during using a multimedia service. Code 1.2 expresses the mandatory behavior of a caller during using the calling service. Execution of the obligation occurs in parallel with using the calling service. The procedure to handle the obligation follows the process shown in Fig. 3. The caller sends an "Invite" massage (request) to set up a conversation. The B2BUA receives the decision along with the detail of the obligation from the PDP. Since the obligation is an ongoing obligation, the B2BUA creates an obligation session between the caller and the obligation authority (in this case an advertisement server). The obligation session should keep alive during the conversion between caller and callee. After establishment of the obligation session, the B2BUA allows to create an access session between caller and callee to use the service. If the caller closes the advertisement window for any reason, the B2BUA realizes the termination of watching the advertisement and sends a "Bye" message to the obligation authority to stop obligation session, followed by a "Bye" message to callee to terminate the access session.

Code 1.2. The BPL description of the obligatory behavior of the intern in scenario 2

```
1  PATTERN  Caller_Behavior ;
2  TYPE  ongoing-obligation ;
3  BEGIN
4     DEFINE  Event = <User , Role , Action , Resource , Time>
5     E [ ]  = new Event  (3) ;
6     set = {E[1] ,E[2] ,E[3]} ;
7     attVal = {<Role ,{" caller " ," calee"}>,<Action ,{" call " ,"
          open" ," watch"}>,<Resource ,{" calling_service " ,"
          advertizement"}>};
8     CALL Op1(set , attVal) ;
9  END
10
11 /* define  operation */
12    DEF Op1  (set , attVal)
13       Set [E1] . Role=attVal [Role ] . value [0] ;
14       Set [E1] . Action=attVal [Action ] . value [0] ;
15       Set [E1] . Resource=attVal [Resource ] . value [0] ;
16
17       Set [E2] . Role=attVal [Role ] . value [0] ;
18       Set [E2] . Action=attVal [Action ] . value [1] ;
19       Set [E2] . Resource=attVal [Resource ] . value [1] ;
20
21       Set [E3] . Role=attVal [Role ] . value [0] ;
22       Set [E3] . Action=attVal [Action ] . value [2] ;
23       Set [E3] . Resource=attVal [Resource ] . value [1] ;
24
25       ASSERT EQUALITY DURATION(E1 , E3) ;
26    END
```

5   Conclusion

This paper addresses the fulfilment of access control obligation during the access to the particular resources. Handling different kinds of obligations goes beyond the capabilities of traditional access control systems. Due to the dynamic nature of pervasive computing entities behavior, protecting resources only by predefining a set of authorization rules is extremely challenging. Moreover, pervasive computing often relies on the heterogeneous environment that exacerbates the incompleteness of access control policy rules. Considering the obligation as a part of authorization policies increases the capability of the access control system to mitigate the misuse of resources. Therefore, obligations are required to force the user to follow specific behaviors in order to access securely the resources and services in pervasive environments.

A model is required to present the obligation in order to dictate the mandatory operations that must be performed by the user before, after, and during the access. Furthermore, due to the incomplete nature of policy languages to cover all aspects of access needs, they cannot specify expressively the features of obligations. Therefore, we first defined a behavior as a sequence of events along with several constraints that show the correlation between events. Then, we modeled the obligation based on the obligatory behavior of a subject in access control system. We also introduced a behavior based language to express the structure and semantics of the mandatory behavior as an obligation.

From the continuity perspective, the fulfillment of ongoing obligation has the main effect on the continuity of the granted access. In the XACML workflow, there is no information for obligation enforcement and the role of obligation for the continuity of granted access. Consequently, we leveraged the capabilities of SIP protocol to handle the obligation. We have developed a structure for obligation service based on XACML reference structure and SIP entities for the purpose of continuity or revocation of granted access.

We aim at extending our approach by provisioning a behavior analysis and testing model in order to find the instances of the user's behavior leading to an obligation violation. Such an extension helps us to cover the fulfillment of the post obligation that cannot be approved appropriately by our current approach due to the durability issue. Meanwhile, PEP needs to monitor the actions of the user to verify the violation of the ongoing obligation. For this purpose, utilizing the complex event processing technology to capture the dynamic nature of user's actions is our next step to accomplish the work.

References

1. eXtensible Access Control Markup Language (XACML), version 3.0, OASIS standard, January 2013. https://www.oasis-open.org/
2. Ardagna, C.A., Cremonini, M., Damiani, E., di Vimercati, S.D.C., Samarati, P.: Supporting location-based conditions in access control policies. In: ACM Symposium on Information, Computer and Communications Security, pp. 212–222. ACM (2006)
3. Cirani, S., Picone, M., Veltri, L.: A session initiation protocol for the internet of things. Sci. Int. J. Parallel Distrib. Comput. Scalable Comput. Pract. Experience 14(4), 249–263 (2015). SCPE
4. Damiani, M.L., Bertino, E., Silvestri, C.: An approach to supporting continuity of usage location-based access control. In: 12th IEEE International Workshop on Future Trends of Distributed Computing Systems, pp. 199–205. IEEE (2008)
5. Elrakaiby, Y., Cuppens, F., Cuppens-Boulahia, N.: Formal enforcement and management of obligation policies. Data Knowl. Eng. 71(1), 127–147 (2012)
6. Feltus, C., Petit, M., Sloman, M.: Enhancement of business IT alignment by including responsibility components in RBAC. In: CAiSE 2010 Workshop Busital 10, Hammamet, Tunisia, pp. 61–75 (2010)

7. Gomez, L., Trabelsi, S.: Obligation based access control. In: Meersman, R. (ed.) On the Move to Meaningful Internet Systems: OTM 2014 Workshops. LNCS, vol. 8842, pp. 108–116. Springer, Heidelberg (2014). doi:10.1007/978-3-662-45550-0_15

8. Rosenberg, J., Schulzrinne, H., Camarillo, G., Johnston, A., Peterson, J., Sparks, R., et al.: SIP: Session initiation protocol. RFC 3261 (2002). https://www.ietf.org/rfc/rfc3261.txt

9. Karopoulos, G., Mori, P., Martinelli, F.: Continuous authorizations in SIP with usage control. In: 20th Euromicro International Conference on Parallel, Distributed and Network-based Processing, pp. 283–287. IEEE (2012)

10. Karopoulos, G., Mori, P., Martinelli, F.: Usage control in SIP-based multimedia delivery. Comput. Secur. **39**, 406–418 (2013). Elsevier

11. Katt, B., Zhang, X., Breu, R., Hafner, M., Seifert, J.P.: A general obligation model and continuity-enhanced policy enforcement engine for usage control. In: The 13th ACM symposium on Access Control Models and Technologies, pp. 123–132. ACM (2008)

12. Kulkarni, D., Tripathi, A.: Context-aware role-based access control in pervasive computing systems. In: 13th ACM symposium on Access Control Models and Technologies, pp. 113–122. ACM (2008)

13. Li, N., Chen, H., Bertino, E.: On practical specification and enforcement of obligations. In: The second ACM conference on Data and Application Security and Privacy, pp. 71–82. ACM (2012)

14. Liscano, R., Dersingh, A., Jost, A.G., Hu, H.: Discovering and managing access to private services in collaborative sessions. IEEE Trans. Syst. Man Cybern. Part A: Syst. Hum. **36**(6), 1086–1097 (2006). IEEE

15. Miskovic, V., Babic, D.: An architecture for pervasive healthcare system based on the IP multimedia subsystem and body sensor network. Facta Univ. Ser. Electron. Energetics **28**(3), 439–456 (2015)

16. Park, J., Sandhu, R.: The UCON$_{ABC}$ usage control model. ACM Trans. Inf. Syst. Secur. **7**(1), 128–174 (2004)

17. Ray, I., Toahchoodee, M.: A spatio-temporal role-based access control model. In: Barker, S., Ahn, G.-J. (eds.) DBSec 2007. LNCS, vol. 4602, pp. 211–226. Springer, Heidelberg (2007). doi:10.1007/978-3-540-73538-0_16

18. Sampemane, G., Naldur, P., Campbellg, R.H.: Access control for active spaces. In: 18th Annual Computer Security Applications Conference. ACM (2002)

19. Schulzrinne, H., Wedlund, E.: Application-layer mobility using SIP. Mob. Comput. Commun. Rev. **4**(3), 47–57 (2000). ACM

20. Sharghi, H., Sartipi, K.: An expressive event-based language for representing user behavior patterns. J. Intell. Inf. Syst. 1–25 (2017). doi:10.1007/s10844-017-0456-5

21. Strembeck, M., Neumann, G.: An integrated approach to engineer and enforce context constraints in RBAC environments. ACM Trans. Inf. Syst. Secur. **7**(3), 392–427 (2004). ACM

22. Toahchoodee, M.: Access control models for pervasive computing environments. Ph.D. thesis, Colorado State University, Fort Collins, Colorado (2010)

23. Toahchoodee, M., Abdunabi, R., Ray, I., Ray, I.: A trust-based access control model for pervasive computing applications. In: Gudes, E., Vaidya, J. (eds.) DBSec 2009. LNCS, vol. 5645, pp. 307–314. Springer, Heidelberg (2009). doi:10.1007/978-3-642-03007-9_22

24. Ulltveit-Moe, N., Oleshchuk, V.: Enforcing mobile security with location-aware role-based access control. Secur. Commun. Netw. **9**(5), 429–439 (2016). Wiley

25. Zhang, X., Parisi-Presicce, F., Sandhu, R., Park, J.: Formal model and policy specification of usage control. ACM Trans. Inf. Syst. Secur. **8**(4), 351–387 (2005)

Privacy Preserving Discovery
of Nearby-Friends

Maryam Hezaveh[(⊠)] and Carlisle Adams

School of Electrical Engineering and Computer Science,
University of Ottawa, Ottawa, Canada
{mheza028, cadams}@uottawa.ca

Abstract. We propose a privacy-preserving protocol for the discovery of
nearby friends. In this scenario, Alice wants to verify whether any of her friends
is close to her or not. This should be done without disclosing any information
about Alice to her friends and also any of the other parties' information to Alice.
In this paper, we present a protocol based on the homomorphic property of
Goldwasser-Micali cryptosystem to protect each user's location in proximity
queries. However, an active adversary could learn, if two users are "close" to
each other due to the vulnerability of the Goldwasser-Micali to IND-CCA2
attacks and malleability of homomorphic encryption schemes. Our protocol
solves this problem with the authenticated encryption scheme called
encrypt-then-mac [5]. We implemented our proposed protocol on the Android
platform and we show that the proposed system and protocol can achieve a high
level of privacy and secrecy.

Keywords: Privacy · Location based services · Goldwasser-Micali
cryptosystem

1 Introduction

Location Based Services (LBSs) use the global positioning systems and the mobile
phone network to calculate the geographical position of mobile phones. If the users
have given that application appropriate permission at the time of application installation, the device automatically releases the user's location to the service provider
applications. By granting this permission, the user's location is sent periodically, or
whenever the service is required, to the service provider. However, revealing accurate
location information in a manner which is completely invisible to the users can give
rise to privacy concerns. While LBS may be useful for mobile users for safety-related
LBS and it is helpful if emergency services know a user's location details, users might
not be aware of the loss of personal information to other third party services. Indeed,
instead of using LBS to improve life, it could easily be misused and turn into a tracking
tool. Hence, an important aspect issue for the research community is protecting the
user's real-time location while they are using LBSs.

Social networking applications have added nearby-friends features by using the
features of LBSs. Some of the more popular applications are Facebook nearby friends,
Loopt, WeChat, etc. These applications have become popular and widely used.

© Springer International Publishing AG 2017
E. Aïmeur et al. (Eds.): MCETECH 2017, LNBIP 289, pp. 41–55, 2017.
DOI: 10.1007/978-3-319-59041-7_3

They need to access the exact (or obfuscated) user's location to calculate the distance between friends and return the result. However, the leakage of the user's precise location to friends and the service provider may be a concern.

Secure LBSs have been proposed using cryptographic and non-cryptographic mechanisms. Most existing solutions are non-cryptographic approaches. These typically use a trusted third party as an anonymizer for K-anonymity approaches or cloaking approaches. The K-anonymity approaches protect a user's location by sending the user's query with the queries of at least K other users within that region. Therefore, the service provider cannot guess the user or the user's location. As an alternative to mixing the user's query with K-1 genuine queries, the user could generate K-1 dummy queries and send these to the service provider. The main goal of cloaking is to deviate or blur the exact location of the user within a certain area from LBS provider.

Both of these approaches may preserve the user's location information in many LBS applications, but none of these are suitable for the nearby-friends application because: the nearby-friend application needs to know the identity of the person who is nearby (therefore, the K-anonymity approach is not an appropriate choice for this application); and the nearby-friend application should protect both friends in the proximity relationship. The approximate location or K-1 dummy query features can be affected by the requested information. The main challenge is to tackle these problems to retrieve required information without disclosing any user's location information.

The cryptographic mechanisms use encryption methods to protect user location. Homomorphic encryption makes it possible to perform addition and/or multiplication over encrypted data. The LBS service provider could, therefore, process the encrypted data and return required information to the user. The user who requested the data is the only one who can decrypt it. Therefore, the user location information can be kept private from the service provider. In nearby-friend applications, cryptographic mechanisms could remove all responsibility for proximity calculation from the server. Friends send their encrypted location directly to each other. On the receiver side, encrypted data is processed and returned to the sender without revealing location information.

1.1 Our Contributions

We propose a homomorphic cryptographic protocols based on the Goldwasser-Micali probabilistic encryption scheme [14, 15] for discovering nearby friends. The protocol possesses a number of advantages over the existing ones: the first is our protocol does not need a trusted third party for processing data; the second one is that the server simply registers users and forwards the encrypted data between them, it cannot collude with friends to learns information about users' location. Finally, our protocol is secure against an active adversary who has access to the ciphertext on the communication channel and the decryption oracle. The adversary cannot forge another ciphertext, which leads him to guess the user's location (IND-CCA2). Moreover, he cannot modify the ciphertext which leads to forge the user's location and affect the outcome of the nearby friend's application (NM-CCA2).

1.2   Organization of This Work

The rest of this paper has the following structure: Sect. 2 presents a brief overview of previous work on privacy-preserving in LBSs; Sect. 3 describes the details of our IND-CCA2 proposed protocol based on the Goldwasser-Micali cryptosystem; Sect. 3.6 presents the security analysis of our protocol; Sect. 4 gives an overview of our prototype implementation on Android, and finally Sect. 5 concludes the paper.

2   Related Work

In this section, we give an overview of the existing location-based schemes for privacy preservation of a user's location as follows: position dummies, K-anonymity, spatial obfuscation, and encryption approaches.

2.1   Dummy Locations

In this approach, the user generates some fake locations which are called dummies and sends them with her real location to the LBS. In this way, LBS would not find out which of them is the user's real location and the location of the user remains secure. The main advantage of this approach is that the user does not need to rely on a trusted third party to produce dummies. The difficult part of this approach is to generate the dummies in such a way that they are not recognizable from the real location. For example, if an adversary tracks the user for a period of time, he should not be able to find out which of the sent locations is the real one. Shankar et al. [25] presented an approach, which assumed that the user generates a database from historical traffic and creates her dummy locations from it. In this way, her dummy locations are indistinguishable from her real location. Obviously, the security of this approach depends on the number of fake requests send to the LBS. The main drawback of this approach is the fact that as the number of requests grows, the LBS may suspect that the user is an adversary and ignore the request. Furthermore, when the number of requests is increased, it slows down the server's response time.

2.2   K-Anonymity

The concept of K-anonymity in location privacy approaches tries to make sure that in a set of K users, a specific user's identity is indistinguishable from K-1 other users. Here, K is the security parameter, which determines the level of anonymity. There are number of other privacy techniques such as entropy-based, differential privacy, probabilistic metrics, etc. However, none of these are relevant to the concept of privacy in location based services. In K-anonymity, often a trusted location anonymizer is responsible for blurring users' locations into cloaked areas, such that the probability of identifying that user is 1/K. In [16], the trusted anonymizer calculates an obfuscation area of a user which includes K-1 other users in that area. By this approach, the trusted anonymizer can provide k-anonymity; that is, hiding the user's actual location by returning an area that has K-1 other people and protecting her location by a pseudonym. This approach assumes that all users have the same K-anonymity requirements and it suffers from scalability because the anonymizer calculates the set of K-1 other users and the obfuscation area for each user individually.

In Casper [22], the anonymizer maintains the locations of the user base in a pyramid data structure, like a Quad-tree. If the calculated obfuscation area contains k users, it will consider it as a cloaking area. Otherwise, the horizontal and vertical neighbors of the obfuscation area add to the obfuscation area to provide enough users to apply k-anonymity. In the worst case, if the number of users is not enough, even with the neighbors, the anonymizer uses the parents of the obfuscation area and repeats this process until enough users are found. This approach guarantees k-anonymity, minimum area and the maximum area within which user wants to hide. In [11], Gedik et al. proposed another K-anonymity scheme to support a personalized level of anonymity where each user is able to define the minimum and the maximum acceptable limits for the obfuscation area size and time periods. These approaches could pose an issue due to the requirement of all the mobile users to periodically report their exact locations to the trusted location anonymizer. Storing the user's exact location at a server is not secure and the user's privacy is clearly impossible because the server could be a single point of attack.

To deal with these problems and remove the trusted anonymizer, Ghinita et al. [12] introduced a decentralized, cooperative, peer-to-peer model. The main idea is the dynamic formation of nearby peer groups that can perform location anonymization for each other to achieve reciprocity of k-clusters. Using this approach, the individual in one k-cluster can cloak their location from all other k-clusters. Although a trusted anonymizer is not required anymore, all users must trust each other.

Similar to k-anonymity clustering, Mescetti et al. [20] presented an approach called historical k-anonymity which takes motion into consideration. They proved that an adversary could make the connection between each user and their location by observing continuous location updates. The Provident Hider [20] algorithm uses historical information of each user to prevent this attack under certain assumptions. However, this approach did not consider query privacy.

To hide the identity of the user who sends the request in a k-anonymity clustering approach, Chow et al. [7] used unstructured peer-to-peer networks. The user uses peer-to-peer communication to find a spatial region that contains k users. After clustering is finished, a random member of the cluster will send the query to the service provider server. Another fully distributed mobile peer-to-peer approach [13] called MobiHide presented Hilbert space-filling curves to anonymize a query by mapping it to a random group of k users. The mobile users should trust each other to exchange their location information and collaborate in computing cloaking regions. The main drawback of clustering k-anonymity is the overhead and latency of the group formation and entire communication.

Hu et al. [18] proposed another decentralized approach in which users collaborate to make a cloaking region without revealing their exact location to other peers. However, like previous ones, this approach considers just a snapshot of user locations and is not secure in continuous location updates.

2.3   Location Obfuscation

"Location obfuscation" approaches try to preserve location privacy by changing, deviating or blurring their exact location. Spatial cloaking approaches rely on a spatial area, not the number of users like K-anonymity. They may even accommodate the case that only one user is located at the spatial obfuscation region. The concept of spatial obfuscation was introduced by Ardagna et al, [2]. The user selects a circular region instead of her exact location and sends it to the LBS. This approach does not require a trusted-third-party to generate the obfuscation location. In addition, the user can choose their obfuscation area. However, the user should be careful about her choice because it affects the returned result. Cheng et al. [6] presented probabilistic cloaking which preserves the privacy of the user's location by uniformly distributing it in a closed region around her. In another approach [9], the obfuscation regions are modeled as a set of vertices in graphs, which provides a more flexible model of geographic space than circles.

Hashem et al. [17] presented a group-based approach which tries to find a location nearest to each of the group members. For example, a group of friends wants to meet in a restaurant which minimizes travel for all of the group members. For privacy preservation of the user's location, they offer to use location region instead of the users' exact locations to the service provider.

Damiani et al. [8] developed a semantic location cloaking framework called Probe (Privacy-aware Obfuscation Environment). The idea here is that the user's location may have a different sensitivity depending on where the user has been. For example being in a hospital is more sensitive than being in a crowded street. By considering this sensitivity, the user can expand their obfuscation area in such a way that the probability of being in a certain sensitive location is less than a defined threshold.

In all these schemes, the size of the obfuscation region can be reduced if the adversary has background knowledge about the users' location. The map-based inference is a particularly strong threat. In order to stop this attack, Ardagna et al. [3] introduced "Landscape-aware Location-Privacy Protection" which aims to provide a map-dependent obfuscation area by considering the probability that a user's location is actually contained in an area.

2.4   Cryptography-Based Approaches

Cryptographic location privacy approaches use encryption to protect user location. Mascetti et al. [21] use symmetric encryption techniques to notify users when their buddies are within their proximity in order to prevent friends and a location-based service provider to find out the actual current user location. However, the location-based service provider could compare the encrypted values if the encrypted scheme is not semantically secure. Therefore, the LSB provider could collude with one of the parties to find out the location of other friends or misinform them that they are far apart from each other while actually, they are nearby.

Zhong et al. [28] proposed three different protocols for location privacy to alert friends if and only if that friend is actually nearby. The protocols are called Louis, Lester, and Pierre. The service provider does not need to be aware of the users' locations. There are some drawbacks of each protocol such as one of the users will learn the exact location or distances with the other user in the Louis and Pierre protocol. The user can add a guessable location to check if her friend is near a special place or not in the Lester protocol. Finally, all of them require the user to calculate distance R, which is computationally expensive.

[23] presented three protocols to enable proximity testing without revealing the mobile users' real location information for privacy preserving distributed social discovery. It allows users to exchange location-based information with friends while protecting their privacy. These schemes allow two parties to exchange privately whether they are close or not, without disclosing any further information to each other, the server or any eavesdropper. With an oblivious server, the protocol cannot guarantee privacy if any two parties collude.

A location-privacy aware friend-locator LBS called FriendLocato, is presented in [26]. Each user encrypts her location with a one-to-one pre-shared key. Later, the server checks for finding a user's proximity by matching the encrypted location into four cells of a grid. This scheme has many flaws, such as lack of flexibility in user preference, dynamic-shape vicinities, and the server learns the information, which was retrieved about the distance between users.

The buddy tracking application [1] presented an efficient algorithm for proximity detection called Strips. This approach focuses on the efficiency in terms of computation cost and communication complexity, such as reducing the messages exchanged between users, rather than location privacy issues. In general, cryptographic approaches are a new research area to determine whether location-based queries such as nearby friends' queries can be provided efficiently over the encrypted data.

3   Proposed Privacy Preserving Protocols

The main aim of cryptographic approaches in nearby friends is to make it possible to automatically detect nearby friends even when the user's location privacy is applied in the application. Our proposed protocols use homomorphic encryption of the Goldwasser-Micali (GM) cryptosystem to achieve this purpose.

3.1   Review of the Goldwasser-Micali Scheme

An important family of homomorphic encryption schemes [24, 27], using the first probabilistic public key encryption system proposed by Goldwasser and Micali in 1982 [14, 15], is described in Table 1. The GM cryptosystem uses probabilistic encryption which is based on randomness. By using randomness in the encryption algorithm every time we encrypt the same message, the ciphertext is different. GM uses two large primes p and q to produce modulus n = pq. The encryption operation is simple; it is the square of a random number r, modulo n. Decryption is the heavier operation, with an exponentiation to determine if the encrypted bit is a quadratic residue or not. With this consideration, the computational complexity of this step can be done in $O(l(p)^2)$, where l(p) denotes the number of bits in p. Note that the computational cost of decrypting k bits plaintext is $O(k.l(p)^2)$. Unfortunately, by increasing the number of bits, this

Table 1. Goldwasser-Micali [14, 15]

Prerequisite:	Alice computed a (public, private) key: she first choses $n = pq$, p and q being large prime numbers and g a quadratic nonresidue modulo n whose Jacobi symbol is 1; her public key is composed of n and g, and her private key is the factorization of n.
Goal:	Anyone can send an encrypted message to Alice.
Principle:	To encrypt a bit b, Bob picks at random an integer $r \in Z_n^*$, and computes $c = g^b r^2 \bmod n$ (remark that c is a quadratic residue if and only if $b = 0$). To get back to the plaintext, Alice determines if c is a quadratic residue or not. To do so, she uses the property that the Jacobi symbol c/p is equal to $(-1)^b$. Please, note that the scheme encrypts 1 bit of information, while its output is at least 1024 bits long!
Security:	This scheme is the first one that was proved semantically secure against a passive adversary (under a computational assumption).

approach has a strong drawback. This is not very efficient for an application with long data input [10]. However, the input data of our proposed protocol does not exceed more than 100 bits per user in the worst case. The idea of how we calculate the input for our nearby-friend's application presents in the grid-based location section in more detail.

In the Goldwasser-Micali cryptosystem, as described in Table 1, if the public key is the modulus n and quadratic non-residue g, then the encryption of a bit b is $\varepsilon(b) = g^b r^2 (mod\ n)$ for some random $r \in \{0, \ldots, n-1\}$. The homomorphic property is then: $\varepsilon(b_1).\varepsilon(b_2) = g^{b_1} r_1^2 g^{b_2} r_2^2 (mod\ n) = g^{b_1+b_2}(r_1 r_2)^2 mod\ n = \varepsilon(b_1 \oplus b_2)$,   where   "." denotes multiplication and "$\oplus$" denotes exclusive-or.

The Goldwasser-Micali encryption scheme is semantically secure. (This notion of security is also commonly referred to as Indistinguishability under chosen-plaintext attack (IND-CPA) [15]). Semantic security means that no partial information about the plaintext can be learned from the ciphertext. However, this definition of secrecy is only valid if the adversary is passive. In the other attack scenario, the attacker who is impersonating the sender is allowed to additionally inject a ciphertext on the communication channel between the sender and receiver. Thereby, it causes the receiver to decrypt the ciphertext and get some information back to the attacker. This attack is called "*passive chosen-ciphertext-attack*" (CCA1), where the attacker can submit any ciphertext of his choice to the decryption oracle, then he learns the entire corresponding plaintext. In this model, the attacker loses the decryption oracle after he receives the challenge ciphertext. There is also "*adaptive chosen-ciphertext attack*" (CCA2), where the attacker can continue querying the decryption oracle with one restriction that he cannot decrypt the challenged ciphertext. This is a quite strong attack; nevertheless, there are real scenarios in which this level of security is required (IND-CCA2).

The main goal to tackle this attack is to define valid ciphertexts in such a way that the adversary cannot forge another ciphertext which leads him to guess the plaintext (IND-CCA2), moreover, he cannot modify the ciphertext which affects the outcome of the protocol (NM-CCA2). In [19], Mao showed the vulnerability of the GM cryptosystem to CCA2. In Sect. 3.5, we show our proposed protocol solves this attack by using authenticated encryption scheme which is called "Encrypt-then-MAC".

3.2   The Vulnerability of the GM Cryptosystem to CCA2

In [19], Mao showed the vulnerability of the GM cryptosystem to CCA2 with an example as follows:

Alice plays a role as a GM decryption oracle, and Malice can send reasonable ciphertext queries to her. If the received ciphertext looks random to Alice, she returns the plaintext to Malice. Supposing that, Malice eavesdropped a ciphertext $C = (c_1, c_2, ..., c_n)$ on a communication channel between Bob and Alice. The main goal of Malice is to find out the plaintext $B = (b_1, b_2, ..., b_n)$. He modifies the ciphertext as follows:

$$C' = (zc_1, zc_2, \ldots, zc_n)(modN).$$

Malice uses a following algebraic property:

$$ab(mod\ N) \in QR_N\ iff \begin{cases} a \in QR_N\ and\ b \in QR_N \\ a \in J_N(1)/QR_N\ and\ b \in J_N(1)/QR_N \end{cases},$$

And he chooses $z \in J_N(1)/QR_N$. Therefore, C' looks random to Alice, and she returns the decryption B' = $(b_1', b_2', ..., b_n')$ to Malice. Then the "multiply-z" attack, cause Malice to learns B = $(b_1, b_2, ..., b_n)$ by complementing each bit of the received B'.

Mao showed that it does not need to have an explicit oracle service. Even if Alice stops to decrypt the Malice's random ciphertext, Malice can still find out the plaintext bit by bit with the following example:

Malice wants to know whether the decryption of c_1 is 0 or 1. He sends an encrypted question concatenate with first bit of C'. If Alice only decrypts the first part of the message correctly and the second part of message is all zeroes, she will ask Malice why his message is uncompleted. Malice will find out the c_1 is residue and the decryption of c_1 is 0. Otherwise, Alice sends decryption correctly and Malice will find out the c_1 is non-residue and the decryption of c_1 is 1.

With these two examples of active attack, Mao showed that the GM cryptosystem is not secure against an active attack. Therefore, notation security of IND-CPA is weak.

3.3   Grid-Based Location

Let us consider a client-server architecture: Alice has a list of friends, $\{U_1, U_2, ..., U_n \in Alice_{FriendList}\}$ and the service provider acts as a registration server. All users can send and receive data through the service provider. Alice would like to be notified when any of her friends is nearby.

Each user extracts her location via GPS, Wi-Fi or cell towers and then the application calculates her grid reference based on the Military Grid Reference System (MGRS). The MGRS is a system to specify point locations on the earth. It uses a grid of squares of lengths 10 km, 1 km, 100 m, 10 m and 1 m depending on the precision used. Our protocol assumes a grid system like MGRS where pairs of friends agree on the grid reference size and they consider that they are nearby if they are located in the same grid square. For example [30], if two friends agree on 100 m, the MGRS will be

"4QFJ 123 678", which includes three parts: "4Q" is the grid zone designator: "FJ" is the 100-meter square identifier; and "123 678" defines a numerical location where east is "123" and north is "678".

3.4   Problem Statement

Alice and her friends have their location as their secret values. This protocol allows Alice and her friends to separately learns whether they are in a same pre-agreed grid reference or not. However, if they are not in the same grid reference, Alice does not learn the location of her friends and her friends do not learn the location of Alice. The proposed protocol is based on the homomorphic feature of the Goldwasser-Micali cryptosystem. We are required the proposed protocol to be secure against active and passive attacks. However, homomorphic encryption schemes are malleable by design [32]. To tackle this problem we use authenticated encryption scheme called Encrypt-then-MAC [5]. Bellare and Namprempre showed that encrypting a message and subsequently applying a MAC to the ciphertext implies security against an adaptive chosen ciphertext attack [5]. We analyze the security of the proposed protocol, and we show an active adversary who has access to the ciphertext on the communication channel and the decryption oracle, cannot forge another ciphertext which leads him to learn Alice's location and her friends' location (IND-CCA2). Moreover, the active adversary cannot modify the ciphertext which leads to affect the result of the protocol (NM-CCA2).

The nearby-friend application notifies Alice if any of her friends is nearby her. The application could run in the background, and whenever it finds a nearby friend, a pop-up notification displays on Alice's phone.

3.5   The Proposed Protocol

Enrollment Phase. Suppose Alice wants to use our nearby-friend's application for the first time. Alice installs the application and logs on to the server by selecting a username and a password. The key generation algorithm generates a public and private key pair, (PU_A, PR_A), based on the Goldwasser-Micali cryptosystem for Alice in her phone. Alice sends a friendship's request and her public key to her friends. Her friends who accepts Alice's request, sends their public key back to her. Note that, the server in our protocol just passes encrypted messages between the users and it does not learn information about user's location and whether they are close to each other or not.

Finding Nearby Friend Phase. Suppose Alice wants to find out whether Bob is nearby her or not. The nearby, process is as follows:

1. Alice first calculates the encryption of her location based on GM, $M_A = \varepsilon(PU_A, L_A)$.
2. Then, she applies Encrypt-then-MAC which is composition of Encryption = (PU, ε, D) and MAC = (K_m, T, V) as follow. She sends "return" to Bob:

$$K_{AB} \leftarrow \varepsilon\,(PU_B, K_m)$$
$$C'_A \leftarrow \varepsilon\,(PU_B, M_A)$$
$$\tau'_A \leftarrow T\,(K_m, C'_A)$$
$$C_A \leftarrow C'_A || \tau'_A$$
$$return\ C_A\ and\ K_{AB}$$

3. Bob calculates MAC to make sure the received message is from Alice, as follow:

$$Parse\ C_A\ as\ C'_A || \tau'_A$$
$$K_m \leftarrow D(PR_B, K_{AB})$$
$$M_A \leftarrow D(PR_B, C'_A)$$
$$v \leftarrow \mathcal{V}(K_m, C'_A, \tau'_A,)$$
$$if\,v = 1\ then\ returns\ M_A\ else\ returns\ \perp$$

4. Bob calculates $M_B = \varepsilon(PU_A, L_B)$ and $M_{AB} = \varepsilon(PU_A, L_B) * \varepsilon(PU_A, L_A)$, and he sends "return" to Alice.

$$C'_{AB} \leftarrow \varepsilon\,(PU_A, M_{AB})$$
$$\tau'_{AB} \leftarrow T\,(K_m, C'_{AB})$$
$$C_{AB} \leftarrow C'_{AB} || \tau'_{AB}$$
$$return\ C_B$$

Note that $M_{AB} = \varepsilon(PU_A, Y \oplus X)$ by the properties of homomorphic encryption.

5. Alice calculates MAC to make sure the received message is from Bob, as follow:

$$Parse\ C_{AB}\ as\ C'_{AB} || \tau'_{AB}$$
$$M_{AB} \leftarrow D\,(PR_A, C'_{AB})$$
$$v \leftarrow \mathcal{V}\,(K_m, C'_{AB}, \tau'_{AB})$$
$$if\,v = 1\ then\ returns\ M_{AB}\ else\ returns\ \perp$$

6. Finally, to prevent Alice from learning Bob's location, our application on Alice's side sets E=0 and OR it with decryption of the received $M_{AB} = \varepsilon(PU_A, Y \oplus X)$ bit by bit. Whenever the first "1" is detected, the decryption process stops. Otherwise, the result is "0" and Alice is notified: "Bob is nearby".

This protocol is asymmetric equality testing, because Alice learns the answer, but Bob does not. Bob should try all processes with his own public key to learn weather Alice is nearby him or not. The protocol is based on the homomorphic feature of the GM, in which the product of the encryptions of two bits is equal to the encryption of their XOR; therefore, if those two bits are the same, the result of XOR will be "zero".

Clearly if Alice and Bob are in the same grid reference, Alice learns Bob's location. If they are not in the same grid location, we have to show Alice does not learn Bob's location. As our stipulation of set E=0 and then OR it with decryption of E (PU$_A$, L$_A$ ⊕ L$_B$) bit by bit, and stops whenever first "1" is detected, Alice does not learn Bob's location if the result of XOR is not zero. However, this stipulation does not prevent a malicious application. This can be addressed by putting the application and Alice's key pair in the secure element (SE) and using attestations. If the risk is considered small, the application can be run by itself; if the risk seems too great, SE is used instead.

3.6   Security Analysis of the Proposed Protocol

For the security proofs of the proposed protocol, we consider two different kind of attacks, passive attacks and active attacks. Note that there is a certain amount of trust required between friends. If Bob uses a fake location, instead of his real location, there is no way to detect it in the proposed protocol. There are some techniques to stop the user from spoofing his location [23, 29, 31]. However, none of these techniques can completely prevent spoofing.

Lemma 1: The proposed protocol is secure against passive attack.

Proof: The GM encryption scheme is semantically secure. This notion of security is also commonly referred to as indistinguishability under chosen plaintext attack (IND-CPA). Semantic security means that no partial information about the plaintext can be learned from the ciphertext. As a property of the GM cryptosystem, each time the user calculates the encryption of her secret value, there is a very different ciphertext. Therefore, the proposed protocol, which is based on GM cryptosystem, is secure against passive attack.   □

Lemma 2: The proposed scheme is IND-CCA2 secure.

Assumption: We assume Malice is an active adversary, which means that he can eavesdrop on the communication channel between Alice and Bob. Therefore, Malice has access to two ciphertexts C_A and C_{AB}, and also the decryption oracle. He can send any modified ciphertext of his choice to the decryption oracle and receives the corresponding plaintext. The main goal of Malice is to find out the Alice's location or Bob's location or whether they are in same location or not.

Proof: Malice tries to modify C_{AB}, as follow, and sends C_M to the decryption oracle.

$$Parse\ C_{AB}\ as\ C'_{AB}||\tau'_{AB}$$
$$C_M = C'_M||\tau'_{AB}$$

The decryption oracle calculates:

$$Parse\ C_M\ as\ C'_M||\tau'_{AB}$$
$$M_M \leftarrow D\left(PR_A, C'_M\right)$$
$$v \leftarrow \mathcal{V}\left(K_m, C'_M, \tau'_{AB}\right)$$
$$if\ v = 1\ then\ returns\ M_M\ else\ returns\ \perp$$

Due to Malice modifies C'_{AB} to C'_M, the value of v is not equle to 1, therefore, the decryption oracle returns $\perp$ to Malice. Bellare et al. proved IND-CCA2 applies NM-CCA2 [4]. Therefore, If the value of v is not equle to 1, the decryption oracle returns $\perp$ to Alice and discard the outcome of protocol. As a result, Malice's modified ciphertext does not affect the result of the protocol.   □

3.7   Efficiency (Performance)

- **Computation time:** Using the Goldwasser-Micali cryptosystem is not efficient, as a ciphertext may be several hundred times larger than the plaintext. However, our defined Android application runs automatically in the background and whenever it finds a nearby friends, it notifies the user. With this perspective, the user is not involved in computation process even if it takes time.
- **Energy consumption:** The amount of data processed is not large, although any computationally-intensive operation that happens continually in the background will significantly impact battery drainage rate. The user can control how much background processing takes place (e.g., she can check for nearby friends every 60 min, or whenever her location changes).

4   Implementation

We implemented a client-server components to show the performance of our proposed protocol. The registration server is a tomcat server which forwards encrypted messages between users. The user application is an android API level 15, IceCreamSandwich, which installs in the user's phone and after registration, user can add her friends. Alice and each of her friends should agree on the grid reference size (e.g.,10 km, 1 km, 100 m or 10 m). As we said before, the user can control when updates her location. For example, she can check for nearby friends every 60 min, or whenever her location changes. We set the application to send the update location every 10 min. Alice's task finishes at this point and the application does the computation part in the background. Whenever the application finds a nearby friend, a notification pops up on the user's phone.

For showing the efficiency of the Goldwasser-Micali algorithm we ran the desktop application which encrypts and decrypts different grid reference sizes: 10 km, 1 km, 0.1 km and 0.01 km. We tried this for different numbers of friends and we ran our application one hundred times to calculate the overall computation time for Goldwasser-Micali. Figure 1a shows the linear increase of calculation time when the

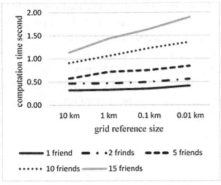

(a) Encryption and decryption time for the Goldwasser-Micali scheme

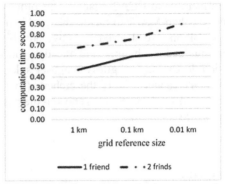

(b) Computation time of the proposed protocol

Fig. 1. Implementation

number of friends increases. As expected, 10 km is the least calculation time since MGRS has only 6 characters (e.g., 4QFJ16); therefore, it reduces the calculation time in Goldwasser-Micali cryptosystem. In the worst case, we have 14 characters for presenting each user's grid reference. Therefore, the computation process does not take long even if the number of friends increases (i.e. less than 2 s in the worst case in Fig. 1a).

We implemented our proposed protocol application and we used two "Samsung S5 neo" phones and one "Sony Ericsson XPERIA TX lt29i" to calculate the computation time for one and two friends in a real scenario. We wanted to make sure the computation time of Goldwasser-Micali on the Android application is practical. We tried it in the Ottawa region where the MGRS is "18TVR 44 14" for 1 km, "18TVR 442 148" for 0.1 km and "18TVR 4420 1489" for 0.01 km. We tried this application 10 times, and the average computation time is shown in Fig. 1b. The worst case occurred for an MGRS grid size of 0.01 km where it is 12 characters. However, the total computation time is sub-second for two friends. This shows that it is computationally possible to use the Goldwasser-Micali cryptosystem for realistic ciphertext sizes. As mentioned before, all these calculation processes take place in background activity, and the user is not stuck waiting for the application to complete processing. The amount of data processed is not large; however, Alice can control how much background processing takes place (e.g., she can check for nearby friends every 60 min, or whenever her location changes).

5   Conclusion

In this paper, we proposed a protocols for a nearby-friend privacy preserving LBS. Our proposed protocols are based on the Goldwasser-Micali probabilistic encryption scheme. The homomorphic property of the Goldwasser-Micali cryptosystem makes the corresponding plaintext equal to the XOR of the two grid references. If two grid reference are equal, the result is "zero". However, the Goldwasser-Micali cryptosystem is vulnerable to CCA2 attacks. Our proposed protocol used authenticated encryption, Encrypt-then-MAC, to tackle this problem. We analyzed the security of the proposed protocol, and we showed an active adversary who has access to the ciphertext on the communication channel and the decryption oracle, cannot forge another ciphertext which leads him to guess the user's location (IND-CCA2). Moreover, the active adversary cannot modify the ciphertext which leads to affect the outcome of the protocol (NM-CCA2). We also showed the performance and practicality of our protocol in real world applications.

References

1. Amir, A., Efrat, A., Myllymaki, J., Palaniappan, L., Wampler, K.: Buddy istracking – efficient proximity detection among mobile friends. Pervasive Mob. Comput. **3**, 489–511 (2007)
2. Ardagna, C.A., Cremonini, M., Damiani, E., Capitani di Vimercati, S., Samarati, P.: Location privacy protection through obfuscation-based techniques. In: Barker, S., Ahn, G.-J. (eds.) DBSec 2007. LNCS, vol. 4602, pp. 47–60. Springer, Heidelberg (2007). doi:10.1007/978-3-540-73538-0_4
3. Ardagna, C.A., Cremonini, M., Gianini, G.: Landscapeaware location-privacy protection in location-based services. J. Syst. Architect. **55**, 243–254 (2009)
4. Bellare, M., Desai, A., Pointcheval, D., Rogaway, P.: Relations among notions of security for public-key encryption schemes. In: Krawczyk, H. (ed.) CRYPTO 1998. LNCS, vol. 1462, pp. 26–45. Springer, Heidelberg (1998). doi:10.1007/BFb0055718
5. Bellare, M., Namprempre, C.: Authenticated encryption: relations among notions and analysis of the generic composition paradigm. J. Cryptology **21**(4), 469–491 (2008)
6. Cheng, R., Zhang, Yu., Bertino, E., Prabhakar, S.: Preserving user location privacy in mobile data management infrastructures. In: Danezis, G., Golle, P. (eds.) PET 2006. LNCS, vol. 4258, pp. 393–412. Springer, Heidelberg (2006). doi:10.1007/11957454_23
7. Chow, C.-Y., Mokbel, M.F., Liu, X.: A peer-to-peer spatial cloaking algorithm for anonymous location based services. In: Proceedings of the ACM Symposium on Advances in Geographic Information Systems, pp. 351–380 (2006)
8. Damiani, M.L., Bertino, E., Silvestri, C.: The probe framework for the personalized cloaking of private locations. Trans. Data Priv. **3**, 123–148 (2010)
9. Duckham, M., Kulik, L.: A Formal Model of Obfuscation and Negotiation for Location Privacy. In: Gellersen, Hans -W., Want, R., Schmidt, A. (eds.) Pervasive 2005. LNCS, vol. 3468, pp. 152–170. Springer, Heidelberg (2005). doi:10.1007/11428572_10
10. Fontaine, C. and Galand, F.: A survey of homomorphic encryption for nonspecialists. Eurasip J. Inform. Security, vol. 10.1155/2007/13801 (2007)
11. Gedik, B., Liu, L.: MobiEyes: distributed processing of continuously moving queries on moving objects in a mobile system. In: Bertino, E., Christodoulakis, S., Plexousakis, D., Christophides, V., Koubarakis, M., Böhm, K., Ferrari, E. (eds.) EDBT 2004. LNCS, vol. 2992, pp. 67–87. Springer, Heidelberg (2004). doi:10.1007/978-3-540-24741-8_6
12. Ghinita, G., Kalnis, P., Skiadopoulos, S.: PRIVE: anonymous Location-based queries in distributed mobile systems. In: Proceedings of World Wide Web Conference (2007) 371–380

13. Ghinita, G., Kalnis, P., Skiadopoulos, S.: MOBIHIDE: a mobilea peer-to-peer system for anonymous location-based queries. In: Papadias, D., Zhang, D., Kollios, G. (eds.) SSTD 2007. LNCS, vol. 4605, pp. 221–238. Springer, Heidelberg (2007). doi:10.1007/978-3-540-73540-3_13

14. Goldwasser, S. and Micali, S.: Probabilistic encryption and how to play mental poker keeping secret all partial information. In: Proceedings of the 14th ACM Symposium on Theory of Computing (STOC 1982), pp. 365–377 (1982)

15. Goldwasser, S., Micali, S.: Probabilistic encryption. J. Comput. Syst. Sci. **28**, 270–299 (1984)

16. Gruteser, M., Grunwald, D.: Anonymous usage of location-based services through spatial and temporal cloaking. In: MobiSys (2003)

17. Hashem, T., Kulik, L., Zhang, R.: Privacy preserving group nearest neighbor queries. In: Proceedings of the 13th International Conference on Extending Database Technology, pp. 489–500 (2010)

18. Hu, H., Xu, J.: Non-exposure location anonymity. In: Proceedings of the 25th IEEE International Conference on Data Engineering, pp. 1120–1131 (2009)

19. Mao, W.: Modern Cryptography: Theory and Practice. Prentice-Hall PTR, Upper Saddle River (2003)

20. Mascetti, S., Bettini, C., Wang, X.S., Freni, D., Jajodia, S.: ProvidentHider: An algorithm to preserve historical k-anonymity in LBS. In: Proceedings of the 10th IEEE International Conference on Mobile Data Management, pp. 172–181 (2009)

21. Mascetti, S., Freni D., Bettini, C., Wang, X., Jajodia, S.: Privacy in geo-social networks: proximity notification with untrusted service providers and curious buddies. VLDB J., 1–26 (2010)

22. Mokbel, M.F., Chow, C.-Y., and Aref, W.G.: The new casper: query processing for location services without compromising privacy. In: International Conference on Very Large Data Bases, Seoul, South Korea, pp. 763–774 (2006)

23. Narayanan, A., Thiagarajan, N., Lakhani, M., Hamburg, M., Boneh, D.: Location privacy via private proximity testing. In: Proceedings of the Network and Distributed System Security Symposium (NDSS) (2011)

24. Sen, J.: Homomorphic encryption: theory & application. In: Theory and Practice of Cryptography and Network Security Protocols and Technologies. InTech, pp. 1–21 (2013)

25. Shankar, P., Ganapathy, V., and Iftode, L.: Privately querying location-based services with sybilquery. In Proceedings of the 11th International Conference on Ubiquitous Computing, pp. 31–40 (2009)

26. Siksnys, L., Thomsen, J.R., Saltenis, S., Yiu, M.L., Andersen, O.: A location privacy aware friend locator. In: Proceedings of the 11th International Symposium Advanced Spatial Temporal Databases, pp. 405–410 (2009)

27. Yi, X., Paulet, R., Bertino, E.: Homomorphic Encryption and Applications. SCS. Springer, Cham (2014). doi:10.1007/978-3-319-12229-8

28. Zhong, G., Goldberg, I., Hengartner, U.: Louis, Lester and Pierre: three protocols for location privacy. In: Borisov, N., Golle, P. (eds.) PET 2007. LNCS, vol. 4776, pp. 62–76. Springer, Heidelberg (2007). doi:10.1007/978-3-540-75551-7_5

29. http://www.klaasnotfound.com/2016/05/27/location-on-android-stop-mocking-me. Web, 29 July 2016

30. https://en.wikipedia.org/wiki/Military_grid_reference_system. Web, 29 July 2016

31. http://www.gpsinformation.org/dale/nmea.htm. Web, 29 July 2016

32. https://en.wikipedia.org/wiki/Homomorphic_encryption. Web, 29 July 2016

AHL: Model-Driven Engineering of Android Applications with BLE Peripherals

Pedram Veisi and Eleni Stroulia[✉]

University of Alberta, Edmonton, Canada
{veisi,stroulia}@ualberta.ca

Abstract. Today, an increasing number of "smart devices" are becoming available to consumers, enabling them to quantify their physical activity and health status and to receive updates from their environment and applications. The preferred method of tethering these devices to the Internet is through the BLE (Bluetooth Low Energy) communication protocol connecting them to special-purpose mobile applications. The efficient development of high-quality applications of this type can present challenges to developers who have to familiarize themselves with a number of new technologies and platform-specific architectural patterns. A combination of domain-specific languages and code-generation techniques is a potential solution to this problem.

In this paper, we present (a) a generic reference architecture for Android BLE-enables applications, and (b) our AHL (Android Health Language), a domain-specific language and a corresponding code-generation framework that enables the easy and rapid development of the core elements of a typical BLE-enabled data-collection application in this architecture. The generated code is functional and does not need any modifications. This model-driven application-construction process relieves developers from the burden of dealing with complex Android concepts and components. Thus, AHL can save time and reduce the cost of Android application development for developers. In this paper, we explain the AHL framework, its models, its underlying DSL, and the methodology we used to design and implement it. We evaluate our work with two functional applications and compare them to the existing ones developed from scratch.

1 Introduction and Motivation

Portability, from a customer's point of view, was the only difference between landline telephones and mobile devices for years. However, with the help of powerful hardware and numerous on-board sensors, smartphones have recently become much more than communication devices, effectively delivering functionalities of desktop and laptop computers, digital cameras, navigation devices, health and fitness gadgets, etc. All these functions in a single portable device have made smartphones irresistible to users. Obviously, these features are only possible with the support of mobile platforms for applications and the business models that allow third parties, including software companies and independent

© Springer International Publishing AG 2017
E. Aïmeur et al. (Eds.): MCETECH 2017, LNBIP 289, pp. 56–74, 2017.
DOI: 10.1007/978-3-319-59041-7_4

developers, to develop applications, improve the platform, and generate revenue. Hence, mobile-applications development is likely the most active area of software development today.

The size of the target market, especially for independent developers and small businesses, is a significant factor considered in choosing the platform for which to develop applications. Android, which currently dominates the world market of smartphones with nearly 83% share of the market [10], is a primary choice for businesses and independent developers. However, despite Google's efforts to make Android development easy, many developers, and especially novices, face major challenges during development. The complexity of the platform in the competitive market calls for tools to make the process easier and faster. Such tools can save time and money and increase the efficiency of development teams.

A burgeoning mobile-application sector today involves the development of health-and-fitness applications that accompany a "smart physical device", such as Fitbit, Garmin, and smart watches. These new devices do not suffer from the limitations of mobile-phone sensors: they can track multiple types of activities and physiological attributes, from counting steps, to measuring heart rate and pulse, to assessing sleep quality. They have minimal energy requirements, easily met by a small rechargeable battery, which may require charging every week or so. Most of these devices are produced as convenient wearables, easy to attach to clothes and sometimes designed to be aesthetically pleasing jewelry. They are typically equipped with on-device storage that can accommodate a few days' worth of data, and they take advantage of BLE (Bluetooth Low Energy) for communication with smartphones and the Web.

However, the convenience of the users, who can quantify a multitude of aspects of their life and health state, comes at the cost of increased software-development complexity. Developers working on such applications have to manage the Bluetooth communication protocol, including implementing low-level functions for coupling the app with the wearable and services for handling the communication between the two, reading from the physical device, and storing the data in a database. This problem can be ideally addressed through a reusable code framework, implementing this set of commonly required functionalities, in support of a family of applications for different wearable sensors. Such a reusble code framework could potentially enable more efficient development, reduced costs, and improved code quality.

Our work provides a tool which generates most of the code for all of the four modules common in this family of applications. A developer specifies the configuration of the system, and our tool generates the code required for database management using Android Content Providers, an Android service and all the other classes related to periodic task scheduling, and all the necessary classes for Bluetooth communication that are not device specific. Our work makes the following contributions.

– **First,** it proposes a modeling language to describe applications that work with a peripheral BLE device.

- **Second,** it offers a development environment and an easy step-by-step process implemented as an IntelliJ IDEA plugin, on which developers, can rely to create their applications.
- **Third,** it evaluates this methodology by creating an example application for a wheelchair usage tracking device (i.e. Redliner) and a BLE Sticker Reader application (i.e. Estimote Stickers) and comparing them with their respective applications developed from scratch.

The rest of this paper is organized as follows. Section 2 places our work in the context of research on model-driven engineering. Section 3 reviews the technical background necessary for understanding our code-generation framework. Section 4 describes a canonical architecture for BLE-aware applications, relying on Android best practices. Section 5 describes our AHL framework. Section 6 reports on two case studies that we conducted to validate the effectiveness and usefulness of our framework. Finally, Sect. 7 concludes with a summary of the lessons we learned from this work and outlines some directions for future research.

2   Related Work

In this section, we first discuss Domain Specific Languages (DSLs), tools for designing DSLs, and model-to-text transformation tools for automatically generating code based on DSL specifications. Next, we review a few popular environments such as Acceleo, Xpand, Xtext, and JetBrains's MPS and explain how they transform models to source code.

Domain Specific Languages (DSLs). General-purpose modeling languages, such as the Unified Modeling Language (UML), are conceived to support the specification and development of all types of software and are, by their nature, agnostic to the requirements specific to any particular application domain. Domain Specific Languages (DSLs), on the other hand, are designed to capture requirements specific to a particular domain, relevant to applications in this domain only. To that end, they typically provide high-level abstractions (and partial and/or generic implementations) of domain concepts and their relations, and they come with associated tools for developing solutions for problems in that domain. SQL, HTML, Verilog, Unix shell scripts, Make and MATLAB, are a few examples of domain-specific languages. Mernik et al. [15] carry out an in-depth survey of when and how to develop DSLs. In our own work, we have developed two DSLs for the development of simple mobile clients as front-ends to REST-based back-ends [4] and for the development of physics-based mobile games [9].

DSLs have many applications but, despite their advantages, they also have some disadvantages. For instance, it takes time to learn them as a new language given their limited applicability. Additionally, designing, implementing and modifying them require expertise, time, and capital.

DSL Design Tools. Designing a DSL requires a deep analysis of the domain and its features, in order to define the right set of abstractions, shared among the applications that the DSL is envisioned to enable. Once this has been accomplished, a number of existing tools can be used to develop an editor for the DSL, which developers can use to specifiy their applications. In principle, DSL editors can be graphical or textual. Graphical editors provide a GUI for modeling the application in terms of the DSL concepts. On the other hand, textual editors provide guidance (such as structured editing and auto-completion tools) to guide developers in constructing a textual specification of their application.

Xtext [27], EMFText [7] and JetBrain's MPS [17] are some examples of popular tools for developing textual editors. Developed as plugins for major IDEs (Xtext and EMFText work with Eclipse, and MPS works with IntelliJ IDEA), they allow developers to define text syntax for a DSL described by metamodels such as Ecore [6]. Each of these tools comes with its own unique features, but all of them offer some standard ones, such as code completion, syntax coloring, quick fixes, etc., that make the development of a correct application speciifcation easier.

Many graphical tools are also available for designing DSLs. Some of the major ones include GMP [8], AToM3 [2], MetaEdit+ [16] and Visual Studio DSL Tools [19]. AToM3 and MetaEdit+ are standalone applications whereas GMF, and Visual Studio DSL Tools are designed as plugins for Eclipse and Visual Studio respectively. MetaEdit+ is a proprietary tool and available with a paid license that makes it more suitable for industrial purposes. However, all other three are free (Visual Studio DSL Tools for Visual Studio users) that makes them a better choice for many researchers and independent developers.

In [22], Pelechano et al. compare Microsoft DSL tools and Eclipse modeling plugins. To evaluate these two, they divided a group of 48 senior undergraduate computer-science students into two groups, and asked each group to develop a DSL (including code generation) with a different tool. After that, they conducted a survey about the experience of working with these tools. The survey includes questions about ease of use, usability and quality of graphical designers, complexity in defining the code generator, etc. Their results show that Eclipse DSL tools have been better accepted than DSL tools and respondents find it more simple, robust, and stable.

In [5], De Smedt compares three graphical DSL editors, AToM3, MetaEdit+ and Poseidon, in terms of speed of development, documentation, platform (Windows, Linux, Mac OS), price, availability of APIs, etc. He concludes that MetaEdit+ is superior to the other two. It is available for all three major operating systems and provides an extensive transformation and generation tool. However, MetaEdit+ is not free and the price of a standard license is high. He also points out that AToM3 offers almost the same functionality as MetaEdit+, free of cost. When it comes to Poseidon, he finds its functionality very limited.

Code Generators. DSLs define a high-level model of a system, and code generators such as Xtend [26], Acceleo [1] and MPS Generator [18] use this model to generate source code. The Xtend language is an extension of Java and generates Java code behind the scenes. Therefore, its basic syntax is Java and it provides additional features such as extension methods and operator overloading with a new syntax. Xtend is used in Xtext DSL projects to define language aspects including typing rules and generators. All generator rules are defined in Xtend, and then, the DSL code is transformed into Java code.

Acceleo and MPS on the other hand, are more general and can generate code in any format (Java, XML, HTML, JSON, plain text, etc.). This flexibility comes with the cost of writing more code. Using these tools, the user defines generator rules for every line of the generated code. In addition to the above mentioned features, MPS enables developers to extend an existing language. This feature offers a great deal of flexibility to DSL designers, and it can be used to add new features to programming languages like Java or another DSL.

Code Generation for Android. Most of the research works targeting code generation for Android focus on Java code that is responsible for functionality rather than UI. One reason for that is the availability of code generators for Java that can be adopted and used to generate Android code.

In [20], a model-driven approach for developing Android applications is proposed. The authors extend the GenCode [21] tool that generates Java code based on UML and sequence diagrams. Their approach is general and does not target any specific family of applications. To demonstrate their work, the authors use one of the available Android SDK samples (Snake), define its behavior using UML and sequence diagrams and generate the Java code for it.

In [14], the authors target high-performance image processing as their domain. They propose a code generator for RenderScript[1], a framework for running computationally intensive tasks on Android, and FileScript, a stricter version of RenderScript that provides wider compatibility with various CPUs and GPUs. They extend the Heterogeneous Image Processing Acceleration (HIPA^{cc}) framework[2] that includes a DSL based on C++ for defining images and filter masks, and integrate a generator for RenderScript and FileScript into the framework. To evaluate their method, they apply image-processing filters and operators (e.g. Sobel and Laplace operators for edge detection and Gaussian blur filter) on a 2048×2048 image using their generated code and compare the results on CPU and GPU with the results from applying the same functions using OpenCL on GPU and OpenCV on CPU. They use an Arndale Board[3] with a Samsung Exynos 5250 running Android 4.2 as their testbed.

In [11], the authors describe an approach that uses ATL and Acceleo to generate code for heterogeneous Android applications. They use ATL to define model-to-model transformation specifications and transform models created by the user into pre-defined intermediate models and then use Acceleo to generate source code from the intermediate models. To demonstrate their work, they generate the code for the Snake sample application included in the Android SDK with some improvement (more directions for movements and new obstacles and entertainment elements) and call it Snake Plus. In [12], the same authors make their work platform-independent and propose sample models for Android and

---

[1] https://developer.android.com/guide/topics/renderscript/compute.html.
[2] http://hipacc-lang.org.
[3] http://www.arndaleboard.org/wiki/index.php/Main_Page.

Windows Phone application development. The process of code generation from models is the same as their previous work.

There are also some works dedicated to generating GUI code for the Android platform. In [24], the authors take a model-driven approach for generating GUI code for multiple platforms. Their code generation happens in three steps. First, the system's GUI is modeled in class and object diagrams. Then, these models are transformed into platform-independent XMI files using JDOM API[4]. Finally, they adopt a model-driven architecture (MDA) approach to transform the models into GUI source code specific to a platform. The transformation rules in the last step are defined using ATL (Atlas Transformation Language). Also, their MDA approach takes scripts that describe the target platform as input. They evaluate their work by demonstrating the process of generating Android GUI code using their framework. Related platform scripts for Android are also provided.

Mohamed Lachgar, et al. [13], take the same approach of model driven code generation, but they provide a DSL, designed using Xtext, for defining the application and generating the UI code. The system is defined in their DSL and this definition is transformed into intermediate models specific to a platform using Xtend. Then, the source code is generated from intermediate models using Xtend generator. Their framework covers a wide range of platforms including web and mobile operating systems. They apply their approach to the Android platform and Server Faces Framework and generate GUI for two sample application to demonstrate their work.

3   Technology Background

Bluetooth Low Energy. Bluetooth Low Energy (BLE, Bluetooth LE or Bluetooth Smart)[5] is a new Bluetooth technology specifically designed for considerably lower energy consumption. BLE is natively supported on all major desktop and mobile operating systems, including Android (version 4.3 and above). Even though there are studies that show that BLE is not as energy efficient as expected [23], it is still quite more efficient than older Bluetooth protocols. For that reason, it is widely adopted by the industry, especially for health and fitness devices that are expected to have a lower power consumption.

Android Content Providers. Content providers are the standard way of handling data access and storage on the Android platform. They provide a layer of abstraction between the underlying data storage and the application code. In this way, the application code is independent of the underlying data persistence approach, and this provides flexibility to developers. Data persistence can be implemented using a common Database Management System (DBMS) such as SQLite, or REST APIs.

---

[4] http://www.jdom.org/.
[5] https://www.bluetooth.com/what-is-bluetooth-technology/
bluetooth-technology-basics/low-energy.

Content providers offer data encapsulation based on URIs. These URIs can be used to perform create, read, update and delete operations in applications. Additionally, and more importantly, implementing content providers makes it possible to share data with other applications in a standard and secure fashion. Access to content providers and possible operations can be managed using Android permission system that works in the same way as requesting access to resources or hardware. So, an application that has the right permissions for accessing or updating the content provider can perform the operation using the designated URI.

Implementing a content provider is a rather complex task and requires experience with Android development. A developer needs extensive knowledge of how they work and how they operate within the Android platform. Also, the necessary implementation results in a substantial amount of code and extensive testing is required to ensure that it works properly. For those reasons, many developers neglect to implement one and write plain SQL in their application code for handling data storage and end up with non-scalable software. Content providers are essential to the scalability of an application and goo data management in Android.

To generate a content provider, we integrated the Android Content Provider Generator[6] tool into our framework. This tool creates both the required *content providers* and a *content resolver*, a singleton that provides access to the various content providers. This tool requires at least two JSON files to function. The first is for defining application-specific configurations that include entries such as package names, database file name, database related class names, etc. It also needs a file for each application table, which includes the definition of the table and the relevant constraints.

Android Services, Alarms, and Broadcast Receivers. Some long-running operations such as network transmissions or data communications with external hardware devices should be done in the background, since they do not involve any interaction with the device user. Android *services* are implemented to perform this kind of operations, and by using them, the lifecycle of the operation does not depend on the application's lifecycle. More importantly, the likelihood of a service being killed is lower than that of an application process being killed, when the device is low on memory and resources need to be reclaimed.

Since periodic data transfers are required between a BLE device and a smartphone, an Android service is the perfect tool for handling communications. Since, BLE supports notifications from the device when data is available, notifications set on different characteristics can wake the application, which, in turn, runs the service to read the data, stores the data in the database, and updates the application.

The scheduling and management of periodic tasks in Android require *alarms* and *broadcast receivers*. Android alarms are designed for running time-based operations outside the lifetime of an application. Developers set an alarm and when it goes off a message is sent to a corresponding broadcast receiver that

---

[6] https://github.com/BoD/android-contentprovider-generator.

is defined for that alarm. Broadcast receivers are Android components that let applications register for application or system-wide events. For periodic tasks such as reading data from a BLE device, an alarm is set that sends a message to a broadcast receiver, which, in turn, runs a service. The service is responsible for actually starting the reading operation.

4 A Canonical Architecture for Android BLE-Aware Applications

To define our DSL for supporting the specification and automatic code generation of BLE-enabled applications that communicate with peripheral devices, we designed a general architecture, diagrammmatically depicted in Fig. 1. This reference architecture consists of the following components.

- The **Device Scanner** is in charge of searching for devices using the BLE component, pairing with them, and storing their information. In effect, this component is responsible for enabling the application to recognize its peripherals.
- The **Service** component handles all the background work and connects all the other components to each other.
- The **BLE** component handles all Bluetooth communications, including searching for devices, connecting to and disconnecting from them, and reading and writing data.
- The **Data Storage** component implements the required content provider(s).

Device Scanner. The device scanner invokes the *BLE scanner*, included in the BLE component, which lists all the nearby devices. The application end user then selects the device they want to pair with the application, and the hardware information about that device is stored in the Android *Shared Preferences*, a shared data structure that of key-value pairs. Later, when the service is started to read the data from the device, this information is retrieved and forwarded to the BLE reader.

Service.   When the boot process is completed in Android, a *BOOT_ COMPLETED* message is broadcast, which can be used by developers as a signal to schedule tasks, including periodic ones. A *boot receiver*, which is a subclass of Android Broadcast Receiver, listens for this message and initiates the application tasks.

For applications that perform time-based operations beyond their lifetime, such as communicating with a peripheral device or periodically communicating with the network, repeating *alarms*[7] should be set for specific periods of time to initiate tasks like running a service, which is done using another broadcast

---

[7] https://developer.android.com/training/scheduling/alarms.html.

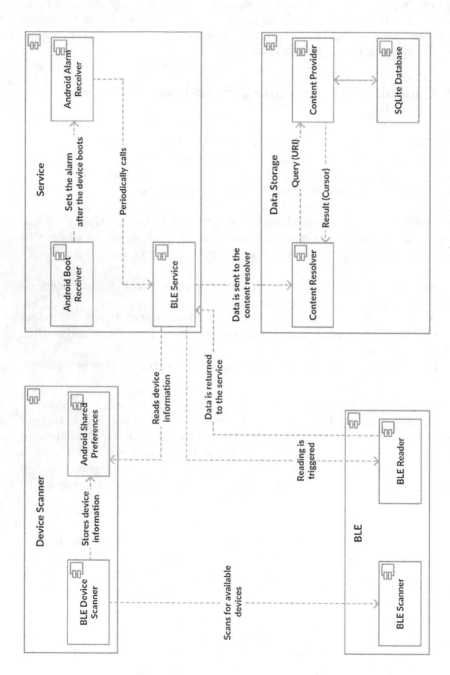

Fig. 1. Common components of android applications working with BLE devices

receiver, the Alarm Receiver class. Together, the boot receiver and alarm receiver classes are usually used for the implementation of periodic tasks in Android.

In our design, when the alarm set by the boot receiver class goes off, the alarm receiver gets the message and invokes the Android service. This service is responsible for collecting and storing data. At first, it reads the device information stored in a shared preferences file by the device scanner component. Then, it triggers the BLE read action and waits for the results to come back from the BLE component. At last, when the data is ready, it will be passed to the content resolver with an insert query by this service. As shown in Fig. 1, the service connects all the components in our architecture to each other.

Data Storage. This component is fully implemented using Android content providers. The data collected by the service running in the background is handed to a content resolver, which is an abstraction layer for content-provider operations. The data is automatically handled by the content provider based on the query from the content resolver. Implementing a content provider makes this architecture more flexible. The data can be shared with other applications if required, and the underlying data persistence mechanism can be any DBMS or REST APIs. We used the lightweight SQLite, which is the default DBMS in Android application.

BLE. The BLE scanner component is used by two other components: the device scanner, which is an activity listing surrounding devices, and the BLE service, which is in charge of reading and storing data periodically. The scanner is generic and can be used in any application that works with BLE devices. On the contrary, the BLE reader is device specific, and its implementation depends heavily on the protocol defined on the physical device. The possibility of accessing each characteristic individually or getting a notification when new data is written to a characteristic are among the main benefits of the BLE standard since they reduce energy consumption. At the same time, reading from a device should be done in a synchronous matter, and characteristics should be read one by one. So, reading the data altogether is not possible, and even if there is a synchronization mechanism in place to do so, it won't be energy efficient. For these reasons, the BLE reader is the only component in our architecture that should be implemented by the user and is neither automatically generated nor pre-written.

5   The AHL Application-Construction Framework

5.1   JetBrains Metaprogramming System (MPS)

We used MPS for implementing the AHL application-construction framework, because it integrates with IntelliJ IDEA, a variant of which is the Android Studio, the official Android IDE. MPS implements a non-textual presentation of code. In this approach that takes advantage of Projectional Editors, developers do not write code in a plain text format. Every expression of a language is broken into cells, and each cell only accepts special keywords or properties that are correct in the context. Since DSLs are mostly being used by domain experts, not professional programmers, projectional editors make things easier by asking for a specific value for each cell. Also, this approach eliminates the need for a parser and provides flexibility for designing languages.

MPS always maintains code in an Abstract Syntax Tree (AST). In this environment, a DSL can be created in one of the following two approaches. First, one can develop a code generator that converts the DSL-specific AST (as it is produced by the DSL code developed in the editor) into an intermediate AST that can be understood and transformed into code by the MPS generator. This method uses model-to-model and model-to-text transformations. Second, one can develop a generator to directly transform the developer's DSL-specific AST into code, which is a model-to-text transformation.

5.2   Designing AHL in MPS

In order to design AHL, we used the following aspects of a language provided in MPS for defining DSLs.

- **Structure:** This part of a language defines all the concepts included in that language. Concepts may be basic, such as a BLE characteristic or a database column, or complex, defined based on the basic ones, such as a database table consisting of multiple database columns, a BLE service consisting of multiple characteristics and characteristic packs, etc.
- **Editor:** Each concept has an editor, which defines how the concept is displayed to the application developer when a file of that concept is created.
- **TextGen:** This aspect defines the model-to-text transformations in MPS. TextGens can generate source-code files or snippets based on the type of the model. There is no limit on the target language or file format since these attributes are defined by the DSL designer.
- **Generator:** Generators in MPS perform model-to-model transformations. A project can have multiple generators, and each generator can have multiple rules including pre- and post-processing scripts, reduction and mapping rules, etc.

AHL Concepts. In MPS, concepts are definitions that describe the abstract structure of a syntax element in a DSL. Therefore, creating a DSL starts with defining its concepts. Our language includes the following concepts (Fig. 2):

- **Characteristic:** This concept defines a single BLE characteristic, namely an attribute type that contains a single logical value. Every Characteristic has three properties: name, uuid, and type.
- **CharacteristicPack:** In some cases, developers bundle related data items in a packet, and access each item within this packet using its start byte and length. The CharacteristicPack concept support this kind of data representation, and has name and uuid properties.

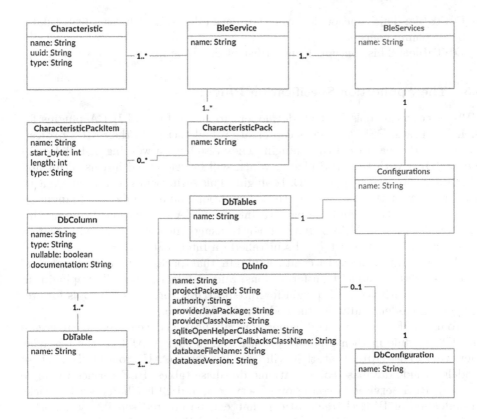

Fig. 2. AHL metamodel

- **CharacteristicPackItem:** This concept defines single items in a Characteristic-Pack and has four properties: name, start_byte, length, and type.
- **BleService:** This concept defines a single BLE service. Each concept of this type includes a list of Characteristics, and, optionally, a list of Characteristic-Packs. Depending on the BLE profile, there can be one or multiple BLE services on the physical peripheral device.
- **BleServices:** This concept aggregates individual BleService concepts. Its main purpose is to support an easier model-to-model transformation process, which will be explained later.
- **Configurations:** This is the biggest concept in our language and includes database configurations, database tables, and BLE services. This concept is designed to enable developers to provide all of the information required for code generation in one single file.
- **DbColumn:** This concept defines a database column, used in the *DbTable* concept. Its properties are: type, nullable and documentation (comment).
- **DbInfo:** This concept defines information about the content provider and database classes to be generated, including database file name and version, class and package names for the content provider, etc.

– **DbTable:** This concept defines a database table and includes a list of database column concepts.
– **DbTables:** This concept defines a list of database tables.

5.3   The Application Specification Plugin

MPS comes with tools for DSL developers to create IntelliiJ IDEA plugins for their languages. DSL developers can create a build script in their MPS project, and define the features of their plugin. They also need a working installation of IntellJ IDEA with the MPS plugin, which will be referenced in this script and will be used for generating the DSL plugin. This script will generate an Apache Ant build script that includes all the information about the designed language, the required features, and the path to IntelliJ IDEA installation. Running this Ant script, either in MPS or independently using Ant build tools, will create a zip file as the plugin which can be installed on IntelliJ IDEA.

We used this feature to create a plugin that packs our language and its concepts, editors, model transformations, and code generators. This plugin, in combination with the MPS plugin for IntelliJ IDEA, provides the tools for creating AHL models and write the code in this language.

To use AHL scripts and code generators, application developers have to create an MPS module in their Android project and to specify AHL as the language they want to use. After that, they will be able to create AHL root models. These models include database configurations, database tables, BLE Service (a single service), BLE Services (a collection of services), and BLE Characteristic Packs (a collection of BLE characteristics) that can be created separately. Another option is to create an AHL configuration model that includes all of the other models. Both methods generate the same code. We provided both options to make organizing and managing models easier for small and big projects.

6   Evaluating the AHL Framework

In this section, we introduce Redliner, an activity monitor for wheelchair users, and compare the application that was generated using our AHL framework with the original Redliner application developed from scratch in terms of functionality and more quantifiable metrics such as line of code and number of classes. To further investigate our AHL framework, we also created an application for a BLE nearable technology called Estimote Stickers and compared to the application developed by another developer it in the same way.

6.1   Redliner vs. AHL Redliner

Redliner is an activity monitor that can measure upper body over-exertion (Redline events) for wheelchair users. By recording a number of different metrics, Redliner allows users to be aware of their activities and to be alerted in case of over-exertion. A peripheral device, which includes multiple sensors and has a BLE module installed on it, is attached to the wheelchair and connects to Android phones. The Redliner activity monitor, in the form of an Android application, periodically connects to this device via BLE, reads the data and stores it in a database on the device. Then the app uses this data to visualize multiple metrics such as Redline events, velocity, the number of pushes, etc.

Functionality Comparison. If we exclude the UI component, most of the other functionalities of the Redliner application are available in AHL Redliner. Listing, pairing and unpairing devices (the background BLE code), data persistence using Android content providers and all the service components are produced by AHL. The only missing part is reading from a BLE device which, as discussed before, is heavily device dependent. We provided a comparison of the two applications in terms of functionality in Table 1. Dashboard and graphical representations are a part of the UI component. Listing devices, pairing and removing a device functionality have both UI code and background code and all of it is produced by the framework.

Table 1. Redliner vs. AHL Redliner in terms of functionality

Functionality	Redliner	AHL Redliner
Dashboard	+	x
Listing nearby devices	+	+
Pairing a device	+	+
Remove a paired device	+	+
Reading from a device	+	x
Data persistence	+	+
Boot receiver	+	+
Alarm receiver	+	+
Android service	+	+
Graphical reperesentations/Charts	+	x

LOC Comparison. In order to evaluate our work in a more quantifiable manner and show the amount of the generated code, we performed a comparison in terms of lines of code (LOC). The results are provided in Table 2. First, this comparison shows all of the classes and nearly all of the code that provide some functionality in the background are generated by AHL. The only background code that must be implemented by the user is a part of the BLE communication class that is responsible for reading from a device. That is the only difference between these two application when it comes to the background code.

Moreover, even though generating UI code is not the focus of our framework, 25% of XML and 24% of Java code for the UI is generated through AHL. Java classes related to UI include activities, fragments and Android list adapters.

Table 2. Redliner vs. AHL Redliner in terms of lines of code (LOC)

	# of classes	# of UI related classes	LOC (Java - Functionality)*	LOC (Java - UI)*	LOC (Java - Total)*	LOC (XML)
Original Redliner	36	14	2235	910	3145	1263
AHL Redliner	25	3	1970	216	2186	315
% of generated code	69%	21%	88%	24%	70%	25%

*Comments and empty lines are not counted.

It is worth mentioning that we excluded all comments and empty lines when counting lines of code to get a better understanding of the actual percentage of the code generated by AHL.

6.2 Estimote Reader vs. AHL Estimote Reader

Estimote Stickers[8] are customizable BLE sensors that can be attached to objects and provide context awareness by broadcasting data packets. These data packets include information like x, y and z accelerometer values, temperature, and a boolean value that indicates whether the sticker is in motion. These stickers are used to track the movements and activities of a home's occupants, in our Smart-Condo project [3,25]. As a part of that project, an Android application connects to the Estimote stickers, collects their data and stores them in a file. This application is in early stages of development, and some of its requirements are not implemented yet. As a method to evaluate our work, we created an Estimote Reader application with AHL and compared it to the original one.

Functionality Comparison. We sat down with the researcher who is working on the Estimote Reader application and managed to develop a fully functional application with AHL in just an hour. In order to adapt the generated application to the project requirements, we had to make some changes. Estimote provides an SDK for handling communications with their devices. This SDK provides function calls for searching for devices and reading from them. Therefore, we removed the BLE Scanner component of our framework. Also, since there is no need to pair stickers with the phone, we also removed the Device Scanner component which was providing an interface for pairing and managing devices.

Other than the BLE Reader component, that is provided by Estimote SDK in this project, AHL covers all the other components of the Estimote Reader application. We compared the original Estimote reader to the AHL produced application in terms of functionality in Table 3.

LOC Comparison. Since the Estimote Reader is in an early stage of development, our framework generated more code than the original application. More

---

[8] http://estimote.com/.

Table 3. Estimote Reader vs. AHL Estimote Reader in terms of functionality

Functionality	Estimote Reader	AHL Estimote Reader
Reading from a device	+	x
Data persistence	+	+
Boot receiver	+	+
Alarm receiver	+	+
Android service	+	+

specifically, there is no service implemented in Estimote Reader and the data persistence mechanism is not standard. Reading from stickers and storing the data is triggered when the application is launched and it stops when the it is closed by the user. This means that there is no background data collection.

Also, this application stores the data in a file and this file is supposed to be transferred to a server over the network for further processing. This is not a standard way of handling data storage in Android; it is instead a temporarily solution. A proper database makes this data exchange much easier, especially when it is done regularly which makes transferring the whole file impractical. The content provider generated by AHL solves this problem and makes data storage standard and scalable in this application.

In terms of user interface, the only UI part in AHL Estimote Reader is the MainActivity class which is the default activity in Android. That explains the generated UI code even though AHL Estimote Reader does not cover any UI requirements. The original application lists the surrounding stickers in the main activity which is not necessary to its functionality and is implemented for debugging purposes. That is the reason for the higher amount of XML and Java UI code in the original Estimote Reader (Table 4).

Table 4. Estimote Reader vs. AHL Estimote Reader in terms of lines of code (LOC)

	# of classes	# of UI related classes	LOC (Java - Functionality)*	LOC (Java - UI)*	LOC (Java - Total)*	LOC (XML)
Estimote Reader	9	4	285	368	653	233
AHL Estimote Reader	21	1	1191	24	1215	112
% of generated code	233%	25%	418%	7%	186%	48%

*Comments and empty lines are not counted.

7 Conclusion and Future Work

In this paper, we introduced the AHL framework that supports a systematic development process of applications working with peripheral BLE devices. We defined a general architecture for applications communicating with such devices and described their common components. Then, using JetBrains MPS, we created a domain specific language that allows developers to define their application requirements in configuration files and generate the code for the components defined in the general architecture. These components include an Android service and related alarm manager and broadcast receivers, a content provider incorporating a content resolver and an SQLite database, and UI elements for detecting and managing Bluetooth devices. Parts of the BLE communications code, which are not device specific, are also generated by our framework.

We provided an IntelliJ IDEA plugin that makes the code generation possible from within an Android application project in IDEA. This plugin includes our domain-specific language and all of its tools and enables application developers to add a model module to their application and define their requirements. After that, the AHL framework uses the defined requirements and adds the generated code to the project.

Using this framework does not require prior knowledge of the generated components and their concepts. These components are complicated and time-consuming to implement. The code generated by AHL is fully functional and does not need any modifications. This means that developers do not have to learn how to implement or modify these components because using them does not require knowledge of how they work.

Our work makes three distinct contributions.

- **We defined a general architecture for Android application working with physical BLE devices.** This architecture laid out all the common components among applications working with BLE devices. Using this, we build other parts of our framework to automate the process of implementing as many of those components as possible.
- **We developed a modeling language that describes the components of an application working with BLE devices.** Using this language developers can define their components' configurations such as database tables and their BLE specifications and the AHL framework takes it from there and produces the application code.
- **We developed a framework that allows Android developers generate code for their application in an easy and efficient way.** AHL turns the tedious task of implementing content providers, services, etc. that usually takes weeks into a fast process that can be done in a few hours. The Redliner Android application is a part of the Redliner platform which will hit the market in the near future. We generated most parts of this application in less than 30 min.
- **We evaluated our framework by developing two applications and comparing them to the applications developed from scratch for the same purpose.** We added the code already written for reading from the Redliner BLE device to the AHL generated Redliner and compared this functional application to the one built from scratch. Furthermore, we developed an application for working with Estimote Stickers in an hour and compared it to the original application developed by another developer.

In the future, we are planning to update our DSL with new syntax, so it is possible to define the order in which BLE characteristics will be read by an application. Using this methodology, our framework will be able to generate some parts of the BLE Reader component. However, the parts related to specific BLE protocol on each physical device will still be left for developers to implement. Also, it is possible to make AHL framework more general in the future. By augmenting it with more auto-generated components, it can be used for other types of applications. Naturally, developers will define the components they need and the code only for those will be generated by the framework.

References

1. Acceleo. https://eclipse.org/acceleo/. Accessed 10 Nov 2016
2. Atom3 a tool for multi-formalism meta-modelling. http://atom3.cs.mcgill.ca/. Accessed 10 Nov 2016
3. Azghandi, M.V., Nikolaidis, I., Stroulia, E.: Multi-occupant movement tracking in smart home environments. In: Inclusive Smart Cities and e-Health - 13th International Conference on Smart Homes and Health Telematics, ICOST 2015, Geneva, Switzerland, 10–12 June 2015, Proceedings, pp. 319–324 (2015)
4. Bazelli, B., Stroulia, E.: WL++: a framework to build cross-platform mobile applications and restful back-ends. IJBPIM 8(1), 1–15 (2017)
5. De Smedt, P.: Comparing three graphical DSL editors: Atom3, metaedit+ and poseidon for DSLs. Preprint, Submitted to Elsevier, University of Antwerp (2011)
6. Eclipse modeling framework. http://www.eclipse.org/modeling/emf/. Accessed 10 Nov 2016
7. Emftext. http://www.emftext.org/index.php/EMFText. Accessed 10 Nov 2016
8. Graphical modeling project. http://www.eclipse.org/modeling/gmp/. Accessed 10 Nov 2016
9. Guana, V., Stroulia, E., Nguyen, V.: Building a game engine: a tale of modern model-driven engineering. In: 4th IEEE/ACM International Workshop on Games and Software Engineering, GAS 2015, Florence, Italy, 18 May 2015, pp. 15–21 (2015)
10. IDC: Smartphone OS market share 2015, 2014, 2013, and 2012. http://www.idc.com/prodserv/smartphone-os-market-share.jsp. Accessed 22 July 2016
11. Kim, W.Y., Son, H.S., Kim, J.S., Kim, R.Y.C.: Adapting model transformation approach for android smartphone application. In: Kim, T., Adeli, H., Robles, R.J., Balitanas, M. (eds.) ACN 2011. CCIS, vol. 199, pp. 421–429. Springer, Heidelberg (2011). doi:10.1007/978-3-642-23312-8_53
12. Kim, W.Y., Son, H.S., Kim, R.Y.C.: Design of code template for automatic code generation of heterogeneous smartphone application. In: Kim, T., Adeli, H., Robles, R.J., Balitanas, M. (eds.) ACN 2011. CCIS, vol. 199, pp. 292–297. Springer, Heidelberg (2011). doi:10.1007/978-3-642-23312-8_37
13. Lachgar, M., Abdali, A.: Modeling and generating the user interface of mobile devices and web development with DSL. J. Theor. Appl. Inf. Technol. 72(1), 124–132 (2015)
14. Membarth, R., Reiche, O., Hannig, F., Teich, J.: Code generation for embedded heterogeneous architectures on android. In: Proceedings of the Conference on Design, Automation & Test in Europe, p. 86. European Design and Automation Association (2014)

15. Mernik, M., Heering, J., Sloane, A.M.: When and how to develop domain-specific languages. ACM Comput. Surv. (CSUR) **37**(4), 316–344 (2005)
16. Metaedit+ domain-specific modeling tools. http://www.metacase.com/products. html. Accessed 10 Nov 2016
17. Jetbrains meta programming system. https://www.jetbrains.com/mps/. Accessed 10 Nov 2016
18. Generator overview mps 3.3 documentation confluence. https://confluence. jetbrains.com/display/MPSD33/Generator+Overview. Accessed 10 Nov 2016
19. Overview of domain-specific language tools. https://msdn.microsoft.com/en-us/ library/bb126327.aspx. Accessed 10 Nov 2016
20. Parada, A.G., de Brisolara, L.B.: A model driven approach for android applications development. In: 2012 Brazilian Symposium on Computing System Engineering (SBESC), pp. 192–197. IEEE (2012)
21. Parada, A.G., Siegert, E., de Brisolara, L.B.: Generating Java code from UML class and sequence diagrams. In: 2011 Brazilian Symposium on Computing System Engineering (2011)
22. Pelechano, V., Albert, M., Muñoz, J., Cetina, C.: Building tools for model driven development. Comparing microsoft DSL tools and eclipse modeling plug-ins. In: DSDM (2006)
23. Radhakrishnan, M., Misra, A., Balan, R.K., Lee, Y.: Smartphones and BLE services: empirical insights. In: 2015 IEEE 12th International Conference on Mobile Ad Hoc and Sensor Systems (MASS), pp. 226–234. IEEE (2015)
24. Sabraoui, A., El Koutbi, M., Khriss, I.: GUI code generation for android applications using a MDA approach. In: 2012 International Conference on Complex Systems (ICCS), pp. 1–6. IEEE (2012)
25. Vlasenko, I., Nikolaidis, I., Stroulia, E.: The smart-condo: optimizing sensor placement for indoor localization. IEEE Trans. Syst. Man Cybern. Syst. **45**(3), 436–453 (2015)
26. Xtend - modernized Java. https://eclipse.org/xtend/index.html. Accessed 10 Nov 2016
27. Xtext - language engineering made easy! https://eclipse.org/Xtext/. Accessed 10 Nov 2016

Security, Privacy and Trust

Insider Threat Likelihood Assessment for Flexible Access Control

Sofiene Boulares[(✉)], Kamel Adi, and Luigi Logrippo

Département d'informatique et d'ingénierie,
Université du Québec en Outaouais, Gatineau, QC, Canada
{bous42,kamel.adi,luigi.logrippo}@uqo.ca

Abstract. Users who request to access protected objects must obtain the authorization of access control systems. Among the elements of decision for such systems should be the risk of authorizing accesses under various assumptions, and one of the notions of risk is threat likelihood. Access control systems deals essentially with insider threats coming from people within the organization, such as employees, business associates or contractors, who could violate access control policies. We present in this paper a new approach for insider threat likelihood assessment for secrecy and integrity properties by considering reading and writing operations within the context of access control systems. Access operations, the trustworthiness of subjects, the sensitivity of objects, and the applied security countermeasures are all considered in the assessment of the likelihood of this category of insider threats. Both qualitative and quantitative assessments are provided. Hence our approach makes it possible to compare and calculate the likelihoods of these insider threats, leading to more flexible and more informed access control decisions in various situations.

Keywords: Information security · Access control · Insider threat · Threat likelihood assessment · Risk assessment

1 Introduction

Access control to data is governed by means of policies determining whether a subject (or user) has the right to execute an action (read, write, etc.) on an object (file, database table, etc.). Conventional access control systems are rather rigid, since they consider only properties of subjects and objects to take decisions. Risk-based access control offers mechanisms to take access decisions by determining the security risks associated with access requests, thus achieving greater flexibility. In the following, we present two examples of situations where this type of access control could be useful. Consider:

Example 1: A situation where a workflow architect asks an IT security specialist to determine which combinations of operations are less risky for the tasks composing a workflow, given the subjects, objects and actions involved in each operation. Which combination should be chosen for each task and on what basis?

© Springer International Publishing AG 2017
E. Aïmeur et al. (Eds.): MCETECH 2017, LNBIP 289, pp. 77–95, 2017.
DOI: 10.1007/978-3-319-59041-7_5

Example 2: An emergency situation where there is an urgent need to consult a patient's file which is classified *Top Secret*. However, of all the doctors present, none has the clearance to read the file. Which of the doctors present should be chosen to read the file and on what basis?

In both examples above, the decision could be based on the evaluation of access risks, by selecting the combination giving the lowest risk value in the first example and the doctor yielding the lowest risk value in the second example.

An access control system that can give employees risky accesses can cause insider security incidents. According to the US firm Forrester Research, insider incidents within organizations represent 46% of security breaches [21]. In addition, the survey Global Corporate IT Security Risks 2013 [10], conducted by Kaspersky Lab, shows that 85% of companies worldwide have experienced an insider computer security incident.

Bishop et al. [2] distinguish two categories of insider threats:

1. violation of access control policy by using authorized access,
2. violation of security policy by obtaining unauthorized access.

The first category includes cases where an employee uses his legitimate access to perform an action that violates the access control policy: discloses sensitive data to a third party, releases information to untrusted environments, provides information to employees who don't have the right to know them, steals property or information for personal gain, etc. The second category includes cases where an employee exploits a vulnerability in the system such as a buffer overflow [14] to obtain an access which he does not have.

The approach for threat likelihood estimation of access requests that we present in this paper deals with the first category of insider threats. Indeed, our method can be seen as an approach to estimate the threat likelihood of the violation of an access control policy, caused by the authorization of other access requests.

This paper is an extended version of our short paper [3]. In this paper, motivational examples, explanations, figures (Figs. 1 and 2), formulae (formulae 4 and 5) and new examples have been added. This paper proves the correctness of formula (2) and presents our write threat likelihood assessment approach when secrecy is intended and our threat likelihood assessment approach when integrity is intended. Furthermore, the literature review has been much enhanced.

The rest of the paper is organized as follows. Section 2 presents an overview of our work and the contribution of this paper. In Sects. 3 and 4, we present respectively our threat likelihood assessment approach for secrecy and integrity. In Sect. 5, we compare our work with notable work of the literature and we present the limitations of our approach. We draw conclusions for this paper and outline opportunities for future work in Sect. 6.

2   Overview and Contribution

The access control model we propose, authorizes accesses that would be refused by the traditional models characterized by predefined access decisions. Assessing the threat likelihood of different types of events with their predicted impacts is a common way to assess IT risks. OWASP [18] defines the risk R as "the product of the likelihood L of a security incident occurring times the impact I that will be incurred by the organization due to the incident, that is: $R = L \times I$". In the following section, we will adapt this risk definition to develop a risk assessment function for access control systems.

Our approach to assess the risk of access requests is based on the Mehari approach that gives guidelines for security assessment [6]. This approach differentiates between the *intrinsic threat likelihood* which is the probability that the risk in question will occur in the absence of security countermeasures and *threat likelihood* which considers the reduction of risk by application of countermeasures [6]. The security countermeasures could be devices, procedures, or techniques that reduce the likelihood of threat on the security of information that is processed, stored or transmitted. Such reduction can be achieved by eliminating or preventing the threat. According to the Glossary presented by Information security Today [11], countermeasures consist in the deployment of security services to protect against a security threat. A synonym for security countermeasure is security control [19,22]. Examples of such countermeasures are enabled access logs, data encryption, etc.

The steps of our approach are summarized in the following:

1. assessment of the *intrinsic threat likelihood* of the access request by considering the information flow which could result if the access was allowed.
2. assessment of the effect of the security countermeasures permitting the mitigation of the *threat likelihood* of an access request.
3. assessment of the *threat likelihood*. In this step we answer the following question: "How likely is the occurrence of the risk made possible by the access request?".
4. assessment of the impact. In this step we answer the following question: "If the request was allowed what would be the extent of the damage?".
5. assessment of the risk.
6. decision on whether the risk is acceptable and hence to allow or deny the request.

Note that steps 4, 5 and 6 are out of the scope of this paper. They will be the subject of future publications.

Let us assume the existence of the following entities: S a set of subjects, O a set of objects, A a set of actions, L_c a set of secrecy levels, L_i a set of integrity levels and SC a set of security criteria. We limit the set A to two actions, read and write, which will be collectively called *accesses* and abbreviated respectively r and w. We limit the set SC to secrecy and integrity abbreviated respectively c and i (confidentiality is a term sometimes used in the literature instead of secrecy.).

We adapt the risk definition presented in this section to define a risk assessment function for access control systems. Specifically, the risk of permitting a subject s to perform an action a on an object o for a security criterion sc can be given by the following function (where × is not necessarily the usual multiplication operator):

$$Risk(s, a, o, sc) = Threat\_likelihood(s, a, o, sc) \times Impact(a, o, sc) \qquad (1)$$

$Threat\_likelihood(s, a, o, sc)$ represents the likelihood of a threat that a subject s (threat source) may present towards an object o (threat target) when it executes an action a in the context of the security criterion sc. $Impact(a, o, sc)$ represents the adverse impact on the satisfaction of security objectives that can result from successfully performing action a on object o in the context of the security criterion sc.

2.1 Contribution

In order to assess the risk of *access requests*, we have focused our effort on developing a qualitative and quantitative approach for determining *threat likelihood* by considering the parameters of information flow, trustworthiness of subjects, sensitivity of objects and security countermeasures. To our knowledge, few works on assessing the risk of access requests have explicitly provided approaches to assess the *threat likelihood* that subjects may present towards data objects [1,5,15,16]. However, in organizational contexts, such assessment is important to make the risk assessment method repeatable and accurate.

3 Assessment of Threat Likelihood when Secrecy is Intended

The assessment of threat likelihood can be done for secrecy or integrity. In this section, we propose our approach to assess threat likelihood on secrecy. We assume that we deal with systems where subjects and objects are classified by secrecy levels. Our approach considers the following factors:

- the intended security criteria (secrecy in this section),
- the requested action (read or write),
- the secrecy level of subjects requesting access,
- the secrecy level of objects to be accessed,
- the security countermeasures.

Information flow is the transfer of information between subjects and objects. Authorizing a read action creates an information flow from an object to a subject and authorizing a write action creates an information flow from a subject to an object. We assume that, when data secrecy is addressed, threat likelihood depends on the importance of information flow between objects and subjects, determined by the difference between their secrecy levels. In other words we can assume a correlation between the information flow that may result from permitted accesses and the threat likelihood.

In this paper, we present an information flow approach to assess the threat likelihood that subjects may present towards objects. Such assessment is needed to evaluate the risk of access requests. According to [20,24], secrecy is related to disclosure of information. In our approach, the likelihood of threat on secrecy increases when information flows down. Consider, for example, the information flow when a *Top Secret* subject writes in a *Public* object, such information flow is more important than the one when the same subject writes in a *Secret* object. In the first case, *Top Secret* information could be leaked to the public, in the second case this information would remain secret. It is reasonable to assume that the threat likelihood would be higher in the first case. The reasoning for integrity is dual.

We define a total order on L_c and for each secrecy level in L_c, we assign a numerical value in accordance with the defined order. For example, if $L_c =$ {Unclassified, Restricted, Classified, Secret, TopSecret}, then the value Unclassified corresponds to the number 1, Restricted corresponds to the number 2 and so on. To simplify the notation, L_c will be considered to be understood and so it won't need to be mentioned: in each system, there is only one L_c which applies to subjects as well as objects. Throughout this paper, the following functions will be needed to develop our approach:

- $csl : S \rightarrow L_c$ formally represents the assignment of secrecy levels to subjects that reflects the trust bestowed upon each of them by the owner of the data.
- $col : O \rightarrow L_c$ formally represents the assignment of secrecy levels to objects that reflects the protection needs of the data.

3.1 Defining "Threat Likelihood"

As discussed earlier in Sect. 2 and precisely in relation to formula (1), threat likelihood metrics are a prerequisite for the computation of risk metrics. To assess likelihood of threat on secrecy, we use the intuition behind the *Bell LaPadula* model including mandatory rules preventing the flow of information from a high level of secrecy to a lower one [20]. This model has a binary view of threat likelihood [5]. In the case of a request from subject s to read object o, *threat likelihood* is equal to 0 if $col(o) \leq csl(s)$ and equal to 1 otherwise. The reverse is true in the case of write requests, threat likelihood is equal to 0 if $csl(s) \leq col(o)$ and equal to 1 otherwise.

Instead of adopting the binary vision of the *Bell LaPadula* model to assess the threat likelihood of read and write requests, we propose to consider the following principles, which replace the properties of the *Bell LaPadula* model: we consider that permitting a subject s to read an object o, such that $csl(s) < col(o)$ or permitting a subject s to write in an object o, such that $csl(s) > col(o)$, presents by itself a measurable threat likelihood, independently of what might happen to the information that is accessed.

In this section, we define the "threat likelihood" in the context of access control systems. In particular, the likelihood of threat on secrecy of accesses is defined as follows:

Case 1: we say that the likelihood of threat on secrecy is non null if a subject $s \in S$ is able to read an object $o \in O$, such that $csl(s) < col(o)$. But for any attempt by a subject s to read an object o, such that $csl(s) \geq col(o)$ the threat likelihood is null. Any measure of read threat likelihood on secrecy in the first case is affected by the following two general principles:

- **Principle 1:** the likelihood of threat on secrecy increases (or decreases) as the object's secrecy level increases (respectively decreases).
- **Principle 2:** the likelihood of threat on secrecy increases (or decreases) as the subject's secrecy level decreases (respectively increases).

Case 2: we also say that the likelihood of threat on secrecy is non null if a subject s is able to write in an object $o \in O$, such that $csl(s) > col(o)$. But for any attempt by a subject s to write in an object o, such that $csl(s) \leq col(o)$ the threat likelihood is null. Any measure of write threat likelihood on secrecy in the second case is affected by the following two general principles:

- **Principle 3:** the likelihood of threat on secrecy increases (or decreases) as the object's secrecy level decreases (respectively increases).
- **Principle 4:** the likelihood of threat on secrecy increases (or decreases) as the subject's secrecy level increases (respectively decreases).

We define a function $Threat\_likelihood : S \times A \times O \times SC \rightarrow [0,1]$ that represents the threat likelihood value of a subject $s \in S$ requesting an action $a \in A$ on an object $o \in O$ when a security criterion $sc \in SC$ is intended (in this section, $sc = c$). We use relation $<_T$ to denote an ordering on *likelihoods of threats* of a set of subject-object accesses. In particular, we define $<_T$ in the following way: $(s, a, o, sc) <_T (s', a', o', sc)$ iff $Threat\_likelihood(s, a, o, sc) < Threat\_likelihood(s', a', o', sc)$. The relation $<_T$ allows threats likelihoods to be compared.

3.2   Read Threat Likelihood Assessment for Secrecy

In this section, we describe the settings of a scenario that will be used in the rest of the paper for motivating our approach. We assume the existence of the following subjects: s_1, s_2, s_3, s_4, s_5 and s_6. Table 1(a) illustrates the secrecy levels of these subjects. Let us also consider three objects o_1, o_2 and o_3. Table 1(b) shows the secrecy levels of these objects.

3.2.1   Read Threat Likelihood Assessment for Secrecy: Qualitative Approach

Assume that access for data objects has been requested by subjects who are employees of the business that owns the requested data objects (trusted and reliable to some degree by the system). In this case, data owners might be more concerned about the secrecy levels of objects than the secrecy levels of subjects. Hence, our approach for threat likelihood assessment in this paper is primarily based on the *secrecy levels of objects*.

Table 1. Secrecy levels for running examples.

Subjects	Secrecy levels
s_1	4
s_2	4
s_3	3
s_4	2
s_5	1
s_6	1

(a)

Objects	Secrecy levels
o_1	4
o_2	3
o_3	2

(b)

Let us consider Table 2 which could be given by a workflow architect to an IT security specialist. The security specialist is asked to define a set of tasks composing a workflow by selecting the least likely threatening combinations of subjects, objects and actions for the secrecy of data. We see that task T_1 can be executed by s_6 reading from objects o_1 or o_2, task T_2 can be executed by either s_4 or s_6 reading from o_2 and task T_3 can be executed by either s_5 or s_6 reading from o_1.

Table 2. Possible accesses by potential subjects to potential objects.

Task	Subjects	Objects	Action
T_1	s_6	o_1, o_2	read
T_2	s_4, s_6	o_2	read
T_3	s_5, s_6	o_1	read

Example 1: According to Principle 1 stated in Sect. 3.1, allowing s_6 to read object o_1 has a greater likelihood of threat on secrecy than allowing s_6 to read object o_2, i.e.:

$$(s_6, r, o_2, c) <_T (s_6, r, o_1, c)$$

This is because the secrecy level of object o_1 is higher than the secrecy level of object o_2. In the above example, we were able to determine which access has a greater threat likelihood by simply comparing the secrecy levels of the two objects. However, such a technique is no longer sufficient when object secrecy levels are the same as we can see in the following example.

Example 2: Determining the least threatening access for task T_2 by using Principle 1 is not possible. This is because the subjects s_4 and s_6 request the access to the same object. In this case we use Principle 2 stated in Sect. 3.1. According to this principle, allowing s_6 to read object o_2 has a greater likelihood of threat on secrecy than allowing s_4 to read object o_2. i.e.:

$$(s_4, r, o_2, c) <_T (s_6, r, o_2, c)$$

This is because s_6 has a secrecy level of 1 which is lower than s_4's secrecy level of 2.

To consider the effect of countermeasures in the reduction of threat likelihood, we define the additional following principle:

Principle 5: The likelihood of threat on data security increases as the effect of security countermeasures reducing the threat likelihood decreases.

The following example shows the importance of the consideration of the countermeasures in our approach:

Example 3: Let us consider task T_3 where allowing s_6 to read object o_1 has the same likelihood of threat on secrecy as allowing s_5 to read object o_1. This is because s_5 and s_6 have the same secrecy level of 1. We also know that all subjects are aware of the terms of the security policy (existence of penalties, etc.) and that all accesses of s_5 are logged whereas access logs are not enabled for subject s_6. Then, according to Principle 5, allowing s_6 to read object o_1 has a greater likelihood of threat on secrecy than allowing s_5 to read object o_1. i.e.:

$$(s_5, r, o_1, c) <_T (s_6, r, o_1, c)$$

This is because enabling access logs represents a dissuasive countermeasure which aims at making it less likely that the subject s_5 will actually perform malicious actions if he is aware that this action can be attributed to him and can lead to severe penalties [6].

Examples 1, 2 and 3 suggest the following method:

Method 1: A read threat likelihood assessment technique that is primarily based on object secrecy levels should support the following:

1. always apply Principle 1 (that is, read threat likelihood always increases as object secrecy level increases),
2. whenever object secrecy levels are the same, apply Principle 2 (that is, read threat likelihood increases as subject secrecy level decreases),
3. apply Principle 5 (that is, threat likelihood of accesses increases (or decreases) as the effect of security countermeasures reducing the threat likelihood decreases (respectively increases).

Based on the above comparisons, the least threatening combinations of subjects, objects and actions on secrecy according to Method 1 are presented in Table 3.

Table 3. The least threatening combinations according to Method 1.

Task	Subjects	Objects	Action
T_1	s_6	o_2	read
T_2	s_4	o_2	read
T_3	s_5	o_1	read

3.2.2   Read Threat Likelihood Assessment for Secrecy: Quantitative Approach

In this section, we present a quantitative approach for threat likelihood assessment and we show why and how it could be useful. To this end, we start with the following example:

Example 4: Table 4 shows that task T_4 can be executed by either s_3 or s_4 reading from o_1. The two subjects request access from two distant sites where s_3 is connected via an unencrypted public network and s_4 via VPN which is a countermeasure that reduces threat likelihood by preventing disclosure of information. Indeed, VPNs typically allow only authenticated remote access using tunnelling protocols and encryption techniques. According to Principles 1 and 2, allowing s_4 to read object o_1 has a greater likelihood of threat on secrecy than allowing s_3 to read object o_1. However, Principle 5 tells us that this may not be true in the presence of countermeasures, that can reduce the threat likelihood of s_4 reading o_1. Hence the need to quantify the countermeasures effect and the threat likelihood of access requests.

Table 4. Possible combinations to define task T_4.

Task	Subjects	Objects	Action
T_4	s_3, s_4	o_1	read

Priority orders only permit a threat likelihood comparison in sets of accesses. However, quantitative measures which correspond to this threat likelihood ordering may be useful, such as in the case where there are many requests that we want to compare. There can be many different formulas which respect the properties of our approach and can measure the threat likelihood of granting access. In this section, we propose a formula and describe its construction.

ISO/IEC 27001 [9] requires regular verification of computer security. In order to determine to which extent the countermeasures are producing the desired outcome to meet the security requirements, the security administrator measures the contribution of the implemented security countermeasures in the reduction of risks. In this work, we adopt the concepts of Mehari methodology [9] to consider the effect of security countermeasures in the calculation of threat likelihood. We introduce a set of rules in Table 5 to determine the countermeasures that reduce threat likelihood of access requests and their effects. Each rule determines a countermeasure and its effect corresponding to an access request identified by the subject's security level, the object's security level, the action requested and the security criteria intended.

The content of Table 5 could be determined by the security administrator. It shows a representation of all possible read accesses by subjects to objects when secrecy is intended. Note that for an attempt by a subject s to read an object o, such that $csl(s) \geq col(o)$ the threat likelihood is null. Hence, Table 5 doesn't show the countermeasures and their values along or below the diagonal of the table. Each table entry $[i, j]$ includes a set of couples (measure, value) that represents the countermeasures and their contribution in the reduction of threat likelihood of a subject s reading an object o, where $csl(s) = i$ and $col(o) = j$. The sum of all countermeasures values in each entry is bound between 0 and 1.

The rule corresponding to the entry $[1, 4]$ shows that if a subject having a secrecy level 1 reads an object having a secrecy level 4, then countermeasure m_3 can reduce the likelihood of threat on secrecy by 0.5. The rule of the entry $[2, 4]$ shows that if a subject having a secrecy level 2 reads an object having a secrecy level 4, then the countermeasures m_3 and m_4 can respectively reduce the likelihood of threat on secrecy by 0.5 and 0.2.

$Counter(s, a, o, sc)$ denotes the sum of the effects of the different implemented countermeasures to reduce threat likelihood if s executes an action a on an object o when the security criteria sc is intended. For example, we can see from Table 5 that if a subject s having a secrecy level of 1 requests to read an object o having a secrecy level of 5 when secrecy is intended and all three countermeasures are applied, we have $Counter(s, r, o, c) = 0.5 + 0.2 + 0.2 = 0.9$. Note that we consider that the countermeasures are independent and perfectly implemented and we don't consider their partial implementation that could result in a lower level of reduction of the threat likelihood.

We define the following additional principles for the calculation of the threat likelihood of access requests:

- **Principle 6:** The threat likelihood of an access request is equal to zero, if the cumulative effect of the corresponding security countermeasures is equal to or greater than the value of the intrinsic threat likelihood.
- **Principle 7:** The threat likelihood of an access request increases (or decreases) when the intrinsic threat likelihood increases (respectively decreases).
- **Principle 8:** The value of the threat likelihood of an access request is bound between 0 and 1.

We now introduce the concept of threat likelihood indexing when secrecy is intended. We assign a numerical value from the set $\{0, \cdots, |L_c| - 1\}$ that represents the threat likelihood index of a secrecy level $clevel$ in L_c. For example, in the case of read accesses when secrecy is intended, from the point of view of subjects, we expect the threat likelihood to increase as subject secrecy levels decrease. Hence, subject threat likelihood index values decrease with subject secrecy levels. We write $\overline{clevel}$ to denote an entity (subject or object) threat likelihood index that decreases with the entity secrecy level. Formally, $\overline{clevel} = |L_c| - clevel$. For example, $(\overline{Secret}) = 5 - 4 = 1$. However, from the point of view of objects, we expect threat likelihood to increase as object secrecy levels increase. Hence, object threat likelihood indexes increase with object secrecy levels. We write $\utilde{clevel}$ to denote an entity threat likelihood index that increases with entity secrecy levels. Formally, $\utilde{clevel} = clevel - 1$. For example, $\utilde{Secret} = 4 - 1 = 3$.

Table 5. The effect of countermeasures in the reduction of the read threat likelihood.

Subjects secrecy levels	Objects secrecy level 1	Objects secrecy level 2	Objects secrecy level 3	Objects secrecy level 4	Objects secrecy level 5
1					$(m_1, 0.5)$
		$(m_5, 0.5)$	$(m_5, 0.5)$	$(m_3, 0.5)$	$(m_2, 0.2)$
					$(m_4, 0.2)$
2			$(m_2, 0.2)$	$(m_3, 0.5)$	$(m_2, 0.2)$
			$(m_4, 0.2)$	$(m_4, 0.2)$	$(m_4, 0.2)$
3				$(m_3, 0.5)$	$(m_4, 0.2)$
4					$(m_4, 0.2)$
5					

In this paper, we assume that $|L_c| = 5$, hence there can be at most $5 \times 5 = 25$ combinations of subject-object accesses. We define a function $Intrinsic : S \times A \times O \times SC \rightarrow [0,1]$ that represents the intrinsic threat likelihood value of a subject $s \in S$ requesting an action $a \in A$ on an object $o \in O$ when a security criterion $sc \in SC$ is intended. In this section, $sc = c$.

$$
Intrinsic(s, r, o, c) = \begin{cases} \frac{(|L_c| \times \overbrace{col(o)} + \widehat{csl(s)})}{(|L_c|)^2 - 1}, & \textbf{if } csl(s) < col(o) \\ 0, & \textbf{Otherwise.} \end{cases} \tag{2}
$$

A formula that respects the principles of Method 1, Principles 6, 7 and 8 for measuring the threat on secrecy likelihood of granting read access to a subject s for an object o, is given below:

$$
Threat\_likelihood(s, r, o, c) = \begin{cases} Intrinsic(s, r, o, c) - Counter(s, r, o, c), \\ \textbf{if } csl(s) < col(o) \textbf{ and} \\ Counter(s, r, o, c) < Intrinsic(s, r, o, c) \\ 0, \quad \textbf{Otherwise.} \end{cases} \tag{3}
$$

The numerator of formula (2) is intuitive. Since we require that more importance be given to the threat likelihood index of objects, we multiply the object threat likelihood index by $|L_c|$ that equals the cardinality of the set of secrecy levels L_c. Then, we add the threat index of the subject. The numerator of the formula maps all possible read accesses by subjects to objects into an interval $[0 \cdots (|L_c|^2) - 1]$, where a higher value represents a greater threat likelihood. In order to have intrinsic likelihood threat values into an interval $[0,1]$, we divide the value obtained from the numerator by $|L_c|^2 - 1$. In formula (3), we subtract the value representing the effect of the different implemented countermeasures corresponding to the request in question. The resultant value represents the object-based read threat likelihood value that respects the principles of Method 1, Principles 6, 7 and 8.

If we apply formula (3) to Example 1 stated in Sect. 3.2.1, we get the following: $Threat\_likelihood(s_6, r, o_1, c) = Intrinsic(s_6, r, o_1, c) - Counter(s_6, r, o_1, c) = 0.79 - 0.5 = 0.29$ (1) and $Threat\_likelihood(s_6, r, o_2, c) = Intrinsic(s_6, r, o_2, c) - Counter(s_6, r, o_2, c) = 0.58 - 0.5 = 0.08$ (2). From (1) and (2), we have $Threat\_likelihood(s_6, r, o_1, c) > Threat\_likelihood(s_6, r, o_2, c)$.

The graph shown in Fig. 1 is obtained by formula (2). It illustrates that the required characteristics are retained. Indeed, for each subject s and object o where $csl(s) \geq col(o)$, the intrinsic threat likelihood is equal to zero. Furthermore, if a subject s attempts to read from an object o, such that $csl(s) < col(o)$ the intrinsic threat likelihood is not null. This satisfies the assumptions of Case 1 stated in Sect. 3.2. The left most side of Fig. 1 shows that with the increase in secrecy levels of objects, and the decrease of secrecy levels of subjects, the intrinsic threat likelihood increases. This satisfies Principles 1 and 2. The right most side of Fig. 1 shows that with the increase of the secrecy levels of subjects, and the decrease of secrecy levels of objects, the intrinsic threat likelihood decreases. This satisfies Principles 1 and 2. The values of Fig. 1 show that the threat likelihood values are bound between 0 and 1. This satisfies Principle 8.

The graph shown in Fig. 2 can be obtained by formula (2). It shows that Principles 5, 6, 7 and 8 are satisfied. The figure shows that when the effect of the security countermeasures increases (or decreases) the threat likelihood decreases (or increases respectively). This satisfies Principle 5. The right most side of the figure shows that the threat likelihood of an access request is null

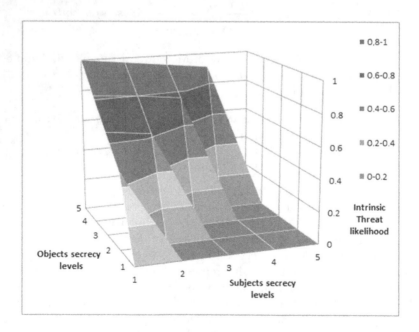

Fig. 1. Behavior of the values of the intrinsic threat likelihood in function of the secrecy levels of subjects and objects.

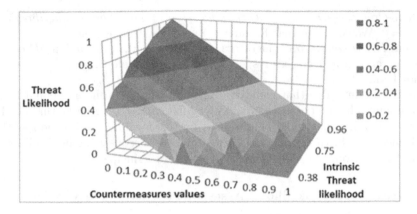

Fig. 2. Behavior of threat likelihood values in function of countermeasures and the intrinsic threat likelihood.

if the value of the corresponding security measures is greater than or equal to the value of the intrinsic threat likelihood. This satisfies Principle 6. The left side of the figure shows that with the increase in the intrinsic threat likelihood and the decrease of the effect of countermeasures values, the threat likelihood increases. This satisfies Principle 7. The right side of the figure shows that, with the decrease of the intrinsic threat likelihood and the increase of the effect of the corresponding countermeasures, the threat likelihood decreases. This satisfies Principle 7. The values of threat likelihood are between 0 and 1. This satisfies Principle 8.

3.2.3   Proof of Correctness

This section shows that formula (2) satisfies Principles 1, 2, 5, 6, 7 and 8. Suppose that $|L_c|$ is fixed, then we have the following:

- When $col(o)$ increases (or decreases), $\widehat{col(o)} = col(o) - 1$ increases (or decreases respectively). Consequently, for any given subject, $Intrinsic$ (s, r, o, c) increases (or decreases) as $col(o)$ increases (or decreases respectively). Hence, $Threat\_likelihood(s, r, o, c)$ increases (or decreases) as $col(o)$ increases (or decreases respectively). We conclude that formula (3) satisfies Principle 1.

- When $csl(s)$ increases (or decreases), $\widehat{csl(s)} = |L_c| - csl(s)$ decreases (or increases respectively). Consequently, for any given object, $Intrinsic(s, r, o, c)$ decreases (or increases) as $csl(s)$ increases (or decreases respectively). Hence, $Threat\_likelihood(s, r, o, c)$ increases (or decreases) as $csl(s)$ decreases (or increases respectively). We conclude that formula (3) satisfies Principle 2.

- If $csl(s) < col(o)$ and $Counter(s, r, o, c) < Intrinsic(s, r, o, c)$, when $Counter$ (s, r, o, c) increases (or decreases), $Threat\_likelihood(s, r, o, c)$ decreases (or increases respectively). We conclude that formula (3) satisfies Principle 5.

- When $Counter(s,r,o,c) \geq Intrinsic(s,r,o,c)$ then $Threat\_likelihood(s,r, o,c) = 0$. We conclude that formula (3) satisfies Principle 6.
- When $Intrinsic(s,r,o,c)$ increases (or decreases), $Threat\_likelihood(s,r, o,c)$ increases (or decreases respectively). We conclude that formula (3) satisfies Principle 7.
- The maximum value that could be obtained by this formula is equal to the maximum value of $Intrinsic(s,r,o,c)$ which cannot be greater than 1. The minimum value that could be obtained by this formula can not be less than 0. Hence, the threat likelihood values of an access request are bound between 0 and 1. We conclude that formula (3) satisfies Principle 8.

3.3 Write Threat Likelihood Assessment when Secrecy is Intended

We can quantify threat likelihood of excessive write accesses, when subjects secrecy levels are higher than objects secrecy levels, by adhering to Principles 3, 4, 5, 6, 7 and 8. For this, we propose the following two formulae which give respectively values representing the intrinsic object_based likelihood of threat on secrecy when write access is requested and the object_based likelihood of threat on secrecy when write access is requested, note the symmetry with respect to formulae (2) and (3):

$$Intrinsic(s,w,o,c) = \begin{cases} \frac{(|L_c| \times \widehat{col(o)} + csl(s))}{(|L_c|)^2 - 1}, & \text{if } csl(s) > col(o) \\ 0, & \textbf{Otherwise.} \end{cases} \quad (4)$$

$$Threat\_likelihood(s,w,o,c) = \begin{cases} Intrinsic(s,w,o,c) - Counter(s,w,o,c), \\ \textbf{if } csl(s) > col(o) \text{ and} \\ Counter(s,w,o,c) < Intrinsic(s,w,o,c) \\ 0, & \textbf{Otherwise.} \end{cases}$$

$$(5)$$

4 Threat Likelihood Assessment when Integrity is Intended

In the previous sections, we have presented an approach for assessing the likelihood of the threat on secrecy. This approach was based on the idea that this likelihood increases when information flows down. In this section we will briefly show how to apply the same concepts to the security criteria of integrity. Our approach is based on the idea that the threat on integrity increases when information flows up. This idea is at the foundation of the well-known Biba model [20]. In the following, we present definitions and principles to be used for the assessment of the likelihoods of threats on integrity. The following functions are needed to develop our approach:

- $isl : S \rightarrow L_i$ formally represents the assignment of integrity levels to subjects that reflects the trust related to data integrity bestowed upon each of them by the organization that owns the data.

- $iol : O \rightarrow L_i$ formally represents the assignment of integrity levels to objects that reflects the data integrity protection needs for each of them.

Clearly, the properties of integrity are dual with respect to the properties of secrecy. We leave it to the reader to modify the definitions and examples in Sect. 3.1 in order to apply them to integrity. Similar formulas can be derived, with the sc parameter set to i. Hence, in this section, we only introduce the concept of threat likelihood indexing when integrity is intended. We assign a numerical value from the set $\{0, \cdots, |L_i| - 1\}$ that represents the threat likelihood index of an integrity level $ilevel$ in L_i. For example, in the case of write accesses when integrity is intended, from the point of view of subjects, we expect the threat likelihood to increase as subject integrity levels decrease. Hence, subject threat likelihood index values decrease with subject integrity levels. We write $\widehat{ilevel}$ to denote an entity (subject or object) threat likelihood index that decreases with the entity integrity level. Formally, $\widehat{ilevel} = |L_i| - ilevel$. However, from the point of view of objects, we expect threat likelihood to increase as object integrity levels increase. Hence, object threat likelihood indexes increase with object integrity levels. We write $\overset{\frown}{ilevel}$ to denote an entity threat likelihood index that increases with entity integrity levels. Formally, $\overset{\frown}{ilevel} = ilevel - 1$.

The following two formulae give respectively values representing the intrinsic object-based likelihood of threat on integrity when read access is requested and the object-based likelihood of threat on integrity when read access is requested.

$$Intrinsic(s, r, o, i) = \begin{cases} \frac{(|L_i| \times \overset{\frown}{iol(o)} + \widehat{isl(s)})}{(|L_i|)^2 - 1}, \text{if}\, isl(s) > icol(o) \\ 0, \quad \textbf{Otherwise.} \end{cases} \quad (6)$$

$$Threat\_likelihood(s, r, o, i) = \begin{cases} Intrinsic(s, r, o, i) - Counter(s, r, o, i), \\ \textbf{if}\, isl(s) > iol(o)\ and \\ Counter(s, r, o, i) < Intrinsic(s, r, o, i) \\ 0, \quad \textbf{Otherwise.} \end{cases} \quad (7)$$

We can derive two formulae giving respectively values representing the intrinsic object-based likelihood of threat on integrity when write access is requested and the object-based likelihood of threat on integrity when write access is requested. Note the symmetry with respect to formulae (6) and (7).

$$Intrinsic(s, w, o, i) = \begin{cases} \frac{(|L_i| \times \widehat{iol(o)} + \overset{\frown}{isl(s)})}{(|L_i|)^2 - 1}, \text{if}\, isl(s) < iol(o) \\ 0, \quad \textbf{Otherwise.} \end{cases} \quad (8)$$

$$Threat\_likelihood(s, w, o, i) = \begin{cases} Intrinsic(s, w, o, i) - Counter(s, w, o, i), \\ \textbf{if}\, isl(s) < iol(o)\ and \\ Counter(s, w, o, i) < Intrinsic(s, w, o, i) \\ 0, \quad \textbf{Otherwise.} \end{cases} \quad (9)$$

5 Related Work and Limitations

In our previous work [15,16], we present a framework for threat likelihood and risk assessment, which includes four different approaches. In this work, our threat likelihood assessment approach is information flow based, makes a distinction between read and write accesses, takes into account security countermeasures and gives different estimates based on the intended security criteria (secrecy or integrity).

Fagade et al. explore the behavioural dimension of compliance to information security standards. Based on an established model of Information Security Governance Framework, they propose how information security may be embedded into organisation security culture [8]. Caputo et al. provide a prototype system for identifying insider threats. This research experimentally studies how malicious insiders behave and how they use information differently from a benign baseline group [4]. Greitzer et al. describe a predictive modeling framework that integrates a set of data sources from the cyber domain, as well as inferred psychological factors that may underlie malicious insider exploits. This threat assessment approach provides automated support for the detection of high-risk behaviors [12]. Hua et al. propose a game theoretical model to study the economic impact of insider threats on information systems security investments. They identify three factors influencing the optimal information systems security investment: breach function sensitivity, deterrence level, and advantage rate. They show that the optimal investment required to protect an information systems infrastructure from insiders is higher than for protecting against external threats [13]. Compared to our approach, none of these works present a qualitative or a quantitative method, to assess insider threat likelihood for access control systems.

Cheng et al. propose Fuzzy Multi-Level Security (Fuzzy MLS), which quantifies the risk of an access request in multi-level security systems as a product of the value of information and probability of unauthorized disclosure [5]. The Fuzzy MLS thesis considers that all subject-object accesses include a temptation to leak information and aims to quantify the risk of "unauthorized disclosure" of information by subjects. In comparison with Fuzzy MLS, the aim of our framework is to assess the threat likelihood posed by subjects towards objects by referring to object sensitivity and subject trustworthiness levels. Unlike Fuzzy MLS which is limited to the estimation of the threat likelihood of read accesses forbidden by Bell Lapadula, our approach estimates the threat likelihood of read and write accesses, is applicable when the objective of integrity is of interest (is not limited to secrecy) and considers security countermeasures mitigating the threat likelihood.

Bartsch proposes a policy override calculus for qualitative risk assessment in the context of role-based access control systems [20]. The risk is equal to the highest value from values estimated for each security objective (secrecy, integrity and availability). This work presents a qualitative estimation of threat likelihood. In comparison with the work of Bartsch, our approach is both qualitative and quantitative, developed in the context of generic access control systems by referring to the sensitivity of objects and trustworthiness of subjects and is not limited to RBAC.

Diep et al. describe an access control model with context-based decisions that includes quantitative risk assessment [7]. However, they do not provide a method for estimating threat likelihood measures.

Wang and Jin propose a method to quantify access risk by considering need-to-know requirements for privacy protection within the context of health information systems [23]. This work exploits the concept of entropy from information theory to compute risk scores of access requests. We believe that our framework could be extended to consider need-to-know requirements while assessing threats of subject-object accesses.

Kandala et al. develop a framework that captures various components and their interactions in order to develop "abstract models" for RAdAC [17]. However, this work does not consider concrete details of assessing threat or risk.

Threat likelihood assessment in our framework cannot cover unexpected threats such as those in which several other socio-technical parameters must be taken into consideration for reflecting the reality of internal threats such as users' access history, behavior, collusion with other users, etc. Hence, all these parameters are outside of the scope of this paper. Similarly, threats related to social engineering concerns and threats posed by Denial of service (Dos) attacks which might compromise the availability criterion by read and write operations, cannot be assessed by our approach.

6   Conclusion

The main contribution of this paper is a qualitative and quantitative approach for insider threat likelihood assessment in the context of access control systems. Our approach considers primarily the security levels of objects, hence giving more priority to the sensitivity of data. Our approach can easily accommodate other views, such as those presented in [15, 16]. In order to obtain realistic values of insider threat likelihood while being compliant with IT Risk standards and guidelines, our approach considers the effect of the security countermeasures mitigating the threat likelihood of access requests.

We believe that this framework is important because it can be used to assess the likelihood of threats posed by subjects towards objects that will subsequently affect the computation of risk metrics. Note that our framework could be extended to also consider need-to-know requirements while assessing threats of subject-object accesses by considering categories of data.

In this paper, we have presented a qualitative and a quantitative threat likelihood assessment approach, which is required for estimating access risks. Nonetheless, our objective is to develop an approach for estimating the risk of access requests by adopting the risk assessment formula (1). This requires us to extend the work reported in this paper by defining formulas for computing impact values in order to quantify the risk of access requests. Future papers will describe this extension.

Acknowledgements. This research was partially supported by the Natural Sciences and Engineering Research Council of Canada.

References

1. Bartsch, S.: A calculus for the qualitative risk assessment of policy override authorization. In: Proceedings of the International Conference on Security of Information and Networks, pp. 62–70 (2010)
2. Bishop, M., Gates, C.: Defining the insider threat. In: Proceedings of the 4th Annual Workshop on Cyber Security and Information Intelligence Research: Developing Strategies to Meet the Cyber Security and Information Intelligence Challenges Ahead, p. 15 (2008)
3. Boulares, S., Adi, K., Logrippo, L.: Insider threat likelihood assessment for access control systems: quantitative approach. In: International Symposium on Foundations and Practice of Security, pp. 135–142 (2016)
4. Caputo, D., Maloof, M., Stephens, G.: Detecting insider theft of trade secrets. IEEE Secur. Priv. **7**(6), 14–21 (2009)
5. Cheng, P., Rohatgi, P., Keser, C., Karger, P., Wagner, G., Reninger, A.: Fuzzy multilevel security: an experiment on quantified risk-adaptive access control. In: Security and Privacy, pp. 222–230 (2007)
6. Clusif. MEHARI 2010 principes fondamentaux et spécification fonctionnelles (2009)
7. Diep, N., Hung, L., Zhung, Y., Lee, S., Lee, Y., Lee, H.: Enforcing access control using risk assessment. In: Fourth European Conference on Universal Multiservice Networks, pp. 419–424 (2007)
8. Fagade, T., Tryfonas, T.: Security by Compliance? A study of insider threat implications for Nigerian banks. In: International Conference on Human Aspects of Information Security, Privacy, and Trust, pp. 128–139 (2016)
9. International Organization for Standardization. ISO/IEC 27001: Information technology - Security techniques - Information security management systems - Requirements (2013)
10. IT Global Corporate. Security risks (2013)
11. INFOSEC Glossary. National information systems security (infosec) glossary (2000)
12. Greitzer, F., Hohimer, R.: Modeling human behavior to anticipate insider attacks. J. Strateg. Secur. **4**(2), 25 (2011)
13. Hua, J., Bapna, S.: Who can we trust? The economic impact of insider threats. J. Global Inf. Technol. Manag. **16**(4), 47–67 (2013)
14. Kandala, S., Sandhu, R., Bhamidipati, V.: An attribute based framework for risk-adaptive access control models. In: Availability, Reliability and Security, pp. 236–241 (2011)
15. Khambhammettu, H., Boulares, S., Adi, K., Logrippo, L.: A framework for threat assessment in access control systems. In: Information Security and Privacy Research, pp. 187–198 (2012)
16. Khambhammettu, H., Boulares, S., Adi, K., Logrippo, L.: A framework for risk assessment in access control systems. Comput. Secur. **39**, 86–103 (2013)
17. McGraw, R.: Risk-adaptable access control (radac). In: Privilege (Access) Management Workshop. National Institute of Standards and Technology (2009)
18. Meucci, M., Muller, A.: The OWASP testing guide 4.0. Open Web Application Security Project, p. 30 (2014)

19. NIST. Risk management guide for information technology systems (2002)
20. Sandhu, R.: Lattice-based access control models. Computer **26**(11), 9–19 (1993)
21. Shey, H., Mak, K., Balaouras, S., Luu, B.: Understand the state of data security and privacy: Forrester Research **10** (2013)
22. Stoneburner, G., Goguen, A., Feringa, A.: Risk management guide for information technology systems (2002)
23. Wang, Q., Jin, H.: Quantified risk-adaptive access control for patient privacy protection in health information systems. In: Proceedings of the ACM Symposium on Information, Computer and Communications Security, pp. 406–410 (2011)
24. Weissman, C.: Security controls in the adept-50 time-sharing system. In: Proceedings of the Fall Joint Computer Conference, pp. 119–133 (1969)

Compliance Verification Algorithm
for Computer Systems Security Policies

Liviu Pene[1(✉)], Lamia Hamza[2], and Kamel Adi[1]

[1] Computer Security Research Laboratory,
Université du Québec en Outaouais, Gatineau, Canada
penl01@uqo.ca
[2] Laboratoire d'Informatique Médicale, Université de Bejaia, Bejaia, Algeria

Abstract. This paper proposes an algebraic formalism and a dedicated logic for computer systems and security policies specifications. A tableau-based proof system is then developed for assessing whether policies are satisfied for a given model of a computer system. A practical example and an implementation within a theorem prover show the effectiveness of our specification and verification technique.

Keywords: Computer security · Formal methods · Process algebra · Modal logic · Security policy · Verification algorithm · Tableau-based proof · Theorem prover

1 Introduction

There are no such things as secure networks. As soon as two or more computer systems are connected, there is a risk associated with the act of communication. The most common security configurations are easily built based on guidelines, standards, and best practices. Still, they are rarely a perfect match of the actual computer system's protection. An ideal framework requires high-level security policies that can be used to automatically derive access control rules. These rules regulate what, when, and how information is processed, stored, or transmitted. They also prevent the exploitation of protected resources by adversaries.

The rulesets are assumed to be correct because they are derived from a valid policy. Oftentimes this is not true and the network is left vulnerable to attacks from malicious intruders. Formal verification of the policies' effectiveness would solve the problem. However, this requires a precise formal description of computer systems and policies, and a methodology for validating compliance. This article proposes a new calculus and an associated logic for the specification and the verification of security policies for computer systems. We specify a system using an algebraic calculus and the desired security policy through a dedicated logic. Policy compliance is formally verified with the aid of a tableau-based deduction algorithm. The algorithm is automated via a theorem prover tool.

This research is supported by a research grant from the Natural Science and Engineering Council of Canada, NSERC.

E. Aïmeur et al. (Eds.): MCETECH 2017, LNBIP 289, pp. 96–115, 2017.
DOI: 10.1007/978-3-319-59041-7_6

The remainder of this paper is organized as follows. Section 2 reviews related works and outlines their limitations that motivated our approach. The new calculus and logic are introduced in Sects. 3 and 4 respectively. The tableau-based proof system for policy satisfaction is presented in Sect. 5. The case study, depicted in Sect. 6, illustrates how the tableau-based proof system works. The implementation of the tableau proof system is presented in Sect. 7. Finally, Sect. 8 summarizes our contributions and discusses directions for future work.

2 Related Work

Access control security policies imply regulated movement in and out of protected boundaries with the purpose of using various resources. Within computer systems, this can be represented in terms of process interactions. A formal specification of such interactions can be accomplished with a process algebra (calculus). While several calculi have been used for this purpose, we found that the mobile ambients of Cardelli and Gordon [1,2] represent a good basis for our objective. Ambients are named locations containing processes and they capture the concepts of administrative scope and mobility in a simple and effective manner. Their hierarchical structures mirror the administrative domains of the system they model, which makes them suitable for representing computers and networks. Properties of processes described with the ambient calculus can be specified using the ambient logic [3].

Furthermore, the mandated behaviour of a system can be prescribed through sets of requirements bundled as security policies. A security policy can be a simple security constraint, such as the ability to execute a particular action, or a collection of conditions for the various components and the whole system. The logic makes use of temporal and spacial modalities to capture the static structure of a system as well as its dynamic evolution [4]. The idea of employing calculi and logics for policy compliance monitoring has been revisited in [5].

The various extensions of the original calculus, such as safe ambients [6,7], security boundary analysis [8], or the ambient guardians [9] show limitations that make them less than ideal for the purpose of security policy verification. The original ambient calculus, for instance, is not refined enough for modeling firewalls and resorts to artificial concepts to simulate a simple accept/deny rule. The derived calculi involve elaborated constructs for verifying relatively simple properties and therefore have limited scalability. The original calculus and logic we propose here are better equipped for expressing access controlled mobility and the associated security policies.

As processes execute actions and systems evolve, they reach states that may or may not comply with a security policy. In order to determine which case stands, static or dynamic policy enforcement needs to be applied. Static enforcement is fairly common and entails verification of system properties applied to a system description (or model). The properties are expressed with logic formulas. The model can be formally analyzed for proof of formula satisfaction with the method of semantic tableaux used by Fitting [10,11] and Cleaveland [12]. Manual proofs can be produced through application of the tableau rules. Universal theorem provers such as Isabel [13], or tableau-specific ones such as Tableau Work Bench [14] and LoTREC [15,16], can be further employed to completely automate the verification process. This is the area addressed by the algorithm proposed in this paper. We define the tableau inference rules for our logic and formally prove the tableau's finiteness, soundness and completeness. A LoTREC implementation of the tableau proof system for our logic is also produced.

Runtime enforcements are preferable for certain policies, as demonstrated by Schneider et al. [17,18], Bauer [19], and Basin et al. [20]. Moreover, non-compliant systems can be modified to accommodate the required policies through program-rewriting, as shown by Hamlen [21], Langar et al. [22], Khoury et al. [23], and by Sui et al. [24]. Our verification technique can be applied independently or corroborated with dynamic enforcement, either at runtime or by program rewriting. The main benefit is that it can lower the number of policies to be enforced dynamically, improving the efficiency of the system.

3   System Specification Calculus

In this section we define the syntax and the semantics of the *Calculus for Specification of Computer Systems* (abbreviated as *CS2*). The calculus allows the description of the relevant components of a computer system's structure in terms of hierarchical domains, communication capabilities and protection mechanisms.

3.1   Syntax

The syntax of *CS2* is presented in Table 1. Let $\mathcal{N}$ be a set of names, $\mathcal{A}$ be a set of all possible process actions, and $\mathcal{K}$ be a set of keys used for protecting domains. In the proposed syntax, process constants 0 and 1 represent deadlock (or blocking) and successful process termination, respectively.

A number of operators are defined as well: "." for sequence, "|" for parallel composition, "+" for nondeterministic choice, and "!" for infinite replication. Ambients are used for delimiting administrative domains. They are identified by names and protected by access keys. For instance, the expression $_n^k[\mathsf{P}]$ depicts an ambient named n, protected by the key k, and containing a process P.

Permission to access resources in actual computer systems can be easily modelled with key possession. For instance, a process is allowed to enter a domain protected by a key k if it has a movement capability with the key k. Let $(\mathcal{K}, \geq)$ be a partial ordered set, and let k, k' in $\mathcal{K}$. The expression $k \geq k'$ means that k is comparable to k', but more powerful, as it can open at least any ambient k' can open. For default ambient protection we use the public key δ, which is the greatest lower bound $glb(\mathcal{K})$.

The ability of processes to move is implemented by the mov_n^k action, where n is the name of a domain for which the access is requested and k is the access key. Note that the same action is used to exit from a domain.

Table 1. Syntax of *CS2*

$n \in \mathcal{N}$		**domain name**
$k \in \mathcal{K}$		**security key**
$a \in \mathcal{A}$		**process action**
P, Q	::=	**processes**
	0	**deadlock**
	| 1	**successful termination**
	| A	**action**
	| P.Q	**sequence**
	| P | Q	**parallel composition**
	| P + Q	**choice**
	| !P	**replication**
	| $_n^k$[P]	**ambient**
A	::=	**process capabilities**
	mov_n^k	**movement**
	| a	**other actions**

General process interactions are expressed through a communication function, γ, which is a partial function of $\mathcal{A} \times \mathcal{A} \rightarrow \mathcal{A}$ that satisfies the two following conditions:

1. $\forall a, b \in \mathcal{A} : \gamma(a, b) = \gamma(b, a)$ (commutativity)
2. $\forall a, b, c \in \mathcal{A} : \gamma(\gamma(a, b), c) = \gamma(a, \gamma(b, c))$ (associativity)

3.2 Semantics

In the remainder of this paper, we note $\mathcal{P}$ the set of processes that can be built using *CS2*. The operational semantics of the calculus is presented in terms of a structural congruence "$\equiv$" and a reduction relation "$\rightarrow$". Table 2 displays a structural congruence on processes and includes, among others, reflexivity, symmetry, transitivity, associativity, and distributivity properties of the ., | and + operators, which are common to most process algebras.

The effect of deadlock is expressed by (2.11) and (2.12). A process will stop any further execution once it encounters a deadlock, and the rest of its actions can be ignored. In case of a choice between a non-blocking process and a deadlock, the non-blocking process will execute. Successful termination, on the other hand, acts as a neutral element and does not change the execution of a process. Its properties are shown in congruences (2.13–2.15).

Table 2. Structural congruence for *CS2*

$$P \equiv P \tag{2.1}$$

$$P \equiv Q \Rightarrow Q \equiv P \tag{2.2}$$

$$P \equiv Q, Q \equiv R \Rightarrow P \equiv R \tag{2.3}$$

$$P \equiv Q \Rightarrow R.P \equiv R.Q \tag{2.4}$$

$$P \equiv Q \Rightarrow P.R \equiv Q.R \tag{2.5}$$

$$P \equiv Q \Rightarrow P \mid R \equiv Q \mid R \tag{2.6}$$

$$(P \mid Q) \mid R \equiv P \mid (Q \mid R) \tag{2.7}$$

$$P \equiv Q \Rightarrow P + R \equiv Q + R \tag{2.8}$$

$$P \equiv Q \Rightarrow !P \equiv !Q \tag{2.9}$$

$$P \equiv Q \Rightarrow {}_n^k[P] \equiv {}_n^k[Q] \tag{2.10}$$

$$0.P \equiv 0 \tag{2.11}$$

$$P + 0 \equiv P \tag{2.12}$$

$$1.P \equiv P \equiv P.1 \tag{2.13}$$

$$P \mid 1 \equiv P \tag{2.14}$$

$$P + 1 \equiv P \tag{2.15}$$

$$P.(Q + R) \equiv P.Q + P.R \tag{2.16}$$

$$(P + Q).R \equiv P.R + Q.R \tag{2.17}$$

$$P \mid Q \equiv Q \mid P \tag{2.18}$$

$$P \mid (Q + R) \equiv (P \mid Q) + (P \mid R) \tag{2.19}$$

$$P + P \equiv P \tag{2.20}$$

$$P + Q \equiv Q + P \tag{2.21}$$

$$!P \equiv P \mid !P \tag{2.22}$$

Process evolutions are captured by the reduction relation defined in Table 3. Most rules are standard and need no explanation. Movement inside and outside ambients is captured by rules (3.8) and (3.9). For instance, rule (3.8) shows that a process can enter an ambient n protected by a key k provided it executes a movement directed into n with a key k' that is equal or superior to k.

System specifications are easy to build and read with our calculus. For instance, the expression ${}_n^\delta[\mathtt{mov}_n^\delta.A]$ models an administrative domain n (a computer, a service, etc.) that is publicly open (uses the public key δ), and contains a process which can exit the domain n and then continue to run as A.

Table 3. Reduction relation for $CS2$

$$\frac{P' \equiv P,\; P \xrightarrow{a} Q,\; Q \equiv Q'}{P' \xrightarrow{a} Q'} \tag{3.1}$$

$$\frac{P \xrightarrow{a} P'}{P+Q \xrightarrow{a} P'} \tag{3.2}$$

$$\frac{P \xrightarrow{a} P'}{P.Q \xrightarrow{a} P'.Q} \tag{3.3}$$

$$\frac{P \xrightarrow{a} P'}{P \mid Q \xrightarrow{a} P' \mid Q} \tag{3.4}$$

$$\frac{P \xrightarrow{a} P',\; Q \xrightarrow{b} Q'}{P \mid Q \xrightarrow{\gamma(a,b)} P' \mid Q'} \tag{3.5}$$

$$\frac{P \xrightarrow{a} P'}{\overset{k}{\underset{n}{}}[P] \xrightarrow{a} \overset{k}{\underset{n}{}}[P']} \tag{3.6}$$

$$\frac{a \neq \mathbf{mov}^-}{a \xrightarrow{a} 1} \tag{3.7}$$

$$\frac{k' \geq k}{\overset{k}{\underset{n}{}}[P] \mid \mathbf{mov}^{k'}_n.Q \xrightarrow{\mathbf{mov}^{k'}_n} \overset{k}{\underset{n}{}}[P \mid Q]} \tag{3.8}$$

$$\frac{k' \geq k}{\overset{k}{\underset{n}{}}[\mathbf{mov}^{k'}_n.Q \mid R] \xrightarrow{\mathbf{mov}^{k'}_n} Q \mid \overset{k}{\underset{n}{}}[R]} \tag{3.9}$$

4   Security Policy Logic

This section introduces a logic tailored for specifying security policies for computer systems described with $CS2$. The logic, named *Security Policy Logic* (or *SPL* in short), needs to be expressive enough to formulate any safety property.

4.1   Logic Syntax and Sematics

The syntax of *SPL* is summarized in Table 4. We define a modal logic with standard propositional connectives ($\neg, \vee$), a temporal operator (.), and a capability operator ($\langle\, \_\, \rangle$). Spatial connectives ($\mid$ and $\overset{\_}{\_}[\,\_\,]$) are also part of the syntax.

The following standard macros are used in the remainder of the paper:

$$\Phi \wedge \Psi \equiv \neg(\neg\Phi \vee \neg\Psi) \quad ff \equiv \neg tt$$

We define the semantics of *SPL* in Table 5, where $a \in \mathcal{A}$, $n \in \mathcal{N}$, and $k \in \mathcal{K}$. The set of logical formulas specified in *SPL* is denoted by $\mathcal{F}$. The semantics of

Table 4. Syntax of *SPL*

$$\Phi, \Psi ::=$$

tt	True
$\mid \quad \neg\Phi$	Negation
$\mid \quad \langle a\rangle\Phi$	Capability
$\mid \quad \Phi.\Psi$	Sequence
$\mid \quad \Phi \mid \Psi$	Parallel Composition
$\mid \quad \Phi \vee \Psi$	Disjunction
$\mid \quad {}^{k}_{n}[\Phi]$	Protected location

Table 5. Semantics of *SPL*

$$[\![\mathit{tt}]\!] \quad = \mathcal{P} \setminus \{0\}$$
$$[\![\neg\Phi]\!] \quad = \mathcal{P} \setminus [\![\Phi]\!]$$
$$[\![\langle a\rangle\Phi]\!] = \{a.P \in \mathcal{P} \ : \ P \in [\![\Phi]\!]\}$$
$$[\![\Phi.\Psi]\!] \quad = \{P.Q \in \mathcal{P} \ : \ P \in [\![\Phi]\!] \wedge Q \in [\![\Psi]\!]\}$$
$$[\![\Phi \mid \Psi]\!] \quad = \{P \mid Q \in \mathcal{P} \ : \ P \in [\![\Phi]\!] \wedge Q \in [\![\Psi]\!]\}$$
$$[\![\Phi \vee \Psi]\!] = [\![\Phi]\!] \cup [\![\Psi]\!]$$
$$[\![{}^{k}_{n}[\Phi]]\!] \quad = \{{}^{k'}_{n}[P] \in \mathcal{P} \ : \ P \in [\![\Phi]\!], \ k' \geq k\}$$

SPL is given by the meaning function $[\![\_]\!] : \mathcal{F} \to 2^{\mathcal{P}}$ defined inductively on the structure of formulas. We say that a process P satisfies the formula Φ and we note $P \models \Phi$ if $P \in [\![\Phi]\!]$.

All processes except for the blocking process satisfy the formula tt. Processes that are not part of the semantics of a certain formula Φ satisfy the negation of the formula. A process satisfies the formula $\Phi \vee \Psi$ if it satisfies either the formula Φ or the formula Ψ. The formula $\langle a\rangle\Phi$ is satisfied by any process of the form a.P, provided that P satisfies Φ. Processes that satisfy the sequence logical formula involve the consecutive execution of two subprocesses, with each one satisfying the respective components of the formula. A process P' satisfies $\Phi \mid \Psi$ if there exists a process P satisfying Φ and a process Q satisfying Ψ such that $P' = P \mid Q$. The protected location logical formula reflects the case when a specific behaviour is required inside an ambient. A compliant process must match both the environment's external parameters (name and key) and the internal formula's semantics.

The syntax and semantics of our logic enable the construction of complex security policies. The logic can be used for expressing safety properties. For instance, to specifically deny access to resources inside a domain n protected by a key k', the following simple formula can be used:

$$\neg\langle \mathrm{mov}^{k}_{n}\rangle\mathit{tt} \ \mid \ {}^{k'}_{n}[\mathit{tt}]$$

Let's take another example by considering a system composed of an anti-virus server and a client:

$$_c^{k_c}[\mathit{tt} \mid {}_v^{k_v}[\mathit{tt}]] \mid {}_s^{k_s}[\langle \mathrm{mov}_s^{k_s}\rangle\langle \mathrm{mov}_c^{k_c}\rangle\langle \mathrm{mov}_v^{k_v}\rangle \mathit{tt} \mid \mathit{tt}]$$

The security policy needs to account for the client and server administrative domains c and s and the anti-virus subsystem v within the client. This translates into three locations protected with the keys k_c, k_v, and k_s, of which two are nested. Another requirement is the server's ability to push virus signature updates. That requirement is represented through a series of movement capabilities. Finally, the rest of the client and server's subsystems have to be represented. As we are not interested in the details of those components, they can be abstracted as True.

Now that the syntax and semantics of the algebraic calculus and the logic are presented, we are able to specify a computer system's structure and behaviour and a desired security policy.

4.2   Formula Closure

In order to perform logical formula manipulations, we introduce some new definitions. They are useful for reasoning about the finite nature of formulas, which plays an important role in model checking. The following definitions are inspired by [12,25] and are given in support of the proofs in the next section.

The evaluation of a system specification with respect to formula satisfaction will be made in Sect. 5 by breaking down complex formulas up to atomic formulas.

Definition 1. *Let Φ and Ψ be two formulas. Ψ is an immediate subterm of Φ, denoted by $\Psi \prec \Phi$, if exactly one of the following hold:*

$$\Phi = \neg\Psi$$
$$\Phi = \langle a\rangle\Psi$$
$$\Phi = \Psi.\Phi' \text{ for some } \Phi'$$
$$\Phi = \Psi \mid \Phi' \text{ for some } \Phi'$$
$$\Phi = \Psi \vee \Phi' \text{ for some } \Phi'$$
$$\Phi = {}_n^k[\Psi]$$

The following definition allows us to determine the length of a formula.

Definition 2. *The size of a formula* Φ, *denoted by* $|\Phi|$, *is equal to the number of subterms and operations, i.e.:*

$$
\begin{aligned}
|tt| &= 1 \\
|\neg\Phi| &= 1 + |\Phi| \\
|\langle a\rangle\Phi| &= 1 + |\Phi| \\
|\Phi.\Psi| &= 1 + |\Phi| + |\Psi| \\
|\Phi \mid \Psi| &= 1 + |\Phi| + |\Psi| \\
|\Phi \vee \Psi| &= 1 + |\Phi| + |\Psi| \\
|{}_n^k[\Phi]| &= 1 + |\Phi|
\end{aligned}
$$

The closure of a formula is defined as the set of all its subterms and their subterms, up to atomic formulas.

Definition 3. *The closure* $CL(\Phi)$ *of a formula* Φ *is defined as follows:*

$$\Phi \in CL(\Phi)$$

$$CL(\neg\Phi) = \{\neg\Phi\} \cup CL(\Phi)$$

$$CL(\langle a\rangle\Phi) = \{\langle a\rangle\Phi\} \cup CL(\Phi)$$

$$CL(\Phi.\Psi) = \{\Phi.\Psi\} \cup CL(\Phi) \cup CL(\Psi)$$

$$CL(\Phi \mid \Psi) = \{\Phi \mid \Psi\} \cup CL(\Phi) \cup CL(\Psi)$$

$$CL(\Phi \vee \Psi)| = \{\Phi \vee \Psi\} \cup CL(\Phi) \cup CL(\Psi)$$

$$CL({}_n^k[\Phi]) = \{{}_n^k[\Phi]\} \cup CL(\Phi)$$

The previous definitions are useful for proving the finiteness of the tableau methodology. Closure can be interpreted as the set of all *SPL* formulas that can be obtained using all the subterms of a formula. Therefore, the cardinal of $CL(\Phi)$ is bounded by the size of the formula, as shown in the following proposition.

Proposition 1. *Let* Φ *be a formula. Then,*

$$|CL(\Phi)| \leq |\Phi|$$

Proof. The proof is by structural induction on Φ. We demonstrate it for capability only, in order to comply with the article size restrictions. The other cases follow exactly the same steps.

Since $CL(\langle a\rangle\Phi) = \{\langle a\rangle\Phi\} \cup CL(\Phi)$, then $|CL(\langle a\rangle\Phi)| = 1 + |CL(\Phi)|$

By induction on the hypothesis $|CL(\Phi)| \leq |\Phi|$, we obtain:

$$|CL(\langle\mathsf{a}\rangle\Phi)| \leq 1 + |\Phi|$$

From the definition of size: $|\langle\mathsf{a}\rangle\Phi| = 1 + |\Phi|$, and therefore:

$$|CL(\langle\mathsf{a}\rangle\Phi)| \leq |\langle\mathsf{a}\rangle\Phi| \qquad\qquad \square$$

5   Tableau-Based Proof System

In this section we define a tableau-based proof system for *SPL*. The tableau system is a model-checking technique that relies on a set of inference rules used for determining automatically whether properties specified as logic formulas are satisfied. Tableaux (or semantic tableaux, as they are also called) have been used successfully in conjunction with modal logics [10,12,25] and are therefore suitable for *SPL*.

5.1   Building the Tableau

Using the logic semantics as defined in Sect. 4 is not very practical. Given a formula Φ, we have to calculate the (possibly infinite) set of processes that satisfy Φ and demonstrate that the model considered is included into that set of processes. However, the tableau based technique considers local model checking. A deductive tableau system needs to provide formal assurance for all scenarios, therefore the reasoning about satisfaction must be made on a tautology. It is often easier to prove a contradiction, so it is a common practice to demonstrate the opposite, namely that the formula negation is unsatisfiable.

Model checking for a given model M is performed on sequents of the form $b \vdash_M s \in [\![\Phi]\!]$, where $s \in \mathcal{S}$ is a specification and $\Phi \in \mathcal{F}$ is a finite formula. The variable b is ranging over $\{\top, \bot\}$. We introduce the operations bb', $b \times b'$, and $b\Phi$ as follows:

bb'	$b \times b'$	$b\Phi$
$\top\top = \top$	$\top \times \top = \top$	$\top\Phi = \Phi$
$\top\bot = \bot$	$\top \times \bot = \bot$	$\bot\Phi = \neg\Phi$
$\bot\top = \bot$	$\bot \times \top = \bot$	$\top\neg\Phi = \neg\Phi$
$\bot\bot = \top$	$\bot \times \bot = \bot$	$\bot\neg\Phi = \Phi$

The inclusion of the variable b is crucial for reasoning on negative forms of the terms and reduces the number of inference rules needed for the tableau proof system introduced in Table 6. Note that our inference rules have the premise at the bottom and the conclusion on top, which permits a more natural way of building the proof tree from the root up, rather then upside down.

Table 6. Tableau rules for SPL

$$R_\neg \quad \frac{\bot b \vdash s \in [\![\Phi]\!]}{b \vdash s \in [\![\neg\Phi]\!]}$$

$$R_{\langle a \rangle} \quad \frac{b \vdash s \in [\![\Phi]\!]}{b \vdash a.s \in [\![\langle a \rangle \Phi]\!]}$$

$$R_{.} \quad \frac{b \vdash s \in [\![\Phi]\!] \quad b \vdash s' \in [\![\Psi]\!]}{b \vdash s.s' \in [\![\Phi.\Psi]\!]}$$

$$R_| \quad \frac{b' \vdash s \in [\![\Phi]\!] \quad b'' \vdash s' \in [\![\Psi]\!]}{b' \times b'' \vdash s \mid s' \in [\![\Phi \mid \Psi]\!]}$$

$$R_{1\vee} \quad \frac{b \vdash s \in [\![\Phi]\!]}{b \vdash s \in [\![\Phi \vee \Psi]\!]}$$

$$R_{2\vee} \quad \frac{b \vdash s \in [\![\Psi]\!]}{b \vdash s \in [\![\Phi \vee \Psi]\!]}$$

$$R_{[]} \quad \frac{b \vdash s \in [\![\Phi]\!]}{b \vdash {}^k_n[s] \in [\![{}^k_n[\Phi]]\!]}$$

The proof is actually based on a refutation tableau that starts with the negation of the formula: $\neg\Phi$. The backward-chaining proof is a tree labeled with formulas at every node and rooted in the original assumption. Branches are built through application of the inference rules and extend until no further inference can be made. The last formula on a branch is called a leaf.

A leaf $b \vdash s \in [\![\Phi]\!]$ is successful if:

- $b = \top \wedge \Phi = tt$
- $b = \bot \wedge \Phi = ff$

Leaves for which no rule can be applied are also successful leaves. A sequent is an unsuccessful leaf, if one of the following conditions holds:

- $b = \top \wedge \Phi = ff$
- $b = \bot \wedge \Phi = tt$
- $s = a.s' \wedge \Phi = \langle a' \rangle \Phi' \wedge a \neq a'$

A tableau is successful when all its leaves are successful. A tableau is unsuccessful if it contains at least one unsuccessful leaf. This means that the original assumption about $\neg\Phi$ is not satisfied, hence the formula Φ holds for the assessed model.

The rule $R_\neg$ makes verification of negative formulas straightforward. Instead of verifying whether $\neg\Phi$ is satisfied by a specification, we verify Φ and conclude the contrary for $\neg\Phi$. This is where variable b comes in handy. The other rules of

Table 6 are intuitive enough to require no particular explanations. For instance the rule $R_{\langle \mathsf{a} \rangle}$ means that if $s \in [\![\Phi]\!]$ then $\mathsf{a}.s \in [\![\langle \mathsf{a} \rangle \Phi]\!]$.

5.2 Tableau Finiteness, Soundness, and Completeness

In this section we demonstrate the tableau system's finiteness, soundness, and completeness. The results are formulated as theorems.

In order to prove the finiteness of the tableau, we have to demonstrate that there is no infinite ascending chain for any sequent that is part of the tableau. The ordering relation for formulas $\prec$ is extended to sequents as follows:

$$\Phi \prec \Phi' \;\Rightarrow\; b \vdash s \in [\![\Phi]\!] \prec b' \vdash s' \in [\![\Phi']\!]$$

Let $R \in \{R_\neg, R_{\langle \mathsf{a} \rangle}, R_., R_|, R_{1\lor}, R_{2\lor}, R_{[]}\}$ be one of the inference rules from Table 6. The notation $\theta_1 \to_R \theta_2$ is used for showing that a parent sequent θ_1 reduces to a child sequent θ_2. The following proposition demonstrates that the number of possible children of a sequent is finite.

Proposition 2. *Let* $\theta_1 = b \vdash s_1 \in [\![\Phi_1]\!]$ *and* $\theta_2 = b \vdash s_2 \in [\![\Phi_2]\!]$. *Then,*

$$\theta_1 \to_R \theta_2 \Rightarrow CL(\Phi_1) \supseteq CL(\Phi_2)$$

Proof. The proof is by induction on formulas and their immediate subterms. We provide only a proof sketch in order to comply with the article size restrictions.

For each rule in Table 6, if $\Phi_1 \to_R \Phi_2$ then $\Phi_2 \prec \Phi_1$. Furthermore, by construction if $\Phi_1 \prec \Phi_2$ then $CL(\Phi_1) \subseteq CL(\Phi_2)$. Therefore, the sequent ordering relation holds for all inference rules $R \in \{R_\neg, R_{\langle \mathsf{a} \rangle}, R_., R_|, R_{1\lor}, R_{2\lor}, R_{[]}\}$. They are the result of reductions of the premise formulas, which decrease the size of the conclusion formulas.   □

We conclude that for a tableau with sequent θ as root, formulas in all sequents derived directly by inference rules belong in $CL(\Phi)$. Informally, since Φ is finite, then $CL(\Phi)$ is finite, which means that there is a bounded number of first-level branches of the tree. Moreover, there will be a bounded number of branches at every level. Therefore, the proposition demonstrates that a tableau built to prove formula Φ from the premise sequent θ has a maximum width. It remains to show that each branch has a finite height.

Proposition 3. *Let* $\theta_1 = b \vdash s \in [\![\Phi_1]\!]$ *be a sequent and let* Θ *be the ordered set* $\{\theta_i : \theta_i \prec \theta_{i+1}, i \geq 1\}$ *of terms of the* θ_1*'s chain in a tableau proof, then,*

$$|\Theta| \leq |CL(\Phi_1)|$$

Proof. The proof is done on sequent chains. The elements of Θ come from the following chain: $\theta_1 \to_{R_1} \theta_2 \to_{R_2} \theta_3 \ldots$, where $R_i \in \{R_\neg, R_{\langle \mathsf{a} \rangle}, R_., R_|, R_{1\lor}, R_{2\lor}, R_{[]}\}$. For the formulas associated with the ordered sequents, this means:

$$|\Phi_1| > |\Phi_2| > |\Phi_3| > \ldots$$

Therefore the set $\{\Phi_1, \Phi_2, \Phi_3, \ldots\}$ is also an ordered set, and it is equivalent to Θ. Moreover, they have the same number of elements:

$$\{\theta_1, \theta_2, \theta_3 \ldots\} \sim \{\Phi_1, \Phi_2, \Phi_3, \ldots\} \leftrightarrow |\{\theta_1, \theta_2, \theta_3 \ldots\}| = |\{\Phi_1, \Phi_2, \Phi_3, \ldots\}|$$

From the definitions of formula subterm, formula closure, and from Proposition 2 we have:

$$\{\Phi_1, \Phi_2, \Phi_3, \ldots\} \subseteq CL(\Phi_1) \Rightarrow |\{\Phi_1, \Phi_2, \Phi_3, \ldots\}| \leq |CL(\Phi_1)|$$

From Proposition 1 we know that: $|CL(\Phi_1)| < |\Phi_1| < \infty$

So finally we have: $|\Theta| \leq |CL(\Phi_1)| < \infty$ □

The two propositions in this section lead to the conclusion that a finite tableau can be built for a given sequent, therefore an assessment of the validity of the formula can be made. In practical terms, this means that we can verify formally whether a set of restrictions (i.e.: security policy) is satisfied by a given model (i.e.: system specification).

Theorem 1 (Finiteness). *For any sequent $\theta = b \vdash s \in [\![\Phi]\!]$, there is a tableau rooted in θ with finite maximum height and width.*

Proof. The proof stems directly from Propositions 2 and 3. The tableau for a sequent with a finite formula Φ has a maximum width and a maximum height bounded by $|CL(\Phi)|$.

Theorem 2 (Soundness). *If $\theta = b \vdash s \in [\![\Phi]\!]$ has a successful tableau, then $s \in [\![b\Phi]\!]$.*

Proof. We need to prove that all successful leaves are semantically valid and all inference rules preserve soundness. Soundness for the inference rules is interpreted as follows. By hypothesis, the sequent of the denominator is sound and the sequent of the numerator has a successful tableau. It remains to prove that the numerator is also sound. We demonstrate it for negation only, in order to comply with the article size restrictions.

- $b = \top \Rightarrow R_\neg$ has the form $\dfrac{\bot \vdash s \in [\![\Phi]\!]}{\top \vdash s \in [\![\neg\Phi]\!]}$

  By hypothesis,

  $$\begin{cases} \top \vdash s \in [\![\neg\Phi]\!] \Rightarrow s \in [\![\neg\Phi]\!] \\[2mm] \bot \vdash s \in [\![\Phi]\!] \Rightarrow s \notin [\![\Phi]\!] \end{cases}$$

  Since $s \notin [\![\Phi]\!] \equiv s \in [\![\neg\Phi]\!] \equiv s \in [\![\top\neg\Phi]\!]$, soundness is preserved.

- $b = \bot \Rightarrow R_\neg$ has the form $\dfrac{\top \vdash s \in [\![\neg\Phi]\!]}{\bot \vdash s \in [\![\Phi]\!]}$

By hypothesis,

$$\begin{cases} \bot \vdash s \in [\![\Phi]\!] \Rightarrow s \in [\![\neg\Phi]\!] \\[2em] \top \vdash s \in [\![\neg\Phi]\!] \Rightarrow s \notin [\![\Phi]\!] \end{cases}$$

Since $s \notin [\![\Phi]\!] \equiv s \in [\![\neg\Phi]\!] \equiv s \in [\![\bot\Phi]\!]$, soundness is preserved. $\qquad\square$

Proposition 4. *Let s be a system specification and Φ be a formula. Then, $b \vdash s \in [\![\Phi]\!]$ has a successful tableau $\Leftrightarrow b \vdash s \in [\![\neg\Phi]\!]$ has no successful tableau.*

Proof. • $\Rightarrow$

By hypothesis, $b \vdash s \in [\![\Phi]\!]$ has a successful tableau and, by Theorem 2, $s \in [\![b\Phi]\!]$.

Suppose that $b \vdash s \in [\![\neg\Phi]\!]$ also has a successful tableau. In this case, Theorem 2 states that $s \in [\![b\neg\Phi]\!]$.

Since $b\neg = \neg b$, then $[\![b\neg\Phi]\!] = [\![\neg b\Phi]\!]$ and, by definition of $[\![\neg b\Phi]\!]$, we deduce that $s \notin [\![b\Phi]\!]$.

This contradicts the hypothesis that $s \in [\![b\Phi]\!]$, and therefore the supposition that $b \vdash s \in [\![\neg\Phi]\!]$ also has a successful tableau is false.

• $\Leftarrow$

We need to prove that if $b \vdash s \in [\![\neg\Phi]\!]$ has no successful tableau, then $b \vdash s \in [\![\Phi]\!]$ must have one.

By hypothesis, $b \vdash s \in [\![\neg\Phi]\!]$ has no successful tableau. This means, by Theorem 2, that $s \notin [\![b\neg\Phi]\!]$. Since $[\![b\neg\Phi]\!] = [\![\neg b\Phi]\!]$, we deduce that which is equivalent $s \notin [\![\neg b\Phi]\!]$.

From the definition of semantics, $s \in [\![\neg\neg b\Phi]\!] = s \in [\![b\Phi]\!]$. Therefore, $b \vdash s \in [\![\Phi]\!]$ has a successful tableau. $\qquad\square$

Theorem 3 (Completeness). *Let s be a system specification and Φ be a formula. Then,*

$$s \in [\![b\Phi]\!] \Rightarrow b \vdash s \in [\![\Phi]\!] \text{ has a successful tableau.}$$

Proof. Suppose that $s \in [\![b\Phi]\!]$, but $b \vdash s \in [\![\Phi]\!]$ does not have a successful tableau.

By Proposition 4, this means that $b \vdash s \in [\![\neg\Phi]\!]$ has a successful tableau.

By Theorem 2, we deduce that $s \in [\![\neg b\Phi]\!]$ which is equivalent to $s \notin [\![b\Phi]\!]$, but this contradicts the hypothesis that $s \in [\![b\Phi]\!]$. $\qquad\square$

6   Case Study

In this section, we illustrate our technique with an example of a medical computer system that allows nurses and doctors to read, create and change prescriptions for their patients. The example demonstrates the use of the *CS2* algebra, the *SPL* logic, and the tableau-based proof method. We show that the system satisfies the security policy.

6.1   System Specification

The emphasis of the case study is the application of the tableau rules and therefore the computer system is kept simple. It includes a desktop computer for the nurse, a tablet for the doctor and a file server for the patient's current prescription, medical test results, allergies, and their medical history.

The hospital system's specification, expressed in *CS2* terms, is as follows:

$$H = {}^{k_n}_n[\text{mov}^{k_n}_n.\text{mov}^{k_p}_p.N] \mid {}^{k_d}_d[\text{mov}^{k_d}_d.\text{mov}^{k_p}_p.(D_1 \mid \text{mov}^{k_f}_f.D_2)] \mid {}^{k_p}_p[P \mid {}^{k_f}_f[F]]$$

$$where\ N, D_1, D_2, P, F \neq 0,\ k_n, k_d, k_p, k_f \neq \delta$$

The three devices, depicted through ambients n, d, and p respectively, are properly safeguarded according to the best industry standards, as symbolized by their access keys k_n, k_d, and k_p. The file server has a general folder for current prescriptions and a restricted one for the patient's more sensitive information. The restricted folder is protected by the key k_f. The nurse can only view current prescriptions (process N), while the doctor can do the same (process D_1) and additionally access the patient's medical history and write new prescriptions or enter new test results (process D_2). Finally, processes P and F represent the prescription and the sensitive information.

The security policy for the system reflects the system's purpose: we require that the nurse and the doctor have their appropriate access levels and that the file server has a restricted area for sensitive data. The *SPL* formula for the system's security policy is:

$$\Phi = {}^{k_n}_n[\langle\text{mov}^{k_n}_n\rangle\langle\text{mov}^{k_p}_p\rangle t\!t] \mid {}^{k_d}_d[\langle\text{mov}^{k_d}_d\rangle\langle\text{mov}^{k_p}_p\rangle(t\!t \mid \langle\text{mov}^{k_f}_f\rangle t\!t)] \mid {}^{k_p}_p[t\!t \mid {}^{k_f}_f[t\!t]]$$

The policy allows us demonstrate the application of 4 different tableau rules and verification of the conditions for both successful and unsuccessful leaves. The case study has a reasonable degree of complexity for a manual proof. At the same time, it is kept legible to prevent from splitting the proof tree on several pages. The same scenario is treated in Sect. 7, where the advantages of automation over manual proofs are highlighted.

6.2   Proof Tree

The hypothesis in this case study have already been presented with the system specification. The initial value of the variable b is $\top$. The sequent to use for

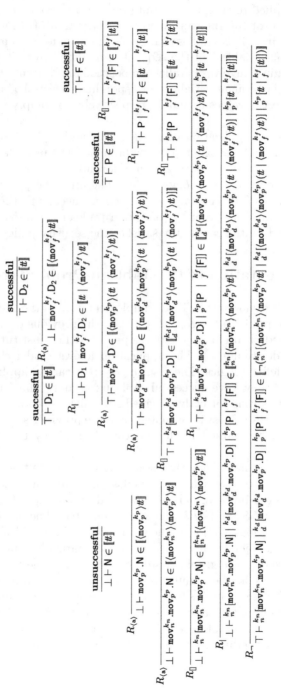

Table 7. Tableau system proof for case study

producing an unsuccessful tableau is $\top \vdash \mathsf{H} \in [\![\neg\Phi]\!]$. The inference rules in Table 6 are applied to the premise and produce the proof tree shown in Table 7.

The premise of the tableau involves the negation of a formula, so the rule $R_\neg$ is invoked first. This implies changes both to the formula and to the variable b. The value of variable b of the sequent is modified from $\top$ to $\bot\top = \bot$. The resulting formula Φ involves parallel composition and the rule $R_|$ is applied. Note the change of the sequent variables corresponding to b' and b'' in the $R_|$ inference rule. They take the values $\bot$ and $\top$, respectively, to comply with the operation $\bot \times \top = \bot$.

The successive application of the $R_{\langle \mathsf{a} \rangle}, R_|$, and $R_{[]}$ tableau rules results in five branches. Finally, at the top of the branches, the proof leads to leafs where processes are evaluated for satisfaction of formula tt. Four of the leaves are successful, since any process belongs to $[\![tt]\!]$. The only exception is $\bot \vdash \mathsf{N} \in [\![tt]\!]$, which is unsuccessful. The tableau is then unsuccessful, the original sequent does not hold, and the proof by refutation tableau is complete. Therefore, the system depicted by the case study satisfies the security policy.

7   Implementation of the Tableau Proof System

In this section we show our LoTREC implementation of the tableau proof system for *SPL* and apply it to the case study from the previous one. LoTREC [15,16] is an automated theorem prover developed at IRIT (Institut de Recherche en Informatique de Toulouse). The application allows model checking on predefined or user-defined logics. The resulting system can be applied to formulas to verify whether they have successful tableaux or not. The formal semantics of LoTREC ensures that correctly specified rules always produce "correct" results. The tableau successfulness is evaluated as in the previous sections, and the truth assessment can be marked in the associated graph by the TRUE or FALSE labels.

The LoTREC implementation starts with the definition of the logic. The syntax uses operators for defining formulas, sequents, and rules. In our case, we needed to express both logical formulas and system specifications. Therefore, elements of both *CS2* and *SPL* were accommodated. The proof tree for the case study in the previous section is shown in Fig. 1. Each tableau rule application corresponds to a label. Branching caused by the parallelism in the security policy is clearly marked in the graph. A step-by-step run of the proof will reveal that the same rules as in the manual proof in Table 7 are applied, exactly in the same order. The tree contains four successful leaves and one unsuccessful leaf, as expected. Therefore, the tree is unsuccessful and the refutation tableau proof is complete. Note that proof generation was significantly faster than building the proof by hand, underlining once more the benefit of automation.

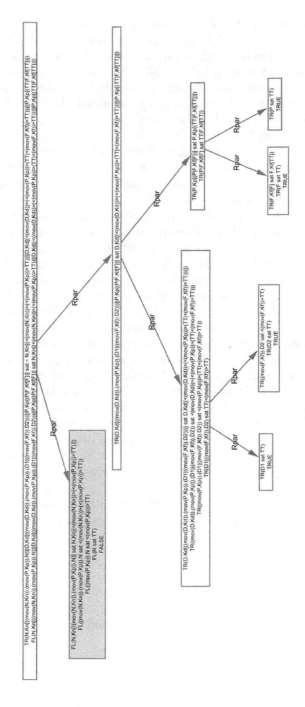

Fig. 1. LoTREC *SPL* tableau proof for the extended case study

8 Conclusion

Formal verification of security policies can ensure that access is provided as intended, with no accidental backdoors or latent vulnerabilities. We are proposing in this paper an automated algorithm for assessing policy implementation. The algorithm employs inference rules applied to logic formulas and systems specifications that we define with our *CS2* process algebra and *SPL* modal logic, respectively. The statement to be evaluated is presented in the form of a sequent, which takes into account a model of the system and a formula representing the policy. A tableau is then built on back-chaining premises and conclusions to determine whether the original statement holds. Formal proofs are given for the finiteness, soundness, and completeness of our tableau methodology. If the tableau is closed, then a conclusion can be reached about the initial sequent, meaning that the verified formula is satisfied (or not) by the model.

The implementation of our tableau-proof system in LoTREC, a tableau theorem prover, is also presented. It allows automatic verification of policy compliance, eliminating the need for manual application of the inference rules. The four components - the algebra, the logic, the proof algorithm, and the implementation - integrate optimally as they are built specifically for the purpose. A set of access permissions and restrictions built as security policies can be checked individually or together. Moreover, the methodology allows verification of any reasoning about the model that can be expressed with *SPL* formulas.

One of the merits of our approach is that it unifies all components in a formal, homogeneous framework. The solutions we have come across so far fall short of our intended objective, as pointed in Sect. 2. In some cases, the system specification and policy logic are well developed, but there is no formal verification. Conversely, formal verification methods are available for several calculi and logics, but do not cover mobility. The framework we propose addresses these shortcomings and advances the solution yet another step through automation. Moreover, tableau finiteness is a guarantee that the algorithm terminates, no matter how complex the initial sequent is. The effectiveness of the implementation has been demonstrated in Sect. 7.

Among the potential directions for extending this work, the automatic enforcement of security policies through program-rewriting is our main priority and our next research endeavour.

References

1. Cardelli, L., Gordon, A.D.: Mobile ambients. In: Nivat, M. (ed.) FoSSaCS 1998. LNCS, vol. 1378, pp. 140–155. Springer, Heidelberg (1998). doi:10.1007/BFb0053547
2. Cardelli, L., Gordon, A.D.: Anytime, anywhere: modal logics for mobile ambients. In: POPL 2000: Proceedings of the 27th ACM SIGPLAN-SIGACT Symposium on Principles of Programming Languages, vol. 365, p. 377 (2000)
3. Cardelli, L., Gordon, A.D.: Ambient logic. Mathematical Structures in Computer Science (2006)

4. Hirschkoff, D., Lozes, E., Sangiorgi, D.: On the expressiveness of the ambient logic. Logical Methods Comput. Sci. **2**(2), 1–35 (2006)
5. Basin, D., Klaedtke, F., Müller, S.: Monitoring security policies with metric first-order temporal logic. In: Proceedings of the 15th ACM Symposium on Access Control Models and Technologies, SACMAT 2010, pp. 23–34. ACM, New York (2010)
6. Degano, P., Levi, F., Bodei, C.: Safe ambients: control flow analysis and security. In: Jifeng, H., Sato, M. (eds.) ASIAN 2000. LNCS, vol. 1961, pp. 199–214. Springer, Heidelberg (2000). doi:10.1007/3-540-44464-5_15
7. Levi, F., Sangiorgi, D.: Mobile safe ambients. ACM Trans. Program. Lang. Syst. **25**(1), 1–69 (2003)
8. Braghin, C., Cortesi, A., Focardi, R.: Control flow analysis of mobile ambients with security boundaries. In: Jacobs, B., Rensink, A. (eds.) FMOODS 2002. ITIFIP, vol. 81, pp. 197–212. Springer, Boston, MA (2002). doi:10.1007/978-0-387-35496-5_14
9. Ferrari, G., Moggi, E., Pugliese, R.: Guardians for ambient-based monitoring. In: F-WAN: Foundations of Wide Area Network Computing, vol. 66 (2002)
10. Fitting, M.: First-Order Logic and Automated Theorem Proving. Springer, New York (1990)
11. Fitting, M.: Prefixed tableaus and nested sequents. Ann. Pure Appl. Logic **163**(3), 291–313 (2012)
12. Cleaveland, R.: Tableau-based model checking in the propositional mu-calculus. Acta Informatica **27**(8), 725–747 (1990)
13. Paulson, L.C.: The isabelle reference manual (2008)
14. Abate, P., Goré, R.: The tableaux work bench. In: Cialdea Mayer, M., Pirri, F. (eds.) TABLEAUX 2003. LNCS, vol. 2796, pp. 230–236. Springer, Heidelberg (2003). doi:10.1007/978-3-540-45206-5_18
15. Cerro, L.F., Fauthoux, D., Gasquet, O., Herzig, A., Longin, D., Massacci, F.: Lotrec: the generic tableau prover for modal and description logics. In: Goré, R., Leitsch, A., Nipkow, T. (eds.) IJCAR 2001. LNCS, vol. 2083, pp. 453–458. Springer, Heidelberg (2001). doi:10.1007/3-540-45744-5_38
16. Gasquet, O., Herzig, A., Longin, D., Sahade, M.: LoTREC: logical tableaux research engineering companion. In: Beckert, B. (ed.) TABLEAUX 2005. LNCS, vol. 3702, pp. 318–322. Springer, Heidelberg (2005). doi:10.1007/11554554_25
17. Schneider, F.B.: Enforceable security policies. ACM Trans. Inf. Syst. Secur. (TISSEC) **3**(1), 30–50 (2000)
18. Hamlen, K.W., Morrisett, G., Schneider, F.B.: Computability classes for enforcement mechanisms. ACM Trans. Program. Lang. Syst. (TOPLAS) **28**(1), 175–205 (2006)
19. Bauer, L., Ligatti, J., Walker, D.: A language and system for enforcing run-time security policies. Technical report TR-699-04, Princeton University (2004)
20. Basin, D., Jugé, V., Klaedtke, F., Zălinescu, E.: Enforceable security policies revisited. ACM Trans. Inf. Syst. Secur. **16**(1), 3:1–3:26 (2013)
21. Hamlen, K.: Security policy enforcement by automated program-rewriting. Ph.D. thesis, Cornell University, Ithaca, NY, USA (2006). AAI3227141
22. Langar, M., Mejri, M., Adi, K.: Formal enforcement of security policies on concurrent systems. J. Symbolic Comput. **3**, 997–1016 (2011)
23. Khoury, R., Tawbi, N.: Equivalence-preserving corrective enforcement of security properties. Int. J. Inf. Comput. Secur. **7**(2/3/4), 113–139 (2015)
24. Sui, G., Mejri, M.: Security enforcement by rewriting: an algebraic approach. In: Garcia-Alfaro, J., Kranakis, E., Bonfante, G. (eds.) FPS 2015. LNCS, vol. 9482, pp. 311–321. Springer, Cham (2016). doi:10.1007/978-3-319-30303-1_22
25. Adi, K., Debbabi, M., Mejri, M.: A new logic for electronic commerce protocols. Int. J. Theor. Comput. Sci. (TCS) **291**, 223–283 (2003)

Review of Existing Analysis Tools
for SELinux Security Policies:
Challenges and a Proposed Solution

Amir Eaman[1,2](✉), Bahman Sistany[2], and Amy Felty[1]

[1] School of Electrical Engineering and Computer Science,
University of Ottawa, Ottawa, Canada
{aeama028,afelty}@uottawa.ca
[2] Irdeto Canada Corporation, Ottawa, Canada
bahman.sistany@irdeto.com

Abstract. Access control policy management is an increasingly hard problem from both the security point of view and the verification point of view. SELinux is a Linux Security Module (LSM) implementing a mandatory access control mechanism. SELinux integrates user identity, roles, and type security attributes for stating rules in security policies. As SELinux policies are developed and maintained by security administrators, they often become quite complex, and it is important to carefully analyze them in order to have high assurance of their correctness. There are many existing analysis tools for modeling and analyzing SELinux policies with the goal of answering specific safety and functionality questions. In this paper, we identify and highlight current gaps in these existing tools for SELinux policy analysis, and propose new tools and technologies with the potential to lead to significant improvements. The proposed solution includes adopting a certified access control policy language such as ACCPL (A Certified Access Core Policy Language). ACCPL comes with formal proofs of important properties, and our proposed solution includes adopting it to facilitate various analyses and proof of reasonability properties. ACCPL is general, and our goal is to design a certified domain-specific policy language based on it, specialized to our task.

Keywords: SELinux · Access control · Security policies · Analysis tools

1 Introduction

On Linux based systems, many security exploits attempt to target system daemons that often run with elevated or even unlimited privileges (e.g. as root). Once the attacker gets access to a daemon, the whole system is compromised since the attacker obtains permanent root privileges on the system. The traditional Discretionary Access Control (DAC) mechanism that Unix/Linux systems use leaves important security decisions up to the discretion of the individual users

© Springer International Publishing AG 2017
E. Aïmeur et al. (Eds.): MCETECH 2017, LNBIP 289, pp. 116–135, 2017.
DOI: 10.1007/978-3-319-59041-7_7

and administrators, resulting in an ad-hoc system where some applications or daemons are well configured whereas others have too many unnecessary permissions. SELinux [18] as an access control mechanism at the operating system level integrates DAC and Mandatory Access Control (MAC). MAC, and in particular SELinux, mandates a central policy-driven approach to access control and regulates DAC's access decisions. SELinux works based on the principle of least privilege, and every grant of access must have the corresponding allow rule in the security policy to permit that access. This means that when DAC allows access to a subject, the access request still needs to be checked by MAC as well. If an access request is denied by DAC, MAC will not get involved.

The policy language used to develop SELinux policies is a complex language encompassing an integration of Role-Based Access Control (RBAC), Type Enforcement (TE), and Multi-Level Security (MLS) [16]. Partly as a result of this fact and partly due to the way the language has been designed to specify fine-grained access control needs (among other reasons), the policies typically are comprised of thousands of policy statements; this makes policy development and analysis very difficult. The complexity of resulting SELinux policies means that for example, safety guarantees cannot be given, defeating the main purpose for SELinux in the first place. Even when a policy is considered both safe and functional, each addition, deletion or modification of the policy has the potential to break the baseline. The need for analysis tools for SELinux policies has been recognized from almost the very beginning with the expectation that such tools would be the silver bullet for SELinux security administrators.

This paper aims to identify and highlight current gaps in existing tools and technologies for SELinux policy analysis, which could potentially lead to improvements and new tools and technologies. A proposal toward closing the gaps identified in the technology and tools discussed in this paper is given. Section 2 describes basic concepts of access control. Section 3 presents the SELinux policy language structures that are used for expressing SELinux policies. In Sect. 4, existing tools developed by different research teams are analyzed, and important problems are identified. Section 5 describes identified challenges for SELinux and proposes a solution for overcoming these challenges by adopting a certified access control policy language. Finally, Sect. 6 concludes.

2 Preliminaries

2.1 Access Control

Access control can be described as a security service that guards protected resources against unauthorized access [4]. Access control, as an IT security service, deals with three primary entities in a system: *subjects* that require access to resources, *objects* or resources that are accessed by subjects, and *actions* that are performed by subjects on objects. Actions can range from being as simple as reading data to sharing or executing data [16]. The final protected system must satisfy information security measures consisting of confidentiality, integrity, and availability (known as the CIA triad).

2.2   Access Control Models

Access control models define the structure and language for describing system policies and relevant procedures for processing them. Three widely used models for different access control policy types were mentioned earlier: Discretionary Access Control (DAC), Mandatory Access Control (MAC), and Role-Based Access Control (RBAC) [23].

RBAC maps users to roles, which are sets of authorized permissions. RBAC lumps users together in bunches and assigns permissions to these groups; thus, a user can have a specific permission if the permission is assigned to a role that is associated with the user.

The traditional DAC model relies heavily on user identity, which can lead to a compromise of the whole system in the case when the attacker obtains root privileges on the system. The owner grants privileged access to objects. DAC defines an access control list for every object in the system. DAC-based systems are coarse-grained since, trivially, DAC cannot provide fine-grained controls using only user identity as the basis of decisions. Two user privileges that are possible in these systems are *admin* and *non-admin*.

MAC overcomes drawbacks of DAC to restrict access to objects solely on user identity by abstracting system resources into subjects and objects. MAC assigns security attributes to system resources and provides a foundation for security administrators to define access control policies for their environments, which requires more systems administration. Different MAC security models target the preservation of different security objectives in the system, provided by defining fixed security rules as their access control policies. Three important security models for MAC include the *Bell-LaPadula* (BLP) model preserving confidentiality, the *Biba* model preserving integrity, and the *Clark-Wilson* model preserving integrity [23]. We describe each in more detail below.

The Bell-LaPadula model ensures confidentiality of information by not allowing a subject to write objects of lower security level and not allowing a subject to read objects of higher security level. BLP security rules restrain the transfer of information from a higher security level subject to a lower security level object in a system.

The Biba integrity model protects the integrity of information by enforcing a policy defined by particular security rules. These security rules include rules that do not allow a subject to read objects of a lower integrity level and do not allow a subject to write objects of a higher integrity level.

The Clark-Wilson model focuses on the integrity of information and uses four security categories as the language for defining access control policy rules [4]. Policy rules control the integrity of the system by ensuring the integrity of the security categories of the model. These categories are:

- Constraint Data Items (CDIs): objects that are integrity protected.
- Unconstrained Data Items (UDIs): objects that are not integrity protected.
- Integrity Verification Procedures (IVPs): verifiers to check CDI integrity.

– Transformation Procedures (TPs): certified procedures to transition CDIs or UDIs to other CDIs. TPs are supposed to be a filter to control information transfers from low or high integrity objects to high integrity objects.

3 SELinux Overview

SELinux is a Linux-based access control framework developed by the United States National Security Agency (NSA) [18]. SELinux is compiled into the kernel and supported through the Linux Security Module (LSM). LSM is a kernel-level security framework that provides the possibility of attaching various security mechanisms to the Linux kernel, such as SELinux, without directly depending on the kernel objects. SELinux implements the MAC model within Linux-based distributions and provides more granular control of security. SELinux primarily involves labeling that divides system resources into subjects, which are processes, and objects, such as files and sockets. Every system resource receives a label which is a combination of values of the user, role, and type attributes. These attribute-value pairs form the *security context* for system resources.

3.1 SELinux Architecture

The SELinux security module implements the Flask architecture in a Linux environment [14]. A feature of the Flask architecture is the separation of security policy logic from the enforcement mechanism. The Security Server is a kernel component responsible for making security decisions, and the Object Manager enforces these security decisions in the system. The Access Vector Cache (AVC), is another component of the SELinux architecture. AVC stores the security policy look-up results to improve the performance of the decision-making procedure. Searching the AVC is faster, so access requests that have been previously processed can be quickly answered without searching the entire security policy again. Figure 1 depicts the core decision-making architecture of SELinux. Attributes used to determine the decisions of the SELinux access control mechanism are described in the following section.

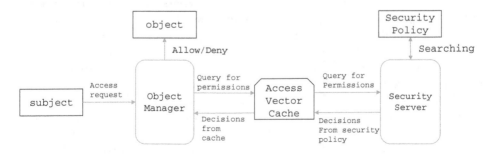

Fig. 1. Core decision-making architecture in SELinux

3.2   SELinux Access Control Criteria

The SELinux attributes include *user*, *role*, *type* or *domain*, and *level*, each described below.

SELinux introduces its own user attribute, and the Linux user attribute is mapped to the SELinux one [16]. The mapping of Linux users to SELinux users can be viewed using the Linux shell command "`semanage login l`."

The role attribute comes from RBAC. The SELinux security policy determines which users are authorized for each role. In particular, these roles are used for making role-based access control decisions. They specify which domains are authorized for which users and thus permit user entry into these domains. The shell command "`seinfo -r`" lists roles that are available in the system.

The SELinux type attribute is the most important attribute within a security context. Terminologically, to help distinguish subjects and objects, types and domains mean the same thing, but domains classify subjects, while types classify objects.

The SELinux level attribute is the final attribute in the security context. This attribute is used only in the MLS access control mechanism, which is not the main policy type of the SELinux access control framework. MLS policies use the level attribute for expressing rules that restrict access requests, which makes it a suitable access control scheme for military type environments. SELinux can be loaded into the Linux kernel without accommodating MLS [8].

Labeling is the main functionality of SELinux with the goal of labeling all system resources with a proper security context. SELinux primarily focuses on Type Enforcement (TE) related to the type/domain field of security contexts. TE allows creation of different domains in the system through assigning subjects to domains, and subsequently associating them with objects. All of these authorized associations are stated in a SELinux security policy by using TE rules. In addition to TE, SELinux allows the expression of restrictions on the other fields of the security context.

3.3   The SELinux Security Policy Language

A SELinux security policy is a collection of statements that defines the threshold for accepting an access request. SELinux denies interaction of subjects and objects by default; in particular, with an empty SELinux policy every access request will be denied. Figure 2 lists syntax of important SELinux security policy rules. Some main rules of the SELinux policy language related to TE, or to user and role components of security context are described.

Type Enforcement (TE) Rules of SELinux mainly include two kinds of rules [16]: Access Vector (AV), and Type Rules, which consist of Object Transition Rules and Domain Transition rules. Access Vector (AV) rules allow, audit, or deny interaction between two types. AV rules include `allow`, `dontaudit`, `auditallow`, and `neverallow` statements [14]. For example, consider the AV rule in Fig. 2 appearing on the first line. This rule allows the process with domain `SourceDType` to have actions `perm1` or `perm2` on the object of type `TargetType`

```
allow SourceDType TargetType : class1 {perm1 perm2};
type_transition SourceDomain TargetType: class1 new_type
type_transition SourceDomain TargetType: process new_type;
constrain classobject_list  permission_list B(t1,r1,u1,t2,r2,u2)
```

Fig. 2. Sample rules of a SELinux security policy

and object class of `class1`. An object class specifies a possible instance of all resources of a certain kind, such as files, sockets, and directories.

Object Transition Rules in SELinux can be used to specify the type of objects that will be created at runtime. For example, consider the object transition rule on the second line in Fig. 2. This type transition means objects of type `TargetType` that are newly created by a process with the domain of `SourceDomain` will take the default type `new_type` instead of `TargetType`. The object class `class1` specifies the object category of `SourceDomain` and `new_type`.

Domain Transition Rules change the domain of a subject to a new domain. For example, consider the domain transition rule on the third line in Fig. 2. This domain transition states that if a process of the domain `SourceDomain` executes a file with the type `TargetType`, the new domain of the process will be `new_type`.

SELinux policies also include Constraints. Software developers use constraints to introduce new criteria for granting access requests to objects. Constraints can refine an explicitly allowed access request through enforcing extra considerations for certain users, roles, and types in the decision-making process of the access, expressed as boolean conditions. For example, consider the fourth line in Fig. 2. `B(t1,r1,u1,t2,r2,u2)` is a boolean expression expressing constraints on the type, role, and user of the source entity security context `(t1,r1,u1)` and target entity security target `(t2,r2,u2)`. This constraint defines the requirements under which the operations in `permission_list` are allowed for the class objects in `classobject_list`. If these requirements are not met by an access request, the operations in `permission_list` will be denied.

The policy language that is used to develop SELinux policies is a complex language consisting of a combination of RBAC, TE, and optionally MLS rules. As mentioned, SELinux policies typically include thousands of policy statements, which makes development and analysis of SELinux policies quite difficult. SELinux policy language statements enable security administrators to configure the required permissions for accesses. Sample policy rules for an application (called App here) are shown in Fig. 3. These rules define a single domain entry to execute App through a domain transition.

3.4 SELinux Policy Analysis Tools

Many analysis tools have been proposed to help policy administrators analyze SELinux policies with respect to these properties. Among existing tools, some are developed while others are at a prototype stage. The typical structure of policy analysis tools is demonstrated in Fig. 4. The complexity of the SELinux

```
require {
attribute domain;
attribute file_type;
attribute exec_type;          Adding types and attributes
type sysadm_t;                that are required by the rules
attribute sysadm_r;
class process transition;
role sysadm_r; }

type app_t;
typeattribute app_t domain;
type app_exec_t;              Declaring new types and
typeattribute app_exec_t file_type;   classify them by attributes
typeattribute app_exec_t exec_type;

role sysadm_r types app_t;         Assigning roles to types
type_transition sysadm_t app_exec_t : process app_t;
allow sysadm_t app_exec_t : file {getatr execute};   Defining default
allow app_t app_exec_t : file entrypoint;            transition and its
allow sysadm_t app_t : process transition;           required access
```

Fig. 3. App program security policy rules in SELinux

policy language makes analyzing SELinux policies and even implementing policies very difficult. As a result, virtually all analysis tools provide some kind of other intermediate language for SELinux security administrators, as shown in Fig. 4.

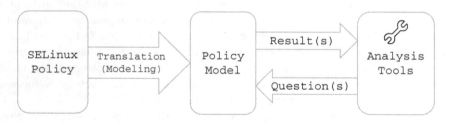

Fig. 4. Typical structure of SELinux analysis tools

3.5   Access Faults

In SELinux, access is a unique combination of (1) a source domain, (2) a destination type, (3) associated action(s), and (4) a destination object class. Almost all policy analysis tools try to detect different access faults that are implicitly leaked through security policy rules. Access faults are caused by implicitly assigning privileges using type attributes or default types available in the security policy [19,20] or generating rules from the SELinux audit log [28].

There are several kinds of access faults. Any access that doesn't meet the security goals of the system is called a *sneak access*. A *backdoor access* occurs when the policy accepts a request that was not explicitly allowed in the specification, but was introduced manually by policy developers or automatically by some tools that audit SELinux logs. These backdoors are usually inserted in a policy in order to run a legitimate program that has some problems reaching its required resources because of SELinux access control. *Wrong actions* are any access in which proper actions are not allowed by the security policy. *Missing actions* are any access in which the intended actions are not allowed because of improper policy rules.

3.6 Answering Security Questions

SELinux analysis tools answer questions about the properties of a policy configuration using two fundamental methods, *Information Flow* [2,8] and *Access Control Spaces* [11].

Information flow is about the reachability of a resource from another resource where some information is transferred by performing a particular operation. For example, there is an information flow between a subject S_1 to a subject S_2 if S_1 can perform a write operation on some objects on which S_2 can perform a read operation [29].

A subject's access control space is composed of all realizable permissions of the subject. The access control space of a subject forms a set which can be classified as the following five subspaces [11].

- Specified Permissions: permissions that are currently assigned to the subject according to the current specification
- Permissible Permissions: permissions assigned to the subject that are authorized by the policy developers
- Prohibited Permissions: permissions whose assignment violates security goals
- Unknown Permissions: permissions that are neither permissible nor prohibited
- Obligated Permissions: permissions that the subject must have according to policy rules

Zanin and Manicini [31] replace the access control space concept by the concept of an *Accessibility Space*, which introduces additional specific sets over possible permissions of an entity. Accessibility spaces remove unknown permissions as SELinux is based on a closed world assumption [31]. Information flow uses abstract views over the possible permissions in the available configuration of a security policy; hence, it can be considered as using just two subspaces, the allowed subspace and the denied subspace, to check the properties of the policy.

3.7 Querying SELinux Security Policies

SELinux analysis tools help identify policy *conflicts* that are caused by policy violation against specifications that describe protection needs of the system. To identify conflicts and check that security goals are achieved, security administrators can query policies about *safety, completeness, integrity, separa-tion of duty* (SoD), as well as some other questions that identify conflicts by posing questions about access faults and other high level security goals.

A policy specification is safe if subjects have no sneak access to resources in the system and all security goals are satisfied by the specification. A policy is complete if all intended permissions are specified in the policy; in other words, all requests are explicitly allowed or prohibited in a complete policy [21]. Integrity and safety have almost the same security aims, but integrity uses security models such as Biba to identify conflicts rather than just focusing on the realization of security specifications to check security goals. Separation of duty can be consid-ered as another kind of integrity checking that is defined with a simple security model. SoD means separating the domain of subjects into those that execute an executable file and those that create or modify the executable files [15].

4   Taxonomy for SELinux Policy Analysis Tools

Table 1 compares eighteen SELinux analysis tools. The comparison considers available features and techniques utilized in the tools. The table shows that dif-ferent analysis tools have different capabilities in terms of providing safety, com-pleteness, integrity, and SoD analyses. The other features that are compared in Table 1 are browsing a policy, rewriting a policy, and building customized queries. The analysis tools employ various forms of query language syntax to allow secu-rity administrators to make queries for checking specific properties of the security policy. Various techniques are utilized as methods of analysis; they model the security policy with well-known concepts such as mathematical sets [31], infor-mation visualization [15,30], and computer security models [1]. Some analy-sis methods expand all macros, while some perform on-demand expansion of macros [2] in the policies. SELint [19] goes further and replaces policy rules with proper macros of the policy rules, which provides the capability to sug-gest improvements. The last three tools in Table 1—SEAL, EASEAndroid, and SELint—are for analyzing Security Enhancements for Android (SEAndroid), which is an Android port of the SELinux MAC mechanism [20]. Because most of the tools in Table 1 are not available publicly, the information provided here is based on the studies conducted for the tools as presented by the authors. In Sect. 4.1, we briefly discuss some aspects of each tool. Other information can be read directly from the table. In Sect. 4.2 we discuss some general problems.

4.1   Tool Descriptions

APOL [25] is a member of the SETools suite [16]. A user loads a SELinux security policy file or a compiled binary policy file to APOL to begin the analysis procedure. By loading the policy file, the user can select attribute items from enabled lists, which are loaded according to the rules in the SELinux security policy file. Then, the user can use regular expressions to specify a search in several analysis modules for particular attributes. A great number of SELinux

Table 1. Analysis tools for SELinux security policies

Analysis tool	Safety analysis	Completeness analysis	Integrity analysis	SoD analysis	Information flow analysis	Method of analysis	Policy browsing	Rewriting the policy	Method of modeling	Query language	Macro expansion
APOL	✓		✓	✓	✓	Information flow	✓		Syntactic analysis	Selecting attributes from menus	✓
SLAT	✓	✓			✓	Information flow-Model checking			XSB logic	✓ (Regular expressions)	✓
XcelLog	✓	✓			✓	Information flow-Deductive spreadsheets			Sets of values	Writing set formulas	✓
GOKYO	✓	✓	✓			AC spaces-TCB			AC spaces-Graphcal AC model (Sets)	✓	✓
PAL	✓	✓	✓	✓	✓	Logic programming			XSB logic	✓	
SELAC	✓				✓	AC spaces-Mathematical set			25 Sets		✓
SPTrack	✓				✓	Data visualization			Graphs		✓
SEGrapher	✓			✓	✓	Data visualization - Clustering			Graphs-Clustering of nodes	Selecting types from menus	✓
SEAnalyzer	✓			✓	✓	Colored Petri nets			Diagrams & Sets	✓	✓
LOPOL	✓				✓	Deductive database		✓	Logical relations	Datalog query	✓
SEEdit	✓			✓	✓	Higher level language, SPDL		✓	Grouping permissions-Access log user decision		
PVA	✓	✓	✓	✓	✓	Information visualization techniques	✓	✓	Semantic substrates - Adjacency matrix	Graphical user interface	✓
GPA	✓		✓		✓	Information visualization techniques			Semantic substrates - Adjacency matrix	Graphical user interface	✓
Sepol2HRU	✓		✓			HRU security model			HRU Model simulation		✓
SCIATool	✓		✓		✓	Colored Petri nets, Information flow, AC space		✓	NA	Wizard-Style query	✓
SEAL	✓		✓		✓	Information flow			Syntactic analysis		✓
EASEAndroid						Semi-supervised learning		✓	Parsing the audit log		✓
SELint	✓					Information flow			Syntactic analysis		✓

analysis tools (e.g., [20,29,30]) use APOL libraries for their development and often a comparison of the ease of use as compared with APOL is carried out.

Guttman and Herzog [8] describe a four-step procedure used in the SLAT tool for verifying security goals in SELinux configurations. These steps include modeling, expressing goals, enforcing goals of the model, and implementation. The language that encodes the security goals is based on information flow diagrams, and security goals are expressed using a language similar to regular expressions. Five different access control relations are defined to model SELinux configurations, which are based on key concepts of SELinux. The authorization relation uses access control relations to authorize class-permission pairs for a process against a resource. Finally, a model checker verifies establishment of security goals of the policy.

XcelLog [21] combines policy rules and deductive spreadsheets (DSS) for taking advantage of deductive reasoning. The transformation of policy rules to deductive spreadsheets is a semi-automated process. Cells of the deductive spreadsheets are capable of containing a set of values or recursive formulas.

GOKYO [12] tries to reveal various conflicts in the policy and find missing or incorrect constraints. GOKYO resolves these constraints, according to the concept of access control spaces, which can reduce the complexity of the policy. The process of resolving conflicts is based on removing the unknown subspace and performing a kind of balancing among different kinds of rules in the policy. The approach creates a near-minimal trusted computing base (TCB) in the SELinux policy model and verifies whether the TCB is integrity-protected.

PAL [2] (Policy Analysis using Logic-Programming) is implemented using the XSB logic programming language. A XSB program translates a policy to a set of facts and builds queries that are answered from these facts. This technique is macro-preserving, which means that the macros in the policy get expanded on demand. As stated in [2], PAL's use of macros that are not fully expanded is efficient and unique in contrast to other tools such as SLAT, APOL, and GOKYO.

SELAC [31] (SELinux Access Control) models each language construct in the security policy language as a mathematical set. A collection of sets is constructed in an incremental way from the specification. As stated in the paper, SELAC has removed the redundant space, unknown space, and general subspaces that are used in GOKYO.

SPTrack [6] represents SELinux security policies as interaction graphs. The nodes in an interaction graph are security contexts made up of subjects or objects. The edges in this graph are possible interactions among nodes, all of which are included according to rules in the policy. The edges of the graph are colored based on the criticality levels of paths between nodes.

SEGrapher [15] begins its analysis with data visualization of the SELinux policy and then generates optimized graphs using the concept of clustering. Cluster-based graphs represent policy analysis results, which have been simplified by the use of clusters. To model a SELinux policy, the tool focuses on the access vector rules within it. These rules are represented as edges in a directed graph.

The building block for clustering the nodes is a focus-graph, based on an object-type set. An object-type set is the set of all types that an object can access [15].

SEAnalyzer [5] utilizes Colored Petri Net (CPN) diagrams for representing SELinux security policies and security goals. A rather complex query language for expressing security goals has been developed for SEAnalyzer with a smaller character count in comparison to PAL and SLAT.

Lopol [13] takes advantage of deductive database analysis and Datalog queries. Lopol policy analysis includes analyzing a collection of logical relations and inference rules. Lopol is capable of rewriting the policy. Rewriting a policy is performed through goal-projection, which involves reverse compilation of the inference rules to the policy.

SEEdit [17] uses the concept of integrated permissions to reduce the number of configuration elements. Integrated permissions group related permissions into a single unit, which causes the removal of the macro entities from the policy. SEEdit creates security policies using a higher-level language called SPDL. SPDL tools consist of two sections including an allow generator and a template generator. The former reads the access log to generate an SPDL based specification for permitting access. The latter uses the user's knowledge to generate an SPDL configuration to make a program that is problematic due to access control restrictions run correctly. Finally, an SPDL converter generates the policy file.

PVA [29] and GPA [30] tools use a visualized-based framework for analyzing, expressing policy queries, and identifying policy violations of a SELinux policy. The concepts and proposed framework in GPA have been slightly enhanced in PVA. The framework begins by representing the policy layout using two visual mechanisms: Semantic Substrates and Adjacency Matrices. The framework provides a visual query formulation that helps system administrators specify precise queries on the policy. Subsequently, the framework generates a policy violation graph to represent the violations that are identified by the integrity model. The integrity model is based on Biba and the concepts of Trusted Computing Base (TCB) and Transaction Procedure in the Clark-Wilson security model. The framework introduces some approaches, such as filtering and ignoring, to modify the policy graph in order to remove any policy violations. GPA proposes identifying and protecting the TCB of a system using the Information Domain.

Sepol2HRU [1] establishes an isomorphic mapping between a SELinux access control system and a HRU security model as defined in [9]. Transforming the SELinux security policy to a HRU model allows the application of the analysis tools available for the HRU model to SELinux security policies. Transforming a policy to a HRU model is a three-step procedure. (1) The elements in an SELinux access control system such as rules and types are mapped to heterogeneous mathematic standard concepts like sets, matrices, and functions. (2) These elements are rewritten to a single composed matrix. (3) The authorization scheme is inferred. Sepol2HRU outputs the SELinux security policy as an HRU model description in a single file in a XML-based format.

SCIATool [32] integrates three policy analysis methods including access control spaces, information flows, and colored Petri-nets. The architectural design of the SCIAtool is based on the modularity principle. SCIATool's approach to integrity analysis is the use of a TCB which means that integrity analysis verifies that subjects inside the TCB are prohibited from reading incorrect information from non-trusted objects.

SEAL [20] is a tool for SEAndroid policy analysis. Finding problematic patterns in SEAndroid policies is the main purpose of the study in [20]. The identified patterns consist of overuse of default types, overuse of predefined domains, forgotten or seemingly useless rules, and potentially dangerous rules.

EASEAndroid [28] proposes a semi-supervised learning approach to refining SEAndroid security policies. SEAndroid security policies require continuous refinements due to continuous updates to Android and to emerging new attacks. A policy is refined based on analyzing the audit log and information in one access event. The tool parses information available on access events, which provides information for building access patterns. These access patterns act as a knowledge base for the learning process of the approach.

SELint [19] helps Original Equipment Manufacturers (OEMs) to produce better SEAndroid policies by optimizing the security policy. SELint has several plugins, including simple macro expansion, parameterized macro expansion, risky rules, unnecessary rules, and user *neverallow* rules. Plugins that operate on macros try to replace certain kinds of rules with macros. In contrast, other analysis tools seek to remove macros because the semantics of the m4-based language, i.e. macro language, is uncertain [10].

4.2 SELinux Security Policy Problems

Analysis tools can help administrators to check system security goals. However, most analysis tools provide some other intermediate language for SELinux security administrators. Although these extra facilities can help with the analysis of policies, at the same time, they often add more complexity to the whole access control process because they require equally complex semantics. On the other hand, developing policies in SELinux leads to quite complex policies, and developing a policy is a cumbersome and error-prone process [10]. Moreover, analysis tools only provide low-level queries, which fail to cover the very large potential query space of SELinux policies [11]. The following is a user's concern about SELinux policies from the Fedora SELinux support mailing list [24]:

> What directories and files does Guix [a package program] need to touch? ... What kinds of labels do I need to introduce to my system? What kinds of tools do I need to use to integrate a Guix policy to the prebuilt policies? ... After all, most software developers ignore SELinux and won't bother publishing a complete access requirement specification.

5 SELinux Challenges and Proposed Solution

The SELinux policy language doesn't have formal semantics. Its semantics is given in terms of a natural language description. Expressing the semantics of an access control policy language in a natural language (e.g. English) results in ambiguity in the specification of behavior of policy statements. For this reason, along with reasons mentioned earlier, i.e. the complexity of the language, and the fact that policies are expressed at a very fine-grained level, both the development and the analysis of policies are difficult. Consider the last three lines of Fig. 3. They are included to protect the `entrypoint access` [16] of the `app_t` domain. Removing any one of these rules will break the intended protection because in order for a domain transition to occur, all three rules are required. The first rule provides execution permission for the domain `sysadm_t` on the file with the type `app_exec_t`; the second rule provides an entrypoint for the domain `app_t`; the third rule provides a type transition to the new type `app_t` from the current type `sysadm_t`. The fact that SELinux rules are so fine-grained adds to the complexity of SELinux. Both writing and analyzing policies are difficult tasks. It is hard for administrators to express the desired protection using such a low-level language.

5.1   Existing SELinux Analysis Tools

As mentioned, the complexity of the SELinux policy language itself complicates both the implementation of policies as well as the ability to analyze them. As a result, many tools are complex and it is difficult to establish the correctness of the analyses they perform. One problem with these tools is that they do not use the same criteria in support of each other; moreover as mentioned, analysis tools try to provide some other intermediate language for SELinux security administrators. Although these extra facilities can help with writing various queries, they require equally complex semantics. Furthermore, existing SELinux analysis tools barely scratch the surface and only offer the possibility of doing simple queries.

5.2   SELinux Policy Language Challenges

As a result of our study described in the previous section, we can summarize the many gaps between the SELinux policy language and current existing analysis tools:

- SELinux as an access control framework requires third-party analysis tools to help security administrators write policies and check various properties.
- The inherent complexity of the SELinux policy language has caused a lot of tools to try to establish intermediate language structures to overcome this complexity; however, they require equally complex semantics and syntax.
- Software developers continually add new rules to SELinux security policies, while fine-tuning the policy to handle access problems of newly installed applications, using the system audit log file. The practice of making every deny access found in the SELinux audit log into new rules in the policy is extremely error prone and can lead to compromising the safety of the system, again due to the complexity of the SELinux access control policy language.

- There is no proof for the correctness of policy analysis tools or formal semantics to make sure their results are reliable. There are informal justifications for results, but no formal justification of results.
- Overall SELinux lacks clarity as an access control language. The clarity of an access control policy language can provide better decision making for incremental policy writing, ease of analysis, and ease of reasoning.

The goal of our proposed solution is to make the process of developing and analyzing policies simpler by adopting a security policy language that is more coarse-grained, in which administrators can more directly express their security goals at a higher level, and providing tools to translate such policies to the more fine-grained level of SELinux

5.3   Ease of Reasoning About SELinux Policies

A particular set of properties which may be used as a basis for formally comparing and contrasting access control policy languages include *safety, independent composition,* and *monotonicity* [26]. An access control policy language that is safe, independently composable and monotonic is said to be most amenable to reasoning as compared to one that does not have any of these properties. In addition, these properties and others mentioned in [22] can be used to classify different access control policy languages along the reasonability spectrum. Being able to reason about policies written in an access control policy language directly leads to another property that is desirable in a policy language. Such a policy language has the property that formal analysis and verification of specific policy statements can determine whether or not the policy meets the high-level goals of the system.

Using the definition of an access control policy language as presented in [26], the SELinux access control policy language can be considered as a tuple $L = (P, Q, G, N, \ll . \gg)$ where P is a set of SELinux policies, Q is a set of requests or queries, G is the granting decisions, and N is the non-granting decisions, with the constraint $G \cap N = \emptyset$. Let D denote the set of decisions $G \cup N$. The last element of L, $\ll . \gg$, is a function taking a policy $p \in P$ to a relation between Q and D. Given a policy $p \in P$, a query $q \in Q$ is assigned a decision of $d \in D$. L also defines a partial order on decisions such that $d \leq d'$ if either $d, d' \in N$ or $d, d' \in G$ or $d \in N$ and $d' \in G$; in other words, non-granting decisions are all the same, granting decisions are all the same, and all granting decisions are considered greater that all non-granting decisions. Note that for SELinux, $D = \{Granted, Denied\}$, $G = \{Granted\}$ and $N = \{Denied\}$. Let DC, TC, CLS, and PRM be the set of all domains, types, object classes, and permissions, respectively, available in a system. Queries are of the form (dc, tc, cls, prm, m) where $dc \in DC$ is the domain type of the subject, $tc \in TC$ is the type of the resource, $cls \in CLS$ is the class of the resource, $prm \in PRM$ is the permission or permissions, and m expresses properties of the query that are not about the Type Enforcement mechanism of SELinux. Two queries $q = (dc, tc, cls, prm, m)$ and $q' = (dc, tc, cls, prm, m')$ have relation $q \trianglelefteq q'$ if $m \implies m'$. In the rest of this section, we assess SELinux with regard to its Type Enforcement (TE) mechanism to determine if it satisfies the three properties mentioned earlier. The TE mechanism is based on TE rules available in SELinux policies. SELinux policies are organized into modules, which allows on-the-fly dynamic loading as needed. Each policy module has its own set of rules.

An access control policy language is considered *safe* if a request with less information will lead to a decision that is less than the decision reached for a request with more information, according to the defined partial order on decisions [27]. For example, requests with incomplete information should only result in a grant of access if a request with more complete information results in a grant of access. Based on this definition, safety can be defined as the following formula:

$$\forall (p \in P), (q, q' \in Q), (d, d' \in D),$$
$$q \trianglelefteq q' \ \& \ q \ll p \gg d \ \& \ q' \ll p \gg d' \implies d \leq d'.$$

Theorem 1. *The SELinux access control policy language is not safe with respect to $\trianglelefteq$.*

Proof. Consider the policy module p_a below along with requests q_a and q_b:

p_a : `allow sAtype_t mytype_t : file read`
     `role sCrole_r type sAtype_t`
$q_a = $ `(sAtype,mytype_t, file, read, {})`
$q_b = $ `(sAtype,mytype_t, file, read, {role ∈ sDrole_r})`

For request q_a, p_a produces *Granted*, while for q_b, it produces *Denied*. Note that $q_a \trianglelefteq q_b$, $q_a \ll p_a \gg$ *Granted*, $q_b \ll p_a \gg$ *Denied*, but *Granted* $\nleq$ *Denied*, which contradicts safety.

An access control policy language has the *independent composition* property if taking into account all policy modules and rendering a decision gives the same result as combining the decisions obtained from each primitive policy in isolation. As a result, independent composition can be defined as the following formula, in which $\Box$ is the decision composition operator for combining policy decisions and $\oplus$ is the composition operator defined in the language for combining policies. Some policy languages, such as FOL [26], allow more than one interpretation of the operator that combines policies, thus preventing them from having the independent composition property.

$$\forall (p_1, \ldots p_n \in P), (q \in Q), (d_1, \ldots d_n, d^* \in D),$$
$$q \ll p_1 \gg d_1 \ \& \cdots \& \ q \ll p_n \gg d_n \ \& \ q \ll \oplus(p_1, \ldots, p_n) \gg d^* \implies$$
$$\Box(d_1, \ldots d_n) = d^*.$$

Composing policies in SELinux simply means adding them together to form one big policy. A request is denied if any *one* of the individual policies produces `denied`. Trivially, SELinux access control always reaches a single decision when combining all policy modules or decisions.

Theorem 2. *The SELinux access control policy language has the independent composition property.*

Proof Sketch. By definition, $\Box(d_1, \ldots d_n)$ is *Denied* if any of $d_1, \ldots, d_n$ are *Denied*. In this case, the combined policy decision d^* will also be *Denied* by the definition of SELinux policy combination. Otherwise, $d_1, \ldots, d_n$ are all *Granted*, and in this case, both $\Box(d_1, \ldots d_n)$ and d^* will be *Granted*, again by definition.

An access control policy language is *monotonic* if adding another primitive policy does not change the combined decision from granting to non-granting.

Theorem 3. *The SELinux access control policy language is not monotonic.*

Proof. Consider policy modules p_c and p_d below along with request q_c :

p_c : allow Dtype1_t type2_t : file open
p_d : constraint process transition
             (u1=user1 and t1=type1 and t2=type2_t)
q_c = (Dtype1_t, type2_t, file, open, {user $\in$ user2})

The policy p_c will result in *Granted* for the request q_c and adding policy module p_d will result in *Denied*, which changes the decision from *Granted* to *Denied*.

5.4   Using a Certified Policy Language to Express SELinux

A small and certifiably correct policy language can be a good candidate for SELinux style access control. ACCPL (A Certified Core Policy Language) [22] is a certified policy language that can be used to represent general access control rules and policies. ACCPL has formal semantics, which include a precise definition of a function that takes a query and returns an allow or deny decision. The Coq Proof Assistant [3,7] has been used to develop proofs for theorems about the expected behavior of ACCPL when evaluating a request according to the given policy and to machine-check the proofs ensuring correctness guarantees are provided. The compactness and verifiability of ACCPL as an access control policy language provides for ease of analysis and reasoning, in comparison to the SELinux policy language. These capabilities are guaranteed because ACCPL satisfies the ease of reasoning properties of [27]. This fact helps system administrators to easily manage and check the intended security level of the system.

ACCPL can be used to encode and implement other policy-based access control languages such as SELinux policy language, taking advantage of its characteristics. We propose to develop a certified domain-specific policy language that appropriately accommodates specialized features of the SELinux Type-Enforcement mechanism. Once we do, we will be able to analyze policies formally using the proof environment for ACCPL implemented in Coq.

6   Conclusion

SELinux is a MAC based access control framework in Linux distributions. The inherent complexity of SELinux and its approach requires additional manual interaction of security administrators to develop or analyze policies. The complexity of the SELinux policy language itself complicates both the implementation of policies as well as the ability to analyze them. Many research projects have included the design and implementation of analysis tools to overcome this problem. Because of the lack of clarity and complexity of the policy language, the implemented tools often utilize languages that are different from but equivalent to SELinux, with equally complex semantics, or they simplify the languages so that they do not implement the full SELinux policy language. Thus, these tools cannot cover the identified SELinux challenges and it is difficult to establish the correctness of the analyses they perform as well. A certified access control policy language can provide ease of use and analysis; moreover, it provides an environment for verification of its properties. ACCPL (A Certified Core Policy Language) is a general certified access control policy language that is more amenable to analysis and reasoning. We plan to design a certified domain-specific policy language based on it for our task. Developing a certified analysis tools base on the certified Type-Enforcement policy language that simplifies and fosters policy analysis will be another direction of future work.

Acknowledgements. Financial support from the Network of Centres of Excellence (MITACS) and Irdeto Canada is gratefully acknowledged.

References

1. Amthor, P., Kühnhauser, W.E., Pölck, A.: Model-based safety analysis of SELinux security policies. In: 5th International Conference on Network and System Security (NSS), pp. 208–215 (2011)
2. Archer, M., Leonard, E.I., Pradella, M.: Modeling security-enhanced Linux policy specifications for analysis. In: 3rd DARPA Information Survivability Conference and Exposition (DISCEX-III), pp. 164–169 (2003)
3. Bertot, Y., Castéran, P.: Interactive Theorem Proving and Program Development. Coq'Art: The Calculus of Inductive Constructions. Springer, Heidelberg (2004)
4. Bishop, M.A.: The Art and Science of Computer Security. Addison-Wesley Longman Publishing Co. Inc., Boston (2002)
5. Chen, Y.-M., Kao, Y.-W.: Information flow query and verification for security policy of Security-Enhanced Linux. In: Yoshiura, H., Sakurai, K., Rannenberg, K., Murayama, Y., Kawamura, S. (eds.) IWSEC 2006. LNCS, vol. 4266, pp. 389–404. Springer, Heidelberg (2006). doi:10.1007/11908739_28
6. Clemente, P., Kaba, B., Rouzaud-Cornabas, J., Alexandre, M., Aujay, G.: SPTrack: visual analysis of information flows within SELinux policies and attack logs. In: Huang, R., Ghorbani, A.A., Pasi, G., Yamaguchi, T., Yen, N.Y., Jin, B. (eds.) AMT 2012. LNCS, vol. 7669, pp. 596–605. Springer, Heidelberg (2012). doi:10.1007/978-3-642-35236-2_60
7. Coq Development Team: The Coq Proof Assistant Reference Manual (Version 8.6) (2016). https://coq.inria.fr/distrib/current/files/Reference-Manual.pdf

8. Guttman, J.D., Herzog, A.L., Ramsdell, J.D., Skorupka, C.W.: Verifying information flow goals in Security-Enhanced Linux. J. Comput. Secur. **13**(1), 115–134 (2005)
9. Harrison, M.A., Ruzzo, W.L., Ullman, J.D.: Protection in operating systems. Commun. ACM **19**(8), 461–471 (1976)
10. Hurd, J., Carlsson, M., Finne, S., Letner, B., Stanley, J., White, P.: Policy DSL: high-level specifications of information flows for security policies. In: High Confidence Software and Systems (HCSS) (2009)
11. Jaeger, T., Edwards, A., Zhang, X.: Managing access control policies using access control spaces. In: 7th ACM Symposium on Access Control Models and Technologies (SACMAT), pp. 3–12. ACM Press (2002)
12. Jaeger, T., Sailer, R., Zhang, X.: Analyzing integrity protection in the SELinux example policy. In: 12th USENIX Security Symposium (2003)
13. Kissinger, A., Hale, J.C.: Lopol: a deductive database approach to policy analysis and rewriting. In: Security-Enhanced Linux Symposium, pp. 388–393 (2006)
14. Loscocco, P., Smalley, S.D.: Meeting critical security objectives with Security-Enhanced Linux. In: Ottawa Linux Symposium, pp. 115–134 (2001)
15. Marouf, S., Shehab, M.: SEGrapher: visualization-based SELinux policy analysis. In: 4th Symposium on Configuration Analytics and Automation (SAFECONFIG), pp. 1–8 (2011)
16. Mayer, F., Caplan, D., MacMillan, K.: SELinux by Example: Using Security Enhance Linux. Prentice Hall, Upper Saddle River (2006)
17. Nakamura, Y., Sameshima, Y., Tabata, T.: SEEdit: SELinux security policy configuration system with higher level language. In: 23rd Large Installation System Administration Conference, pp. 107–117 (2009)
18. National Security Agency: Security-Enhanced Linux (2016). https://www.nsa.gov/what-we-do/research/selinux/
19. Reshetova, E., Bonazzi, F., Asokan, N.: SELint: an SEAndroid policy analysis tool. CoRR abs/1608.02339 (2016)
20. Reshetova, E., Bonazzi, F., Nyman, T., Borgaonkar, R., Asokan, N.: Characterizing SEAndroid policies in the wild. CoRR abs/1510.05497 (2015)
21. Singh, A., Ramakrishnan, C.R., Ramakrishnan, I.V., Stoller, S.D., Warren, D.S.: Security policy analysis using deductive spreadsheets. In: ACM Workshop on Formal Methods in Security Engineering (FMSE), pp. 42–50 (2007)
22. Sistany, B.: A certified core policy language. Ph.D. thesis, University of Ottawa (2016). https://www.ruor.uottawa.ca/handle/10393/34865
23. Stallings, W., Brown, L.: Computer Security, Principles and Practices. Pearson Education, New York (2008)
24. The Fedora-SELinux Support List: Fedora SELinux Support. https://lists.fedoraproject.org/admin/lists/selinux.lists.fedoraproject.org/
25. Tresys Technology: APOL (2016). https://github.com/TresysTechnology/setools3
26. Tschantz, M.C.: The clarity of languages for access-control policies. Ph.D. thesis, Brown University (2005)
27. Tschantz, M.C., Krishnamurthi, S.: Towards reasonability properties for access-control policy languages. In: 11th ACM Symposium on Access Control Models and Technologies (SACMAT), pp. 160–169 (2006)
28. Wang, R., Enck, W., Reeves, D.S., Zhang, X., Ning, P., Xu, D., Zhou, W., Azab, A.M.: EASEAndroid: automatic policy analysis and refinement for Security-Enhanced Android via large-scale semi-supervised learning. In: 24th USENIX Security Symposium, pp. 351–366 (2015)

29. Xu, W., Shehab, M., Ahn, G.: Visualization-based policy analysis for SELinux: framework and user study. Int. J. Inf. Secur. **12**(3), 155–171 (2013)
30. Xu, W., Zhang, X., Ahn, G.: Towards system integrity protection with graph-based policy analysis. In: 23rd Annual International Federation for Information Processing (IFIP), Data and Applications Security XXIII, pp. 65–80 (2009)
31. Zanin, G., Mancini, L.V.: Towards a formal model for security policies specification and validation in the SELinux system. In: 9th ACM Symposium on Access Control Models and Technologies (SACMAT), pp. 136–145. ACM Press (2004)
32. Zhai, G., Guo, T., Huang, J.: SCIATool: a tool for analyzing SELinux policies based on access control spaces, information flows and CPNs. In: Yung, M., Zhu, L., Yang, Y. (eds.) INTRUST 2014. LNCS, vol. 9473, pp. 294–309. Springer, Cham (2015). doi:10.1007/978-3-319-27998-5_19

A Supervised Approach for Spam Detection Using Text-Based Semantic Representation

Nadjate Saidani[✉], Kamel Adi, and Mouhand Said Allili

Department of Computer Science and Engineering,
University de Quebec en Outaouais, Gatineau, Canada
{sain06,Kamel.Adi,MohandSaid.allili}@uqo.ca

Abstract. In this paper, we propose an approach for email spam detection based on text semantic analysis at two levels. The first level allows categorization of emails by specific domains (e.g., health, education, finance, etc.). The second level uses semantic features for spam detection in each specific domain. We show that the proposed method provides an efficient representation of internal semantic structure of email content which allows for more precise and interpretable spam filtering results compared to existing methods.

Keywords: Email spam detection · Domain categorization · Semantic features

1 Introduction

Email is one of the most used services on the Internet given the advantages it offers in terms of transmission speed, the ability to handle multimedia documents and broadcast emails to groups of people. By its popularity, the email generates its biggest disadvantage, which is the overload of the mailboxes with unwanted messages called spam. Among others, it favors the fast distribution of false information and malicious codes. According to a study of Kaspersky Lab in 2014, spam represented a share of over 70% of unwanted email in the traffic. These emails not only cause a waste of time and resources (storage: disk and transmission: bandwidth) but can also cause a major problem in computer security with billions of dollars and productivity loss [1].

Several spam detection methods have been proposed in the literature [2]. Among recent approaches, learning-based methods using text mining have gained more and more popularity [9]. These methods generally represent email content using text features such as words, n-grams, etc., which aim to distinguish between spam and legitimate emails (ham). These methods have proven good efficiency compared with other methods relying only on network analysis or black lists, for example [16]. However, these methods have also their limitations since textual features that are extracted independently can usually miss features correlation and semantic content description of the email. Indeed, spam content can be very dependent on the domain and the targeted users. For example, in health subject,

© Springer International Publishing AG 2017
E. Aïmeur et al. (Eds.): MCETECH 2017, LNBIP 289, pp. 136–148, 2017.
DOI: 10.1007/978-3-319-59041-7_8

spams can be targeted to medicine or false therapy campaigns advertisement, whereas in finance, spams can carry advertisement for dubious financial services and products. Therefore, using a specific spam discrimination for each domain can be more efficient than a general-purpose spam filter. Moreover, using more semantic cues for each domain in addition to raw text features can offer better discrimination between legitimate and spam emails. For example, emails advertising health products can be of interest if they are only informative and not targeting money extortion.

In this paper, we propose a general approach for incorporating semantic analysis for spam detection. Semantic analysis of email content is carried out at two levels. These levels consist respectively on first categorizing emails by domains and then extracting explicit semantic features within each domain to classify emails into spam and ham categories. For email domain categorization, without loss of generality, we have considered five domains: (1) Computer, (2) Adult, (3) Education, (4) Finance, and (5) Health. These categories are among the most targeted by spams [7,8,15]. To assign emails to these domains, we train a supervised classifier on labeled data after operating feature selection on the vocabulary of email text content using information gain. Semantic features are then extracted automatically for each domain using CN2-SD method [12], which will serve as weak spam classifiers with outputs combined in a more general and robust classifier for discriminating spams from legitimate emails. Experiments on a large corpus of emails have shown that our approach yields very good spam classification results compared to recent text-based filtering techniques.

The rest of the paper is organized as follows: in Sect. 2 we give a brief overview of related work. In Sect. 3 we discuss our contribution to spam detection using text-based semantic representation. We report our evaluation results in Sect. 4. Finally, Sect. 5 presents our conclusions and some directions for future work.

2   Related Work

Various spam filtering methods have been proposed in the literature for spam detection. Most of these methods have some success for filtering specific spams, but fail to solve efficiently the problem. Recently, machine learning algorithms were widely used for spam filtering, after their indisputable success in text categorization [9]. In fact, spam filtering can be seen as a text categorization with two classes {*spam, ham*} and several classifiers were applied such as Support Vector Machines (SVM) [17], Naïve Bayes (NB) [18], Artificial Neural Networks (ANN) [13], etc.

For spam filters, features are usually obtained from the body, the subject or the header of emails. Thus, email text-content plays an important role in any categorization process. One of the most popular representation for email categorization is the Vector-Space Model (VSM), also called Bag-of-Words (BoW) [9]. This model, describes the text of an email as a vector of words where each word represents an individual feature of the email. However, this representation is very high-dimensional and may incur an important loss in the semantic of the email since words are taken independently. To overcome this issue, some works has used n-gram models instead of individual words [6]. In this representation, emails are represented by sequences of words which leads to more refined models. However, this approach increases exponentially the size of the vocabulary which leads to highly sparse spaces for representing email documents. Several works have proved that complex representations of texts do not always improve the efficiency of the classification and sometimes may even deteriorate it [5].

Given the limitations of above mentioned methods, some researchers have recently investigated semantic-based approaches for improving emails classification [2]. Here, we refer to the semantic approach as the ability to depict and capture, in an explicit way, the information conveyed by emails. Authors in [11] explored the use of semantic manipulations for spam filtering by introducing a Word Sense Disambiguation (WSD) as a preprocessing step. The task of disambiguating words senses is the process of identifying the most appropriate meaning of a polysemous word for a specific context. In [14], the authors introduce a model called "enhanced Topic-based Vector Space Model" (eTVSM) which uses a semantic ontology to deal with synonyms. These methods can have some success in narrowing the semantic meaning of words, depending on the email content. However, they do not extract higher level semantic concepts of emails which can be helpful for discriminating legitimate and spam emails.

3   Our Approach

In our approach for spam detection, a fundamental step is the semantic characterization of the considered specific domains (computer, adult, education, finance and health), each described by a set of semantic features. Each set of semantic features is then used to provide basic attributes for building a domain specific classifier for spam detection. Figure 1 summarizes our overall approach. As we can see in Fig. 1, we proceed by two levels of semantic analysis. In the first level, we use a classification algorithm to automatically partition a global training dataset (emails) into the considered five domains. In the second level, we automatically extract a set of semantic features from the dataset in each domain. The semantic features are then used to build specialized classifiers for detecting domain specific spams.

3.1   Email Categorization by Domains

Today, spam is used in a myriad of goals, through the unsolicited advertising, phishing, to the dissemination of malicious code. Targeted domains are many: medicine, education, finance, etc. The annual reports on spam by Kaspersky [7,8] and Symantec [15] contain a deep analysis of the new targeted domains with the different techniques used to send spams. Those reports have been used, in our work, to fix the spammers' most targeted domains and five domains were considered.

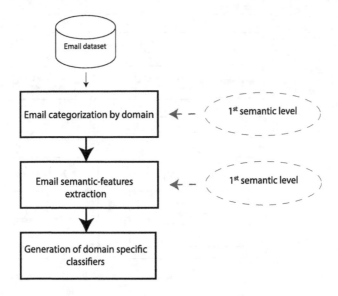

Fig. 1. General model of our approach.

In the domain of health, typical spams include advertisements for weight loss, skin care, improved posture, nutritional supplements, alternative medicine, etc. In the domain of finance, we can find offers for insurance, debt reduction services, loans at competitive interest rates, etc. The computer domain includes software, cheap equipment and services for website owners such as accommodation, registration areas, optimizing websites, etc. In the adult domain, typical spams are those offering products to increase or improve sexual ability, links to pornographic sites or pornographic advertising, etc. The education domain includes offers for seminars, training courses, evening classes, etc. It is worth to mention that spammers are constantly seeking to target new domains and develop new techniques, some sectors are quickly evolving and should be monitored closely (e.g., politics).

For email categorization by domain, we assign a category to each email of the global training dataset. Notice that an appropriate email preprocessing steps are required before we can efficiently exploit the information contained in the subject and the body of emails for the categorization. We present in Fig. 2 the global process for email categorization.

Let $D = \{d_1, \cdots, d_n\}$ be the set of email documents, $C = \{c_1, \cdots, c_p\}$ be the set of categories and $T = \{t_1, \cdots, t_m\}$ be the set of characteristics called terms. Note that in the present work, we consider five categories ($p = 5$) and each document $d \in D$ is associated to a unique category $c(d) \in C$. For the categorization process, we consider three main steps. The first step allows text preprocessing on documents in D, where each document is represented by a vector of terms. The second step is used to extract the relevant features. A special attention is paid for the reduction of data dimensionality to avoid deterioration

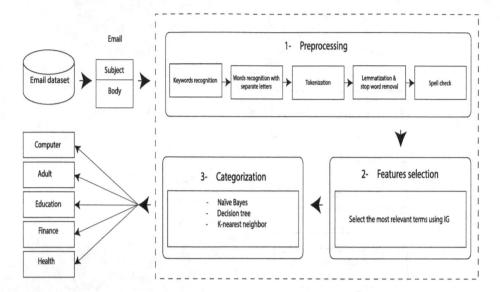

Fig. 2. An outline of the different steps used for email categorization by domain.

of classification accuracy in the presence of noisy data. The third step consists of learning a classifier to build a better classification model for categorizing email documents by domain.

Preprocessing. The preprocessing phase includes the following steps:

- *Keywords recognition:* used to recognize keywords and abbreviations in the emails with the help of a dictionary of keywords for each category. For instance, in the computer science category, we identified the abbreviations VLC, CD, PDF, etc.; in the adult category, we spot the taboo words, etc. Keywords are coded by using regular expressions.
- *Words recognition with separate letters:* this step is important for text segmentation phase (tokenization), which is the next phase of our process. The goal of this phase is to avoid alphabet letters in the feature vectors at the end of this process. Indeed, while referring to a dictionary of natural language, we implemented a tree search algorithm of the longest word on segments of text strings.
- *Tokenization:* is the step of text segmentation to extract the words or the terms of the email. Our algorithm performs a text division into tokens by using white space as a separator. So each email is coded as a vector of tokens representing the vocabulary used in the email.
- *Stop-word removal:* allows to eliminate some words that often occur in messages (e.g., "to", "a", "for").

- *Lemmatization:* allows to reduce words to their root forms (e.g., "extracting" to "extract"), at this stage we use the algorithm PorterStemmer[1].
- *Spell check:* allows to check the spelling of words in the vocabulary vector (vector of characteristics), we used a function to call Microsoft Word spell checker in order to correct misspellings especially those of spammers. This step enhances the recognition of key words in each category.

The removal of the stop words and the standardization (lemmatization) are very useful as they allow dimensionality reduction of the feature vector. However, this still remain insufficient and to solve the problem, we used a statistical method for selecting relevant features.

Feature Selection. Feature selection is an important step and aims to reduce the number of features for improving classifier performance. To select the most representative terms we used the Information Gain (IG) which is widely recognized in the spam detection literature [9]. It measures the discriminating power of a word, i.e.: the information amount provided by the knowledge of the appearance or not of a term in the decision process. Given the set T containing all email's terms obtained during the preprocessing phase from D and a set of categories C, the IG provided by a term $t \in T$ for a category $c \in C$ is defined as follows:

$$IG(t, c) = \sum_{\acute{c} \in \{c, \bar{c}\}} \sum_{\acute{t} \in \{t, \bar{t}\}} p(\acute{t}, \acute{c}) log \left(\frac{p(\acute{t}, \acute{c})}{p(\acute{t})p(\acute{c})} \right) \tag{1}$$

Where $\bar{t}$ indicates the absence of a term t and $\bar{c} \in C \setminus \{c\}$ and:

- (t, c): represent the presence of t and a membership in c.
- $(t, \bar{c})$: represent the presence of t and a non-membership in c.
- $(\bar{t}, c)$: represent the absence of t and a membership in c.
- $(\bar{t}, \bar{c})$: represent the absence of t and a non-membership in c.

The first and last tuples represent the positive dependencies between t and c, while the other two represent the negative dependencies and $p(\acute{t}, \acute{c})$ is the occurrence frequencies of the four-tuples in the corpus D. $p(\acute{t})$ and $p(\acute{c})$ represent term and class probabilities in the collection. Finally, we chose the 500 terms having the highest information gain for each category.

Categorization. After performing feature relevance analysis, various classification algorithms are applied to categorize email documents by domain. We compared the following classification methods in our experiments:

- *Bayesian classifier:* is based on the theorem of Bayes. For a set of training data D, the classifier calculates for each category, the probability that a document $d \in D$ represented as a vector of m terms $d = (t_1, \cdots, t_m)$, belongs to a category $c \in C$. This calculation is done for each category, and we consider the highest probability to select the category of an email.

---

[1] http://tartarus.org/martin/PorterStemmer/index-old.html.

- *K-nearest neighbor (Knn):* is one of the most popular used methods for text classification. The approach looks at the K email documents in the training dataset that are the closest to the email under classification: it is classified according to the class to which the majority of the K-nearest neighbors belong.
- *Decision tree:* is a structure that includes a root node, branch with internal nodes and leaf nodes. Each internal node denotes a test on an attribute, each branch denotes the outcome of a test, and each leaf node holds a class label.

3.2   Email Semantic Features Extraction

This step aims at extracting semantic meanings for email text. As semantics of emails, we mean a set of hidden concepts describing the email's content. The final goal is to create a very precise semantic representation for an efficient detection of spams. In this regard, we applied CN2-SD algorithm [12] for an automatic extraction of semantic features. In our case, these features are represented in the form of rules which are a conjunction of a set of terms. Each rule describes some semantic meaning in the text and its output takes on binary values (1 if the rule is satisfied and 0 otherwise).

The CN2-SD algorithm is built on top of two algorithms: CN2 [3,4] and SD [10]. SD is used to discover subgroups on a set of data and CN2 is used to induce classification rules. The main difference between a classification and a discovery of subgroups is that classification is a predictive task, while discovering subgroups is a descriptive task. The main reasons behind our choice of CN2-SD algorithm are as follows:

- allows an efficient and automatic induction of rules.
- allows an automatic generation of population description. This is particularly useful for the extraction of the semantic features.
- ensures precise discrimination between populations.

CN2-SD Algorithm. The idea of CN2-SD is to adapt the classifier CN2 to the task of subgroup discovery. CN2 sequentially builds a set of classification rules from a training dataset. At each iteration, generating a rule, CN2 removes the rule covered subset from the training dataset. Rule candidates are constructed based on a beam search strategy and a selection metric. One of the most used selection metrics is the accuracy, it is defined as follows:

$$Acc(Cond \rightarrow Class) = \frac{n(Class.Cond)}{n(Cond)} \qquad (2)$$

where $n(Cond)$ represents the number of examples (emails) covered by the rule $Cond \rightarrow Class$ and $n(Class.Cond)$ is the number of correctly classified examples (true positives).

The main modifications of the CN2 algorithm, making it appropriate for SD, involve the implementation of the weighted covering algorithm by incorporating example weights into the Weighted Relative Accuracy (WRAcc) heuristic.

In the first iteration of the algorithm, all examples are assigned to the same weight: $w(d_i, \ 0) = 1$, which means the email d_i have not been covered by any rule. In the following iterations, weights of emails covered by one or more rules will decrease according to a weighting scheme. Two weighting schemes can be used in CN2-SD, the additive weights and the multiplicative weights. In our spam detection framework, we used the additive weights method, whose equation is defined as follows:

$$w(d_i, \ j) = \frac{1}{j+1} \tag{3}$$

the WRAcc is defined as follows:

$$\text{WRAcc}(Cond \rightarrow Class) = \frac{s(Cond)}{S} \left(\frac{s(Class.Cond)}{s(Cond)} - \frac{s(Class)}{S} \right) \tag{4}$$

Where S is the sum of the weights of all the examples, $s(Cond)$ represents the sum of the weights of all the examples covered by the induced rule, and $s(Class.Cond)$ is the sum of the weights of all correctly covered examples by the rule.

The algorithm CN2-SD uses the metric WRAcc to select rule candidates. It also yields unordered sets of rules, but combines them in terms of a uniform weighting scheme. Furthermore, covered examples at each iteration are not removed, but only re-weighted.

3.3 Generation of Domain-Specific Classifiers

For each specific domain, the set of semantic features extracted from the previous step is used as learning attributes to build a domain specific classifier. To this end, we use a labeled training set of emails in each domain and perform a supervised learning of candidate classifiers such as Naïve Bayes, decision trees and Knn.

Whence domain-specific classifiers are generated, a newly coming email should be first automatically assigned to one of the considered domains. The domain-specific classifier is, then, used to classify the email as legitimate or spam. See Fig. 3 for the process of spam detection.

4   Experimental Results

To evaluate our approach, we collected a dataset containing spam and legitimate emails from several public sources: Enron[2], Ling-spam[3] and some specialized forums. Ling-spam corpus contains messages collected from a mailing list on the science and profession of linguistics. The corpus comprises 2893 messages, of which 2412 are legitimate and 481 are spam. Enron corpus is a large dataset of $200,399$ real emails, owned by Enron's employees. The corpus contains a variety

---

[2] https://www.cs.cmu.edu/./enron/.
[3] http://csmining.org/index.php/lingspam-datasets.html.

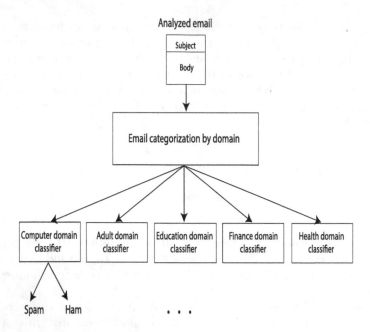

Fig. 3. An outline of the approach for spam detection using domain-specific classifiers.

of topics, mainly in business such as energy trading and considerable number of personal messages.

In our collection, spam emails come from the two datasets, Enron and Ling-spam. The ham emails come from specialized discussion forums and the two datasets Enron and Ling-spam. The use of the forums for ham collection is made necessary due to the insufficiency hams in Enron and Ling-spam databases. We chose raw folders of these two datasets without prior preprocessing. We labeled manually the selected emails according to their domain. We used a total of 6679 emails distributed according to their content in the five pre-selected categories. The overall collection includes 3475 ham emails and 3204 spam emails.

We compared three classifiers: Knn, Naïve Bayes and decision tree to categorize emails by domains. Then we applied the same classifiers to separate spam from legitimate emails in each of the considered domains. In order to evaluate the performance of the machine learning classifiers, we apply the k-fold cross validation model with $k = 10$, which randomly divides the dataset into k subsets. Each classifier is trained on $k - 1$ sets and evaluated on the remaining set. The final estimation of the classifier is the average of the k results from the subsets. We consider the following metrics: *Precision, Recall, Accuracy* and *F1-measure* metrics to evaluate the generated classifiers. These are defined as follows:

$$Precision = \frac{TP}{TP + FP} \tag{5}$$

$$Recall = \frac{TP}{TP + FN} \tag{6}$$

$$Accuracy = \frac{TP + TN}{TP + TN + FP + FN} \tag{7}$$

$$F1 - measure = \frac{2.Precision.Recall}{Precision + Recall} \tag{8}$$

where TP, TN, FP and FN are the obtained true positives, true negatives, false positives and false negatives after classification.

Table 1 shows the obtained evaluation results for email categorization by domains. Knn, Decision tree and Naïve Bayes classifiers were capable of achieving more than 80% of good prediction. Naïve Bayes gives the best results with an accuracy of 0.9684, a recall of 0.9684 and a precision of 0.9745.

Table 1. Quantitative evaluation of machine-learning classifiers for the categorization of emails by domains.

Classifier	Accuracy	Recall	Precision	F1-measure
Knn	0.8182	0.8758	0.5482	0.6743
Naïve Bayes	0.9684	0.9684	0.9745	0.9714
Decision tree	0.9416	0.8994	0.9718	0.9342

Table 2 summarizes the results for spam detection on each considered domain. We can see that Naïve Bayes almost achieved a higher accuracy, recall and precision in all the specified domains (computer, adult, education, finance, health). The last row of the table "Average" represents the overall evaluation results of our approach which are given by computing the average of the obtained results in the five domains. According to the results, Naïve Bayes classifier clearly outperforms the other algorithms. This achieved an accuracy of 0.9772, a recall of 0.9771 and a considerably high precision of 0.9705.

To prove that domain-based detection allows better prediction of spam, we used a direct approach, where the semantic attributes of all the domains are used to detect spam without going through specific domains. The obtained results are shown in Table 3. We can see clearly that the spam detection after categorization by domain outperforms the direct approach.

We compare the filtering capabilities of our approach with two different approaches, eTVSM and VSM. The approach eTVSM use semantic relationships between terms and the approach VSM uses terms as a bag of words. As it can be seen in Table 4, our method produce a batter performance compared to other methods. Additionally, our approach does not extract high dimensional feature dataset which makes the system more efficient.

Table 2. Quantitative evaluation of machine-learning classifiers using our semantic approach for spam detection.

	Classifier	Accuracy	Recall	Precision	F1-measure
Computer	Knn	0.9424	0.9448	0.9278	0.9362
	Naïve Bayes	0.9633	0.9611	0.9722	0.9666
	Decision tree	0.9677	0.9725	0.9692	0.9708
Adult	Knn	0.9782	0.9710	0.9678	0.9694
	Naïve Bayes	0.9759	0.9745	0.9736	0.9740
	Decision tree	0.8763	0.8613	0.8042	0.8318
Education	Knn	0.9565	0.9696	0.9759	0.9727
	Naïve Bayes	0.9779	0.9954	0.9774	0.9863
	Decision tree	0.9786	0.9963	0.9774	0.9868
Finance	Knn	0.9669	0.9888	0.9566	0.9724
	Naïve Bayes	0.9707	0.9888	0.9626	0.9755
	Decision tree	0.9698	0.9856	0.9639	0.9746
Health	Knn	0.9729	0.9735	0.9620	0.9677
	Naïve Bayes	0.9718	0.9655	0.9668	0.9661
	Decision tree	0.9751	0.9655	0.9746	0.9700
Average	Knn	0.9634	0.9695	0.9580	0.9637
	Naïve Bayes	0.9772	0.9771	0.9705	0.9738
	Decision tree	0.9554	0.9562	0.9378	0.9469

Table 3. Results for spam detection without categorization by domains.

Classifier	Accuracy	Recall	Precision	F1-measure
Knn	0.9070	0.9301	0.8953	0.9124
Naïve Bayes	0.8534	0.9494	0.8043	0.8708
Decision tree	0.9175	0.9197	0.9216	0.9206

Table 4. Comparative evaluation with other methods.

Model	Classifier	Accuracy	Recall	Precision	F1-measure
eTVSM [14]	Knn	0.9355	0.9067	0.9565	0.9309
	Naïve Bayes	0.9739	0.9650	0.9674	0.9662
	Decision tree	0.9657	0.9638	0.9658	0.9670
VSM [9]	Knn	0.8512	0.7709	0.9312	0.8435
	Naïve Bayes	0.9361	0.9784	0.9062	0.9409
	Decision tree	0.9088	0.9102	0.9142	0.9122

5   Conclusion

We have proposed a new approach for exploiting semantic information for spam detection. This is achieved by extracting semantic features specific to email domains. For this purpose, we first assign emails to their domains by training a supervised classifier. Next, we apply the algorithm CN2-SD on each domain to extract semantic features to form a more general and robust spam classifier specific to each domain. Conducted experiments have shown that our approach yields better results in terms of spam detection in comparison with approaches based on bag-of-words and/or extracting word-based semantic information (eTVSM). Future work will focus on enhancing our model using more elaborated semantic features like ontologies and word sense disambiguation.

References

1. Bratko, A., Cormack, G.V., et al.: Spam filtering using statistical data compression models. J. Mach. Learn. Res. **7**, 2673–2698 (2006)
2. Caruana, G., Li, M.: A survey of emerging approaches to spam filtering. ACM Comput. Surv. (CSUR) **44**(2), 1–27 (2012)
3. Clark, P., Boswell, R.: Rule induction with CN2: some recent improvements. In: Kodratoff, Y. (ed.) EWSL 1991. LNCS, vol. 482, pp. 151–163. Springer, Heidelberg (1991). doi:10.1007/BFb0017011
4. Clark, P., Niblett, T.: The CN2 induction algorithm. Mach. Learn. **3**(4), 261–283 (1989)
5. Cormack, G.V.: Email spam filtering: a systematic review. Found. Trends Inf. Retrieval **1**(4), 335–455 (2007)
6. Çiltik, A., Güngör, T.: Time-efficient spam e-mail filtering using n-gram models. Pattern Recogn. Lett. **29**(1), 19–33 (2008)
7. Gudkova, D., Vergelis, M., et al.: Spam and phishing in Q2 2016, pp. 1–22. Kaspersky Lab (2016)
8. Gudkova, D., Vergelis, M., Demidova, N.: Spam and phishing in Q2 2015, pp. 1–19. Kaspersky Lab (2015)
9. Guzella, T.S., Caminhas, W.M.: A review of machine learning approaches to spam filtering. Expert Syst. Appl. **36**(7), 10206–10222 (2009)
10. Herrera, F., Carmona del Jesus, C.J., et al.: An overview on subgroup discovery: foundations and applications. Knowl. Inf. Syst. **29**(3), 495–525 (2010). Published online first
11. Laorden, C., Santos, I., et al.: Word sense disambiguation for spam filtering. Electron. Commer. Res. Appl. **11**(3), 290–298 (2012)
12. Lavrac, N., Kavsek, B., Flach, P., Todorovski, L.: Subgroup discovery with CN2-SD. J. Mach. Learn. Res. **5**(2), 153–188 (2004)
13. Renuka, D.K., Hamsapriya, T., et al.: Spam classification based on supervised learning using machine learning techniques. In: International Conference on Process Automation, Control and Computing (PACC), pp. 1–7. IEEE (2011)
14. Santos, I., Laorden, C., Sanz, B., Bringas, P.G.: Enhanced topic-based vector space model for semantics aware spam filtering. Expert Syst. Appl. **39**(1), 437–444 (2012)
15. Symantec. Internet Security Threat Report, vol. 21, pp. 1–77, April 2016
16. Tang, G., Pei, J., Luk, W.S.: Email mining: tasks, common techniques, and tools. Knowl. Inf. Syst. **41**(1), 1–31 (2014)

17. Torabi, Z.S., Nadimi-Shahraki, M.H., et al.: Efficient support vector machines for spam detection: a survey. Int. J. Comput. Sci. Inf. Secur. **13**(1), 11 (2015)
18. Wang, H., Zheng, G., He, Y.: The improved bayesian algorithm to spam filtering. In: Wong, W.E. (ed.) Proceedings of the 4th International Conference on Computer Engineering and Networks, pp. 37–44. Springer, Cham (2015). doi:10.1007/978-3-319-11104-9_5

Process Modeling and Adaptation

Activity-based Process Integration in Healthcare with the User Requirements Notation

Malak Baslyman[1], Basmah Almoaber[1,2], Daniel Amyot[1,4(✉)],
and El Mostafa Bouattane[3,4]

[1] School of Computer Science and Electrical Engineering,
University of Ottawa, Ottawa, Canada
{mbasl071,balmo036,damyot}@uottawa.ca
[2] King Khalid University, Abha, Saudi Arabia
[3] Montfort Hospital, Ottawa, Canada
mostafabouattane@montfort.on.ca
[4] Institut du savoir Montfort, Hôpital Montfort, Ottawa, Canada

Abstract. The healthcare sector faces important challenges in evaluating and improving its services to meet desired targets, patient needs, and government requirements. In particular, the introduction of a new process or information system in healthcare is a challenging task, especially in the absence of mature practices for requirements engineering and process modeling. Most of today's healthcare process research is focused on mappings between existing processes and new ones without considering the different needs of multiple stakeholders and the satisfaction of organizational goals. In this paper, we introduce a novel *Activity-based Process Integration* (AbPI) approach that highlights integration opportunities of each new activity into current processes. AbPI exploits the User Requirements Notation (URN) language to model, analyze, and estimate the potential impact of each integration opportunity on performance objectives, organizational goals, and stakeholder satisfaction. We demonstrate the capabilities of the proposed approach with an illustrative example (increasing patient satisfaction in an Emergency Room). Preliminary results show the feasibility of the approach as well as many potential benefits over existing approaches.

Keywords: Healthcare processes · Process integration · Process integration analysis · Process modeling · Requirements engineering · URN

1 Introduction

Hospitals are facing many challenges such as wait time, an aging population, and increasing service demand. Hospitals are trying to improve their performance while controlling budgets. Governments also impose new rules and guidelines to ensure that hospitals provide better and more efficient health services. For example, the Government of Ontario changed their purchasing system from using service-based payments to using *value-based* payments, which forces hospitals to question their practices and often restructure their processes to reach the desired performance levels [1].

© Springer International Publishing AG 2017
E. Aïmeur et al. (Eds.): MCETECH 2017, LNBIP 289, pp. 151–169, 2017.
DOI: 10.1007/978-3-319-59041-7_9

However, redesigning workflows or proposing new structures is not straightforward in healthcare, in part due to its multidisciplinary nature. A process may require multiple units (e.g., clinical services, clinics, and administration) to collaborate, while each unit has its own interests and objectives when participating to the process. In such a case, modeling is a common approach used to understand and combine different process views, as well as to define measurements and quality criteria to evaluate these views and the way they interact [2]. Yet, process modeling is not widely used in healthcare. One more key to better cope with performance challenges is to consider technology-based solutions. Similarly, technology alone does not represent a perfect solution to healthcare problems due to disruptions to current practices, users' resistance to change, and large deployment/integration/operations efforts.

Requirements engineering (RE) regroups proven practices for the elicitation, modeling, analysis, specification, validation, and management of requirements. These practices aim in part to give a comprehensive view of different units/stakeholders along with their intentions and workflows, and to estimate the impact of alternatives during decision making, prior to system implementation. The absence of suitable RE practices can lead to systems that result in unsatisfied users, time/effort lost, low performance, or harmful ignorance about changes. This could also lead (in a multidisciplinary environment) to situations where we miss engaging a party/unit in decision making opportunities or where we unconsciously force changes on others [3]. As the focus of e-health system development must move away from a single viewpoint to multiple views and user intentions, we see an opportunity to introduce better RE practices in healthcare along with intention-driven process modeling approaches.

The main objective of this paper is to investigate the usefulness of model-based RE practices in improving technology-dependent healthcare processes by introducing a new *Activity-based Process Integration* (AbPI) approach. AbPI enables the modeling and assessment of alternative activity-based integrations of proposed processes into current practices while minimizing disturbances to work routines. AbPI can be used to estimate the impact of integrating the activities on the satisfaction of users and organizational goals.

The rest of the paper is organized as follows. Section 2 provides background on value-based healthcare and the modeling notation underlying AbPI, namely the User Requirements Notation (URN). Section 3 presents related work that uses RE techniques to introduce new systems and re-engineer processes. Section 4 explains the Activity-based Process Integration approach, which is applied in Sect. 5 to an illustrative example of a new technology-dependent process that targets the increase of patient satisfaction in the emergency room (ER) unit at Montfort hospital. Section 6 discusses the relevance of AbPI in healthcare, its limitations, and threats to the validity of our observations. Finally, the paper concludes with a conclusions and future work in Sect. 7.

2   Background

This section covers the essence of value-based healthcare and URN modeling.

2.1   Value-Based Healthcare

Value-based healthcare is an emerging approach that focuses on addressing issues of current Ontario healthcare systems such as growing care costs, clinical inefficiency, and duplication of services. The main strategy behind value-based healthcare is to make *value* the overreaching goal [4]. Controlling costs, improving outcomes, increasing value for patients by making them the center of the healthcare experience, and ensuring an efficient use of individual and social resources are all anticipated results of adopting this new healthcare value-based system.

The fundamental goal of value-based healthcare is to maximize value for patients by achieving the best outcomes at the lowest cost. Maximizing value involves either improving outcomes without raising costs or lowering costs without compromising outcomes, or improving outcomes and lowering costs at the same time [5].

In order to enable improved value for patients, healthcare systems should adopt a number of changes for their different units/services, including restructuring health organizations, measuring outcomes and cost, and changing reimbursement systems.

Working towards such improvements is challenging. This requires appropriate tools and approaches that can describe the current system as it is now in order to identify its weaknesses and opportunities for improvement, and then describe how it should be like, so stakeholders will be aware of and validate what is needed and how these needs can be met. The required tools should also be able to explore new ways of doing things in the system, to eliminate bad ideas, and to refine good ideas to be implemented. Modeling is one of the tools that support decisions in healthcare systems on which ideas are worth deploying to create effective and yet affordable healthcare.

Modeling is the process of representing the relevant parts of a real-world situation to characterize a given problem and find ways to solve it. In many cases, modeling is used to support the decision-making process by providing the information required to make informed decisions about the current system or about options for the future [6].

The introduction of a new process or a new information system to the current healthcare system is not a trivial procedure. Such introduction requires tremendous efforts just to convince stakeholders to accept the change and actively participate in implementing it. Moreover, the transformation process involves much decision making that has a significant impact on healthcare delivery processes, clinical operations, and resources utilization. Modeling here is a great tool to support the evolution of current systems towards value-based healthcare in many ways, including optimizing and streamlining different healthcare processes and supporting the management of different technical and social aspects during the various phases of the change.

2.2   User Requirements Notation (URN)

The *User Requirements Notation* is a standard graphical language that enables modelers to capture, analyze, specify and validate requirements. URN combines complementary sub-languages: the *Goal-oriented Requirement Language* (GRL) for modeling systems and stakeholders, their intentions, and their relationships, and *Use Case Maps* (UCM) for workflows. The GRL and UCM view can be aligned with each other, such that processes are linked to the goals that justify their existence. URN models can also be used to reason about different design alternatives with regards to users, business processes [7], and organizational goals. We believe that URN can be used to model and measure value (with GRL intentions and actors) and processes (with UCM), as well as their evolution in a healthcare context.

GRL provides a graphical representation of systems and stakeholders (actors ⌒), their intentions (goals ⊂⊃, qualitative softgoals ⊂⌒, tasks ◇, and resources ▭) indicators (⬦), and the links connecting these model elements (AND/OR/XOR decompositions ╂, contributions ⟶, and dependencies ▬▶). Requirements can be inferred from the selection of alternatives for system functionalities and qualities that provide the best trade-off among the various conflicting intentions of the stakeholders. Trade-off and what-if analyses are enabled by GRL *strategies*, which offer initial satisfaction values to some of the intentions or observable values to indicators, and *propagation algorithms*, which propagate (through the links) satisfaction to the other intentional elements of the model and ultimately to the actors themselves [8].

UCM is used to model the behavioral structure of functional and operational goals in a process-oriented way. UCM's graphical representation shows processes that evolve from *start points* (●) to *end points* (▮) through causal sequences of *responsibilities* (✖) bound to a structure of *components* (▭). The responsibilities often operationalize the GRL goals and their tasks. Guarded alternative flows (⟍, ⟍), concurrent flows (╪, ╪), and *timers* (⧖) with timeout paths can also be modeled. Complex processes can be decomposed into submaps contained into *stubs* (◇). UCM models can be explored and analyzed using *scenario definitions*, which specify initial values for the variables used in guarding conditions and responsibilities, as well as the start points triggered. A traversal algorithm then highlights the paths traversed for this scenario. Such analysis can be used to understand complex scenarios, find unexpected interactions between processes, and ensure quality during process evolution.

jUCMNav is a free Eclipse plug-in that supports URN modeling and analysis [9].

3   Related Work

In healthcare, few studies have used requirements engineering practices or process modeling to propose new systems/processes or introduce change. Teixeira et al. [10] attempted to show how human and non-technology factors can be used to enhance the requirements engineering process in the design process of a web-based information system for hemophilia. They used both a user-centered design approach and grounded theory to gather user and organizational requirements about the context and the process. Then, they used three methods to model the elicited requirements: (1) UML use cases, (2) task analysis, and (3) prototyping. Their results showed that combining these approaches gives an opportunity to look at the process from different angles and decide on the critical requirements. In addition, it confirms that it was hard for healthcare providers to express their needs or to understand abstract models with UML diagrams. On the other hand, Hayes et al. [11] proposed the use of narrative networks to analyze the adaptation variability of new technologies into current practices. They claim that this approach is better than traditional business process modeling (BPM) as it considers multiple views and provides a generic overview of the process. The effectiveness of the approach was validated with two case studies. However, the authors recommended using narrative networks with traditional process modeling because narrative networks are only a representation to assist in analysis and decision making and do not measure the effect of changes on the organizational goals.

Hübner et al. [12] attempted to answer: "how to appropriately capture information and process requirements that are both generally applicable and practically useful". There are two contributions: (1) collecting requirements and information about the current practices by conducting expert interviews and Delphi surveys along with collecting medical guidelines about the topic; (2) modeling the collected information using a standard language (UML).

Moving into process modeling, Damas et al. [13] focused on modeling different workflows of various units and pathologies based on non-functional requirements. They proposed two categories of logical operators. *Composition* operators are used to compose Message Sequence Charts (akin to UML sequence diagrams) for intersectional processes and tasks, whereas *decomposition* operators are used to separate irrelevant components from the charts to improve separation of concerns. A labeled transition system logic is then applied to demonstrate transitions between activities.

There are more mature approaches that combined the view of process modeling and requirements engineering outside the healthcare domain. They mainly lay under two categories: business processes improvement and redesign, and IT alignment with business processes. In the former category, Santos et al. [14] proposed a variability analysis approach to update business strategies or transform them into software. The *Business Process Model and Notation* (BPMN) was used to demonstrate business strategies and goal-oriented modeling was used for capturing goals. The approach identifies alternatives for configuring business processes based on the variability of concerns. The study did not investigate requirements variability itself due to its complexity.

Some studies are URN-based. Kuziemsky et al. [15] used URN to show the possible impact of healthcare information systems (HIS) on business operations and goals. The approach evaluated the impact of adapting the IS based on performance indicators and the satisfaction of business goals. They applied the framework on a palliative care process, and the results showed that the framework was effective in identifying and prioritizing indicators to support the decision of adapting the IS. However, the approach did not consider how current practices may change to accommodate the new tasks brought by the HIS and what the impact of these changes is on the satisfaction of stakeholders and of non-business goals. Another interesting work proposed by Pourshahid et al. [16, 17] defines a set of improvement patterns to identify improvement opportunities in business processes that may lead to more effective and efficient performance. They used GRL to model performance and business goals, UCM to model business processes, and *Aspect-oriented URN* (AoURN) to model patterns. The main drawback of this approach is the high complexity of using this extended AoURN in practice.

One of the challenges in requirements engineering relates to the complexity of developing or evaluating models. Rungworawut et al. [18] attempted to tackle this issue partially by proposing the use of *genetic algorithms* (GA) to introduce better requirements satisfying the design goals of business process components. The study recommended the use of GA to find optimal process components as they consider the design process to be artistic, needing human expert interventions, to make better decisions.

Also relevant is the work done on the alignment of IT with business processes. Bleistein et al. [19] addressed the alignment of requirements with competitive business strategies. They proposed a *Business Strategy, Context, and Process* (B-SCP) framework. They used the *i** goal modeling (similar to GRL) to represent business strategy as requirements, Jackson context diagrams to represent business contexts, and activity role diagrams to model processes. The authors mapped activity role diagrams to goal models and context diagrams so that analysts can check whether the business process belongs to the intended business context and serves its business goals. They evaluated this approach using a case study, which highlights the complexity of their approach, especially when demonstrating business strategies. Decreus and Poels [20] further contributed a B-SCP metamodel, an Eclipse-based B-SCP editor, and a (non-validated) BPMN generator that requires a human to complete the model.

This literature review shows that, in healthcare, there is a gap related to the integration of new systems or processes into current practices. Also, goals are rarely considered, and estimates of user/stakeholder satisfaction levels are absent. On the other hand, there is some work outside the healthcare area that focuses on business processes or goals. In our paper, we attempt to fill the gap in healthcare by introducing an Activity-based Process Integration approach (presented next) that is based on requirements engineering techniques to model goals, requirements, and processes. In addition, the approach permits the continuous evaluation of the impact of each integrated activity on the satisfaction of goals and stakeholders. AbPI provides integration alternatives and trade-off analysis to support integration decisions.

4   Activity-based Process Integration (AbPI)

4.1   Concepts and Relationships

AbPI is a model-driven, analysis-enabled process integration approach that supports the sequential integration of activities from a *proposed process* into a *current process*, one activity at a time. AbPI also supports the investigation of the potential effect of a single activity on entire processes, other activities, organizational goals, or stakeholders. It also shows the roles (i.e., who performs a certain activity) and the execution ordering of a group of activities when a single process cuts across multiple units or teams. AbPI aims to integrate the proposed process by maximizing the level of familiarity with the current process, which is an essential factor to gain user acceptance.

When integrating an activity into a current/existing process, four types of relationships can be introduced (see Table 1):

- *Activity-process*: defines how the activity is connected to the current process. An activity-process relationship also identifies the changes that may be introduced to the structure of the process after the activity integration.
- *Activity-role*: shows how an activity can affect (change, eliminate, or add) a role in the current process.
- *Activity-goal*: shows the impact of an activity on the satisfaction level of a goal.

Table 1. Activity relationships in AbPI

Type	Description
Activity – Process relationship	
Current	An activity is currently part of a process
New	A new activity does not exist yet in the current process, but there is a possibility to integrate that activity in the process
Integrated	A new activity is integrated into the current process
Activity – Role relationship	
Change	An activity can change a role in the current process to another (change a nurse role to a physician role, for example)
Eliminate	An activity can eliminate a role in the current process
Add	A new activity can introduce a new role to the process
Activity – Goal relationship	
Contribute	An activity may contribute positively or negatively to a goal, to some level
Activity – Activity relationship	
Replace	A new activity replaces a set of activities in the current process
Eliminate	A new activity eliminates a set of activities in the current process
Compose	A new activity is combined with a set of current activities. There are six types of possible composition: • New; Current // sequential composition, before • Current; New // sequential composition, after • New **OR** Current // alternative composition • New **PAR** Current // parallel composition • Merged // new activity that is neither New nor Current

- *Activity-activity*: shows which activities will be affected by the integration of a new one, and how (replace, eliminate, or compose).

4.2   Inputs, Output, and Roles

The AbPI approach consists of two main methods: *integration* and *analysis*. For each method, there are inputs, outputs, and roles. The integration method has two *Goal-Process Models* (GPM), composed of goal views and of process views, as inputs. One is the current GPM and the other is the proposed GPM. The goal view of a GPM consists of the organizational goals, user requirements, and stakeholders, along with their relationships (contributions), importance values, and current benefits they bring to the organization. The process view of a GPM is composed of sequenced activities performed by roles. In a GPM, activities contribute to the satisfaction of goals and criteria can be defined to evaluate the satisfaction levels. URN can be used as a language to capture and formalize GPMs.

Regarding the creation of GPMs, an analyst (who models the GPMs and who manage the integration of processes) and domain experts can collaborate to define the context in which a new process is proposed that includes developing the current and proposed GPMs. In the last step, if the current process is complex, it may be decomposed into sub-processes each of which corresponds to a proposed process.

In the integration method, the analyst and the domain experts collaborate to define the integration opportunities of the proposed GPM into the current GPM and develop a new, resulting GPM after the integration. The new GPM consists of the possible integration alternatives and the new contribution levels from activities to goals. The main role of the domain expert is to ensure that the integration result complies with the organization policy and guidelines.

In the analysis method, the new GPM is analyzed and evaluated by the analyst, the domain experts, and stakeholders. The output of this step is a new GPM that contains integration alternatives achieving the desired outcomes.

4.3   Integration Method

There are three major steps in this method.

(1) **Identifying opportunities:** An integration opportunity highlights a possible spot in the current process in which a new activity can be integrated in a way that preserves the process flow properties and keeps it logically sound. An activity can have multiple integration opportunities. In this step, the domain experts decide on the potential opportunities to integrate.

(2) **Identifying the type of activity-activity integration:** For each potential opportunity resulting from the previous step, the relations between the *new* activity to be integrated and other *current* activities in the current process should be defined. There are three possible relations: replace, eliminate and compose. If the relation is either *replace* or *eliminate*, dependencies (if any) between the current activity to be eliminated or replaced and other current activities in the current process should be defined. Then, the analyst and the domain experts investigate the possibility of transferring those dependencies to the new activity, or the new activity will eliminate those current activities as well. On the other hand, if the relation is *Compose*, the analyst and the domain experts not only investigate the effect on an activity brought by another, but they also consider the possible change that may happen to the process structure such as changing roles or adding a new role.

(3) **Design a new process model:** In this step, the analyst models the alternatives discussed above. The analyst modifies the current process to reflect the changes introduced by each integration opportunity and its relation to other activities. The analyst and the domain experts modify the goals linked to the activities with the new values of contributions. The developed integration alternatives model (GPM) in this step will be the input of the analysis method.

4.4   Analysis Method

The analysis method helps reason about the designed process alternatives in terms of goal satisfaction. It answers important questions, such as *"how will a goal be satisfied?"*

and *"why is an alternative better than another?"*. The analyst, the domain experts, and stakeholders should be involved to reason about trade-offs and resolve early conflicts. The aim of the analysis method is to illustrate the impact of the changes, introduced by the integration, on three levels:

- **Goal level:** the evaluation will show the impact of the new integration on the goal satisfaction levels that might have been affected by the contributions coming from activities. The evaluation helps decide keeping an integration if it is helping to achieve the organizational goals and performance objectives.
- **Process level:** the evaluation helps estimate the impact of the activity integration on the process performance, which contributes to the evaluation of the satisfaction levels of performance goals. In addition, the evaluation shows the impact of the newly brought changes on the process structure and roles.
- **Stakeholder level:** this evaluation targets the satisfaction levels of stakeholders, which could be defined at a department, unit, or personnel level, while considering their importance levels. As a result, this will help decide whether to keep, modify, or reject an integration to maximize the satisfaction level of an important stakeholder or to resolve conflicts between stakeholders. The satisfaction level of a stakeholder can be obtained by the importance of goals to stakeholders.

These three levels together give a comprehensive evaluation of the integration alternatives to reason about trade-offs and decision support in a holistic way. The analysis method has three main steps:

1. Set the evaluation values and contribution levels of activities that will affect the goals.
2. Propagate satisfaction levels to goals and actors.
3. Validate the integrated models against predefined criteria and desired outcomes.

The following section will illustrate the AbPI approach with a practical healthcare example.

5 Illustrative Example: Patient Satisfaction in an Emergency Room (ER)

The section illustrates the AbPI approach (and its integration and analysis methods) with a realistic example from Montfort Hospital.

5.1 Problem Definition

The example's context is defined as follows. The current workflow in an emergency room (ER) involves three main stages. First, the patient is triaged by a nurse to assess the acuity level. Once the acuity level is assigned, the patient is moved to the waiting area or examination room until seen by a physician. The physician at this stage may order some tests, or may request a specialist consultation. Once results are obtained, the patient is either discharged from the ER or admitted to the hospital for further treatment.

One problem with the current flow is the lack of efficient information communication with patients. Presently, patients need to ask the round nurse about updates on their status, e.g., when the lab test will arrive, or how long the wait time is.

The quality of care in value-based hospitals is indicated by the patient experience with the provided care. The lack of real-time information about wait times and intended plans during ER visits can increase patients' anxiety, which then reflects negatively on the satisfaction level of these patients. At Montfort Hospital, expectations on wait time are posted on a white board manually at different times during the day. There is no specific process to inform patients of updates in real time. Thus, patients in the ER complain mostly about being unaware of what is the current status of the process and how long it will take them to reach a specific step.

To help patients dealing with the unknown about their health and manage their anxiety, the introduction of a new system, the *Wait Time Estimation System* (WTES), is considered. WTES aims to provide patients with an up-to-date view of their status and wait time. Caregivers will interact with WTES to insert and update the status and wait time of patients during their visits. In this example, our focus is on the interaction between caregivers and WTES and on activities that will be added to the current ER process. To simplify the integration, the example will cover only the first and second steps in the ER process (triage and physician assessment), as Fig. 1 illustrates with a UCM view of the current GPM. We used the jUCMNav tool [9] to illustrate the use of the AbPI approach in integrating WTES in the ER.

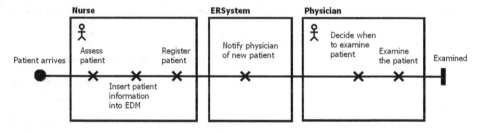

Fig. 1. Current ER process with the triage (initial nurse assessment) and physician assessment tasks

Figure 2 presents the proposed process to interact with WTES. The process starts with Register patient to WTES. Then, the nurse gives an access code to the patient to track the process in the system. This step is required to comply with privacy requirements. The nurse shall set the current status and expected time to reach the next expected step (such as Physician assessment in the current process). The time starts and ends either by moving to the expected step or timeout. If further examination (such as a lab test or imaging) is required, the nurse has to update the status and set the expected time again.

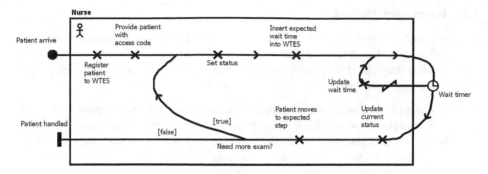

Fig. 2. The proposed process of WTES

Figure 3 shows the goal view of the GPM, which includes Montfort Hospital, caregivers, and patient, in the context of keeping patients updated. The WTESystem actor shows the goals newly combined with the current goals of other stakeholders.

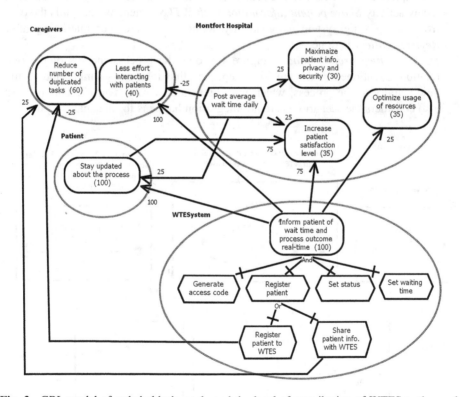

Fig. 3. GRL model of stakeholder's goals and the level of contribution of WTES to the goals

5.2   Integration Method

As mentioned in Sect. 4.1, each activity in the new process is integrated separately. However, one exception is when that activity cannot be separated from other activities, such as when they are in loops or guarded branches. The three steps of the integration method are discussed here.

(1) ***Identifying integration opportunities:*** The first activity in the proposed process is *Patient registration to WTES*, which happens after the patient arrival to the ER. In the current process, there is ideally only one opportunity to integrate the activity that is either before or after the *Register patient* activity, because they both should be performed after the nurse assessment.

(2) ***Identifying type of activity-activity integration:*** For the *Patient registration to WTES* activity, there are two possible relations: Compose (New; Current) or Compose (Current; New). This implies simply adding the new activity to *Register patient* where a caregiver will perform them both separately. The order here does not make much of a difference as the nurse should perform both activities to accomplish the registration. The second relation is Compose (Merged), producing a new activity *Share patient information with WTES*, where WTES pulls the data from the existing system automatically without the caregiver interfering after *Register patient* is done.

(3) ***Design a new process model:*** Figure 4 shows the process models of the two relations mentioned in the previous step. The first relation is simply adding the new activity to the process, which introduces a new role "Nurse". This process also considers the scenario where no integration happens for the analysis purpose.

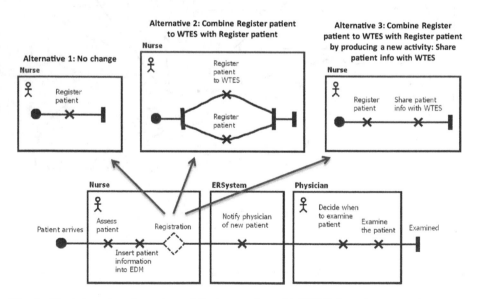

Fig. 4. The integration alternatives of *Register patient* with WTES from the proposed process to the current one

The other activities in the proposed process will be integrated following the same steps performed with the first integration. The produced relations between the proposed activities and the existing activities in the current process will be simply adding the activities as shown in Fig. 5. There are also dependency relationships involved as some activities must be performed together or not at all.

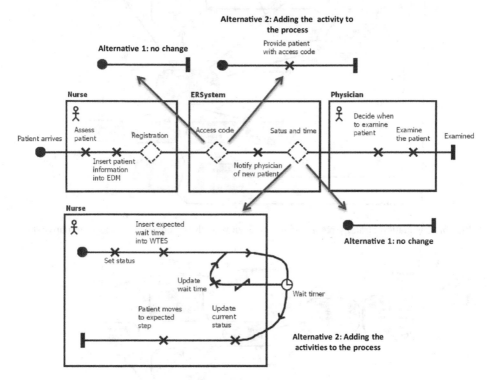

Fig. 5. The integration alternatives of the other activities in the proposed process after integrating them sequentially. Alternative 2 in the *Status and time* stub is a process that consists of dependent activates that cannot be separated

5.3   Analysis Method

As mentioned in Sect. 4.2, we follow three steps: set up values and contributions, evaluate the trade-offs, and choose the best alternative that achieves the desired outcome. In the previous example, all activities are depended on *Register patient to WTES* and also on *Share patient info. with WTES*. Thus, there will be three main alternatives (processes) to evaluate based on the choice of the sub-process in the *Register patient* stub (Fig. 4).

First integrated process: this is the current process with no changes. Figure 6 shows the satisfaction of the goals and stakeholders after applying the corresponding GRL evaluation strategy in jUCMNav. The WTES and the Caregivers (nurses) are not satisfied at all, and the Hospital and Patient actors have a very low satisfaction level.

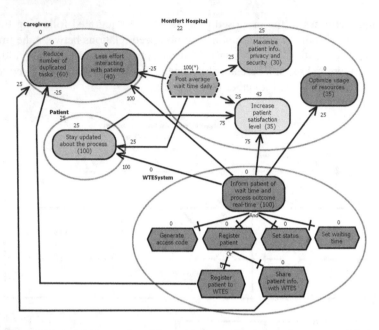

Fig. 6. Evaluation strategy results of the goal view with the current process (alternative 1)

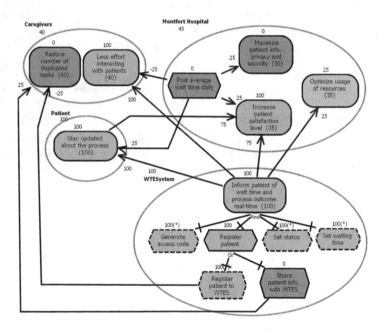

Fig. 7. Evaluation strategy results of the goal view with alternative 2 in the first integration

Second integrated process: this one uses alternative 2 (Register patient to WTES) in Fig. 4 and alternative 2 in the two stubs of Fig. 5. The impact of an activity is represented in the tasks in the GRL model. If the activity is chosen, the evaluation value of the equivalent task is set to 100 (and 0 otherwise). Figure 7 shows that the Patient and WTES actors are satisfied, but that there is room for improvement for the other actors.

Third integrated process: this one corresponds to alternative 3 (Share patient info with WTES) in Fig. 4 and to the two alternative 2 in Fig. 5. This integrated process is better than the second one because the Caregivers are more satisfied while the other actors have kept the same levels of satisfaction (see Fig. 8).

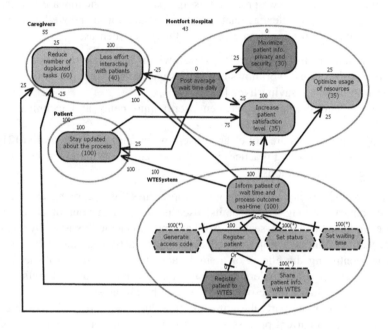

Fig. 8. Evaluation strategy results of the goal view with alternative 3 in the first integration

This analysis approach helps reason about trade-offs. As seen in the previous figures, the goal about maximizing patients' information privacy and security was better satisfied with the current process. On the other hand, nurses are more satisfied with sharing patients' information with WTES (automatically) than by inserting the information manually in the *Register patient to WTES* activity. Patients are fully satisfied, and so is the *Increasing patient satisfaction level* goal in Montfort Hospital. However, it is worth mentioning that even if the Caregivers are more satisfied with the proposed process, the satisfaction level is only 55, so there is still room for improvement.

The analysis outcome should be presented to the hospital stakeholders to guide them on the best alternative to choose. Note that the results may not always be as clear as in this example. For example, one integration could lead to actor X being satisfied at level 80 and actor Y at 60, while another integration would lead to the opposite (X at 60 and Y at 80). In such cases, each actor can be given a certain weight, so the analyst can choose the integration that satisfies the highest weighted sum of actor satisfactions. It is worth mentioning that all the contributions and importance values are estimated and driven from the problem definition provided by Montfort Hospital.

6 Discussion

6.1 AbPI in Healthcare

The design of AbPI is not specific to healthcare; it is generic and can likely be applied in other domains. However, we propose this approach for the healthcare field because there are several grand challenges related to the introduction of new e-health systems and processes that often remain unresolved in that field, such as:

- Caregivers already follow particular workflows. In most cases, introducing a new system disturbs current workflows and brings undesirable changes in the routine of people who are busy saving lives [21].
- There is an undesirable gap between user requirements and technical requirements [22].
- The long-term benefits are not clear to users when changes are required [21].
- Requirements engineering practices in healthcare are not as mature as in other fields such as telecommunications.

The healthcare field is hence lacking good approaches for proposing changes along with their impact on long-term benefits, user needs, and current practices, as was highlighted in the related work section. AbPI attempts to tackle this issue by identifying the elements of current and proposed processes (goals, activities, and stakeholders), in addition to identifying the effects of a single activity integration on those elements. AbPI aims to enable stakeholders to reason more clearly about trade-offs and integration alternatives that achieve outcomes desired by all, as shown in the example in Sect. 5. The approach supports the transition to value-based hospitals as the changes and improvements to current processes are introduced incrementally and are based on measurable goals.

6.2 Limitations

There are many limitations to the AbPI approach. One of them is that the evaluation does not reflect the real impact of changes on caregivers' performance (for example, time and effort). Considering only the abstract satisfaction levels (on a 0..100 scale) is not sufficient in the real world. More precise performance information is needed.

Another challenge is the high number of possible integration alternatives with which analysts may end up. Evaluating all these alternatives manually may be a time-consuming and error-prone task. Defining criteria to choose among these alternatives for evaluation would be a solution. Another potential solution is to automate the evaluation process using techniques such as genetic algorithms or constraint-based solving.

The usability and usefulness of the AbPI approach are unknown. We illustrated the feasibility of the approach in Sect. 5, but a usability study should be conducted to explore the acceptance and areas of improvement of the approach by healthcare professionals, and case studies are needed to evaluate the complexity and the applicability of the approach in real-world cases. Another important limitation is that the chosen example may not reflect the complexity and subtleties of real healthcare processes and integration challenges. Additional validation work is hence needed here.

7   Conclusions and Future Work

In this paper, we proposed a new Activity-based Process Integration approach. We argue that our approach improves upon the others by focusing on engaging stakeholders (not only focusing on the business side) and introducing integrations incrementally. The approach also includes a comprehensive evaluation of each integration for trade-off analysis, which is essential to hospitals in order to move towards a value-based payment system efficiently. AbPI also attempt to provide the missing link between delivering a new e-service, considering caregivers' interaction with it, and meeting the goals of the users and organizations involved. The feasibility of the approach was illustrated by modeling and analyzing the potential integrations of a Wait Time Estimation System (with its goals and processes) to the current ER process at Montfort Hospital, in order to keep patients updated about the delays and status of the process in real time.

While AbPI provides some original means of tackling the process integration problem, several limitations have been observed. In order to overcome some of them, we are currently working on adding *indicators* to the models in order to have more precise evaluations (observed values compared to targets) than with abstract satisfaction levels. We are also considering automating the evaluation process to reduce its complexity in case there are many potential integrations. We finally intend to formalize the methods (PGM metamodel and mapping from URN's, constraints specifications, integration and analysis algorithms, etc.), provide tool support, and do a deeper evaluation of the approach, including additional healthcare-related case studies and usability studies.

Acknowledgments. Malak Baslyman is sponsored by the Ministry of Education of Saudi Arabia and Basmah Almoaber is sponsored by King Khalid University, Abha, Saudi Arabia.

References

1. Burwitz, M., Schlieter, H., Esswein, W.: Modeling clinical pathways-design and application of a domain-specific modeling language. In: Wirtschaftsinformatik 2013, AISeL, paper 83 (2013)
2. Jun, G.T., Ward, J., Morris, Z., Clarkson, J.: Health care process modelling: which method when? Int. J. Qual. Health Care **21**(3), 214–224 (2009). doi:10.1093/intqhc/mzp016

3. Alahmadi, A., Soh, B., Ullah, A.: Automated health business process modelling and analysis for e-health system requirements elicitation. In: 18th Pacific Asia Conference on Information Systems (PACIS), AISeL, paper 213 (2014)
4. Hillary, W., Justin, G., Bharat, M., Jitendra, M.: Value based Healthcare. Adv. Manag. 9(1), 1 (2016)
5. Porter, M.E., Lee, T.H.: The strategy that will fix health care. Harvard Bus. Rev. 91(12), 24 (2013)
6. Alimadad, A., Borwein, A., Borwein, P., Dabbaghian, V., Drakes, C., Ferguson, R., Ghaseminejad, A.H., Gusev, Y., Hare, W., Li, J., Mitrovic-Minic, S., Rutherford, A., van der Waall, A., Vásárhelyi, K., Vertesi, L.: Complex Systems Modelling Group (CSMG) Modelling in Healthcare. American Mathematical Society, Providence (2010)
7. Weiss, M., Amyot, D.: Business process modeling with URN. Int. J. E-Business Res. (IJEBR) 1(3), 63–90 (2005). doi:10.4018/jebr.2005070104
8. Amyot, D., Mussbacher, G.: User requirements notation: the first ten years, the next ten years. J. Softw. (JSW) 6(5), 747–768 (2011). doi:10.4304/jsw.6.5.747-768
9. Amyot, D., et al.: Towards advanced goal model analysis with jUCMNav. In: Castano, S., Vassiliadis, P., Lakshmanan, L.V., Lee, M.L. (eds.) ER 2012. LNCS, vol. 7518, pp. 201–210. Springer, Heidelberg (2012). doi:10.1007/978-3-642-33999-8_25. http://softwareengineering.ca/jucmnav
10. Teixeira, L., Ferreira, C., Santos, B.S.: User-centered requirements engineering in health information systems: a study in the hemophilia field. Comput. Methods Programs Biomed. 106(3), 160–174 (2012). doi:10.1016/j.cmpb.2010.10.007
11. Hayes, G.R., Lee, C.P., Dourish, P.: Organizational routines, innovation, and flexibility: the application of narrative networks to dynamic workflow. Int. J. Med. Inf. 80(8), 161–177 (2011). doi:10.1016/j.ijmedinf.2011.01.005
12. Hübner, U., Cruel, E., Gök, M., Garthaus, M., Zimansky, M., Remmers, H., Rienhoff, O.: Requirements engineering for cross-sectional information chain models. In: Proceedings of the 11th International Congress on Nursing Informatics, paper 176. American Medical Informatics Association (2012)
13. Damas, C., Lambeau, B., van Lamsweerde, A.: Transformation operators for easier engineering of medical process models. In: 5th International Workshop on Software Engineering in Health Care (SEHC), pp. 39–45. IEEE CS (2013). doi:10.1109/SEHC.2013.6602476
14. Santos, E., Castro, J., Sanchez, J., Pastor, O.: A goal-oriented approach for variability in BPMN. In: 13th Workshop on Requirements Engineering, Ecuador, pp. 17–28 (2010)
15. Kuziemsky, C., Liu, X., Peyton, L.: Leveraging goal models and performance indicators to assess health care information systems. In: 7th International Conference on the Quality of Information and Communications Technology, pp. 222–227. IEEE CS (2010). doi:10.1109/QUATIC.2010.37
16. Pourshahid, A., Amyot, D., Peyton, L., Ghanavati, S., Chen, P., Weiss, M., Forster, A.J.: Business process management with the user requirements notation. Electron. Commer. Res. 9(4), 269–316 (2009). doi:10.1007/s10660-009-9039-z
17. Pourshahid, A., Mussbacher, G., Amyot, D., Weiss, M.: Requirements for a modeling language to specify and match business process improvement patterns. In: 3rd International Workshop on Model-Driven Requirements Engineering (MoDRE), pp. 10–19. IEEE (2013) doi:10.1109/MoDRE.2013.6597259
18. Rungworawut, W., Senivongse, T., Cox, K.: Achieving managerial goals in business process components design using genetic algorithms. In: 5th ACIS International Conference on Software Engineering Research, Management & Applications (SERA), pp. 409–418. IEEE CS (2007). doi:10.1109/SERA.2007.38

19. Bleistein, S.J., Cox, K., Verner, J., Phalp, K.T.: B-SCP: a requirements analysis framework for validating strategic alignment of organizational IT based on strategy, context, and process. Inf. Softw. Technol. **48**(9), 846–868 (2006). doi:10.1016/j.infsof.2005.12.001

20. Decreus, K., Poels, G.: A goal-oriented requirements engineering method for business processes. In: Soffer, P., Proper, E. (eds.) CAiSE Forum 2010. LNBIP, vol. 72, pp. 29–43. Springer, Heidelberg (2011). doi:10.1007/978-3-642-17722-4_3

21. Holden, R.J.: What stands in the way of technology-mediated patient safety improvements? A study of facilitators and barriers to physicians' use of electronic health records. J. Patient Saf. **7**(4), 193–203 (2011). doi:10.1097/PTS.0b013e3182388cfa

22. Vermeulen, J., Verwey, R., Hochstenbach, L.M., van der Weegen, S., Man, Y.P., de Witte, L.P.: Experiences of multidisciplinary development team members during user-centered design of telecare products and services: a qualitative study. J. Med. Internet Res. **16**(5), e124 (2014). doi:10.2196/jmir.3195

A Business Process Re-Engineering Approach to Transform BPMN Models to Software Artifacts

Javier Gonzalez-Huerta[1,2], Anis Boubaker[1(✉)], and Hafedh Mili[1]

[1] LATECE Laboratory, Université du Québec à Montréal, Montreal, Canada
anis@boubaker.ca
[2] Software Engineering Research Lab Sweden,
Blekinge Institute of Technology, Karlskrona, Sweden

Abstract. Business Process Model and Notation (BPMN) is becoming a de-facto standard for the specification of organizational business processes. In most cases, business processes are modeled in order to build software that may support or automate specific parts of those processes. In this work, we aim at refining BPMN models in order to automatically derive software analysis and design artifacts (e.g., UML Class Diagrams or Use Cases) from a given BPMN. These artifacts will be later on used to develop the software components (not necessarily services) automating or supporting business process activities. Our envisioned approach is based on a three-steps model transformation chain: (1) we refine the BPMN *as-is* model; (2) we apply process re-engineering and automation patterns to generate the BPMN *to-be* model; and (3) we use the resulting *to-be* BPMN model to derive analysis and design software artifacts. In this paper, we focus on the first two steps of the approach.

1 Introduction

Business Processes are primary assets within organizations as they embed their differential characteristics that distinguish them from their competitors. The field of Business Process Management (BPM) had recognized the need to document these processes, usually through models using visual and semi-formal languages such as the Business Process Model and Notation (BPMN) [15], which is becoming a de-facto standard. These process models are then analyzed in order to ensure alignment with company objectives and to identify improvement opportunities. One of these improvement opportunities is building information systems that support or automate (parts of) the business processes [13]. In fact, business and software analysts have long recognized that understanding the business processes that an information system has to support is key to eliciting its requirements [8,14]. Therefore, our objective through this work is to contribute answering the following question: *How to leverage business process models to derive, semi-automatically, the set of analysis and design software artifacts that will help us build the supporting software?*

© Springer International Publishing AG 2017
E. Aïmeur et al. (Eds.): MCETECH 2017, LNBIP 289, pp. 170–184, 2017.
DOI: 10.1007/978-3-319-59041-7_10

Several proposed approaches deal with the automatic derivation of software artifacts from BPMN process models (e.g., [5,12,18]). However, these work try to define one-to-one mappings between the BPMN model to analysis and design artifacts (e.g., use case diagrams or UML class diagrams or WS-BPEL specifications) assuming that the BPMN input models are correct, complete and represent the *to-be* Business Process to be supported. Yet, business process models are usually defined and specified to reflect the reality of the process as it is *currently* being implemented at the organization (*as-is* model). In the process of automating/providing support to some of the business process activities, we should not replicate what is being done manually or with the current *as-is* system (if any). The focus should be on trying to improve the current process by optimizing/rearranging some of the activities being performed into a new *to-be* model.

Therefore, in this idea paper, we propose a three-step approach relying on a semi-automatic model transformation chain, starting from a given BPMN *as-is* model. The first step intends to refine the business process model by detecting missing model elements or inconsistencies. In the second step, we apply a set of process re-engineering and automation patterns to generate the BPMN *to-be* model. Finally, in the third step we use the resulting *to-be* BPMN model to derive analysis and design software artifacts, usually as a set UML diagrams (Use cases, class, sequence and finite-state diagrams). These artifacts will be later on used to develop the software components (not necessarily services) that will automate or support business process activities. This paper focuses on the first two steps of the approach, i.e., producing the *to-be* model from an *as-is* business process model, for which we lay our ground ideas, and describe our prototype implementation.

The rest of the paper is organized as follows: Sect. 2 gives an overview of the approach. Section 3 describes the strategy to correct and/or complete the BPMN input model by applying BPMN and domain specific correction patterns. Section 4 introduces the re-engineering patterns and their application strategy. Section 5 describes the use of a Rule Engine to support the question-based transformation approach. Section 6 discusses existing approaches that deal with the derivation of software artifacts from BPMN specifications. Finally, Sect. 7 discusses the next steps and challenges to be faced.

2   An Approach to Refine and Transform BPMN Specifications

A precise modeling of the organizational business processes and their translation into software models is key for aligning information systems with organizational business goals. Traditional approaches try to build a generic catalog of software components that are combined to match organization's specific requirements [13]. However, if these software components have to be developed from scratch, or if parts of the business process model do not match any of the existing components, we will need to establish a mapping between the organization-specific business processes and the information system analysis and design artifacts.

This mapping will vary depending on: (i) how each process accommodates the business objective; (ii) the application domain; and (iii) the different levels of automation, ranging from simply recording the occurrence of tasks to the full automation of the different activities [13].

2.1   Our Solution Approach

The process towards obtaining a first version of the analysis and design artifacts starts with an incomplete - and sometimes incorrect- *as-is* BPMN model [1]. Our input *Computation Independent* BPMN *as-is* model is refined through a series of intermediary steps (as shown in Fig. 1). We apply a question/answer-based metaphor in which the tool keeps checking for patterns, and asks generic questions or makes suggestions to the business analyst. In the case of (e.g.) incomplete models, the tool could ask the business analyst for ways to complete the model (e.g., by adding a missing Data Store). In the case of incorrect models, we would ask or suggest ways to correct the model (e.g., by asking if there are missing data objects or missing data inputs/outputs). This way, we introduce computation dependent details to the *as-is* BPMN model. Once we have a complete and "correct" *as-is* model, the tool tries to match a set of automation patterns, suggesting ways to provide certain degree of automation to the (manual or partially automated) model, considering the *as-is* model as a suboptimal model.

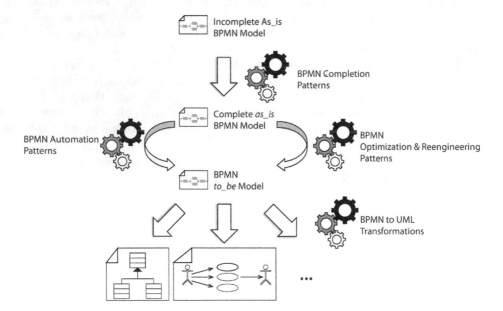

Fig. 1. Transformation chain to refine the BPMN model and derive UML models

---

[1] By incorrect or incomplete, we de not necessarily mean that the model does not conform to BPMN specifications, but might lack certain details or be *computational-independent*.

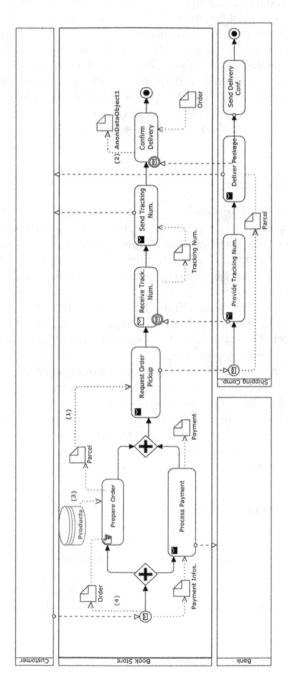

Fig. 2. Book store Example BPMN *as-is* model

In parallel, we might also suggest ways to optimize the process (e.g., merging tasks). However, in the latter the business analyst will have a more involved role.

With regards to the implementation, we envision our approach to be integrated within a business process modeling tool as a modeling support module suggesting patterns as the model is constructed, in the image of what is found in integrated programming environment. When a given pattern is detected, the analyst is notified and the model transformation will be done according to his answers to pattern specific questions. We present in Sect. 5 a console-mode proof of concept that loads a process model and tries to match a set of patterns, described in the next section, then makes necessary transformations in the input process model.

2.2   A Running Example

To illustrate the envisioned approach, we will use the sample book store process model illustrated in Fig. 2. The process has four main participants: the customer, the book store, the bank and the shipping company. The process starts by receiving an order from the Customer. Then two activities will be performed concurrently: the order is packaged into a parcel ready for shipping and the payment is processed through the Bank. Once these activities are completed, the process continues on by requesting a Shipping Company to perform the delivery. A tracking number is then received from the Shipping Company that is, in turn, sent to the Customer. Once the parcel is delivered, the Book Store receives a delivery confirmation and the process ends.

The model, as portrayed in Fig. 2, contains a *partial* specification of the data involved in the *Store* swimlane (e.g., products or packaging) and lacks certain data associations. Moreover, there is no data store that permits the persistence to the orders allowing for their usage beyond the scope of this process [15]. Therefore, we must first complete the model by expliciting additional information required to produce the supporting software and eliminate structural and semantic (business) inconsistencies. This will be covered in the next section.

3   Fixing the *as-is* model

As a first step to our approach, we seek to fix the input *as-is* model in order to complete missing information that would be required to produce the UML analysis models. To do so, we rely on a pattern recognition approach and according to patterns we identified and classified into two categories: BPMN correction patterns and domain specific correction patterns. In the following, we describe these sets in turn.

3.1   BPMN Correction Patterns

At this step, our main objective is to identify any inconsistencies or missing information with regards to process' sequence flow and data flow. Several authors (e.g., [20]) have addressed sequence flow inconsistencies, detecting such situations that might lead the business process execution to deadlocks – i.e., the process stalls at some point because a condition could never be met – or livelocks – i.e., the business process never reaches a state that permits it end. However, to the best of our knowledge, data flow inconsistencies have not attracted researcher's attention yet and we propose to fill that gap.

Modeling the data flow in a BPMN process model is done implicitly as BPMN's main modeling concern is the sequence flow. The BPMN standard defines explicit representation of tasks' data inputs and outputs as Data Objects and/or Data Stores. Constructs as Data Object Reference and Data Store Reference could also be used to handle access/modification of a given data source by multiple tasks [15]. However, nothing prevents the business analyst to partially specify the data flow in a given business process (e.g., not relating Data Object to flow elements or doing it partially). Thus, we propose a set of BPMN Data Correction patterns aiming at completing and correcting the BPMN model by adding missed Data Objects/Data Sources, as well as missed Data Input and Outputs. In the remainder of this subsection, we present two Data Correction patterns.

Message with No Content

Description: Business process models often involve several participants and the BPMN standard makes provision to model business process collaborations through message exchanges between participants and using constructs such as Message Sending/Receiving activities and events.

Context: A sent or received message usually embeds business objects and process-related information. However, the BPMN standard does not require these exchanged data objects to be modeled explicitly (mainly because BPMN permits different abstraction levels). As per BPMN execution semantics, a Data Object sent (resp. received) by message to another process participant should appear as a data input (resp. output) to the artifact sending (resp. receiving) the message (see [15, pp. 225]).

Structure: This pattern detects any message sending/receiving activities and events that do not refer to any Data Object. If such an element is detected, the analyst is asked whether a data flow link should be added to an existing Data Object within process' scope or if a new data object should be created.

Examples: An example of this pattern is illustrated in blue in Fig. 2: the first data input flow between *Parcel* and *Request Order Pickup* illustrates the first situation (i.e., linking to an existing Data Object) while the second blue link, out of *Confirm Delivery*, shows the creation of a new Data Object.

Data Object Coming from Nowhere

Description: This pattern intends to identify data objects that appear in the business process without being produced by any task or being received through a message. Going back to our Book Store process (Fig. 2), the *Products* and *Order* Data Objects, shown in red, illustrate this situation and will trigger this pattern.

Context: Even though BPMN specifications permits this modeling *shortcut*, we need to determine the source of such Data Objects. Indeed, for us to derive (e.g.) a class diagram that corresponds to the data model supporting a given BPMN model, all Data Input and Data Output Associations should be explicit in the BPMN model.

Structure: To do so, we suggest to the analyst one of three possibilities: (1) to connect the Data Object to a message receiving activity or event, (2) to transform the Data Object into a Data Store if the information comes from a global data store that persists the data beyond the scope of the business process or (3) to define them as global process Data Inputs.

Examples: Going back to our Book Store example, the red annotation num. 3 in the model (Fig. 2) shows an example of transforming a Data Object into a Data Store (second case scenario). In the red annotation numbered 4, we see Data Objects being set as process global Data Input.

3.2   Domain Specific Correction Patterns

We also propose to rely on business domain specific patterns (e.g., see [11]) to complete the business process. One interesting example, proposed by Koschmider and Reijers is the shipment pattern [11]. If we go back to our example in Fig. 2, we can see that shipment is handled by a shipping company and, relying on the as-is model, the act of shipping simply comes down to requesting the shipment. However and as described in [11], many shipping variations could be considered, thus raising several questions:

1. Is there a contract with a specific shipping company or should the best shipping company be selected based (e.g.) on the type of parcel or its destination? The latter would involve adding a Business Rule Activity for selecting the shipping company.
2. Does the Book Store or its customer wants to have a saying on the shipping schedule? In which case shipping company selection could have to be done at order time.

Another aspect we should consider is the absence of error-handling for key activities. Indeed, studies have shown (e.g., see [2]) that business analysts tend to overlook error handling, relegating them as implementation details. However, we argued in [3] that error handling is most and foremost a business problem that should be tackled by the analyst, and proposed a business oriented app-roach to model semi-automatically compensation paths (returning the process to a stable state after abortion).

In implementing domain specific patterns, the main problem we will encounter is matching patterns with a given activity (or a set thereof). In [11], the authors suggested an algorithm based on a noun-verb labeling style. Although this approach has its merits, its main drawback lies in the error-prone assump-tion that the analyst will comply with a strict naming pattern. We would also consider two other approaches. In the first approach we would rely on a classi-fication of process model elements using a domain specific ontology. While this approach avoids naming mistakes, it relies on the existence of an ontology and implies a heavier modeling effort. The second approach we propose is by lever-aging other business process views as the value model, the goal model or the decision model. For example, we proposed in [4] an approach to extract a value model from a business process model. The value model gives another perspective on the business and permits to answer such questions as *what are the economic resources involved? how are they transformed/consumed? by whom? and why?*. As a shipment involves the transfer of custody over resources between three par-ticipants *and* the consumption of another economic resource, we could identify a shipping activity as these information are readily available in the value model.

4   Re-engineering Patterns

Once we have a "correct" *as-is* model, the last step towards producing the *to-be* model involves transforming the result through the application of re-engineering patterns. We distinguish between two types of patterns: (1) *Automation Patterns* – i.e., those focused on certain aspects of the process to be automated, or (2) pure *Optimization Patterns* – i.e., changes affecting the organization of tasks in order to increase the effectiveness and efficiency of the process.

Automation patterns are computation dependent patterns and are treated by following the same strategy as for the Correction and Completion patterns: asking a question to the business analyst and parameterizing the pattern based on his/her responses. As an example of such patterns, the *Compose Message* pattern is illustrated in Fig. 3. This pattern seeks to include explicitly in the business process model computer support (e.g.: a web form) to produce a message for messages sent with no apparent activity producing them (Fig. 3a). To apply the transformation shown in Fig. 3b, the analyst should answer positively the question: "Does the system need to provide support to compose the message that starts the process on Company?".

With regards to *Optimization Patterns*, we are looking into maximizing a certain fitness function that could be reducing the process lead time or reducing error-prone activities, to name a few. Many authors proposed different business process modeling metrics measuring business processes structural aspects. For example, Balasubramanian *et al.* propose a set of metrics to approximate com-mon performance goals [1]. From these metrics, the branching automation fac-tor measures the extent to which process flow decisions are determined through

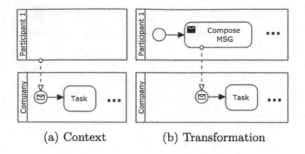

(a) Context   (b) Transformation

Fig. 3. The compose message automation pattern

definite business rules (rather than human involvement), whereas the role integration factor "denotes the extent of integration in the activities carried out by a role within the process" [1]. Gruhn et al. also proposed a set of metrics transposed from traditional software engineering into business process modeling as McCabe complexity metric and nesting depth calculations [9]. We propose to derive from these metrics a set of optimization patterns in which we define a general process structure that might lead to inefficiencies and propose the corresponding re-engineering transformation. In Fig. 4, we illustrate an example of an optimization pattern derived from the integration factor metric [1]. This pattern seeks to minimize the number of *Unnecessary handovers of Data Objects* between business process pools or swimlanes through a data flow analysis. Following the detection of such pattern, we could re-arrange process activities so that activities assigned to a pool/swimlane that manipulate a given data object follow one another, thus reducing the handovers[2]

Other authors proposed some generic business process optimization heuristics (e.g., see [10,17]). Some of these heuristics include, for example, the *Outsourcing* [17] of activities – i.e., delegating part of the activities to an external participant – or the *Composition* [17] – i.e., combining some activities to be performed more

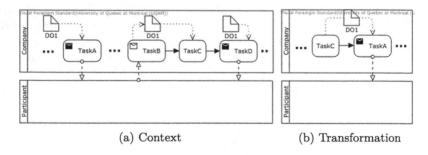

(a) Context   (b) Transformation

Fig. 4. The unnecessary handover of data objects optimization pattern

---

[2] This transformation will not always be feasible as other dependencies to activities and data objects might prevent it.

efficiently. However, these heuristics are presented in a purely informal fashion, and require more complex interaction with the business analyst to be applied systematically as process transformations.

5   Implementation

In this section we discuss the implementation of a first prototype of the approach that is able to apply some of the patterns described in Sects. 3 and 4. The implementation follows a two-staged transformation schema: the first stage is intended to parse the model, and the second stage applies the actual modifications to the model. The proposed patterns are implemented as a set of rules, where the left-hand-side of the rules describes the BPMN structure to be matched and the right-hand-side defines a set of transformations to be applied. In the first stage, when the left hand side of a given rule is matched, the tool asks questions to the analyst to complement the information available in the BPMN model. These questions aim at parameterizing the pattern, and once parameterized, the pattern occurrence is inserted in the transformation's knowledge base. At the second stage, each time the tool finds an instance of a given pattern in the knowledge base, it applies the model modifications associated to the right hand side of the pattern. This two staged strategy that interacts with the transformation knowledge base lets us establish the relevancy of the questions to be asked to the analyst, discarding those that are not.

5.1   Representing Process Models

We implemented our prototype on top of the Eclipse Modeling Framework (EMF) [19] to be able to manipulate the instances of BPMN2 and UML2 models. We use the Eclipse BPMN2 modeler [7] metamodel to be able to retrieve and modify the BPMN2 model structure in the BPMN completion and in the application of BPMN automation and reengineering patterns. We also rely on the EMF UML2 [6] implementation to create and handle the output models after the BPMN2UML transformations. By using an EMF-based third party toolset compliant with the standard, we allow the users to use other tools to edit their models at the same time. The toolset also provides us with the Java^{TM} EMF manipulation classes to be able to manipulate the models.

We extended these manipulation classes by creating adapters that allow us to create the BPMN2 constructs (e.g., tasks, data objects, data stores or data associations between tasks and data objects or data stores) and also to create the UML class models and UML use case diagrams in the BPMN2UML transformations.

Finally, we also have extended modeling capabilities by using BPMN extension mechanisms provided by the standard and supported by the Eclipse BPMN2 Modeler. These extension mechanisms allows us to create approach-specific metaclasses (e.g., *Automatable Task* to represent the tasks the system is going to automate).

5.2   Representing Patterns

We explicitly represent the occurrence of the patterns to be inserted in the transformation knowledge base. This representation contains both the question provided to, and answer provided by, the business analyst as well as the source model elements of interest in each pattern. The addition of the source model elements will be accessed later by other rules, that will eventually trigger the addition of new patterns/facts to the knowledge base (e.g., the addition of all the tasks that interact with a new data store added to support the whole process) or that will perform the actual modification/creation of entities in the model. This modification/creation of entities will occur either in the BPMN model for the BPMN correction/automation or reengineering patterns, or in the UML.

5.3   Model Transformations

For supporting the different model transformations that constitute our approach (described in Sect. 2) we rely on the Drools engine. Drools is a rule engine that extends the Rete algorithm for its use in object oriented systems. On the one hand, Drools allows to exercise control over the knowledge base (the working memory in Drools terms) and, on the other hand, to group rules into *ruleflow* groups and a *ruleflow* sequence that prescribes the order in which the rule groups will be executed. This sequencing capability allows us to orchestrate the rules that perform each of the transformation processes described in Sect. 2.

```
 1  rule "DataObject-from-Nowhere" ruleflow-group "BPMNParsing"
 2  when
 3      $dataObject:DataObject()  &&     not( $dataoutput:
 4          DataOutputAssociation(getTargetRef()==$dataObject))
 5      ...
 6      && $Event: StartEvent(eContainer()==$dataObject.eContainer())
 7  then
 8      ...
 9      if (inputValue.equals("yes")) {
10          Pattern p = new Pattern("q1", "yes");
11          p.add("Event",$Event);
12          p.add("DataObject",$dataObject);
13          insert(p);}
14  end;
15  ...
16
17  rule "CreateDataAssociation" ruleflow-group "BPMNTransformation"
18  when
19      $pattern: Pattern(getQuestion().equals("q1") &&
20          getResponse().equals("yes") &&
21          getType().equals("DataObjectFromNowhere")
22      )
23  then
24      Bpmn2Adapter.createDataOutputAssociationCatchEventDataObject
25      ( (StartEvent) $pattern.get("Event"),
26          (DataObject) $pattern.get("DataObject") );
27      retract($pattern);
28  end;
```

Fig. 5. Transformation rules

Figure 5 shows a code snippet of two Drools rules in different *ruleflow* groups implementing a BPMN Completion pattern. The first rule belongs to the *BPMNParsing* rule-group, and defines that, once detected, a given structure in the source model (a data object that has no incoming data association), inserts an occurrence of the pattern in the knowledge base. The second rule belongs to the *BPMNTransformation* and applies modifications in the BPMN model when the representation of the pattern is found in the knowledge base. Using Drools we are able to establish a *ruleflow* sequence that starts by parsing the model and, after instantiating all the possible rule matches, instantiates the *BPMNTransformation* rules. All resulting transformations are valid BPMN models.

6 Related Work

Producing software artifacts from a high level specification is a problem that attracted the attention of many authors during the past decades. Several approaches focused on producing the software artifacts from an abstract high level structured specification expressed as business process models (BPMN, UML Activity Diagrams, etc.). In this category, we distinguish between those who tried to operationalize the abstract specification by deriving an executable software relying on the SOA paradigm (e.g., [16]), presuming the existence of a set of services matching business process activities. Others focused on producing traditional software engineering artifacts (i.e., UML diagrams) following a model driven engineering approach. Our work falls in the latter category and we describe below some of the related work.

In [12], Cruz *et al.* proposed an approach to derive use cases from BPMN models. Each business process activity is derived into a use case. Then, use case description is gathered from different connections the activity has within the BPMN model. Finally, using a use case template, they fill in the blanks from activity's connections to other elements from the model relying on a simple set of rules. This approach was then extended in [5] to produce class diagrams through a three-steps rule-based framework using a company's full business process landscape (the set of all business processes). First, they identify the entities through a set of rules such as *creating an entity for each datastore/agent/activity*. Then, the second step aims at identifying entity attributes from datastore descriptions. In the last step, they propose a set of rules to generate associations between entities/classes. An example of such rules is *associating an activity class with the agent in charge of performing it*. Although we recognize the quality of the approach and the encouraging results obtained by applying it on a toy example, requiring the process landscape could be a strong limitation. With no such requirement, our approach builds on business process best practices and analyst involvement to complement the initial as-is model and would produce more accurate software models (at the expense of analyst involvement).

Rodriguez et al. [18] used a formal model transformation approach focusing specifically on security aspects expressed through a BPMN profile metamodel, BPSec. In their approach, they generate software artifacts through a set of QVT transformations. They start with a basic transformation of process models into class diagrams where participants and DataStores are transformed into analysis classes and business process tasks transformed into class operations assigned to their corresponding participant. Then, these classes are associated to security-specific classes (e.g., access control, integrity, non-repudiation) generated through the analysis of the annotations related to BPSec. Although this approach produces interesting analysis class models regarding software security aspects, the class model produced remain fairly simple and associations between classes are overlooked (except for specializations gathered from swimlanes included within pools).

7   Discussion

Understanding the business processes that a given software system needs to support is key to elicit its requirements. In this scenario, BPMN represents a common dialect that can be used to communicate the early requirements between stakeholders. But once we have produced a detailed BPMN representation of the business process that a given software system is going to support, it is worth deriving as much information as possible in form of design and analysis artifacts. However, even though there are several approaches that try to map certain constructs of the BPMN models directly into use case diagrams or pure data models, less attention has been paid to the refinement of the BPMN process models to: (i) correct and complete the *as-is* model; and (ii) produce the *to-be* model by applying reengineering patterns that take into account the software system to be developed.

In this paper, we have presented our envisioned approach that aims at deriving analysis and design artifacts from the *to-be* model through model transformations. To do so, we first apply BPMN completion and correction patterns to the *as-is* model. This *as-is* model is refined into a *to-be* model by applying automation and optimization patterns that consider the peculiarities of the software system/automation to be developed. Once refined, different analysis and design artifacts are derived through model transformations. Our approach is question based and requires the involvement of the business analyst to parameterize the different transformation patterns to be applied. We have introduced the mechanisms that provide support to our approach, such as the explicit representation of the patterns to be applied and how we plan to exercise control over the knowledge base to be able to decide which questions/patterns might raise new questions to be asked to the business analyst.

This paper presents an early work and we are currently extending the set of patterns considered in each of the BPMN refinement stages. In addition, although the prototype proves our ability to derive UML use case and class diagrams, the maps are yet to be evolved in order to derive a more complete, realistic, and cohesive set of analysis and design artifacts. We also aim at performing case studies to evaluate the extent to which the derived models are useful in the development of the final information systems.

References

1. Balasubramanian, S., Gupta, M.: Structural metrics for goal based business process design and evaluation. Bus. Process Manage. J. **11**(6), 680–694 (2005). ISSN 1463-7154. doi:10.1108/14637150510630855
2. Ben-Eliahu, Z., Elhadad, M.: Semantic business process for improved exception handling. Technical report. Ben Gurion University, Dept. of Comp. Sci. (2009)
3. Boubaker, A.: La modélisation semi-automatisee de la compensation dans les processus d'affaires. PhD thesis, Université du Québec à Montréal (2016). http://www.archipel.uqam.ca/9271/
4. Boubaker, A., Leshob, A., Mili, H., Charif, Y.: A pattern-based approach to extract REA value models from business process models. Intelligent Systems in Accounting, Finance and Management (2017). ISSN 1055615X. doi:10.1002/isaf.1402. http://doi.wiley.com/10.1002/isaf.1402
5. Cruz, E.F., Machado, R.J., Santos, M.Y.: Deriving a data model from a set of inter-related business process models. In: 17th International Conference on Enterprise Information Systems (ICEIS 2015), Barcelona, Spain, pp. 49–59 (2015)
6. Eclipse Foundation. Eclipse Model Development Tools - MDT - UML2 (2016)
7. Eclipse Foundation. Eclipse BPMN2 Modeler (2016)
8. Eriksson, H.-E., Penker, M.: Business Modeling with UML: Business Patterns at Work. Wiley, New York (2000)
9. Gruhn, V., Laue, R.: Approaches for business process model complexity metrics. In: Technologies for Business Information Systems, Chap. 2, pp. 13–24. Springer, Netherlands (2007). ISBN 978-1-4020-5633-8
10. Hammer, M.: Reengineering work: don't automate, obliterate. Harvard Bus. Rev. **7–8**, 105–114 (1990)
11. Koschmider, A., Reijers, H.: Improving the process of process modelling by the use of domain process patterns. Enterp. Inf. Syst. **9**(1), 1–29 (2013)
12. Cruz, E.F., Machado, R.J., Santos, M.Y.: From business process models to use case models: a systematic approach. In: Aveiro, D., Tribolet, J., Gouveia, D. (eds.) EEWC 2014. LNBIP, vol. 174, pp. 167–181. Springer, Cham (2014). doi:10.1007/978-3-319-06505-2_12
13. Mili, H., Valtchev, P., Leshob, A., Obaid, A., Ghislain, L.: Towards building software systems from the specification of the supported business processes. In: OOPSLA Workshop on Domain-Specific Modeling (2007)
14. Mili, H., Tremblay, G., Bou Jaoude, G., Lefebvre, E., Elabed, L., El Boussaidi, G.: Business process modeling languages: sorting through the alphabet soup. ACM Comput. Surv. **43**(1), 1–56 (2010)
15. Object Management Group. Business Process Model and Notation (BPMN) Version 2.0 (2011)
16. Ouyang, C., Van Der Aalst, W.M.P., Arthur, H.M.: From business process models to process-oriented software systems: the BPMN to BPEL way. ACM Trans. Softw. Eng. Methodol. **19**, 1–37 (2009)
17. Reijers, H.: Design and Control of Workflow Processes: Business Process Management for the Service Industry (2003)
18. Rodríguez, A., García Rodríguez de Guzmán, I., Fernández-Medina, E., Piattini, M.: Semi-formal transformation of secure business processes into analysis class and use case models. Inf. Softw. Technol. **52**(9), 945–971 (2010)

19. Steinberg, D., Budinsky, F., Paternostro, M., Merks, E.: Eclipse Modeling Framework. Addison-Wesley, London (2008)
20. Aalst, W.M.P., Hirnschall, A., Verbeek, H.M.W.: An alternative way to analyze workflow graphs. In: Pidduck, A.B., Ozsu, M.T., Mylopoulos, J., Woo, C.C. (eds.) CAiSE 2002. LNCS, vol. 2348, pp. 535–552. Springer, Heidelberg (2002). doi:10.1007/3-540-47961-9_37

Evaluating the Potential of Technology in Justice Systems Using Goal Modeling

Sanaa Alwidian[1], Daniel Amyot[1(✉)], and Gilbert Babin[2]

[1] School of Computer Science and Electrical Engineering,
University of Ottawa, Ottawa, Canada
{salwidia,damyot}@uottawa.ca
[2] Department of Information Technology, HEC Montréal, Montreal, Canada
gilbert.babin@hec.ca

Abstract. Context: In Canada, the justice system suffers from performance and efficiency issues as indicated by long wait time before trial. Actors in the justice system are seeking solutions involving emerging information technology. Problem: There is need to guide the selection of appropriate combinations of technologies supporting or improving justice systems, yet there is no adapted approach focusing on this concern. Objective: This paper aims to develop the basis of a modeling approach supporting the selection of technologies relevant to justice systems. Method: Goal-oriented requirements modeling is used to describe and evaluate the contribution of technology in the context of justice systems, with the help of an illustrative example targeting the improvement of access to justice. Results: The example shows that it is feasible to model the technology alternatives and their contributions to the goals of different stakeholders in justice systems so that selected technologies are well-aligned with the needs of such systems. Goal models also support trade-off analysis in this context. Conclusion: A justice-aware modeling approach has the potential of helping justice stakeholders to better reason about technology selection and document the rationale of their choices. There are however many remaining challenges in the generalization of the approach to other cases and in its validation in practice.

Keywords: Access to justice · Cyberjustice · Goal-oriented requirement language · Justice systems · Requirement engineering · Technology selection

1 Introduction

Justice systems, all over the world, are the results of many decades, or even centuries of development, revision and evaluation of rival rules and laws. In the last decades, the interfaces through which individuals had access to justice systems were based on oral and written procedures. For instance, civil and criminal justice procedures were depending solely on the paper work and the physical existence of participating parties [34]. Being face-to-face and paper-based, access to justice systems becomes more and more cumbersome. In Canada, the Chief Justice has referred to these issues as the "access to justice crisis" [38]. This crisis has culminated with a decision from the Supreme Court of Canada prescribing that there is "… a presumptive ceiling of 18

© Springer International Publishing AG 2017
E. Aïmeur et al. (Eds.): MCETECH 2017, LNBIP 289, pp. 185–202, 2017.
DOI: 10.1007/978-3-319-59041-7_11

months on the length of the criminal case in provincial courts, from the charge to the end of trial" [33]. For federal cases, the prescribed limit was set to 30 months. The access to justice problem is further magnified by the following factors: the physical inaccessibility to courts (caused by geographical remoteness) and the high costs of litigation (which may prohibit most citizens from accessing courts) [7].

To overcome these challenges, the legal community in Canada called for the integration of *Alternative Dispute Resolution* (ADR) into the state and federal trial court systems [28]. ADR is a process, such as arbitration or mediation, which takes place out of the court through a pre-authorized third party [2]. ADR has been adapted in courts' case management programs to provide litigants with alternative means of resolving their disputes, either in a paper-based format or with computers. The paper-based, face-to-face ADR approaches can outperform the traditional court-based ones in terms of their time efficiency. Nevertheless, they remain costly and still require the presence of participants [29]. Computer-based ADR, also referred to as *Online Dispute Resolution* (ODR), is a mechanism for resolving disputes through the use of information and communications technology to process, store, organize, and communicate data globally through the internet, with high speed [39]. ODR has been introduced to solve particular disputes, such as e-commerce conflicts [25]. With ODR, arbitration and mediation are performed online. In addition, other innovative online processes are developed such as automated negotiation techniques, including "blind-bidding", where each party makes monetary settlement offers in isolation of the other party and then a settlement is reached if the bids come within close reach of each other) [26]. Other examples include mock trial systems such as eJury [16] and VirtualJury™ [41], where a jury of online volunteers gives a verdict based on a set of facts as a form of crowd sourcing [40].

Despite the obvious contribution technology has had on judicial systems (from supporting the day-to-day court activities to enabling a trial judge to handle the many cases stacked in her court), there still remains the question as to how technology can be selected appropriately to facilitate their performance while being aligned with their goals. In this paper, we investigate ways of evaluating, at selection time, the potential of technologies to support judicial systems and increase access to justice. Particularly, we explore the use of a requirements engineering methodology based on the Goal-oriented Requirement Language (GRL) for goal modeling. This paper refines the models envisioned in [3] by including the goals of judicial system stakeholders inferred from a literature review and by enabling the indicator-based assessment of how well technology and products can support these goals.

The rest of this paper is organized as follows. Section 2 reviews background work related to technology selection and evaluation, and work related to the use of goal models in support of justice systems and legal compliance. Section 3 presents our technology selection approach for justice systems, which exploits the Goal-oriented Requirement language (GRL) for modeling and analysis. Section 4 provides an illustrative example based on the evaluation of a specific ODR technology in a provincial justice system. Section 5 provides a discussion of the benefits and limitations of the approach, and then Sect. 6 concludes the paper and presents future work items.

2 Related Work

In this section, we provide a brief introduction to technology selection and to the use of the goal modeling in relation to justice systems.

2.1 Technology Selection and Evaluation

With the rapid development of technologies, along with their increased variety and complexity, the task of technology selection becomes non-trivial. Technology selection is concerned with the choice of the best technology from a number of available options or alternatives [35]. Of course, the selection of the "best" technology varies depending on the requirements of the organization. Lamb and Gregory [27] defined technology selection as "gathering information from various sources about the alternatives, and the evaluation of alternatives against each other or some set of criteria". According to the authors, the evaluation of technological alternatives is concerned with the notions of cost, benefit, and risk.

Current approaches to technology selection are often either based on generic decision support tools (that are not fully adapted for technology selection) or narrowly focus on the financial/technological feasibility of technology options and/or the traditional investment justification factors [15, 35], most of these criteria being objectively measurable. They are however limited when it comes to take into account the subjective assessment of stakeholder goals and side-effects of the technology on these goals.

A variety of approaches for the identification, selection and evaluation of the appropriate single/combination of technology have been developed by various organizations and researchers with different models and goals for different domains (which are beyond the scope of this paper). Examples include public transportation [37], aeronautics [21], and mobile phones [31]. In the information technology domain, some approaches have even been standardized, for instance to select security products [19] or computer-aided software engineering tools [23]. Some large companies and organizations such as The MITRE Corporation also have their own documented technology selection processes [13].

In addition, the domain of requirements engineering (which is of a particular concern of this paper) has adapted strategies for technology selection to support some of the RE activities. For instance, Aranda et al. [5] proposed an approach for technology selection based on techniques from the field of cognitive psychology to support the process of requirements elicitation in the global distributed software development projects, where communication of virtual teams is a challenge that needs to be solved or minimized through the appropriate selection of technology.

We argue that current technology selection approaches could be enhanced to better analyze the impact of a specific technology or product on stakeholder goals in the context of very complex stakeholder goal networks, which is typically the case in public services in general, and more specifically in judicial systems.

2.2   Goal Models for Justice Systems

Goal models define the goals of systems and stakeholders, together with their rela-tionships such as decompositions, contributions, and dependencies. They are typically used to share the understanding of who wants what, and they can be analyzed to determine satisfaction and discuss trade-offs.

The early identification of goals has the potential to help stakeholders, inside and outside justice systems, to better understand and evaluate the role of technology to improve specific qualities such as access to justice. In addition, goal modeling could be used by decision makers in insuring that the information technology-enabled processes and tools are aligned with the goals of justice systems. Finally, goal modeling can formalize requirements independently from the actual technology being assessed.

Over the years, many goal-oriented modeling languages have been proposed by the requirements engineering community, but only one has been standardized at this point, namely the *Goal-oriented Requirement Language* (GRL), part of ITU-T's User Requirements Notation [24].

In the legal and regulatory domain, goal models have been used in multiple contexts such as modeling the objectives and clauses of laws and regulations [36], deriving system or software requirements from laws and regulations [22], and evaluating the compliance of systems and processes to laws and regulations [17]. They have shown interesting benefits in enabling the monitoring of compliance levels, providing guidance as to what areas of non-compliance should be focused on, and how to detect and reason about trade-offs related to conflicting regulations from different jurisdictions [18].

Goal modeling was also suggested as a means to support some aspects of tech-nology selection. Ayala and Franch pioneered this area with a goal-oriented method targeting the selection of commercial off-the-shelf (COTS) components [6]. Cares and Franch furthered some of these selection ideas in the domain of mobile office devices [14]. However, to our knowledge, goal modeling has never been used to support technology selection targeting the specificities of the legal/justice domain. In addition, no technology selection method has taken advantage of the advanced modeling and analysis features of GRL (e.g., indicators, strategies, and contribution overrides) yet.

3   Goal-Oriented Technology Selection for Justice System

The objective of this section is to develop a preliminary goal model as a framework for selection of technologies relevant to justice systems. In essence, we exploit the inherent capabilities of goal-oriented languages to facilitate the rapid identification of require-ments about stakeholders (the who), goals and quality criteria they have (the what), and the combination of enabling technologies to meet and satisfy these goals (the how).

3.1   Generic Goal-Oriented Modeling Structure for Technology Selection

Figure 1 illustrates the overall structure of a goal model for technology selection using GRL [24]. A selection model should include all relevant stakeholders (represented as actors ⬭) and their goals (with hard goals ⬭ and qualitative softgoals ⬭) regarding

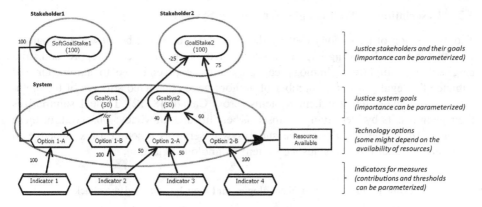

Fig. 1. Generic goal model for technology selection

the system under study. It should also show the goal(s) of the system and the general technological services that the system can/should provide (with tasks ⬭). Assessment of the technological alternatives is performed with indicators (⬬), which measure observable values and convert them to GRL satisfaction values (from 0 for denied, to 100 for satisfied) that can be propagated to other model elements through links. All these components (actors, goals, tasks and indicators) can be structured through AND/OR/XOR decomposition links (+——). Contribution links (——→) indicate the positive or negative impact of the satisfaction of one element on the satisfaction of another element. Finally, dependency links (—▶—) model dependencies between elements, often across two different actors or, in the case of technology selection, from tasks/goals to resources (☐) required for the services to be selected.

To evaluate a specific technology product, current measures must be determined for the different indicators, for example, through testing, documentation, or experts' opinions. Goal achievement levels are then obtained by propagating these current values in the model. The level of satisfaction of the stakeholders is derived from the level of goal achievement and the relative importance of these goals (indicated between parentheses) for the containing stakeholder. The modeler can also adapt the model to the current context (e.g., a specific provincial) jurisdiction by changing the values of: (i) the indicator definitions (e.g., their targets), (ii) the weights of the contribution from indicators to technology options, and (iii) the importance values of the goals to their containing actor.

One particular challenge of such goal model is the determination of appropriate contribution weights. However, many approaches now exist to build consensus over their values [1]. In addition, the validation of the whole GRL model can also be done by inspection, or through more advanced mechanisms for reaching consensus on a per-stakeholder basis (e.g., using the questionnaire generation and analysis approach for conflict detection and resolution in [20]).

3.2   Description of Technologies for Justice Systems

The application of technology in the judicial contexts must not be viewed in a narrow way that is limited to using large computer systems to produce court reports and store caseload data. In fact, technology can play a more pivotal role to administer and enhance the legal process. A number of authors have conducted surveys of technologies used by the different judicial systems across Canada [8, 12]. Table 1 summarizes their main results by identifying a subset of benefits and drawbacks observed for these systems. This table and the source surveys will serve as a source of knowledge to elaborate the goal model for justice system technology selection.

Table 1. Justice system technologies and their benefits and drawbacks

Technology	Benefits	Drawbacks
Electronic records	− Improved access to critical court records anytime and anywhere − Enhanced preparation of judge for next day hearings − Ability to prepare orders that can be instantly filed and served − Expanded ability of judge to balance workday requirements	− Inefficiency of the system − Unauthorized access to documents − Security and privacy concerns of critical court records
Video conferencing	− Serve people with geographical constraints − Allow for remote participation in court proceedings − Facilitate trial preparation	− Lack of face-to-face presence of disputants − Loss of visible body language of disputants − Unreliability of technology − Fairness issues for accused parties as compared to face-to-face presence − Cost issues
e-filing	− File documents efficiently − Limit the number of errors contained in the documents − Save time and cost to process the filings	− Privacy concerns − Lack of trust in electronic filing systems
Websites	− Facilitate adjudication of cases by expanding the scope of information that a judge may find useful	− Websites could be hacked, affecting the privacy and security of stakeholders
Real-time court reporting	− Create and produce transcripts − Enhance preparation for the trial − Enhance functionality of judges to expeditiously finalize their orders	− Inconsistency of transcripts and case records
Case management systems	− Manage the court case files by facilitating functionalities such as: managing the calendar and creating documents (e.g., orders, opinions, memoranda, letters, etc.), viewing multiple pages on one screen or multiple documents, reviewing of files, and enabling the judge to officially file final orders electronically	− Concerns with security and efficiency of the systems

3.3   A Goal Model for Canada's Justice System

In this section, we present a technology selection goal model for Canada's justice system created using the generic structure discussed in Sect. 3.1. A high-level subset of the resulting model is presented in Fig. 2. The complete model was constructed manually, as an illustrative example, based on our interpretation of the judicial domain literature and the Cyberjustice literature and its surveys (see Table 1).

In Fig. 2, we see some of the most important stakeholders (judges, disputants, the court, lawyers, witnesses, clerks of court) of the judicial system. For each stakeholder, we identified goals that emerged from the benefits and drawbacks identified in Table 1. The judicial system itself is also represented as a stakeholder. The GRL model in Fig. 2 captures the various technological alternatives (presented as tasks) that can be performed to increase access to justice, and the relationships between these alternatives. Many local alternatives can have various impacts on different concerns of the stakeholders involved, with no obvious global solution that would satisfy everyone.

Looking at Fig. 2, we can see that *reach a settlement* is a very important goal for the disputants involved (as indicated by the 100 importance value), because an efficient settlement is one that saves disputants' time and money. From the judicial system's point of view, *increasing access to justice* is a very important goal (importance = 50 as there are other important goal); this goal can be realized by reducing the cost of litigation, reducing delays, increasing the ability to access information, increasing the physical accessibility to courts, or simplifying the process of litigation. These options are not mutually exclusive. Achieving this goal can be done by using technology or applying one of the ADR methods (negotiation, mediation, or arbitration). The model view in Fig. 2 specifies the impact of alternatives on some of the goals (other goals and weighted positive or negative contributions exist in the model).

As indicated in Fig. 2, judicial systems in Canada rely on various technological means of increasing access to justice and use various alternative dispute resolution mechanisms to resolve disputes faster and at a lower cost. The most commonly adopted electronic-based legal services include: videoconferencing, electronic filing, electronic access to court records, electronic discovery, social media, online access to court decisions, and/or the utilization of one of the Cyberjustice technologies. The latter in turn also includes several technical alternatives, such as case file management systems, communication technologies, and auto court reporting.

The model also shows that justice systems technologies depend on a secure, Internet-based connection that allows the litigants or their legal representatives to file or access court documents electronically. However, these systems vary with respect to several aspects such as the format of the documents that can be filed, the program/service provider, and the level of security provided.

The goal model illustrated in Fig. 2 is useful for identifying stakeholders and for gaining a common understanding of their concerns/goals. In addition, this model assists in documenting decision rationales and enables trade-off analysis based on GRL what-if strategies and tool-supported satisfaction propagation algorithms. For example, the model can help analyze and understand the trade-offs between using paper-based or computer-based dispute resolutions as two forms of ADR, and the impact of either alternative on achieving the "increase access to justice" goal. The model analyst does

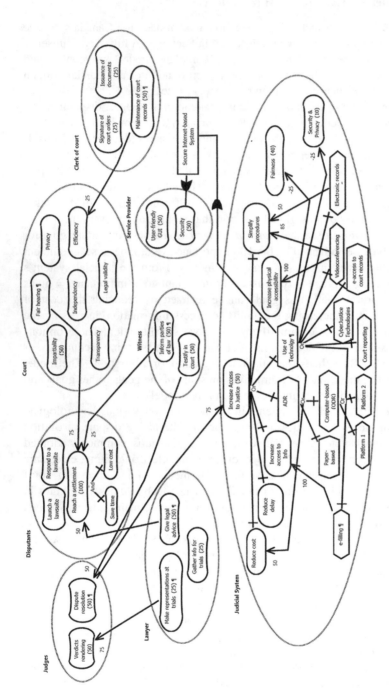

Fig. 2. Goal model for technology selection in Canada's judicial system

this by defining different GRL strategies and, using the jUCMNav tool [30], evaluating their impact on the satisfaction of higher-level goals and of stakeholders.

As GRL models are analyzable with tools, they often allow stakeholders to *disagree* on parts that are ill-defined or misunderstood *sooner* than with textual, paper-based descriptions of the same information. New model iterations can then help solve these disagreements and reach a clear consensus. GRL also supports mechanisms to capture remaining disagreements, for example with *contribution overrides*, which allow the definition of alternative sets of contribution levels for selected contribution links, which can be applied in conjunction with evaluation strategies [4].

4   Illustrative Product Selection Example

In addition to the potential advantages of using goal models for documenting stakeholders, goals, technologies and impacts (discussed in Sect. 3.3), these models can also be used to assess the impact of and identify trade-offs for specific technological *products*. In this case, dealing only with abstract satisfaction values on a [0...100] is insufficient as the model analyst needs to better relate observations about the real-world products under review to the goal model. The model needs to handle domain-specific units such as durations (e.g. the time needed to resolve disputes or to reach a settlement, in days), costs (e.g., the cost of litigation in Canadian dollars), or counts (e.g., the number of successfully mediated cases).

GRL supports this kind of information through the integration of *Key Performance Indicators* (KPIs) to the rest of the goal model [32]. KPIs, which form the bottom layer of the model structure in Fig. 1, can be associated through decomposition and contributions links to GRL intentional elements. KPIs are functions that compare an observable *evaluation value* (defined in a GRL strategy by an expert or provided by an external source of information such as a database, a web service, or a sensor) to other parameters to infer a GRL satisfaction value, propagatable to the other model elements. These parameters are the *target* value (the KPI is fully satisfied if the evaluation value reaches it), the *worst-case* value (the KPI is fully denied if the evaluation value reaches it), and a *threshold* value (the KPI is neutral if the evaluation value equals it), all measured in a concrete *unit* (e.g., hours).

In this section, we illustrate this last usage of the goal model with a real-time ODR platform called *PARLe* (Platform to Assist in the Resolution of Litigation Electronically). This software is the product of research on ODR conducted at the Cyberjustice Laboratory [10, 11]. PARLe supports conflict resolution in three basic steps: (1) negotiation, where participants get to submit viable solutions to the conflict, (2) mediation, for inviting a trusted third-party to facilitate dialogue and discussion between the participants, and (3) transfer of the file to an arbitrator or to a court of competent jurisdiction when the conflict could not be resolved in the previous two steps. PARLe offers the following services [10, 11]: memory aids regarding rights and obligations of participants, uploading electronic documents, secure instant messaging, a private discussion forum, a calendar tool, "blind" negotiation, case management system, payment system, electronic signature, hearing date planner, e-filing and indexing. Finally, this cloud-based system is accessible 24/7 from a computer or a mobile device.

To illustrate the use of KPIs, we need, as a *first step*, to define the suitable indicators and their parameters for a particular context. Then, as a *second step,* we need to use the GRL quantitative algorithm to evaluate the satisfaction levels of the goals connected to indicators. Regarding the first step, Fig. 3 shows a portion of the generic goal model presented in Sect. 3.3, augmented with KPIs and customized to a specific context. This portion represents the Judicial System contextualized to the province of Ontario, including the main actors, their goals, tasks performed to achieve these goals, and KPIs measuring these tasks. The figure also shows a revised importance level for each goal derived from our observations about goals and their importance in Ontario. The Ontario jurisdiction has set many important goals, including increasing access to justice, decreasing cost, and reducing delays. Based on these goals, the KPIs used to measure and monitor the impact of using the PARLe technology in that context are: (1) cost of litigation (in $), (2) time needed to successfully resolve a dispute (in days) and (3) the proportion of successfully resolved cases (in percentage).

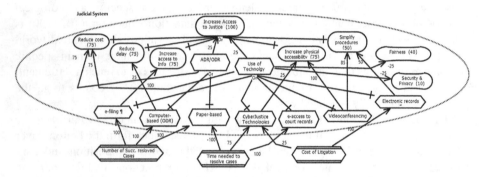

Fig. 3. The use of key performance indicators for Ontario's judicial system

Current parameters of the three indicators are summarized in Table 2. We mainly depend on documentations about several jurisdictions in Ontario (such as the Supreme Court of Canada) to obtain their values. Documents provide insights about the targeted values of litigation cost, number of successfully resolved/settled cases per month, and the time needed for dispute resolution. In addition, the worst-case situations that decision makers are trying to avoid are also obtained from these documentations. To simplify the example, only three KPIs are used here, but dozens would be needed in practice to evaluate technologies that are as complex as PARLe. Also, note that some technology aspects can be evaluated through multiple KPIs, and that one KPI can help measure multiple technology aspects.

Table 2. Key performance indicators' parameters

KPI	Target	Threshold	Worst
Cost ($)	1000	1500	2500
Time (days)	90	150	360
Cases (#/month)	80	75	30

It is worthwhile to mention here that the current evaluation value of KPIs is normalized to a satisfaction scale of 0 to 100 by the indicator. If the result is higher than 100, then it becomes 100. Normalization enables the KPI to be used like any other intentional element in a GRL model. For example, let us assume that the "cost of litigation" KPI shown in Fig. 3 have a target value of $1000, a threshold value of $1,500, a worst-case value of $2,500 and a current evaluation value of $1,300. Given these inputs, and knowing that the current evaluation value is between the target value and the threshold value, the normalization function is calculated as $|threshold-current|/|threshold-target|*100$, and the resulting satisfaction level of the KPI is 40 (|1500 −1300|/|1500−1000|*100). For other cases, however, when the current evaluation value is higher than the threshold value and lower than the worse value ($2,500), the normalization function becomes: $|threshold-current|/|worst-threshold| * (-100)$.

For the second step, and after the addition of customized KPIs, current values are computed for the KPIs (e.g., by testing the product under investigation, by measuring its performance, or by inferring values from documentation or public comments). This in turn produces satisfaction values, and then the usual GRL quantitative algorithm can be used to evaluate the impact of using the product (the PARLe platform here) on the satisfaction level of the goals connected to the KPIs. For this purpose, the generic goal model of the justice system (presented in Fig. 2) is re-illustrated in Fig. 4, but this time with the refinement (goals and new KPIs) for Ontario modeled in Fig. 3. The evaluation of one GRL strategy, where the KPIs are fed current values, is also done, leading to satisfaction values with corresponding colors.

In Fig. 4, the parameters of indicators are set according to Table 2. Calculating the current measures of indicators and feeding them to the GRL model allows us to make global assessment about how well high-level goals are met. Then, the satisfaction level of each stakeholder can be obtained from the sum of theirs goal satisfactions (weighted using the importance value of each goal). For example, Fig. 4 illustrates the result of a strategy for our example where:

- The current value of the "cost of litigation" KPI using PARLe is $900, leading to a GRL satisfaction level of 100 (as $900 is better than the $1000 target);
- The current value of the "time needed to resolve disputes" KPI using PARLe is expected to be 120 days, leading to a GRL satisfaction level of 75 (midway between the threshold and the target); and
- The current value of the "number of successfully resolved cases" KPI using PARLe in this context is estimated to be 47 case/month, leading to a GRL satisfaction level of 38 (closer to the worst case than to the threshold).

In the Eclipse-based modeling tool we use (jUCMNav), a color-coding scheme allows to highlight satisfaction levels (red for denied, yellow for neutral, and green for satisfied, with various shades for values in between).

As can be seen from the figure, running this strategy eventually leads to a weakly satisfied "Reduced delay" softgoal (22), "Increase access to information" softgoal (38) and a completely satisfied (i.e., 100) "Increased access to Justice" goal in the judicial system actor. According to Fig. 4, the following observations can also be made about the impact of using PARLe on the satisfaction of other stakeholders and their goals:

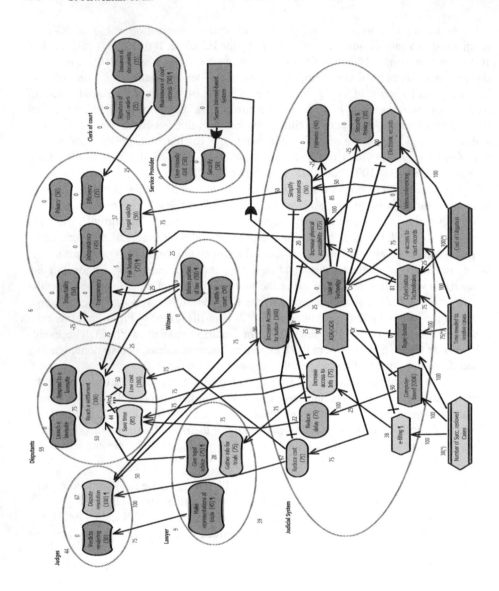

Fig. 4. Assessing the impact of selecting the PARLe platform on Ontario's judicial system (Color figure online)

1. The model indicates that disputants will find that using PARLe platform meets the threshold in terms of saving their time and money (with level of satisfaction of 50) and does a reasonable job at resolving their disputes (75).
2. Judges are weakly dissatisfied with PARLe (44), while their goal "dispute resolution" is partially satisfied (67).

3. The "Gather information for trial" softgoal of lawyers is weakly dissatisfied (28). This is because the satisfaction of this goal is affected by the satisfaction of the "Increase access to information" goal in the judicial system actor (as indicated by the contribution link).
4. Since using PARLe does not involve the physical existence of disputants and their witnesses, the goal "Fair hearing" made by courts is almost completely denied (5).
5. PARLe is meant to serve disputants resolve their problem through negotiation and/or mediation (with the use of a variety of enabling technologies such as e-filing) *before* going to courts. Therefore, the stakeholders courts, witnesses, and clerk of court are not involved in the PARLe platform. As a result, running the evaluation strategy with PARLe scores leads to a fully denied satisfaction (0) of the goals for the court, witness, and clerk of court actors. This results from evaluating PARLe on its own. Another strategy could evaluate PARLe *in combination* with existing tools or practices of the organization, to get a holistic understanding of which goals would be improved (or hurt) by the introduction of this new technology.

It is worth mentioning here that other strategies can be defined to evaluate other types of ODR technologies and find the most suitable candidate (or candidates if multiple sets of technologies are considered at once). The resulting satisfaction values of stakeholders and their goals should be used to compare different strategies and find suitable trade-offs, at the technology selection level, between PARLe and other competing ODR platforms rather than be interpreted as some sort of satisfaction percentage. Moreover, as mentioned previously, the modeler can adapt the model to the current context (e.g., a specific province) jurisdiction by changing the values of the indicator definitions, the weights of the contribution from indicators to technology options, and the importance values of the goals to their containing actor.

A limitation worth mentioning in the context of the PARLe product is that the current values of the KPIs are inferred from documentation and public comments, which are not necessarily accurate. Consequently, the satisfaction values that are computed based on these KPIs using GRL's quantitative algorithm (to evaluate the impact of using the PARLe platform on the goals connected to the KPIs) could be inaccurate as well. Better and more precise values for KPIs could be obtained by testing the PARLe platform and measuring its performance. However, this level of accuracy is not necessary here to demonstrate the feasibility of our approach.

5   Discussion

This section briefly discusses how this new approach represents a step forward compared to what currently exists, as well as the main limitations of the approach.

5.1   Contributions

This paper raises awareness about research issues related to technology selection in the context of justice systems, and pinpoints the potential opportunities for contributions associated with the use of goal-oriented requirements modeling, which goes beyond the conventional fields explored in the past. Exploiting the early analysis and evaluation capabilities of goal modeling, with GRL, we describe and evaluate the contribution of technology in justice systems. This is done through modeling technology alternatives and their contributions to the goals of different stakeholders in justice systems so as to perform trade-off analysis between the different technology options and to assure that the selected technologies are well-aligned with the needs of such systems. Our goal-oriented modeling approach contributes to justice systems stakeholders to better reason about technology selection and document the rationale of decisions taken. Furthermore, the use of KPIs helps measure goals and quality requirements with quantifiable metrics, which is one benefit of GRL over most other goal modeling languages. There are however many remaining challenges in the generalization of the approach to other cases and in its validation in practice.

5.2 Limitations and Threats to Validity

The goal models presented in this paper are constructed manually based on our interpretation and understanding of the judicial domain and the Cyberjustice literature and its surveys. In addition, the relationships (i.e., decomposition and contribution links) defined between the various components of goal models are set based on findings we observed from the literature rather than empirically. Since contribution values could have a significant positive or negative impact on linked intentional elements, we acknowledge that our work needs further validation with this regard. To obtain a more appropriate justification of contribution levels that technology has on the satisfaction of stakeholders' goals, we envision the use of group-based consensus-building approaches such as those discussed by Akhigbe et al. for GRL [1].

Moreover, the parameters of KPIs (i.e. current evaluation value, target, threshold and worst values) were concluded from the information published on judicial websites (such as Supreme Court of Canada), which are not necessarily accurate. To enhance the accuracy of such metrics, we should consult experts from the judicial domain (such as lawyers and judges) to elicit more precise values about indicators. In fact, the goal model could benefit from a rigorous stakeholder-oriented validation, as suggested in the questionnaire-based approach in [20].

In addition to model validity issues, we recognize that the example models presented in the paper illustrate concerns in particular judicial contexts in Canada, which cannot necessarily be generalized to other jurisdictions. Our literature survey was also biased towards technologies for managing low-intensity disputes, so additional sources of information would be needed to generalize the results in terms of available technologies and their impact for, say, criminal cases or constitutional cases. However, our intent in this paper was to indicate how goal-based technology selection could be beneficial in the context of justice systems and to explain how to produce useful models and analysis results, not to be complete.

6 Conclusions and Future Work

There is a need to provide the justice community with suitable requirements/modeling approaches to solve their needs (for example, technology selection). In this paper, we elaborated an approach that uses goal modeling with GRL to model both the goals of justice systems stakeholders and the alternative technological means of satisfying their needs, with an emphasis on improving access to justice through online dispute resolution.

The paper also introduced the use of Key Performance Indicators (KPI) to monitor, measure, and evaluate the technologies as part of the selection process (Fig. 1). We consider KPIs as means of measuring how well justice systems goals and performance requirements are satisfied. Feeding this type of information into goal models provides us with capabilities to analyze the contributions (or consequences) of selecting a particular technology on goals, which can be used for technology alignment thereafter.

Although our work is still preliminary and requires further validation, the models presented in the paper illustrate that the use of goal modeling with GRL for administering and evaluating the selection of technology in the context of justice systems goes beyond other conventional approaches used for technology selection. For the future, there are opportunities, using goal models, to support aspects of justice systems other than technology selection. Furthermore, successful approaches for technology selection could be validated and generalized for jurisdictions other than just Canada. Finally, the use of fuzzy logic could be investigated in the context of goal models [9] in order to determine if this could help cope with some of the arbitrariness of the models and values used in our context.

Acknowledgements. This work was supported by the *Towards Cyberjustice* project, funded by Canada's SSHRC Major Collaborative Research Initiative program. We also thank Jane Bailey for her support and for useful discussions.

References

1. Akhigbe, O., Alhaj, M., Amyot, D., Badreddin, O., Braun, E., Cartwright, N., Richards, G., Mussbacher, G.: Creating quantitative goal models: governmental experience. In: Yu, E., Dobbie, G., Jarke, M., Purao, S. (eds.) ER 2014. LNCS, vol. 8824, pp. 466–473. Springer, Cham (2014). doi:10.1007/978-3-319-12206-9_40
2. Alleweldt, F., et al.: Cross-border alternative dispute resolution in the european union. Directorate-General for Internal Policies, European Parliament, IP/A/IMCO/ST/2010-15 PE464.424 (2011). http://www.europarl.europa.eu/meetdocs/2009_2014/documents/imco/dv/adr_study_/adr_study_en.pdf. Last Accessed 24 Jan 2017
3. Alwidian, S.A., Amyot, D.: Towards systems for increased access to justice using goal modeling. In: Eight International Workshop on Requirements Engineering and Law (RELAW 2015), pp. 33–36. IEEE CS (2015). doi:10.1109/RELAW.2015.7330209

4. Amyot, D., Shamsaei, A., Kealey, J., Tremblay, E., Miga, A., Mussbacher, G., Alhaj, M., Tawhid, R., Braun, E., Cartwright, N.: Towards Advanced Goal Model Analysis with jUCMNav. In: Castano, S., Vassiliadis, P., Lakshmanan, Laks V., Lee, M.L. (eds.) ER 2012. LNCS, vol. 7518, pp. 201–210. Springer, Heidelberg (2012). doi:10.1007/978-3-642-33999-8_25

5. Aranda, G.N., Vizcaino, A., Echich, A., Piattini, M.: Technology selection to improve global collaboration. In: International Conference on Global Software Engineering (ICGSE 2006), pp. 223–232. IEEE CS (2006). doi:10.1109/ICGSE.2006.261236

6. Ayala, C., Franch, X.: A goal-oriented strategy for supporting commercial off-the-shelf components selection. In: Morisio, M. (ed.) ICSR 2006. LNCS, vol. 4039, pp. 1–15. Springer, Heidelberg (2006). doi:10.1007/11763864_1

7. Bailey, J.: Reopening law's gate: public interest standing and access to justice. UBC Law Rev. 44, 255–285 (2011). https://ssrn.com/abstract=2279632. Last Accessed 24 Jan 2017

8. Bailey, J.: Digitization of court processes in Canada. Working Paper no. 2, Cyberjustice Laboratory, Canada, 23 October 2012. http://www.cyberjustice.ca/files/sites/102/WP002_CanadaDigitizationOfCourtProcesses20121023.pdf. Last Accessed 24 Jan 2017

9. Baresi, L., Pasquale, L., Spoletini, P.: Fuzzy goals for requirements-driven adaptation. In: Proceedings of the 18th IEEE International Requirements Engineering Conference, pp. 125–134. IEEE CS (2010). doi:10.1109/RE.2010.25

10. Benyekhlef, K., Amar, E., Callipel, V.: ICT-driven strategies for reforming access to justice mechanisms in developing Countries. World Bank Leg. Rev. 6, 325–343 (2015). doi:10.1596/978-1-4648-0378-9_ch15

11. Benyekhlef, K., Callipel, V., Amar, E.: La médiation en ligne pour les conflits de basse intensité. Gazette du Palais 87, 17–22 (2015)

12. Bridenback, M.L.: Study of state trial courts use of remote technology. NAPCO, Final report, April 2016. http://napco4courtleaders.org/wp-content/uploads/2016/08/Emerging-Court-Technologies-9-27-Bridenback.pdf. Last Accessed 27 Jan 2017

13. Brown, S.: Standardized technology evaluation process (step) user's guide and methodology for evaluation teams. Mitre Corporation (2007). http://www2.mitre.org/work/sepo/toolkits/STEP/files/StepUsersGuide_09.pdf. Last Accessed 17 Jan 2017

14. Cares, C., Franch, X.: 3MSF: a framework to select mobile office devices. Int. J. Comput. Sci. Appl. 6(5), 121–144 (2009)

15. Chan, F.T.S., Chan, M.H., Tang, N.K.H.: Evaluation methodologies for technology selection. J. Mater. Process. Technol. 107(1–3), 330–337 (2000). doi:10.1016/S0924-0136(00)00679-8

16. eJury, L.L.C.: eJury – the online trial experience. http://www.ejury.com. Last Accessed 24 Jan 2017

17. Ghanavati, S., Amyot, D., Peyton, L.: A systematic review of goal-oriented requirements management frameworks for business process compliance. In: 4th International Workshop on Requirements Engineering and Law (RELAW), pp. 25–34. IEEE CS (2011). doi:10.1109/RELAW.2011.6050270

18. Ghanavati, S., Amyot, D., Rifaut, A., Dubois, E.: Goal-oriented compliance with multiple regulations. In: 22nd IEEE International Requirements Engineering Conference (RE 2014), pp. 73–82. IEEE CS (2014). doi:10.1109/RE.2014.6912249

19. Grance, T., Stevens, M., Myers, M.: Guide to selecting information technology security products. Recommendations of the National Institute of Standards and Technology, NIST Special Publication 800-36 (2003). http://nvlpubs.nist.gov/nistpubs/Legacy/SP/nistspecialvpublication800-36.pdf. Last Accessed 17 Jan 2017

20. Hassine, J., Amyot, D.: A questionnaire-based survey methodology for systematically validating goal-oriented models. Requirements Eng. **21**(2), 285–308 (2016). doi:10.1007/s00766-015-0221-7. Springer
21. Houseman, O., Tiwari, A., Roy, R.: A methodology for the selection of new technologies in the aviation industry. Decision Engineering Report Series. Cranfield University, UK (2004)
22. Ingolfo, S., Jureta, I., Siena, A., Perini, A., Susi, A.: Nòmos 3: legal compliance of roles and requirements. In: Yu, E., Dobbie, G., Jarke, M., Purao, S. (eds.) ER 2014. LNCS, vol. 8824, pp. 275–288. Springer, Cham (2014). doi:10.1007/978-3-319-12206-9_22
23. ISO/IEC: ISO/IEC 14102:2008, Information technology – Guideline for the evaluation and selection of CASE tools (2008)
24. ITU-T, Recommendation Z.151 (10/12): User Requirements Notation (URN) - Language Definition, Geneva, Switzerland (2012). http://www.itu.int/rec/T-REC-Z.151/en
25. Katsh, E., Rifkin, J.: Online Dispute Resolution: Resolving Conflicts in Cyberspace. Jossey-Bass, Wiley (2001)
26. Kaufmann-Kohler, G., Schultz, T.: Online Dispute Resolution: Challenges for Contemporary Justice. Kluwer Law International, The Hague (2004)
27. Lamb, M., Gregory M.J.: Industrial concerns in technology selection. In: Portland International Conference on Management of Engineering and Technology (PICMET 1997), pp. 206–212. IEEE CS (1997). doi:10.1109/PICMET.1997.653333
28. MacCoun, R.J., Lind, E.A., Tyler, T.R.: Alternative dispute resolution in trial and appellate courts. In: Kagehiro, D.K., Laufer, W.S. (eds.) Handbook of Psychology and Law, Part 2, pp. 95–118. Springer, New York, (1992). doi:10.1007/978-1-4757-4038-7_6
29. Maeno, Y., Nitta, K., Ohsawa, Y.: Reflective visualization of dispute resolution. In: IEEE SMC 2009, pp. 1698–1703. IEEE CS (2009). doi:10.1109/ICSMC.2009.5346821
30. Mussbacher, G., Ghanavati, S., Amyot, D.: Modeling and analysis of urn goals and scenarios with jUCMNav. In: 17th IEEE International Requirements Engineering Conference (RE 2009), pp. 383–384. IEEE CS (2009). doi:10.1109/RE.2009.56. http://softwareengineering.ca/jucmnav/
31. Ondrus, J., Bui, T., Pigneur, Y.: A multi-actor, multi-criteria approach for technology selection when designing mobile information systems. In: Krogstie, J., Kautz, K., Allen, D. (eds.) MOBIS 2005. ITIFIP, vol. 191, pp. 271–278. Springer, Boston, MA (2005). doi:10.1007/0-387-31166-1_19
32. Pourshahid, A., Chen, P., Amyot, D., Forster, A.J., Ghanavati, S., Peyton, L., Weiss, M.: Business process management with the user requirements notation. Electron. Commer. Res. **9**(4), 269–316 (2009). doi:10.1007/s10660-009-9039-z. Springer US
33. Supreme Court of Canada: R. v. Jordan, 2016 SCC 27. http://scc-csc.lexum.com/scc-csc/scc-csc/en/item/16060/index.do. Last Accessed 17 Jan 2017
34. Senécal, F., Benyekhlef, K.: Groundwork for assessing the legal risks of cyberjustice. Can. J. Law Technol. **7**(1), 41–56 (2009)
35. Shehabuddeen, N., Probert, D., Phaal, R.: From theory to practice: challenges in operationalizing a technology selection framework. Technovation **26**(3), 324–335 (2006). doi:10.1016/j.technovation.2004.10.017
36. Tawhid, R., Alhaj, M., Mussbacher, G., Braun, E., Cartwright, N., Shamsaei, A., Amyot, D., Behnam, S.A., Richards, G.: Towards outcome-based regulatory compliance in aviation security. In: 20th IEEE International Requirements Engineering Conference (RE 2012), pp. 267–272. IEEE CS (2012). doi:10.1109/RE.2012.6345813
37. Tan, K.H., Noble, J., Sato, Y., Tse, Y.K.: A marginal analysis guided technology evaluation and selection. Int. J. Prod. Econ. **131**(1), 15–21 (2011). doi:10.1016/j.ijpe.2010.09.027
38. Tyler, T.: Access to justice a 'basic right'. The Toronto Star, Canada, 12 August 2007. http://www.thestar.com/News/Canada/article/245548

39. UNCITRAL: Working Group III, Online Dispute Resolution. United Nations Commission on International Trade Law, Vienna, Austria (2016). http://www.uncitral.org/uncitral/commission/working_groups/3Online_Dispute_Resolution.html
40. van den Herik, J.: Towards crowd sourced online dispute resolution. J. Int. Commercial Technol. **7**(2), 99–111 (2012)
41. VirtualJury™. http://www.virtualjury.com

Data Analytics and Machine Learning

An OLAP Rule Environment for Reactive Performance Monitoring

Katherine Chengli and Liam Peyton(⊠)

University of Ottawa, Ottawa, Canada
katchengli@gmail.com, lpeyton@uottawa.ca

Abstract. Organizations are increasingly focused on using data to make their operational business processes more intelligent and reactive. Reactive performance monitoring consists of automating strategic decisions into rule-based actions when appropriate. Often there is a response gap, where there is unnecessary latency or missing detail, as the mapping between the strategic, the operational and the analytical is complex, labor intensive and not clearly defined. This paper presents an OLAP-modeled rule environment that leverages Complex Event Processing (CEP), multi-dimensionally modeled On-line Analytical Processing (OLAP) databases and Business Process Management (BPM) to provide reactive performance monitoring. We use two case studies to evaluate our proposed architecture for an OLAP-modeled rule environment. The first case study prototyped the environment using IBM PMQ, while the second prototyped the environment using QuickForms and a custom-built OLAP rule engine. Predictive modeling, traditional rule engines, and our OLAP rule engine are compared in terms of their support for reactive performance monitoring.

Keywords: Performance monitoring · Rule engines · Complex Event Processing · Business Process Management · Predictive modeling · OLAP

1 Introduction

Organizations are increasingly focused on using data to make their operational business processes more intelligent and reactive. Reactive performance monitoring [1] consists of automating strategic decisions into rule-based actions when appropriate. In any organization, there is a strategic level where the business goals that the organization wishes to achieve are determined by senior executives. As shown in Fig. 1, actions are directed at the operational level to achieve those strategic goals. At the same time, actions are directed at the analytic level to log operational events as data and runs reports to measure how well the operational is performing. The analytical provides feedback to the strategic level to determine what actions might be needed operationally to improve performance. The question mark dashed line indicates an opportunity for reactive performance monitoring to close the "response gap" by triggering an operational response in situations where the interaction between the strategic, the operational and the analytical is well understood [2] and can be replaced with an automated rule-based response.

© Springer International Publishing AG 2017
E. Aïmeur et al. (Eds.): MCETECH 2017, LNBIP 289, pp. 205–212, 2017.
DOI: 10.1007/978-3-319-59041-7_12

Fig. 1. Reactive performance monitoring

There are several approaches to reactive performance monitoring in the literature. An application meta-model for healthcare process monitoring was proposed that maps operational events to performance metrics using business rules to infer transitions between process states [3, 4]. However, there was no attempt to define appropriate actions that could be taken in response to poor performance (e.g. a patient is waiting too long). In other work, predictive modeling [5] is used to analyze event data and predict when actions are needed. And complex event processing (CEP) has been used to process operational event data with rules to infer when complex events have occurred and trigger actions [6]. Business process management (BPM) is a technology to automate online business processes [7] that could be triggered as actions. Most rule engines used in complex event processing are based on simple object models that are independent of the rich multidimensional OLAP databases used in the analytical layer [8] even though there has been work on streaming event data into OLAP databases in real-time [9]. This paper demonstrates how an OLAP-modeled rule environment can provide a better framework for reactive performance monitoring.

2   OLAP-Modeled Rule Environment

As shown in Fig. 2, our OLAP-modeled Rule Environment is composed of 4 main components: Operational Event Sources, Analytical Data Warehouse, a Rule Environment that mediates between them, and Actions that can be invoked for automated feedback between the analytical and the operational. Fact Events are received from Operational Event Sources by the Application Management module in the Rule Environment and logged in dimensional fact tables in the Analytical Data Warehouse by a Data Access Object (DAO) module. The Application Management module also forwards the Fact Events in parallel to one or more Rule Engine modules for processing. The Rule Engine can make Conditional Queries against any OLAP Database in the Analytical Data Warehouse to determine how to react to the Fact Events it is receiving. A Condition Query returns a Facts Set which the Rule Engine can use to generate Reports that it sends as notification messages to trigger operational Actions.

The OLAP-modeled Rule Environment addresses the opportunity shown in Fig. 1. The Analytical Data Warehouse contains all the data that the analytical uses to

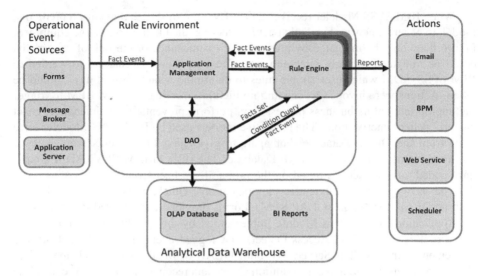

Fig. 2. OLAP-modeled rule environment.

understand the operational. An OLAP Database is dimensionally modeled to optimize it for reporting and analysis, so that Fact Events are stored in Fact Tables linked to Measures (like Cost and Duration) and Dimensions (like Date, Location, Age, Gender, Diagnosis, Procedure) [14].

The Operational Event Sources provide data from the operational to the analytical, and the Actions automate feedback from the analytical to the operational, by-passing the strategic, when the appropriate response can be encoded in business rules. Operational Event Sources can be: Forms filled by people; a Message Broker that forwards Fact Events; or an Application Server that sends Fact Events directly to the Rule Environment. Possible Actions which can receive Reports sent as notification messages include: Email sent directly to an operational person for action; BPM to trigger a business process that acts based on the Report; a Web Service interface that can be used as a gateway to trigger any service; and a Scheduler that can be used to schedule an Action or schedule the generation of a future internal Fact Event in the Rule Environment (this is represented by the dashed line from the Rule Engine module to the Application Management module).

3 Case Studies

We used two case studies to evaluate our proposed OLAP-modeled rule environment. The first case study prototyped the environment using IBM PMQ [12] (which bundles several IBM products). A Message broker implemented by IBM Integration Bus provided Fact Events (from sensors or user inputs) to an Application Management Module implemented by IBM SPSS C&D which logged events to an OLAP Database implemented in IBM DB2. There were two Rule Engines: a predictive engine implemented by IBM SPSS Modeler and a CEP engine implemented by IBM SPSS ADM.

When IBM SPSS Modeler receives a Fact Event, it evaluates it against a predictive model, to generate new probabilistic Fact Events (e.g. the likelihood of large equipment failure that could be mitigated by preventative maintenance or the risk of cancer that could be mitigated by early interventions). These new Fact Events are forwarded to IBM SPSS ADM which uses simple rules to determine what action, if any, should be taken. Actions were invoked by sending notification messages to IBM BPM to trigger the appropriate online business process (e.g. perform preventative maintenance, enact an early patient intervention). The predictive models used by IBM SPSS Modeler were built from the OLAP Database, but apart from logging Fact Events there was no real-time interaction with the OLAP Database. The rules in IBM SPSS ADM simply hard-coded possible actions based on the probabilistic Fact Events.

The second case study extended the open source QuickForms framework [10, 11] with an OLAP rule engine (OLAP RPM). Forms provided user-entered Fact Events to an Application Management Module implemented by the QuickForms Server which has a built-in DAO (Data Access Object) that logged events to an OLAP Database implemented in MS SQL Server. We built OLAP RPM to interact with the OLAP Database in real-time to make a Condition Query and receive a Facts Set in return. The Facts Set was used to generate reports that could be sent to trigger actions (e.g. notify someone of the need to perform preventative maintenance or enact an early patient intervention) via an Email Service or a Web Service. We also prototyped a Scheduler that could schedule actions or generate internal Fact Events (e.g. do not sent emails continuously for routine actions, but schedule them to be sent at specific times on specific days).

We also looked at two different examples of reactive performance monitoring. The first was typical of the applications supported by IBM PMQ while the second was typical of the applications supported by QuickForms. The first example was the detection of patients with a higher risk of cancer recurrence to improve the timeliness of doctor visits. More specifically, we needed rules to start the cancer recurrence hospital process for all patients whose risk of recurrence was higher than 60%. For example, if IBM SPSS Modeler received repeated high blood pressure Fact Events for Olivia who was 54, female, and overweight, it would generate a probabilistic Fact Event for cancer recurrence with a risk of 62%. When IBM SPSS ADM received this event it would determine what action should be taken by sending IBM BPM a notification message to trigger a cancer recurrence business process for Olivia.

1. BloodPressureEvent
        in - > IBMSPSS Prediction Model - > out

                                        CancerRecurrenceRiskEvent

2. IF CancerRecurrenceRiskEvent > 60%
        THEN CancerRecurrenceBusinessProcess

At first glance, the QuickForms rule environment cannot duplicate the IBM PMQ functionality because it does not have a predictive engine. However, similar function-ality can be approximated using the OLAP RPM rule engine, if one analyzes the predictive model used in IBM PMQ and characterizes the patterns used by the predictive model. After all health care professionals would want to understand the basis for

IBM PMQ recommendations. For example, one could characterize that patients who are female, middle-aged (age > 50), over-weight (BMI > 30) and have an elevated blood pressure 3 weeks in a row have a risk of cancer that should be treated proactively. Such a characterization could be formulated as a FemaleAtRisk QueryCondition that returned a Facts Set of all women in the OLAP DB matching the condition. Then, we could have a scheduled internal Fact Event, which triggered a rule to notify the person's physician:

1. Every Sunday at 3am:
      generate FemaleReportReminderEvent
2. IF SendFemaleReportReminderEvent and QueryCondition (FemaleAtRisk)
      THEN For each Female in FemaleAtRisk :

      SendEmail (CancerRecurrenceCase, Female)

Clearly, this would not be as optimal or as dynamic as the IBM RPM rule. However, for many applications (including this health care example), it would be sufficient and more easily understood, maintained and updated as new medical research was done.

In our second example, the QuickForms environment was used to proactively inform women from at risk populations of the progress of their pregnancy on a weekly basis by reminding them to review the content in a pregnancy coach app for the current week of their pregnancy. For example, if Amelia's due date is October 18th, then, on August 16th, send Amelia an email reminder with a link to week 31 content. This was achieved by defining a DueDate QueryCondition that could be run daily to return all women whose due date was on that day of the week and calculate how many weeks pregnant each woman was.

1. Every Day at 3am:
      SendEmailReminderEvent
2. If SendEmailReminderEvent and QueryCondition(DueDate):
      THEN For each Female in DueDate :

      SendEmails (WeeklyReminder, Female)

The DueDate Facts Set has the following fields: Name, Email, Due Date, and Week. If the rule condition passes, the action "SendEmails" is enacted. This action simply consists of sending an Email for every Female in the DueDate Facts set using the "WeeklyReminder" Email template. For example:

"Hello [Name],
Since your due date is [Due Date],
here is your weekly content associated with week [Week] of your pregnancy:
      http://www.example.com/week[Week]"

Unfortunately, because the IBM PMQ implementation does not interact with the OLAP DB in real-time (no support for Query Conditions) and does not have support for a Scheduler, there is no easy way for it to support this type of reactive performance monitoring. In theory, IBM SPSS Modeler could be trained with data to know when to send such Emails. Presumably, this is possible, if a few weeks' worth of emails had already been sent manually, but this seems unnecessarily awkward.

4 Evaluation

Using our two case studies and two examples of reactive performance monitoring, we have found our proposed architecture for an OLAP-modeled rule environment effective. However, we struggled to use existing predictive modeling and CEP rule engines in IBM PMQ to achieve all the desired functionality, so we build our own RPM OLAP rule engine as an extension to QuickForms.

Figure 3 below compares the different types of rule engines we investigated: IBM SPSS ADM, IBM SPSS Modeler, Drools, and our custom built rule engine RPM OLAP. Drools [13] is an open source rule engine similar in functionality to IBM SPSS ADM, which we investigated after the case studies were completed. Rather than building a complete new rule engine on our own, it seemed worthwhile to investigate if there was an extendible open source rule engine that might be a suitable starting point for building a fully featured RPM OLAP.

Criteria	IBM SPSS ADM	IBM SPSS Modeler	Drools	RPM OLAP
Open Source	No	No	Yes	Yes
Actions	No	No	Extendible	Yes
Scheduled	No	No	Yes	Yes
OLAP	No	Yes	No	Yes
Predictive	No	Yes	No	No

Fig. 3. Comparison of rule engines

There were five criteria we considered in evaluating the rule engines. First, it was important that a rule engine be open source so that we could experiment with enhanced support for reactive performance monitoring based on our architecture for OLAP-modeled rule environments. Both of the IBM rule engines were not open source but Drools and RPM OLAP rule engine were.

Second, it was important that the rule engines supported direct invocation of actions to automate immediate feedback from the analytical to the operational. Both of the IBM rule engines did not have direct support for actions. They simply generated facts with certain probabilities based on a prediction model (IBM SPSS Modeler) or inferred facts based on rules (IBM SPSS ADM). We had to extend IBM PMQ with a custom BPM integration module that mapped inferred facts (e.g. CancerRecurrenceBusinessProcess) to the actual invocation of IBM BPM to launch the associated business process. In RPM OLAP we provided a library of functions to support actions for Email, Web Service and Schedule, that could be incorporated directly into the rules so that actions could be invoked directly without any specialized coding. Drools does not currently ship with such a library of functions, but it is extendible and we could provide a similar library of functions just like we did in RPM OLAP.

The third criterion is the ability to schedule facts. Both the IBM SPSS ADM and the IBM SPSS Modeler do not have this capability at all and would have to depend on an external action or other operational event source to schedule something. Drools has integrated scheduling capabilities as does RPM OLAP.

The fourth criterion was a key focus of this research: real-time integration of OLAP Databases to provide full support for complete feedback from the analytical to the operational. This is fully supported by RPM OLAP. For IBM SPSS ADM and Drools, there is no direct support for OLAP Databases. Since Drools is open source, it would be possible to provide a library of functions for Query Conditions as is supported by RPM OLAP. However, Drools does not have a built-in DAO module which would be needed to log Fact Events and execute Query Conditions, so this would have to be added to Drools as well. IBM SPSS modeler is highly integrated with OLAP, logging events and building its predictive models based on the Fact Events stored in the OLAP Database. However, the predictive models are not updated in real-time, nor is there any support for Query Conditions that return a Facts Set.

Finally, only SPSS Modeler supports predictive modeling. This is a very sophisticated feature that is very useful for reactive performance monitoring. Because predictive modeling is quite different from both traditional CEP and our concept of an OLAP rule engine, it is important that our architecture for OLAP-modeled rule environment allow for multiple rule engines of different types. More work is needed to better understand how to integrate these different technologies.

5 Conclusions

We have preliminary results that demonstrate the viability of reactive performance monitoring using our proposed OLAP-modeled rule environment to close the response gap between the analytical and the operational. It provides automated logging and monitoring of operational events as they occur with the full analytic power of OLAP databases available to interpret the events and generate notification messages when appropriate to trigger immediate operational actions in response. More case studies for different types of reactive performance monitoring are still needed to fully evaluate the architecture. We have, however, identified a coherent set of features that should be incorporated into rule engines to better support reactive performance modeling including built-in support for triggering actions and real-time interaction with OLAP databases. Future work is also needed to better understand how to integrate predictive modeling, CEP, and OLAP in this context as well.

References

1. Chenglie, K.: A Reactive Performance Monitoring Framework, Thesis, University of Ottawa (2016). https://www.ruor.uottawa.ca/handle/10393/34839. Last accessed March 2017
2. Barone, D., Peyton, L., Rizzolo, F., Amyot, D., Mylopoulos, J., Badreddin, O.: Model-based management of strategic initiatives. J. Data Semant. 4(3), 149–165 (2015)
3. Mata, P., Baarah, A., Kuziemsky, C., Peyton, L.: An application meta-model for community care. Procedia Comput. Sci. 37, 465–472 (2014). doi:10.1016/j.procs.2014.08.070

4. Baraah, A., Badreddin, O., Mouttham, A., Peyton, L.: An application meta-model for real-time monitoring of care processes. Int. J. Adv. Comput. Sci. **4**(5), 203–213 (2014)

5. zur Mühlen, M., Shapiro, R.: Business Process Analytics. In: vom Brocke, J., Rosemann, M. (eds.) Handbook on Business Process Management 2. International Handbooks on Information Systems, pp. 137–157. Springer, Heidelberg (2010)

6. Luckham, D.C.: First Concepts in Event Processing. Event Processing for Business: Organizing the Real Time Strategy Enterprise, pp. 49–76. Wiley, Hoboken (2012)

7. van der Aalst, W.M.P.: Business process management: a comprehensive survey. ISRN Softw Eng. **2013**, 1–37 (2013)

8. Abdelfattah, M.: A comparison of several performance dashboards architectures. Intell. Inf. Manag. **5**(2), 35–41 (2013)

9. Costa, J., Cecílio, J., Martins, P., Furtado, P.: Blending OLAP processing with real-time data streams. In: Yu, J.X., Kim, M.H., Unland, R. (eds.) DASFAA 2011. LNCS, vol. 6588, pp. 446–449. Springer, Heidelberg (2011). doi:10.1007/978-3-642-20152-3_36

10. QuickForms (uOttawa). QuickForms Wiki. https://github.com/uoForms/quickforms3/wiki. Accessed March 2017

11. Mata, P., Chamney, A., Viner, G., Archibald, D., Peyton, L.: A development framework for mobile healthcare monitoring apps. Pers. Ubiquit. Comput. **19**(3), 623–633 (2015). Elsevier

12. Noller, D., Rajasekharan, A., Peters, P.: IBM Predictive Maintenance and Quality. IBM Redbooks Solution Guide (2014). http://www.redbooks.ibm.com/abstracts/tips1130.html. Accessed March 2017

13. Drools. Drools Business Rules Management System. http://www.drools.org. Accessed March 2017

14. Kimball, R., Ross, M.: The Data Warehouse Toolkit: The Complete Guide to Dimensional Modeling, 3rd edn. John Wiley & Sons, Hoboken (2013)

Supervised Methods to Support Online Scientific Data Triage

Hayda Almeida[1], Marc Queudot[1], Leila Kosseim[2], and Marie-Jean Meurs[1(✉)]

[1] Université du Québec à Montréal, Montreal, QC, Canada
meurs.marie-jean@uqam.ca
[2] Concordia University, Montreal, QC, Canada

Abstract. This paper presents machine learning approaches based on supervised methods applied to triage of health and biomedical data. We discuss the applications of such approaches in three different tasks, and evaluate the usage of triage pipelines, as well as data sampling and feature selection methods to improve performance on each task. The scientific data triage systems are based on a generic and light pipeline, and yet flexible enough to perform triage on distinct data. The presented approaches were developed to be integrated as a part of web-based systems, providing real time feedback to health and biomedical professionals. All systems are publicly available as open-source.

1 Introduction

Scientific data processing is a very important and often critical step in the routine of life science practitioners. In certain cases, the ability to find crucial information quickly can be decisive to help patients, or to avoid bottlenecks in the scientific research workflow. Health care and biomedical professionals can make use of many online data sources, which can provide them with essential information. For example, scientific researchers constantly rely on online literature databases to support their work, while health care professionals have the opportunity of following up closely on patient conditions through their interactions on health forum posts. Going through these large sets of data to fetch critical pieces of information can be overwhelming. Systems that perform scientific data triage automatically can therefore be a powerful tool for health and biomedical professionals, since they can help with identifying relevant information faster in large datasets. Additionally, the automatic triage when integrated in web-based systems, can provide a data relevance feedback in real time for life-science professionals.

In this paper, we present three automatic approaches based on supervised machine learning to perform scientific data triage. Supervised methods make use of relevant data that was previously labeled by the subject experts to derive a pattern, used as a model. This model is applied to predict the relevance of new data that needs to be analyzed. We present three supervised learning approaches for automatic triage of biomedical and health data, that are suitable for web-based systems. First, we describe an approach to select scientific

© Springer International Publishing AG 2017
E. Aïmeur et al. (Eds.): MCETECH 2017, LNBIP 289, pp. 213–221, 2017.
DOI: 10.1007/978-3-319-59041-7_13

literature related to fungal enzymes that can be used in bioproduct conversion processes. Second, an approach to support scientific literature screening for HIV systematic reviews is described. Finally, we present an on-going project to predict the severity of user posts in the ReachOut mental health forum. These approaches were developed using open access data, and are based on light and generic methods. Their design allow for their usage on various data, as well as their integration in online platforms.

2 Related Work

Systems developed to support health and biomedical practitioners are important tools to help dealing with large amounts of scientific data in a responsive and efficient manner [8,15]. Health and biomedical data available online represent a highly valuable, often essential, resource in the routine of science professionals and researchers [9,14].

Data triage systems can assist these professionals in acquiring knowledge from scientific data, allowing them to save time, scale up their work, and reduce bottlenecks in their knowledge discovery or response workflow [16,20]. More importantly, health and biomedical triage tools can be decisive to keep up with the quick pace of scientific research, and the need of timely responses in health care when data are found in online platforms. Studies have investigated several approaches to better performing scientific data triage. Machine learning methods have been applied to handle large biological datasets [21], sort scientific literature in systematic review workflows [5,21], help identify mental health issues [18], and recognize user sentiments [19]. Previous works have evaluated the importance of integrating intelligent systems to web-based environments to assist scientific data processing. Their applications are numerous, such as heart disease automatic classification [17], literature mining [12], or even finding patterns in bioimages [10]. In this context, specific strategies to process data can be substantially beneficial for integrating supervised learning methods into online platforms. Methods such as data sampling [7] and feature selection [11] have been shown to reduce the computational cost of learning tasks, while still maintaining or even improving performance [4,22].

Here, we describe the methods implemented to tackle the scientific data triage in three different tasks, using supervised machine learning, data sampling and feature selection. The approaches were developed to be integrated in web-based systems.

3 Proposed Triage Approaches

We describe here three approaches proposed to handle the task of health and biomedical data triage. The tasks presented are (1) *Discovery of fungal enzymes*, (2) *HIV systematic review*, and (3) *Response urgency of mental health forum posts*. These approaches were developed to meet the specific requirements of each application, such as utilizing the most fitting feature set, and handling different data inputs. However, the presented systems are based on a generic pipeline and architecture. This allows them to be used in other applications and domains. Such approaches can not only be applied in tasks handling data regarding new topics, but can also be easily integrated in online and real-time systems.

The pipeline of the data triage systems is based on a supervised machine learning approach, which is divided in two phases: training and testing. Before being able to provide relevance predictions for new data, the triage systems have to be trained based on manually labeled corpora. Documents in the training corpora were labeled according to their relevance for health and biomedical practitioners, given a certain topic. In task (1), documents were labeled as either *positive* or *negative*. In task (2), documents were labeled as either *included* or *excluded*. For these cases, *positive* or *included* documents were the ones of potential interest. In task (3), documents were labeled as *crisis*, *red*, *amber* or *green*, to indicate the urgency of a forum moderator to intervene. After being trained, the systems are capable of outputting predictions for new data. The data triage systems presented here were applied in different tasks. However their architecture follows the same pipeline, divided into four lightweight and generic main modules:

Data Handling: this module is responsible for processing the data, by handling all input documents, labeled or unlabeled. During this step, selected content from documents is gathered, after going through normalization processes.

Feature Extraction: at this step, discriminative features are extracted from the training data. Multiple feature extraction methods can be applied, and they can be used in an combined manner, creating a feature set. The usage of different features yields distinct performances depending on the task subject. Additionally, features can also go through a filtering process, where feature selection algorithms are used to identify which features seem more discriminative for a given task.

Model Building: this module represents the task data in terms of the feature set chosen. At this step, a model is generated after processing the features representing the data, using a classification algorithm. The model generated by the training data and selected feature set is what provides knowledge to the triage systems, since it depicts the underlying pattern in the task data.

Document Predictor: the prediction module relies on the model generated by the *Model Building* module. Once new unlabeled input data are represented in the same manner as the training data (using the same feature set), the triage systems make use of the generated model to output relevance predictions regarding these new data.

The data triage approaches can be easily integrated in online platforms, and provide real-time feedback for new input data. Each triage system was incorporated in web-based applications, to support professionals in going through large volumes of health and biomedical data. In the following Sections, we provide further details regarding the approach adopted in each of the three triage tasks.

3.1 Discovery of Fungal Enzymes

The task of discovering fungal enzymes [2] aimed at selecting relevant literature to support the identification of fungal enzymes used in industrial processes. To identify the most fitting set-up for this task, over 100 classification models were designed and evaluated, using 4 feature settings, 3 supervised learning algorithms, and 9 differently balanced corpora.

The feature settings were composed of Enzyme Commission (EC) numbers, Bag-of-Words (BOW) representation of the document content, and annotated bio-entities, which were extracted from documents with the help of the mycoMINE [13] annotation tool. The different corpora were generated based on a data sampling technique, applied to study the usage of corpora with more equally balanced class distributions. The three algorithms used in this task were Naïve Bayes (NB), Logistic Model Trees (LMT), and Support Vector Machine (SVM).

The system for discovery of fungal enzymes was created to be integrated with the Proxiris [6] web-based tool, which supports scientific data mining by identifying entities of interest in web literature. Combining both approaches facilitates the discovery process of candidate fungal enzymes, since users can visualize entities of interest in the literature, and have a relevance prediction about the whole document in real-time.

3.2 HIV Systematic Review

The process of systematic reviews entails finding studies that can answer a given research problem. The HIV systematic review triage [3] was developed to support researchers working on the SHARE[1] database in identifying potentially relevant literature.

Over 100 classification models were analyzed to identify the most appropriate configuration to address the problem, using 3 feature types, 2 feature selection methods, 5 differently balanced corpora, and 3 classification algorithms: NB, LMT, and SVM.

The different corpora used in this task were also generated based on sampling techniques, to analyze the results of training based on various class distributions. The feature sets were composed of different combinations of a BOW representation of the document content, SHARE experts selected keywords, and Medical Subject Headings[2] (MeSH) terms found in documents. Two methods were used to filter out features according to their discriminative power, : Inverse Document Frequency (IDF) and Odds Ratio (OR).

The HIV systematic reviews triage was designed to be integrated in the SHARE web-based tool, to help researchers in the process of quickly determining if new documents should be reviewed by SHARE curators.

---

[1] http://www.hivevidence.ca.
[2] https://www.ncbi.nlm.nih.gov/mesh.

3.3   Response Urgency of Mental Health Forum Posts

The third system, for triage of mental health forum posts [1], was developed for the CLPsych Shared Task[3]. The goal of the system is to guide forum moderators to quickly assess the response urgency required from a post, given the content that the user has posted.

A specific normalization method was created to handle the forum data. User posts contained images, URLs, and emoticons, which were replaced by a corresponding word, since they could be helpful to indicate the sentiment related to a post.

The feature set used in this task was made of bigrams (consecutive word pairs), Part-of-Speech (POS) tags, and sentiments. The vocabulary of two sentiment libraries was selected to annotate post sentiments, while the POSTaggerAnnotator[4] was used to annotate POS tags in posts. All feature types were filtered using a Correlation-based Feature Selection (CFS).

The automatic classification of posts was performed by Bayesian Network (BN), Sequential Minimal Optimization (SMO), and LMT algorithms. A rule-based classification method was merged with the automatic classification output to finally provide risk predictions for each post. The rules were based on a discriminative vocabulary selected from the least represented (and more urgent) post labels: *red* and *crisis*.

One of the CLPsych task interests is to integrate the proposed techniques in the web forum ReachOut[5], so forum moderators can assess in real time if user posts need to be treated urgently.

4   Experimental Results

We present here the summary of results for each of the three tasks described in this paper. Since over 100 models were evaluated for some of these tasks, we will only present the models that yielded the best performances, in addition to an explanation of the best result obtained on each triage.

Discovery of Fungal Enzymes. The experiments ran for the discovery of fungal enzymes (see Sect. 3.1) evaluated the usage of different balance ratios for the training corpora (using various ratios of *positive* labeled documents), classification algorithms, and feature combinations.

The performance is shown for the least represented *positive* label. Table 1 shows that the best results were achieved with training corpora presenting a balanced distribution of labels, the LMT and SVM classification algorithms, and either the BOW representation of documents or all the features combined. The results are ranked by F-2 score, a generalization of the F-measure (harmonic mean of Precision and Recall) using twice the weight for Recall than Precision.

---

[3] http://clpsych.org/shared-task-2016/.

[4] http://nlp.stanford.edu/software/tagger.shtml.

[5] http://au.reachout.com/.

Table 1. Task (1): best results on the discovery of fungal enzymes

Positive label %	Feature set	Classifier	Precision	Recall	F-m	F-2
40%	All features	LMT	0.361	0.847	0.506	0.670
30%	All features	LMT	0.398	0.780	0.527	0.650
35%	BOW	SVM	0.369	0.800	0.505	0.650
35%	BOW	LMT	0.359	0.807	0.497	0.650
35%	All features	SVM	0.357	0.793	0.493	0.640

The model that yields the best performance is composed of the LMT classifier, using a balanced dataset (containing 40% of *positive* documents), and represented by a combination of all the feature types. Another model that yields similar performance, is composed of the SVM classifier, a balanced dataset (containing 35% of *positive* documents), and BOW features.

HIV Systematic Review. The triage for HIV systematic reviews (see Sect. 3.2) also evaluated training data sampling, along with a comparison between the use of SHARE keywords, BOW or BOW with MeSH terms as features. The usage of BOW and MeSH terms was also analyzed before and after IDF and OR feature selection methods. Table 2 reports the results obtained with LMT and SVM models, which demonstrated better performance.

Table 2. Task (2): best results on HIV systematic review

Positive label %	Feature set	Feature selection	Classifier	Precision	Recall	F-m	F-2
40%	BOW + MeSH	N/A	LMT	0.467	0.900	0.615	0.759
40%	BOW + MeSH	OR	LMT	0.445	0.882	0.591	0.737
30%	BOW	N/A	SVM	0.540	0.800	0.645	0.730
30%	BOW	OR	SVM	0.497	0.827	0.621	0.730

Models using OR as feature selection used ≈80% less features than models without any feature selection, and yet yielded comparable results. Also in this task, performance metrics are shown for the least represented *included* label.

The best model is composed of the LMT classifier, a balanced dataset (containing 40% of *positive* documents), and no feature selection. The model composed of the same configurations, but utilizing OR as feature selection, achieves similar performance, but the process considerably less data after filtering out features.

Response Urgency of Mental Health Forum Posts. The approaches that best suited the triage of mental health forum posts were chosen after performing experiments evaluating different techniques. At first, a relevant set of features was selected, based on the CFS method. The relevant features were used to generate a supervised classification model, and get predictions on the data. Additional predictions were obtained through a rule-based classification approach. Finally, the supervised and rule-based classification predictions were merged to produce the final predictions.

Performance is presented in terms of the official CLPsych metrics, which included accuracy and macro-averaged F-score (macro F-m). The task metrics are based on the system capability of highlighting the labels of higher interest (*crisis*, *red*, and *amber*). Table 3 shows that the best results were achieved using the merged approach, using SMO and a set of 5 rules, and LMT using a set of 3 rules.

Table 3. Task (3): best results on response urgency of mental health forum posts

Approach	Macro F-m	Accuracy	Non-green vs. Green macro F-m	Non-green vs. Green accuracy
SMO + 5 rules	0.29	0.74	0.68	0.82
LMT + 3 rules	0.27	0.72	0.72	0.83
LMT + 5 rules	0.26	0.72	0.72	0.83
LMT only	0.25	0.75	0.75	0.85

5   Conclusion

In this paper we presented an overview of three different approaches to perform triage of scientific data. We evaluated the performance of several supervised learning models by using a common data triage pipeline between all tasks. At the same time we applied specific methods to meet the requirements of each task, such as data sampling and feature selection. The scientific data triage pipeline is based on light and generic modules, allowing the systems to be used to process other data types, and to be integrated in online platforms.

Generally, models using the LMT classifier outperformed all other models. Models based on SVM, however, yielded similar performance to LMT models, and can be suitable if an even shorter response time is required. The usage of dataset sampling yielded better performance on tasks (1) and (2), and feature selection methods improved performance on tasks (2) and (3). Such techniques allow the classification models to perform well using less computational resources, providing lightweight solutions that can respond efficiently in real-time and online systems.

Ongoing work. Novel classification approaches are being developed to improve the results on task (3). Along with evaluating the system with a new dataset, two different methods are currently under development and testing: ensemble classification and deep neural networks.

The systems presented in this paper are publicly available, and can be found at:
https://github.com/TsangLab/triage.
https://github.com/TsangLab/mycoSORT.
https://github.com/BigMiners/CLPsych2016_Shared_Task.

References

1. Almeida, H., Meurs, M.-J.: Automatic triage of mental health online forum posts - NAACL-CLPsych 2016 system description. Red **110**(11.61), 27 (2016)
2. Almeida, H., Meurs, M.-J., Kosseim, L., Butler, G., Tsang, A.: Machine learning for biomedical literature triage. PLOS ONE **9**(12), e115892 (2014)
3. Almeida, H., Meurs, M.-J., Kosseim, L., Tsang, A.: Data sampling and supervised learning for HIV literature screening. IEEE Trans. NanoBiosci. **15**(4), 354–361 (2016)
4. Basu, T., Murthy, C.: Effective text classification by a supervised feature selection approach. In: Proceedings of the IEEE 12th International Conference on Data Mining Workshops (ICDMW), December 10, Brussels, Belgium, pp. 918–925. IEEE (2012)
5. Bekhuis, T., Demner-Fushman, D.: Screening nonrandomized studies for medical systematic reviews: a comparative study of classifiers. Artif. Intell. Med. **55**(3), 197–207 (2012)
6. Chahinian, V., Meurs, M.-J., Mason, D.H., McDonnell, E., Morgenstern, I., Butler, G., Tsang, A.: Proxiris, an augmented browsing tool for literature curation. In: Proceedings of 9th International Conference on Data Integration in the Life Sciences, DILS 2013. CEUR, July 2013
7. Chawla, N.V., Bowyer, K.W., Hall, L.O., Kegelmeyer, W.P.: SMOTE: synthetic minority over-sampling technique. J. Artif. Intell. Res. **16**, 341–378 (2002)
8. Holzinger, A., Jurisica, I.: Knowledge discovery and data mining in biomedical informatics: the future is in integrative, interactive machine learning solutions. In: Holzinger, A., Jurisica, I. (eds.) Interactive Knowledge Discovery and Data Mining in Biomedical Informatics. LNCS, vol. 8401, pp. 1–18. Springer, Heidelberg (2014). doi:10.1007/978-3-662-43968-5_1
9. Howe, D., Costanzo, M., Fey, P., Gojobori, T., Hannick, L., Hide, W., Hill, D.P., Kania, R., Schaeffer, M., St Pierre, S., Twigger, S., White, O., Yon Rhee, S.: Big data: the future of biocuration. Nature **455**(7209), 47–50 (2008)
10. Kölling, J., Langenkämper, D., Abouna, S., Khan, M., Nattkemper, T.W.: WHIDE - a web tool for visual data mining colocation patterns in multivariate bioimages. Bioinformatics **28**(8), 1143–1150 (2012)
11. Liu, H., Motoda, H., Setiono, R., Zhao, Z., Selection, F.: An ever evolving frontier in data mining. In: Proceedings of the 4th Workshop on Feature Selection in Data Mining, June 21, Hyderabad, India, pp. 4–13 (2010)
12. Lu, Z.: PubMed and beyond: a survey of web tools for searching biomedical literature. Database **2011**, baq036 (2011)
13. Meurs, M.-J., Murphy, C., Morgenstern, I., Butler, G., Powlowski, J., Tsang, A., Witte, R.: Semantic text mining support for lignocellulose research. BMC Med. Inf. Decis. Making **12**(1), S5 (2012)
14. Moorhead, S.A., Hazlett, D.E., Harrison, L., Carroll, J.K., Irwin, A., Hoving, C.: A new dimension of health care: systematic review of the uses, benefits, and limitations of social media for health communication. J. Med. Internet Res. **15**(4), e85 (2013)

15. Murdoch, T.B., Detsky, A.S.: The inevitable application of big data to health care. JAMA J. Am. Med. Assoc. **309**(13), 1351–1352 (2013)
16. O'Mara-Eves, A., Thomas, J., McNaught, J., Miwa, M., Ananiadou, S.: Using text mining for study identification in systematic reviews: a systematic review of current approaches. Syst. Rev. **4**(1), 5 (2015)
17. Palaniappan, S., Awang, R.: Intelligent heart disease prediction system using data mining techniques. In: IEEE/ACS International Conference on Computer Systems and Applications, 2008, pp. 108–115. IEEE (2008)
18. Saleem, S., Prasad, R., Vitaladevuni, S.N.P., Pacula, M., Crystal, M., Marx, B., Sloan, D., Vasterling, J., Speroff, T.: Automatic detection of psychological distress indicators and severity assessment from online forum posts. In: The International Conference on Computational Linguistics, COLING, pp. 2375–2388 (2012)
19. Thelwall, M., Buckley, K., Paltoglou, G.: Sentiment strength detection for the social web. J. Am. Soc. Inf. Sci. Technol. **63**(1), 163–173 (2012)
20. Tuarob, S., Tucker, C.S., Salathe, M., Ram, N.: An ensemble heterogeneous classification methodology for discovering health-related knowledge in social media messages. J. Biomed. Inf. **49**, 255–268 (2014)
21. Wang, M., Zhang, W., Ding, W., Dai, D., Zhang, H., Xie, H., Chen, L., Guo, Y., Xie, J.: Parallel clustering algorithm for large-scale biological data sets. PLOS ONE **9**(4), e91315 (2014)
22. Weiss, G.M., McCarthy, K., Zabar, B.: Cost-sensitive learning vs. sampling: which is best for handling unbalanced classes with unequal error costs? In: DMIN-International Conference on Data Mining, pp. 35–41 (2007)

A New Scalable and Performance-Enhancing Bootstrap Aggregating Scheme for Variables Selection
Taking Real-World Web Services Resources as a Case

Choukri Djellali[✉] and Mehdi Adda

Mathematics, Computer Science and Engineering Department,
University of Québec At Rimouski, 300, Allée des Ursulines,
Rimouski, QC G5L 3A1, Canada
{Choukri.Djellali,mehdi_adda}@uqar.ca

Abstract. Variables selection is a vital Data Mining technique which is used to select the cost-effective predictors by discarding variables with little or no predictive power.

In this paper, we introduce a new conceptual model for variables selection which includes subset generation, Ensemble learning, models selection and validation. Particularly, we addressed the problem of searching for and discarding irrelevant variables, scoring variables by relevance and selecting a subset of the cost-effective predictors. The generalization was seen to improve significantly in terms of recognition accuracy when the proposed system, which is named $SPAS$, is tested on QoS for Real-World Web Services. Good experimental studies demonstrate the effectiveness of our Wrapper model.

Keywords: Data mining · Pattern recognition · Ensemble learning · Models selection · Variables selection · Bagging · Wrapper · Web service

1 Introduction

Several studies of machine learning focused on identifying and selecting the relevant knowledge to provide a rich understanding to a particular application domain. However, the dimension of the variables space often exceeds the number of patterns (also known as Bellmans curse of dimensionality). This represents a increasingly encountered obstacle to machine learning algorithms.

Most machine learning algorithms exhibit a lower prediction performance when faced with many irrelevant (or redundant) variables. Thus, it is necessary to reduce the size of the variables space before applying the inductive models training.

Variables selection (also known as subset selection or features selection) is used to identify and select the subset of relevant variables that have the greatest predictive information. It is defined as follows: is a process that chooses a subset of variables by eliminating features with little or no predictive information [16].

© Springer International Publishing AG 2017
E. Aïmeur et al. (Eds.): MCETECH 2017, LNBIP 289, pp. 222–235, 2017.
DOI: 10.1007/978-3-319-59041-7_14

The variables selection has a positive impact on efficiency of machine learning algorithms and, thus, it arises in many engineering systems, including, Big Data [19], e-Health [22], Pervasive and Ubiquitous Computing [20], Wireless communications [5], network-based technologies [15], magnetic resonance imaging [1], Chemometrics [4], bioinformatic [2], Robotics [3], Information retrieval or (IR) [14] and many other fields [17]. All these disciplines show the practical importance of variables selection algorithms.

The purpose of variable selection is to select the cost-effective predictors by discarding variables with little or no predictive information. However, the problem of variable subset selection is known to be NP-hard due mainly to huge search space and, thus, an exhaustive search is too prohibitively time-consuming. In other words, search space increases exponentially with respect to the number of possible combinations.

On one hand, irrelevant/redundant or noisy variables induce a high computational cost, and so reduce the convergence speed to achieve the neighborhood of the solution.

On the other hand, most machine learning algorithms degrade their learning performance while irrelevant variables are introduced in pattern representation. Moreover, irrelevant variables may lead to over fitting and noisy decision boundaries.

In order to avoid these limitations, we used a new variables selection scheme based on variables generation, efficient Wrapper models, Ensemble learning, Bootstrap aggregating scheme and subset validity assessment criterion.

This paper is structured as follows: In Sect. 2, we present the current state of the art, our research questions and the problematic of variables selection. The conceptual architecture of our Wrapper model is given in Sect. 3. We present in Sect. 4 a short evaluation with a benchmarking model for variables selection.

Lastly, a conclusion (Sect. 5) ends the paper with future works.

2   State of the Art, Problem and Research Questions

In machine learning, Data representation generates a highly dimensional space even after pretreatment and cleaning, where the number of variables is larger than the number of patterns available for learning.

In order to avoid the effects of the curse of dimensionality, variables selection is used to identify and select a subset of cost-effective predictors for use in model training.

Formally, the optimization problem of variables selection is the process of selecting a subset D' from the original variables D. The candidate subset $D' \subset D$ $(|D'| \prec |D|)$ can be generated under the following considerations:

$$\begin{cases} \psi(D') = Z \subset D, |Z| = k\max(\psi(Z)) \\ |D'| = k, |D| = m, k \leq m \\ \psi(Z) \prec \psi(Z \cup \{x\}) \end{cases} \tag{1}$$

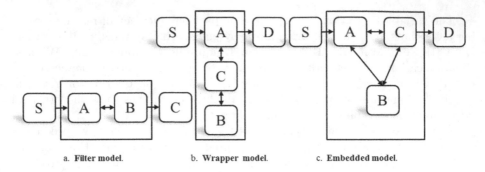

a. **Filter model.**   b. **Wrapper model.**   c. **Embedded model.**

Fig. 1. Filter, Wrapper, and Embedded variables selection models.

where:

Z: set of variables.

ψ: is a monotone increasing selection criterion function.

As shown in Fig. 1, there are three general models of variable selection algorithms, namely Filter model, Wrapper model, and Embedded model. First, Filter model use an independent criteria to score each variable individually. Second, Wrapper model use a predictive model to score variable subsets and consider the model biases when exploring the variables space. Finally, Embedded model takes advantage of Filter and Wrapper models and scores variables subset by using performance measures that are generated during model construction [7, 23].

A: subset generation.

B: subset evaluation.

C: Data Mining algorithms.

D: Data Mining Suite.

S: variables set.

However, the Wrapper model is one of the most popular models for dimensionality reduction. Hence, there is growing interest in the use of Wrapper models during the last few decades.

For instance, Kabir et al. (2010) [10] described a variables selection process based on a combined Filter and Wrapper models. In order to identify variable subsets and present the NN input patterns, the authors propose a non-parametric, iterative Filter based on combination of Euclidean distance estimation and MultiLayer Perceptron or (MLP) Neural Networks or (NNs). Rolling forecasts model selection is used to compare inductive models. The evaluation step is based on a set of synthetic time series and ESTSP08 Data sets.

Panthong et al. (2015) [8] introduced a Wrapper variables selection process for dimensionality reduction based on Ensemble learning algorithm. The predictive accuracies of different machine learning algorithms are calculated using 10-fold cross validation. The evaluation step used 13 Data sets from Machine Learning Repository or (UCI). The experimental study showed that the Sequential

Feature Selection or (SFS) using bagging method and Decision Tree obtained better recognition accuracy (89.60%) than other learning algorithms.

Liu et al. (2006) [11] presented a new feature selection model for Support Vector Machines or SVM. In order to filter out irrelevant variables and improve computational cost, this approach used a variable pruning process into a Wrapper model. Support Vector Machine is used to perform categorization of the reduced space. The Filtered and Supported Sequential Forward Search or (FS-SFS) is tested on ten synthetic and real-world Data sets coming from Machine Learning Repository.

Kabir et al. (2012) [12] proposed a new hybrid Ant Colony Optimization or (ACO) named ACOFS, for variables selection, using a Neural Network. The generation strategy used a combination of Filter and Wrapper models. In order to monitor the search strategy, this model used a set of rules for pheromone update and heuristic information measurement. The model performance is evaluated on gene expression Data sets.

Jingu et al. (2008) [18] studied Non-negative matrix factorization or (NMF) as a clustering method. By analyzing the relationship between NMF and K-means, some constraints can be relaxed to achieve NMF formulation. Experimental study with synthetic and text Data showed that Sparse NMF is a consistent solution to Data clustering.

Most previous approaches provide limited support for all activities of variables selection, in particular, the generation strategy. The precision and computational cost do not meet the demands of actual applications. In these approaches, there are no built-in methods or tools that combine different decisions to accelerate the learning process and there are usually several ways of variables selection. Moreover, traditional variables selection models are not intended to discern correctly the hidden information in a collection of patterns because they are heavily dependent on the used patterns, user defined parameters, architecture configuration and scalability.

In order to overcome the obstacles mentioned above, we present in this paper a new Wrapper model for variables selection, using subset generation, Ensemble learning, models selection and validation.

The next section explores how patterns are moved across our Wrapper model and introduce the rules of generation strategy, Ensemble learning and models selection.

3   Architecture of Our Wrapper Model

Our conceptual model for variables selection use a predictive model to score variable subsets, which is composed of four process, namely variable generation, Ensemble learning, models selection and finally, validation.

The variable selection process starts with Data set presentation and then adjusts it performance related to models construction by adding or discarding variables, as shown in Fig. 2.

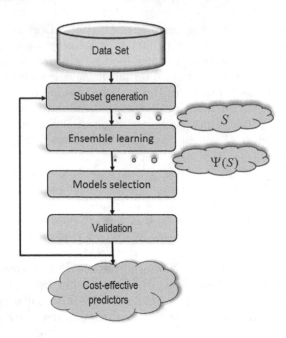

Fig. 2. Wrapper model.

Instead of using original variables, the cost-effective predictors are chosen on the basis of their distinctive scores according to basis factors defined by two inductive models based on Singular Value Decomposition or SVD [13] and Non-negative Matrix Factorization or NMF [18]. This Ensemble learning scheme is designed to improve stability and accuracy of our Wrapper model.

Basically, SVD and NMF discard variables that are weakly correlated with the most important basic factors. The variables related to small factors are almost irrelevant and do not affect the similarity measures, i.e., they explain a small amount of the variance. In other words, the selected factor vectors point into the direction of the largest variance of the original Data. We can see this projection as a process that selects the variables that are more relevant than others based on the variance amount representing the Data set. The maintained variables have the greatest influence on patterns position in the reduced space. This compactly generated space improves pattern clustering and reduces computational cost.

The introduction of a slight bias in SVD and NMF estimators lead to a significant reduction of its variance (a decrease of error), and thus to improve its performance. Hence, we used models selection technique to choose the best model from a set of candidate models. The optimal choice of variables subset is correlated with representation-induction bias. Each variables subset is used to learn a Wrapper model, which is tested on 10-fold cross-validation. The relevance of variable subsets is estimated by recognition accuracies of the inductive models.

The obtained estimation of recognition accuracy from cross-validation is not based on a selected model, but the average accuracies of trained models.

4   Experimentation

4.1   Data Set

We used in our experiments the QoS Data set for Web Service[1], which is the most widely used test collection for Web service and cloud computing. Each pattern contains 5825 variables representing the response time values of Web services, i.e., the time duration between request sending and response receiving. The average response time is equal to 0.8111 ms and the standard deviation is equal to 1.9670 ms.

As shown in Fig. 3, from the 339 service users, we select the first tree service users and we plot their response time value. X-axis represents the Web service and the Y-axis shows the response time value.

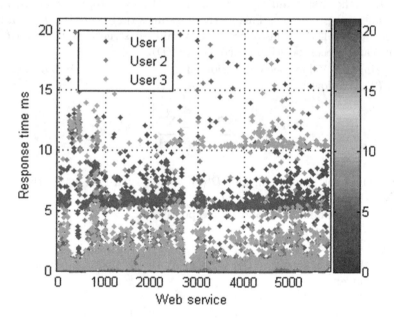

Fig. 3. Response time *vs.* Web service

---

[1] http://wsdream.github.io/dataset/wsdream_dataset1.html.

4.2   Configuration

The experimental system used to assess the efficiency of our Wrapper model
was run on a computer with an AMD A69-3400M APU with Radeon(tm) HP
Graphics 1.40 GHz, Installed Physical Memory (RAM) 4.00 GB, Windows 10
Pro 64-bit Operating System, x64-based processor.

Our variables selection scheme is developed with Java under Neon.1a Release
(4.6.1) eclipse integrated development environment 64-bit and some library functions such as JDK 8u111 + Java EE, Java Matrix Package or JAMA[2], etc.

4.3   Subset Generation

Exhaustive generation strategy enumerates $2^{5825} - 1 = 2.147.483.646$ combinations and the time-consuming have exponential growth with an increasing
number of variables.

In order to avoid the effects of the Bellmans curse of dimensionality, two
Wrappers models are performed using SVD and NMF.

SVD: in the first evaluation, we used SVD as a Wrapper model to select
the cost-effective predictors. This method assumes that there is a hidden latent
structure behind Data. The uncovering of hidden structures is performed by
Singular Value Decomposition process or (SVD).

The Singular Value Decomposition of D is a rank-matrix $\widehat{D}_r$ defined by
formula (2) as follows:

$$\widehat{D}_r = U_r \sum_r V_r^T = \sum_{i=1}^r u_i \sigma_i v_i^T \tag{2}$$

where,
D represents a set of pattern, i.e., $D[i,j] = v_{ij}$, such that v_{ij} is the jth time
response value of Web service used by i^{th} user.
u_i and v_i: are columns of U_r and V_r^T (respectively).
σ_i: the ith singular value.
$\sum_r = diag(\sigma_1, \sigma_2, ..., \sigma_r)$.

The rank of $\widehat{D}$ ($r = rank(|\widehat{D}|)$ is given by the number of singular values σ_i
those are non-zero.
$\sigma_1 \geq \sigma_2 \geq ... \geq \sigma_k... \geq \sigma_r > 0$.
$\sum_r$: diagonal singular values matrix containing the square roots of eigenval-
ues in descending order.
The singular vector $(\sigma_1, \sigma_2, ..., \sigma_r), 1 \leq i \leq r$ of the matrix $\sum_r$ is unique.
The first r columns of V are eigenvectors of $\widehat{D}^T \widehat{D}$.
$U_r U_r^T = I_m \wedge V_r^T V_r = I_n$.
$I_m(I_n)$: identity matrix of size $m(n)$.

---

[2] http://math.nist.gov/javanumerics/jama/.

Hence, the SVD Wrapper model to select the relevant variable subset S' given the set of singular values $S = diag(\sum_k) = \{\sigma_1, \sigma_2, ...\sigma_r\}$ is defined by the following formula:

$$
\begin{cases}
\psi(S') = Z \subset S, |Z| = k\max(\psi(\dfrac{\sum\limits_{i=1}^{i=k}\sigma_i^2}{\sum\limits_{j=1}^{j=r}\sigma_j^2})) \\[4ex]
|S'| = k, |S| = r, k \leq r \\[1ex]
\psi(Z) \prec \psi(Z \cup \{x\})
\end{cases}
\tag{3}
$$

The monotone increasing selection criterion function ψ measures the cumulative variance generated by k cost-effective predictors.

Algorithm 1 shows the iterative pseudo-code of Singular Value Decomposition.

Algorithm 1. Pseudo code of $SVD(D, \delta, var\ k)$

Input $D(p_1, p_2, ...p_n); p_i(v_{i1}, v_{i2}, ...v_{im})$; threshold δ

Begin

   Step 1 /* SVD*/

   $$D \to \widehat{D}_r; \widehat{D}_r = U_r \sum_r V_r^T = \sum_{i=1}^{r} u_i \sigma_i v_i^T$$

   Step 2 /* TSVD*/

   While $(\dfrac{\sum\limits_{i=1}^{i=k}\sigma_i^2}{\sum\limits_{j=1}^{j=r}\sigma_j^2} \prec \delta)$

   $$D \to \widehat{D}_k; \widehat{D}_k = U_k \sum_k V_k^T = \sum_{i=1}^{k} u_i \sigma_i v_i^T$$

   $r \leq min(m, n), rang(\widehat{D}) =| \{\sigma_i\} |$

   end while

Step 3 /* Dimensionality reduction */

   $\sum_k V_k^T$

Step 4 /* Clustering and ranking */

   $sim(p_i, p_j) = (p_i U_k)(\sum_k V_k^T)$

Output

   Write (k)

End

Figure 4 shows the rank approximation of the [user, time response value] matrix D. Singular values (also known as canonical multipliers) are positive real numbers and by convention they are sorted in descending order along the diagonal of singular values matrix $\sum_r$.

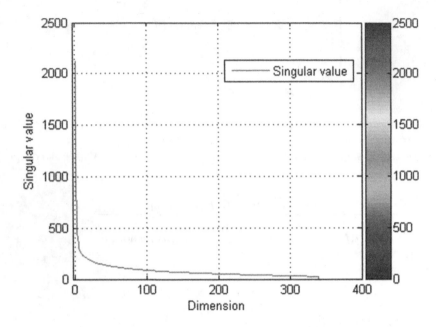

Fig. 4. Rank approximation

NMF: in the second evaluation, variables selection is performed by Nonnegative Matrix Factorization. NMF select sparse variables from a nonnegative high-dimensional Data, and it is represented mathematically as follows:

$$\widehat{D}_k = FW \tag{4}$$

$$\underbrace{\begin{pmatrix} v_{11} & v_{12} & .. & v_{1m} \\ . & . & .. & . \\ . & . & .. & . \\ . & . & .. & . \\ v_{n1} & v_{n2} & .. & v_{nm} \end{pmatrix}}_{D[n,m]} = \underbrace{\begin{pmatrix} f_{11} & .. & f_{1k} \\ . & .. & . \\ . & .. & . \\ . & .. & . \\ f_{n1} & .. & f_{nk} \end{pmatrix}}_{F[n,k]} \underbrace{\begin{pmatrix} w_{11} & ... & w_{1m} \\ . & .... & . \\ . & .... & . \\ w_{k1} & ... & w_{km} \end{pmatrix}}_{W[k,m]}$$

where,
n and m: are the number of patterns and the number of variables (respectively),
$k \prec min(n, m)$.

Formally, the Non-Negative Matrix Factorization provides a low rank approximation defined by the following non-convex optimization problem:

$$\begin{cases} FW\min(f(F,W)) = \dfrac{1}{2}\|D - FW\|_F^2 \\[2ex] W_{ij}, H_{ij} \geq 0, \forall ij. \end{cases} \qquad (5)$$

where,
F: is the underlying basis vectors or basic factors.
W: encoding or weight column.

NMF produces a lower rank approximation matrices W and F, such that D is approximated to $W.F$. Each pattern $D(i:)$ can be built from k basic factors (columns) of F as defined by the following equation.

$$\underbrace{D(i:)}_{\text{Pattern}_i} \approx \sum_{j=1}^{k} \underbrace{F(k,j)}_{\text{Basis vectors}} \underbrace{W(:,k)}_{\text{Weight column}} = \underbrace{WH(i:)}_{\text{Pattern}_i \; approximation} \qquad (6)$$

We applied the amplitude error as a stopping criterion and we set the convergence of learning when $\delta = 0.064$.
This nonlinear criterion is defined as follows:

$$\Theta^k = \frac{1}{2}\|D_{ij}^k - F_{ij}^k W_{ij}^k\|_F^2 \qquad (7)$$

$$e^k = |\;\Theta^{k+1} - \Theta^k\;| \qquad (8)$$

where,
e^k: error at k iteration.

In Fig. 5, we illustrate the learning phase of NMF Wrapper model. The estimate generalization error is based on a loss function. The learning is performed dependently in each Wrapper model. All patterns are presented to each Wrapper model and each output is calculated individually. The objective is to adjust F and W matrixes to find the better fitting of Data, i.e., $D \approx FW$. X-axis represents epoch number (or iteration) and Y-axis shows the final value of the amplitude error e^k after patterns presentation.

4.4   Models Selection

Models selection is the most common technique in machine leaning, which is a meta-model or a Bootstrap aggregating scheme designed to assess the stability of the discovered clusters, and to improve the clustering accuracy.

To overcome the problem of clustering instability, we used models selection technique based on 10 fold-cross validation.

As shown in Fig. 6, nine folds $\{L\}$ are used as training samples sets and the remaining out-of-bag vectors $\{T\}$ are the set of samples used for model testing.

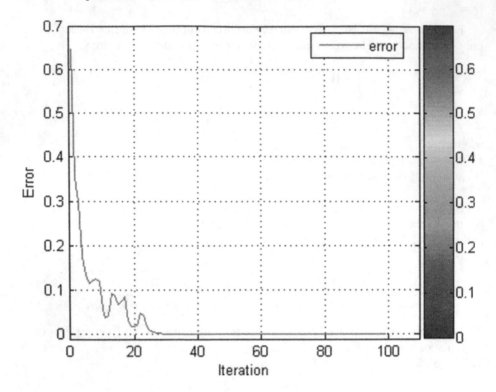

Fig. 5. Iteration *vs.* Error

$$\textbf{B.S [1]} \begin{bmatrix} \underbrace{L}_{Training\ Set} & L\ L\ L\ L\ L\ L\ L\ L & \underbrace{\textbf{T}}_{Test\ Set} \end{bmatrix}$$

$$\textbf{B.S [2]} \begin{bmatrix} L & \underbrace{L}_{Training\ Set} & L\ L\ L\ L\ L\ L & \underbrace{\textbf{T}}_{Test\ Set} & L \end{bmatrix}$$

$$\cdot \qquad \cdot \qquad \cdot$$
$$\cdot \qquad \cdot \qquad \cdot$$

$$\textbf{B.S [10]} \begin{bmatrix} \underbrace{\textbf{T}}_{Test\ Set} & L\ L\ L\ L\ L\ L\ L\ L & \underbrace{L}_{Training\ Set} \end{bmatrix}$$

Fig. 6. Cross-validation scheme

In order to evaluate our variable selection models, two Wrapper models were evaluated on the task of pattern clustering. They correspond to Self-Organizing Map [21] and our Wrapper model *SPAS*.

A Self-Organizing Map (also known as Kohonen Feature Map) is a Neural Network using competitive unsupervised learning to provide a reduced dimensional space. Each input neuron is fully connected to all neurons in the output layer. The output vector implements a winner-takes all mechanism.

To evaluate the effectiveness of our Wrapper, we used recognition accuracy measures that are widely used in machine learning, information retrieval, and pattern recognition.

The learning performance of the ith Wrapper model is computed as the number of correctly recognized patterns divided by the total number of patterns. The recognition accuracy measure is defined by formula (9) as follows:

$$accuracy_i = \frac{\# \ recognized \ pattern}{\# \ presented \ pattern} \times 100 \tag{9}$$

However, the average accuracy (AC) from prediction scores is the most widely used measure in models selection technique.

We computed the AC measure as the average over 10 accuracy estimates for SVD and NMF, as described by the following formula.

$$AC = \frac{1}{k} \sum_{i=1}^{k} \frac{1}{c} \sum_{j=1}^{c} (\frac{\# \ recognized \ pattern}{\# \ presented \ pattern}) \times 100 \tag{10}$$

where,
k: is the number of folds.
c: number of Wrapper models.

Table 1 show that our $SPAS$ Wrapper model has good performance, which provides an efficient system for cost-effective predictors selection.

Table 1. Recognition accuracy

Wrapper model	Accuracy AC
$SPAS$	95.87%
SOM	94.79%

One of the main advantages of our Wrapper model is the construction of compactly generated space by Ensemble learning and models selection. This feature was an ingredient key in the identification of relevant variables. Hence, Ensemble learning and models selection have a positive impact on the stability and accuracy of our Wrapper model.

5   Conclusion

In this paper, we have presented a new conceptual model for variables selection in Web service Data set. Our Wrapper model is composed of subset generation, Ensemble inductive models learning, models selection and clustering. The subset generation is performed by Non-Negative Matrix Factorization and Singular

Value Decomposition techniques. The SVD and NMF Wrapper Models use a reduced space to represent the relations between variables, and thus, reduce the noise and computational cost.

In order to improve stability and accuracy of variables selection process, we used Ensemble learning scheme.

A models selection technique is used for accuracy estimation and model selection. This technique has two main advantages over conventional methods: automatic (accuracy estimation) and optimal (model selection with an extremely optimistic bias). Performance and results of different trained models from cross-validation were considered in recognition accuracy of the selected model. Furthermore, Ensemble learning and models selection are indispensable to reduce variance and improve generalization ability.

6   Future Works

The purpose of our next work is to improve generalization capability, i.e., choose the best model that satisfy the trade-off bias-variance. A new algorithm can be designed based on boosting and Ensemble learning techniques.

References

1. Smith, M.S., Fahrmeir, L.: Spatial Bayesian variable selection with application to functional magnetic resonance imaging. J. Am. Stat. Assoc. **102**(478), 417–431 (2007). Taylor & Francis
2. Long, N., Gianola, D., Rosa, G.J.M., Weigel, K.A.: Dimension reduction and variable selection for genomic selection: application to predicting milk yield in Holsteins. J. Anim. Breed. Genet. **128**(4), 247–257 (2011). Wiley Online Library
3. Chagas, C.M., Koike, C.: Bayesian Approach to Action Selection and Attention Focusing: An Application in Autonomous Robot Programming. Institut National Polytechnique de Grenoble-INPG (2005)
4. Lloyd, G.R., Wongravee, K., Silwood, C.J.L., Grootveld, M., Brereton, R.G.: Self organising maps for variable selection: application to human saliva analysed by nuclear magnetic resonance spectroscopy to investigate the effect of an oral healthcare product. Chemometr. Intell. Lab. Syst. **98**(2), 149–161 (2009). Elsevier
5. Zhang, Y., Lee, W., Huang, Y.A.: Intrusion detection techniques for mobile wireless networks. Wireless Netw. **9**(5), 545–556 (2003). Springer, New York
6. Deepa, T., Punithavalli, M.: A GLFES and DFT technique for feature selection in high-dimensional imbalanced dataset. IJCSE **3**(2), 336–343 (2012)
7. Chandrashekar, G., Sahin, F.: A survey on feature selection methods. Comput. Electr. Eng. **40**(1), 16–28 (2014). Elsevier
8. Panthong, R., Srivihok, A.: Wrapper feature subset selection for dimension reduction based on ensemble learning algorithm. Procedia Comput. Sci. **72**, 162–169 (2015). Elsevier
9. Lin, C.-J.: Projected gradient methods for nonnegative matrix factorization. Neural Comput. **19**(10), 2756–2779 (2007). MIT Press
10. Kabir, M.M., Islam, M.M., Murase, K.: A new Wrapper feature selection approach using neural network. Neurocomputing **73**(16), 3273–3283 (2010). Elsevier

11. Liu, Y., Zheng, Y.F.: FS_SFS: a novel feature selection method for support vector machines. Pattern Recogn. **39**(7), 1333–1345 (2006). Elsevier
12. Kabir, M.M., Shahjahan, M., Murase, K.: A new hybrid ant colony optimization algorithm for feature selection. Expert Syst. Appl. **39**, 3747–3763 (2012). Elsevier
13. Lu, C.-J., Tsai, D.-M.: Automatic defect inspection for LCDs using singular value decomposition. Int. J. Adv. Manuf. Technol. **25**(1–2), 53–61 (2005). Springer
14. Mladenić, D., Grobelnik, M.: Feature selection on hierarchy of web documents. Decis. Support Syst. **35**(1), 45–87 (2003). Elsevier
15. Amiri, F., Yousefi, M.R., Lucas, C., Shakery, A., Yazdani, N.: Mutual information-based feature selection for intrusion detection systems. J. Netw. Comput. Appl. **34**(4), 1184–1199 (2011). Elsevier
16. Azevedo, A.: Integration of Data Mining in Business Intelligence Systems. IGI Global, Hershey (2014)
17. Jovic, A., Brkić, K., Bogunovic, N.: A review of feature selection methods with applications. In: 2015 38th International Convention on Information and Communication Technology, Electronics and Microelectronics (MIPRO), pp. 1200–1205. IEEE (2015)
18. Jingu, K., Haesun, P.: Sparse nonnegative matrix factorization for clustering. Georgia Institute of Technology (2008)
19. Hoi, S.C.H., Wang, J., Zhao, P., Jin, R.: Online feature selection for mining big data. In: Proceedings of the 1st International Workshop on Big Data, Streams and Heterogeneous Source Mining: Algorithms, Systems, Programming Models and Applications, pp. 93–100. ACM (2012)
20. Choudhury, T., Consolvo, S., Harrison, B., Hightower, J., LaMarca, A., LeGrand, L., Rahimi, A., Rea, A., Bordello, G., Hemingway, B., et al.: The mobile sensing platform: an embedded activity recognition system. IEEE Pervasive Comput. **7**(2), 32–41 (2008). IEEE
21. Xia, J., Nick, P., Young, N., Wishart, D.S.: MetaboAnalyst: a web server for metabolomic data analysis and interpretation. Nucleic Acids Res. **37**(suppl 2), W652–W660 (2009). Oxford Univ. Press
22. Kaur, P.D., Chana, I.: Cloud based intelligent system for delivering health care as a service. Comput. Methods Program. Biomed. **113**(1), 346–359 (2014)
23. Zhao, J., Wang, G.-Y., Wu, Z.-F., Tang, H., Li, H.: The study on technologies for feature selection. In: Proceedings of the 2002 International Conference on Machine Learning and Cybernetics 2002, vol. 2, pp. 689–693. IEEE (2002)

Towards an Adaptive Learning Framework for MOOCs

Soufiane Ardchir$^{(\boxtimes)}$ (iD), Mohamed Amine Talhaoui (iD),
and Mohamed Azzouazi (iD)

Faculty of Sciences Ben M'Sik, Hassan II University of Casablanca,
Casablanca, Morocco
soufiane79@gmail.com, t.med.amine@gmail.com,
azouazii@gmail.com

Abstract. Massive Open Online Courses (MOOCs) are a new shaking development in higher education. They combine openness and scalability in a most energetic way. They have the capacity to broaden participation in higher education. In this way, they help to achieve social inclusion, the dissemination of knowledge and pedagogical innovation and also the internationalization of higher education institutions. However, one of the most essential elements for a massive open language learning experience to be efficient is to enhance learners and to facilitate networked learning experiences. In fact, MOOCs are meant to serve an undefined number of participants, thus serving a high heterogeneity of profiles, with various learning styles and schemata, and also contexts of contribution and diversity of online platforms. Personalization can play a primary role in this process. Accordingly, adaptive MOOCs use adaptive techniques so as to present personalized learning experiences, having as basis dynamic assessment and data collecting on the course. They count on networks of prerequisites and deal with learners according to their different personalized paths through the content. This has been described by the Gates Foundation as an essential novelty in the area for large-scale productivity in online courses. Analytics are also to be credited with bringing about change and improvement of the course in the future. This paper looks into the MOOCs system by reviewing the available literature, spotting the various limitations of traditional MOOC system and suggesting a proposed framework for adaptive MOOCs based on hybrid techniques. By so doing, we generate suggestions of learning paths adapted to the competences profile of each participant with a focus on objectives, such as reducing the rate of dropout and improving MOOCs quality.

Keywords: MOOCs · Big data · Adaptive learning · Student modeling · System recommender

1 Introduction

MOOCs or massive open online courses have become a fashionable theme of debate about online education. MOOCs can be defined as online courses that rely on open educational resources (OER), with a wide number of simultaneous participants, and including interaction among participants using social tools.

© Springer International Publishing AG 2017
E. Aïmeur et al. (Eds.): MCETECH 2017, LNBIP 289, pp. 236–251, 2017.
DOI: 10.1007/978-3-319-59041-7_15

According to Siemens, a key figure in the field, MOOCs are a continuation of the trend in innovation, experimentation and the use of technology initiated by distance and online learning in order to provide large numbers of learners with a variety of opportunities [1]. MOOCs have been subject to controversy. In fact, some supported them; others had doubt about them; whereas traditional academic community dealt with them cautiously. One of the credits of MOOCs is that they offered the chance for numerous people to take part in true "education for all". Up to December 2015 there have been more than 4,000 active MOOC courses worldwide, and the trend continues to enhance as new institutions start further courses in more languages [2]. The key elements of MOOCs stand for:

- Massive: unlimited attendance.
- Open: participants are not charge and access is possible to anyone with internet connection.
- Online: distance learning, delivered via the internet.
- Courses: streamlined around a set of goals in a specific area of study.

In the literature, we distinguish between two pedagogical forms of MOOCs; these are explained below and might be seen as 'process' or 'content-based' approaches [5]:

- cMOOCs: The early MOOCs were 'connectivist' [1], described as cMOOCs, it is based on a participatory approach, where each learner performs their own information research, exchange with other participants, and publishes their own conclusions. This goes hand in hand with the idea that learning occurs within a network, where learners use digital platforms such as blogs, wikis, social media platforms to make connections with content, learning communities and other learners to create and construct knowledge. It is worth mentioning that cMOOCs are usually not sponsored by higher education institutions, but are rather organized by individuals with passion for a specific subject. The time allotted by the organizers aims at creating a framework for learning, where students worldwide can connect, share, contribute and collaborate, while at the same time learn about a specific subject and enlarge their network of professional and personal contacts [3].
- xMOOCs: The most instructivist models have been labeled xMOOCs. These have a tendency to employ a knowledge transmission model, by dint of video recordings of classroom lectures or custom produced mini-lectures. Besides, xMOOCs are the most popular type of MOOCs, for higher education, last but not least, xMOOCs are the most widely known because they are closer to the traditional education.

Despite their common goal of providing open and free (or relatively cheap) education to the public, xMOOCs and cMOOCs have distinctly different structures and qualities. Each form of MOOC sets up a different type of learning environment and is suitable for distinct methods of knowledge acquisition. Generally speaking, on the one hand, cMOOCs reflect the new learning environments characterized by flexibility and openness. On the other hand, xMOOCs offer high quality content as compared to cMOOCs [4]. Ultimately, the purpose of MOOCs was to open up education and cater free access to university level education for as many students as possible. The development of MOOCs is rooted within the basic ideal of openness in education. In other words, knowledge should be shared freely, and the desire to learn should not be

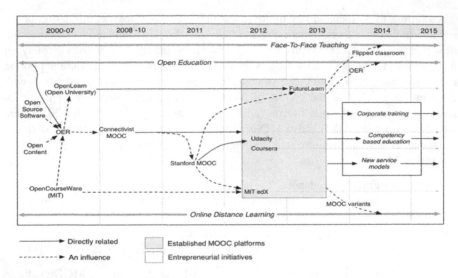

Fig. 1. Potential impact and trends of MOOC on education [5].

hampered by any demographic, economic, or geographical hindrances. As Fig. 1 shows [5], since 2000 the concept of openness in education has witnessed fast evolution. Accordingly, Massachusetts Institute of Technology (MIT) launched Open-CourseWare in 2002 followed by the Open University which started OpenLearn in 2006, representing a continuous evolution of the open education movement. As a result of this early development of MOOCs, various open learning platforms have been founded by leading institutions. MIT edX and OU's Futurelearn in 2012 can be given as an illustration.

Several types of MOOC platforms provide courses open to the public, either for free or for credit. The most lively ones these days are Coursera, Udacity, and edX. Table 1 is a good illustration of a sample and brief description of some features of the many MOOC Providers offering courses today. Table 1 is also an evidence that shows most platforms are made in such a way that they imitate the traditional features of pedagogy in electronic form [6], so the completion rate for most courses is below 13%. We believe that adaptive learning has the potential to take part in important key aspects of MOOCs and can overcome the current problems of high dropout rate in MOOCs.

In this research, we propose a framework based on a hybrid technique to provide students with an adapting content of MOOC according to the participant's competences, taking into account their prior knowledge. The proposed framework is based on two essential topics in personalization learning system such as student modeling and system recommender, having as an objective to provide adaptation mechanisms for MOOC platforms which integrates machine learning and soft computing. The paper is organized as follows: Sect. 2 for literature review on learning adaptivity, Sect. 3 describes our proposed system. Finally, in Sect. 4, we summarize our work and provide an outlook on the future related to this area of research.

Table 1. Summary of features supported by various MOOCs platforms [6]

	edX	Coursera	Udacity	Future-Learn	Canvas Network
1. Learning Methods					
Video with audio	✓	✓	✓	✓	✓
Audio only	✗	✗	✗	✓	✗
Articles	✓	✓	✗	✓	✓
Projects	✗	✗	✓	✗	✗
Discussions	✓	✓	✓	✓	✓
2. Assignments	✓	✓	✓	✓	✓
3. Quiz tests	✓	✓	✓	✓	✓
4. Transcriptions	✓	✗	✓	✓	✗
5. Video with interactive transcription	✓	✗	✗	✗	✗
6. Certificate	✓	✓	✓	✓	✓
7. Peer Assessment	✗	✓	✗	✗	✗
8. Adaptive learning	✗	✗	✗	✗	✓
9. Course joining timings	Scheduled Anytime	Scheduled Anytime	Scheduled Anytime	Scheduled	Scheduled
10. Target Users	Anyone	Anyone	Professionals	Anyone	Anyone

2 Literature Review

Web systems generally suffer from their incapacity to meet the heterogeneous needs of many users. To tackle this challenge, a special trend of research that has been called adaptive web systems; Adaptive systems makes it easier for users to find appropriate items in a commonly large information space, by basically engaging three main adaptation technologies [7]: adaptive content selection, adaptive navigation support, and adaptive presentation.

Adaptation is a key topic in traditional e-learning systems and different concepts have been used for this purpose. George Siemens, the authority of the MOOC, was quoted in The New York Times in December 2013 saying, "the next challenge will be scaling creativity, and finding a way that even in a class of 100,000, adaptive learning can give each student a personal experience." [1]. Adaptive learning develops a model of a learner's understanding of topics and concepts, permitting detailed feedback on progress and supplying personalized pathways to attain learning outcomes. Nevertheless, adaptation is not very developed in MOOCs, where it has gained even more ground as they commonly have more participants whose profiles are more varied. Moreover, many frameworks have also been suggested, Daradoumis et al. [8] use software agents to ameliorate and personalize management, delivery and evaluation of massive online courses on an individual level basis. This framework takes into account the participants schemata which is very important because most MOOCs incorporate lectures formatted as short videos. Bassi et al. [9] propose an agent-based framework for MOOCs. Agents gather data and analyze them based on different perspectives including educational objective, time management, pedagogical preferences, etc. The analyzed data is used by other agents for content personalization, teaching feedback; the authors contend that intelligent agents could also be used for cutting down cheating and fraud during quizz and online tests. Lerís et al. [10] propose a construct of adaptivity for MOOCs to detect some specific personalizing indicators. These indicators are selected as a consequence of previous work done and are based on two aspects of learning: self-regulation and cooperation. Sonwalkar [11] suggests an adaptive system with web services and computer architecture, which counts on diagnostic assessment adapted to five learning styles. In addition, Onah [12] recommends systems by which users create their own learning paths, making choices based on their own objectives and preferences. Teixeira et al. [13] add to the pedagogical model for MOOCs, with content adaptation aiming at making compatible initial knowledge and the device used. Adaptive MOOCs can be defined as an intelligent system that allows personalization for each individual user, its content and its presentation according to user preferences and characteristics. The process of personalization of MOOCs is implemented through a decision making and personalization engine which adapts the contents according to a user model. In this context, it is clear that the key element of an adaptive e-learning system is the user model.

2.1   Student Modeling

Building of the student model and following related cognitive processes are important aspects in providing personalization. The student model is a representation of information about an individual learner that is essential for an adaptive system. The system uses that information from student model so as to predict the learner's behavior, and there by adapt to his/her individual needs. Data from student model is classified along three layers that are suggested in [14]:

- Objective information, which incorporate data provided directly by the learner like: personal data, previous knowledge, preferences, etc. The learner edits this data during his/her registration on the system.
- Learner's performance, which includes data about level of knowledge of the subject domain, his/her misconceptions, progress and the general performance for particular learner.
- Learning history, which includes information about lessons and tests learner has already studied, his/her interaction with system, the assessments he/she went through, etc.

2.2 Student Modeling Techniques and Methods

Machine Learning Techniques. The concept of machine learning (ML) has been around for decades. What's new is that it can now be applied to huge quantities of complex data. Less expensive data storage, distributed processing, more powerful computers, and the analytical opportunities available have dramatically increased interest in machine learning systems. There is no denying that learning is the process of acquiring knowledge. On the one hand, humans naturally learn from experience by dint of their ability to reason. On the other hand, computers do not learn by reasoning, but learn with algorithms. Today, there are a large number of ML algorithms found in the literature. The main machine learning methods which are used in MOOC data analysis enable us to do prediction, clustering, relationship mining, discovery with models and data distillation for human judgment.

Two main branches of machine learning can be identified: on the one hand, supervised learning and unsupervised learning. Supervised learning is used when the algorithms are provided on the basis of training data and correct answers. The task of the ML algorithm is to learn on the training data and apply the knowledge acquired in the real data; the goal was to identify patterns within independent variables to explain a dependent variable. The key example here is the linear regression and logistic regression, known from classical statistics. Recent techniques such as support vector machines, random forests, and generalized boosted regression are gaining popularity due to their robustness, computational feasibility, and effectiveness [15]. On the other hand, in unsupervised learning, ML algorithms have not a training set. They are used with some data about the real world and have to learn from that data on their own. Unsupervised learning algorithms are mainly axed on finding hidden patterns in data, there is no dependent variable and we want to investigate patterns in the data, most commonly clusters similar observations. Clustering is realized by the simple k-means or k-medoid.

Modeling the Uncertainty of Learning. One of the most important problems encountered when constructing a student model is uncertainty [16]. The processes of learning and student's diagnosis are complex. They are defined by many factors and depend on tasks and facts that are uncertain and, usually, unmeasured. The determination of the student's knowledge, mental state and behavior is not a straightforward task, it is rather based on uncertain observations, measurements, assumptions and inferences. The presence of uncertainty in student's diagnosis is increased in an adaptive/personalized tutoring system due to either the indirect interaction between the learner and the teacher or the technical difficulties [16].

The limitations of traditional machine learning techniques for modeling human behavior led to the introduction of Soft Computing (SC) for User Modeling (UM). The most common used techniques to face this kind of uncertainty are fuzzy logic (FL), Bayesian Networks and neural network. FL is not a machine learning technique; nevertheless due to its ability to handle uncertainty it is used in combination with other machine learning techniques in order to produce behavior models that are able to capture and to manage the uncertainty of human behavior [17].

The knowledge domain representation in an adaptive and/or personalized tutoring system is a key factor for providing adaptivity. The most usual used techniques of knowledge domain representation are hierarchies and networks of concepts. The knowledge representation approach enables the system to identify the domain concepts that are already partly or completely known for a learner, or the domain concepts that the student has forgotten, while taking into consideration the learner's knowledge level of the related concepts. Therefore, the representation of dependencies between the domain concepts of the learning material comprises uncertain and imprecise information. Consequently, an effective solution for dealing with this uncertainty is to use fuzzy logic techniques in the representation of the knowledge domain. In fact, Fuzzy Cognitive Maps (FCMs) is a way to represent real-world dynamic systems (Fig. 2); in a form that corresponds tightly to the way humans think of it [18]. A FCM is a network of nodes ($N_1, N_2, \ldots N_n$) which represent the important concepts of the mapped system and oriented arcs representing the causal relationships between two nodes (N_i, N_j). The directed arcs are marked with fuzzy values (f_{ij}) in the interval [−1, 1] that show the "strength of impact" of node N_i on node N_j.

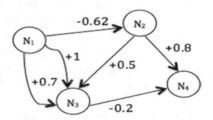

Fig. 2. Fuzzy cognitive maps [18]

Ontology-Based Student Modeling. Recently, a lot of research has been done around the modeling of users and web ontologies. Due to the fact that adaptive and/or customized teaching systems try to model learning processes in the real world and as they are web applications, so they can be combined with Web ontologies. These allow the representation of abstract properties and concepts and make them expanded and reusable in different applications [18]. These characteristics of ontologies can participate in the modeling of students, find a solution to describe the learning preferences of the learners and are also used for searching and indexing various educational resources. The main advantages of ontological models are: formal semantics, reuse of domain knowledge, domain knowledge from the operational knowledge.

2.3   Recommendation System

The main goal of recommender systems in web-based learning system, such as MOOC is to assist users by providing personalized recommendations related to content and services. Recommender systems are increasingly being adopted in E-commerce for recommending movies, books, music, TV shows or different types of items. Such successful implementation of recommender systems in the e-commerce domain has encouraged researchers to explore similar benefits in the e-learning domain since the implementation of recommender systems in e-learning has high potential for achieving advanced personalization. Recommendation system is the most popular application for personalization and recommendation techniques. In this regard, there are several techniques used in the learning system [19]. The following section will discuss the most used techniques and their efficiencies to improve learners' experiences.

Collaborative Filtering (CF). Collaborative filtering focuses on identifying of learners with similar learning patterns and uses their learning methods to recommend contents to others [20]. The CF technique can be divided into user-based and item-based CF approaches [21]. In the user-based CF approach, a user will receive recommendations of items liked by similar users. In the item-based CF approach, a user will receive recommendations of items that are similar to those they have loved in the past. The similarity between users or items can be calculated by Pearson correlation-based similarity [19], constrained Pearson correlation (CPC)-based similarity, cosine-based similarity, or adjusted cosine-based measures.

Content-Based. The system learns to recommend items that are similar to the ones that the user liked in the past taking into account the object content analysis that the user has evaluated in the past. The similarity of items is calculated based on the features associated with the compared items. Clustering was proposed by [22] to group learning documents based on their topics and similarities. In fact, the existing metrics in content based filtering only detect similarity between items that share the same attributes. Indeed, the basic process performed by a content-based recommender consists in matching up the attributes of a user profile in which preferences and interests are stored with the attributes of a content object (item). The objective is to recommend to the user new interesting items. In CB recommender systems, two techniques have been used to generate recommendations. One technique generates recommendations heuristically using traditional information retrieval methods, such as cosine similarity measure. The other technique generates recommendations using statistical learning and machine learning methods, largely building models that are capable of learning users' interests from the historical data (training data) of users.

Knowledge-Based Recommendation System. This system recommends contents based on specific domain knowledge on the usefulness of the contents to the learners needs and preferences [23]. The knowledge-based systems are case-based systems which use a similarity function to access the needs of the learners and provide recommendations. Another example of knowledge-based system is a constraint-based system, which collect learners' requirement and re-adjust the preferences for consistency, and also automatically suggest recommendation if none is offered originally. While case-based recommenders offer recommendation based on similarity matrices, constraints-based recommenders exploit predefined knowledge bases with explicit rules to suggest contents to learners suitable to their learning needs. However, in [23] authors, argue that knowledge-based systems tend to be more efficient as compared to the others at the early stages or phases of their application, but there exists some criticisms, which they argue that if knowledge-based systems are not properly "equipped with learning components", they certainly can be overshadowed by other methods such as collaborative filtering which can exploit both human and computer interactions.

In this section, we have presented a review of principal techniques for adaptation in e-learning, such as system student model and recommendation technique. We believe that many combined powerful techniques can improve adaptation for MOOCs. We have also showed that machine learning and fuzzy logic technique can provide a robust user model which can be useful to recommender system so as to provide dynamic feedback and suggest the suitable resources to the MOOC learner.

3 Proposed Framework

MOOC user behaviors are also a big part of massive MOOC data. User behavior real-time data (study process, assignment achievement, test score, etc.) mean the effect of MOOC learning. Therefore, identifying the learning problems during the course as early as possible enables educators to apply the intervention or the suitable measures to achieve improvement in online learning. In this respect, there are a wide variety of current techniques popular within educational big data analytics. Most used techniques are statistics and machine learning. Figure 3 shows the classical learning workflow in the MOOC environment. The course material is made of lecture videos, exercises, assignments etc., which is generally split on a week basis. At the start of the week, the learner has access to the above mentioned material during the current week. In other words, the learner watches video lectures, does exercises, debates in the provided

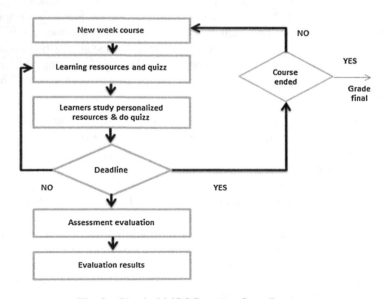

Fig. 3. Classical MOOC system flow diagram.

discussion forum, completes assignments etc. Once the deadline is reached, the learners' assignments are subjected to an evaluation procedure, which is mostly peer evaluation. The same procedure is repeated for the next week as long as the course is not completed.

One of the shortcomings of MOOC implementation system is the fact that learners attend the same course, without taking in consideration the features and behavior of each learner. In order to cope with this pitfall in the traditional MOOC system, there is a need for an adaptive system that takes into account the specificities of each learner before the beginning of each week. This adaptation should take the form of some suggestive tasks or readings to be performed based on the interaction with the system. Figure 4 is an illustration of the adaptive MOOC system. This adaptive MOOC system is to be credited with two fold advantages. Firstly, it is personalized as it takes into consideration the particularities of each learner. Secondly, the learner is aware of his weaknesses and thus provided with recommended tasks to overcome them. This adaptive MOOC system manages to achieve this by analyzing the behavior and characteristics of each learner at the beginning of each week which enables it to suggest the suitable and efficient tasks to be performed. More importantly, this behavior analysis is done continuously and recurrently throughout the week while the learner is interacting with the system which makes it possible to renew and revise the recommended tasks to fit the learner's individual needs.

For more details, this section describes the adaptive learning framework that could cater for improved and personalized recommendations for MOOCs. Our framework structured in four layers (Fig. 5).

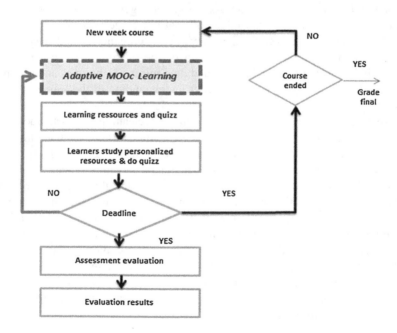

Fig. 4. Proposed adaptive MOOC flow diagram

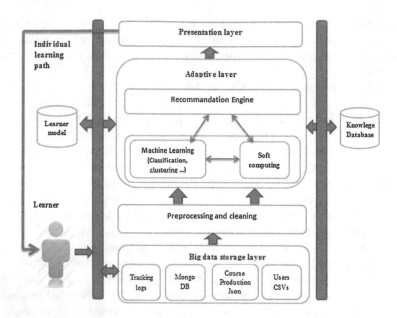

Fig. 5. The proposed framework for an adaptive learning of MOOCs.

As concerns the first layer, while users work with the adaptive framework system, it logs and stores all their actions. When scheduled, the storage system retrieves usage data, preprocesses them and stores them into different types of files, namely log files, Json files and database (storage layer). As the systems generate daily due to learner's interaction with the system, the quantities of data get bigger which makes it hard to analyze them manually, especially that they are heterogeneous and need speed to manage. So as to reach deeper understanding of the outcomes, we can rely on the existing analytical techniques for big data and data mining techniques and use them in the teaching courses. This can help in a better understanding of the learner's behavior and interaction.

The second layer consists of preprocessing and cleaning. In fact, tracking logs provide a lot of useful information. However, the format of tracking logs is semi-structured. To understand the pattern and classify these logs based on their events, it is necessary to preprocess and clean them. The major benefit of processing the record of every user interaction in entire course is to gain more insights into learner behavior. Nevertheless, in relationship with the cleaning process, it is worth mentioning that finding meaningful interpretation from clickstream data is challenging task. This challenge lies in the difficulty to transform clickstream data into more understandable data. Data cleaning extracts valuable row data to draw meaningful interpretation thought it is not directly possible to apply these data for interpretation process. As result, we first need to identify the characteristics of the database and extract features out of it. By extracting each feature and applying data mining process, we get further valuable information from data.

As regards the third layer, the adaptive layer is responsible for building and updating learner's model characteristics and also for personalization of content to be given to the learner. Moreover, it treats changes of learner's characteristics in accordance with the learner's activities as well as providing ways to adapt visible aspects of the system with specific learner. Among its main tasks, we can find also storage and management of learning material, presenting that material to learners, generating of reports and test results etc. During each session, the system gradually re-builds the learner model in order to follow the learner's actions and his/her progress, identify and correct his/her errors and possibly redirect the session accordingly. As the session ends, all of learners' preferences are recorded in learner model.

Machine learning algorithms are executed on stored usage data and usage patterns are found out and saved in the knowledge base. With clustering algorithm, learners are grouped into recognizable and manageable clusters according to their common attributes and based on the privileged categories of content delivery. Parts of the instruction are then tailored to the groups and are carried out similarly to all members of a segmented group. That segmentation is accomplished by different surveys that the learner has to complete during the registration on the system and optionally after every sequence and by following the learner's actions, progress and general performance. Assessment techniques such as homework, quizzes, to name only a few can be used to evaluate concepts causing difficulties for learning.

The shortcomings of traditional machine learning techniques for modeling human behavior have led to the introduction of Soft Computing (SC) technologies that provide an approximate solution to wrongly defined problem and can create user models in an environment, such as a e-learning system, in which users are reluctant to give feedback on their actions and/or designers are not able to completely define all possible interactions. Human interaction is an essential component of MOOC system, which means that the data available will be usually inaccurate, incomplete and heterogeneous. In this context SC seems to be the convenient paradigm to deal with the uncertainty and fuzziness of the information available to create user models [15]. The elements that a user model captures, namely goals, plans, preferences, common characteristics of users can utilize the ability of SC of combining various behaviors and capturing human decision processes so as to carry out a system that is more flexible and sensible in relation to user interests.

Different techniques cater for different capacities. For example, Fuzzy Logic provides a mechanism to imitate human decision-making for the purpose of inferring goals and plans. Neural Networks is an adjustable mechanism for the representation of common characteristics of a learner and the definition of sophisticated stereotypes. Another technique is Fuzzy Clustering which is a mechanism in which a learner can be part of more than one stereotype at the same time and NeuroFuzzy systems is a mechanism to detect and tune expert knowledge which can be used to get assumptions about the learner. In this regard, Frías-Martínez et al. [17] draw a comparison of different SC techniques and allow to have guidelines to choose the most appropriate technique, and show that Fuzzy logic is best suited for the task of recommendations. Thus, we suggest selecting fuzzy clustering to categorize the learner of one or multiple group.

The task of recommending system in MOOC is to suggest for a learner a based individual learning path on the tasks already performed by the learner and based also on tasks done by other similar learners. These similar learners are incorporated in the profiles. The chief objective is to recommend a sequence of pertaining concepts for particular learner, based on the learner's current needs obtained from the system-user interactions. Accordingly, we propose a fuzzy-based system for MOOC learners to retrieve optimal resources.

It is worth mentioning that the knowledge domain is responsible for the representation of the subject being dealt with that can take the shape of course modules, which involve domain concepts which include sub objectives. Figure 6 is an illustration of the course module components. The primary objective of knowledge representation is to display it in a way that makes reasoning an easy task. In an adaptive system, adaptation relies on the type of knowledge representation technique chosen. Thus Fuzzy Cognitive Mapping (FCM) is a way to represent knowledge of systems which are characterized by uncertainty and complex processes. FCM consists of concepts and relations among each other when it is used to present learning resource. Furthermore, FCM can represent not only causal relations between concepts but also knowledge of various granularity levels. However, learning resources should be organized in some semantic forms in order to back up high efficient searching and recommendation.

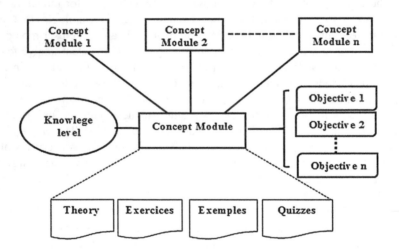

Fig. 6. Knowledge representation

Capturing initial data about the user occurs at the starting point of the system. This data includes user preferences, learning style, knowledge level about all the concepts taught in the week. At this initial stage the focus is on knowledge level of all the concepts previously taught in the week. This knowledge level can be captured by using exercises and quizzes of the week. The structure of the quizzes and exercises should be pre-defined and the structure in a way that each question must be mapped to a given objective of a given concept.

This system can use various recommendation techniques so as to propose online learning tasks or optimal browsing pathways to students. These systems use various machine learning algorithms, for example, clustering and sequential pattern mining combined with fuzzy logic. In this way, they can find out clusters of students showing common behavior and/or knowledge and then they are able to discover the sequential patterns of each cluster. This type of recommender system can personalize the recommendations. First, it categorizes the new students in one or more groups of students (fuzzy clusters). Then, it only uses the sequential patterns of the corresponding group to personalize the recommendations based on other similar students and his current navigation. The recommender module creates a sequence of recommended concepts based on the current session of a learner and the knowledge saved in the knowledge database. The concepts in the current user session are associated with the ones in patterns of the knowledge database. When corresponding (similar) patterns are found, the concept recommendation is implemented. The result is a sequence of recommended concepts and the evaluation of their appropriateness and relevance for the user. This sequence is generated as a response to MOOC system (each time the user shifts to another concept or fragment, or after some time period or at the beginning of each session). [24]

4   Conclusion and Future Work

In this paper, we have proposed an adaptive learning framework of massive open online courses (MOOCs), which is based on existing adaptive methodologies of adaptation model development using machine learning techniques, soft computing and recommender system. Therefore, the framework proposed is able to generate suggestions of learning paths adapted to the competences profile of each participant so as to allow for an increased personalization and contextualization of learning experiences. The framework is also flexible as it has the ability to adapt the content for MOOCs learners. In other words, we believe that the combination of these SC techniques among themselves and with other machine learning techniques will provide a useful framework to efficiently capture the natural complexity of human behavior and recommend useful personalized content for each student.

Future development of the recommender system will focus on enhancing the set of data mining algorithms, e.g., to use fuzzy clustering techniques in order to discover user clusters according to their learning styles. We also plan to evaluate quality of recommendations carried out by our recommender system using data produced by MOOCs provider. The evaluation will be based on a feedback from students as well as on results of the recommendation performed on a testing set of data.

References

1. Siemens, G.: Massive Open Online Courses: Innovation in education? In: Open Educational Resources: Innovation, Research and Practice, p. 5 (2013)
2. State of the MOOC 2016: A Year of Massive Landscape Change For Massive Open Online Courses. http://www.onlinecoursereport.com/state-of-the-mooc-2016-a-year-of-massive-landscape-change-for-massive-open-online-courses/

3. Petkovska, B., Delipetrev, B.J., Zdravev, Z.: MOOCS in higher education – state of the art review. In: ITRO 2014
4. Yousef, A.M.F., Chatti, M.A., Schroeder, U., Wosnitza, M., Jakobs, H.: A review of the state-of-the-art. In: Proceedings of the 6th International Conference on Computer Supported Education, CSEDU 2014, pp. 9–20 (2014)
5. MOOCs and Open Education Timeline (updated!). http://blogs.cetis.org.uk/cetisli/
6. Thakkar, S.R., Joshi, H.D.: E-learning systems: a review. In: 2015 IEEE Seventh International Conference on Technology for Education (T4E), pp. 37–40 (2015). doi:10.1109/T4E.2015.6
7. Brusilovsky, P., Nejdl, W.: Adaptive hypermedia and adaptive web. In: Miscellaneous 2004. http://www.kbs.uni-hannover.de/Arbeiten/Publikationen/2003/brusilovsky-nejdl.pdf
8. Daradoumis, T., Bassi, R., Xhafa, F., Caballé, S.: A review on massive e-learning (MOOC) design, delivery and assessment. In: Proceedings of the 2013 8th International Conference on P2P, Parallel, Grid, Cloud and Internet Computing, 3PGCIC 2013, pp. 208–213 (2013). doi:10.1109/3PGCIC.2013.37
9. Bassi, R., Daradoumis, T., Xhafa, F., Caballé, S., Sula, A.: Software agents in large scale open e-learning: a critical component for the future of massive online courses (MOOCs). In: Proceedings of the 2014 International Conference on Intelligent Networking and Collaborative Systems, INCoS 2014, pp. 184–188. IEEE (2014). doi:10.1109/INCoS.2014.15
10. Lerís, D., Sein-Echaluce, M.L., Hernandez, M., Bueno, C.: Validation of indicators for implementing an adaptive platform for MOOCs. In: Computers in Human Behavior (2016). doi:10.1016/j.chb.2016.07.054
11. Sonwalkar, N.: The first adaptive mooc: a case study on pedagogy framework and scalable cloud architecture-part I. In: MOOCs Forum, pp. 22–29 (2013). doi:10.1089/mooc.2013.0007
12. Onah, D.F.O., Sinclair, J.E.: Massive open online courses – an adaptive learning framework. In: The University of Warwick, INTED 2015, pp. 1258–1266. doi:10.13140/RG.2.1.4237.0083
13. Teixeira, A., Mota, J., García-Cabot, A., García-Lopéz, E., De-Marcos, L.: A new competence-based approach for personalizing MOOCs in a mobile collaborative and networked environment. In: Revista Iberoamericana de Educación a Distancia, vol 19, pp. 143–160 (2016). doi:10.5944/ried.19.1.14578
14. Milićević, A.K., Vesin, B., Ivanović, M.: Integration of recommendations and adaptive hypermedia into Java tutoring system. doi:10.2298/CSIS090608021K
15. Kidziński, Ł., Giannakos, M., Sampson, D.G., Dillenbourg, P.: A tutorial on machine learning in educational science. In: Li, Y., et al. (eds.) State-of-the-Art and Future Directions of Smart Learning. Lecture Notes in Educational Technology, pp. 453–459. Springer, Singapore (2015)
16. Chrysafiadi, K., Virvou, M.: Fuzzy Logic in Student Modeling. In: Bra, Paul M.E., Chrysafiadi, K., Virvou, M. (eds.) Advances in Personalized Web-Based Education. Intelligent Systems Reference Library, vol. 78, pp. 25–60. Springer International Publishing, Cham (2015)
17. Frías-Martínez, E., Magoulas, G., Chen, S., Macredie, R.: Recent soft computing approaches to user modeling in adaptive hypermedia. In: Bra, Paul M.E., Nejdl, W. (eds.) AH 2004. LNCS, vol. 3137, pp. 104–114. Springer, Heidelberg (2004). doi:10.1007/978-3-540-27780-4_14
18. Chrysafiadi, K., Virvou, M.: Student modeling approaches: a literature review for the last decade. In: Expert Systems with Applications, vol. 40, pp. 4715–4729. Elsevier Ltd. (2013). doi:10.1016/j.eswa.2013.02.007

19. Sikka, R., Dhankhar, A., Rana, C.: A survey paper on e-learning recommender system. Int. J. Comput. Appl. **47**, 27–30 (2012). doi:10.5120/7218-0024
20. Onah, D.F.O., Sinclair, J.E.: Collaborative filtering recommendation system: a framework in massive open online courses, pp. 1249–1257 (2015)
21. Vesin, B., Klašnja-Milićević, A., Ivanović, M., Budimac, Z.: Applying recommender systems and adaptive hypermedia for e-learning personalization. In: Computing and Informatics, vol. 32, pp. 629–659 (2013)
22. Hammouda, K.: Collaborative document clustering. In: Sixth SIAM International Conference on Data Mining, pp. 451–461 (2006)
23. Schafer, J.B.: The application of data-mining to recommender systems. In: Encyclopedia of Data Warehousing and Mining, pp. 44–48 (2009)
24. Krištofič, A.: Recommender system for adaptive hypermedia applications. In: Student Research Conference, IIT. SRC 2005 pp. 229–234 (2005). http://www.fiit.stuba.sk/iit-src/2005/zbornik.pdf#page=243

E-Health and E-Commerce

A Virtual Patient Navigation Application for Lung Cancer Assessment Patients

Gursimran Singh Chandhoke[1], Ajaydeep Singh Grewal[1],
Venus Pathak[1], Simrandeep Singh[1], Mir Kamyar Ziabari[1],
Daniel Amyot[1(✉)], Hussein Mouftah[1], Wojtek Michalowski[2],
Michael Fung-Kee-Fung[2,3], Jennifer Smylie[3], and Salome Shin[3]

[1] School of Computer Science and Electrical Engineering,
University of Ottawa, Ottawa, Canada
{gchandho, agrewl00, vpath031, ssingl36,
mziab054, damyot, mouftah}@uottawa.ca
[2] Telfer School of Management, University of Ottawa, Ottawa, Canada
wojtek@telfer.uottawa.ca
[3] The Ottawa Hospital, Ottawa, Canada
{mfung, jesmylie, sshin}@toh.ca

Abstract. A *virtual patient navigator* is a web/mobile application that helps patients with lung cancer diagnosis reduce their anxiety and uncertainties. In particular, lung cancer patients easily become overwhelmed when having to manage information overload, many appointments with different instructions and locations, and recommendations on how to improve their lifestyle. Existing solutions such as paper-based patient navigators provide much reliable information but are limited in terms of dynamic updates and do not provide opportunities for interactions between care providers and patients. In this paper, we propose a new web-based, mobile, and user-friendly virtual patient navigator application named *Care Ami*, which incorporates the information found in an existing paper-based navigator along with new features such as remote updates to personal care paths and calendars, personalized navigation guidance, sharing of symptom/medication information, and peer group support. The architecture and main features of this application are presented. Based on the identified requirements, *Care Ami* compares favorably against related work and solutions.

Keywords: Drupal · eHealth · Lung cancer · Uncertainties · Virtual patient navigation

1 Introduction

Lung cancer is one of the leading types of cancer in Canada, and one of the deadliest. In Ontario, lung cancer represents 25% of all cancer deaths and is considered to be the type of cancer with the lowest survival rate [7]. Smoking causes most lung cancers, but lung cancer can also affect individuals who have never smoked in their lifetime [31].

When diagnosing lung cancer, a patient has to undergo several tests and consults (e.g., biopsy for diagnostics, staging, and others related to treatment options) over a period of several weeks. Patients find such journey complex: they become uncertain

© Springer International Publishing AG 2017
E. Aïmeur et al. (Eds.): MCETECH 2017, LNBIP 289, pp. 255–272, 2017.
DOI: 10.1007/978-3-319-59041-7_16

about what to do as they have to manage a significant amount of diversified information, complex appointments schedule (which may be changing), many instructions (e.g., fasting before a particular test, and finding where to get a test in a large hospital), and recommendations on how to have a healthy lifestyle. In this context, there is a need for *patient navigation* that can guide the patients through their complex cancer care journey. Patient navigation eliminates the barriers faced by the patients during their diagnosis and treatment of cancer [13]. A patient navigation may also help providing information to the patients, support during their treatment, and assistance with survivorship issues [28]. Several studies have shown the positive impact of patient navigation programs on patients [5, 15, 27, 34, 39].

According to the Canadian Partnership Against Cancer, patient navigation (PN) systems are of three kinds: professional, peer-based, or virtual [33]. In a professional PN, the patient navigators are trained professionals (e.g., case managers or nurses) who possess broad knowledge about the healthcare system. In a peer-based PN, the patient navigators are community health workers who share similarities with patients regarding language, social, and cultural background [12]. A virtual PN system connects the patients (or their families) online through a web or mobile application, hence simplifying their journey by providing convenient access to services while enabling patients and healthcare providers to save time [19]. In addition, virtual PN systems provide patients with reliable and comprehensive information [20, 29].

In the recent past, The Ottawa Hospital (TOH), located in Ottawa, Ontario, Canada, used a systems approach to re-engineer its lung cancer diagnosis process in a way that has improved the overall patient experience, mainly by reducing the total wait time from referral to the first treatment [14]. In addition, TOH started providing patients undergoing lung cancer assessment a paper-based *passport* [43], shown in Fig. 1, in order to support their care journey and to reduce their fears and uncertainties. This passport provides much reliable information about tests and medical terms, and it enables the patient to collect information about his/her medications, symptoms, appointments, questions for physicians, etc.

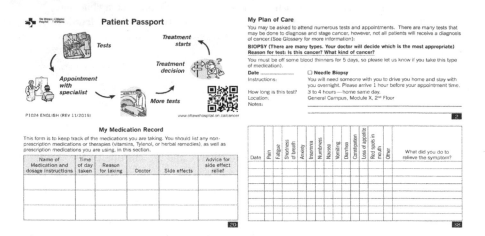

Fig. 1. Four sample pages from TOH's existing paper-based passport

However, such paper-based solution cannot provide a direct contact between the providers and the patients, nor can it adapt dynamically to changes in patients' journey. Therefore, to further improve the patient experience, an online-based solution can be used to address such issues, and in addition provide map-based navigation guidance, peer communication between patients, and support for decision making.

This paper presents a new virtual patient navigator application called *Care Ami* ("ami" meaning "friend" in French), developed for TOH, a bilingual hospital. Care Ami aims to improve the patient experience by providing on-line access to the information that was included in the paper-based passport while addressing many of the issues raised above. This application is also meant to be used on computers, tablets, and mobile phones. Hevner's Design Science methodology was used to guide our research activities [21].

The rest of the paper is organized as follows. Section 2 discusses the related work on virtual patient navigation systems. Section 3 explores the application's requirements, architecture, and technology choices. Section 4 highlights the implementation of the Care Ami application. Section 5 compares Care Ami with related work and, finally, Sect. 6 discusses conclusions and future work.

2 Literature Review

Our review methodology is inspired from the systematic literature review approach for software engineering developed by Kitchenham et al. [30]. Four steps are used here: finding keywords, searching queries, gathering, and filtering papers by applying inclusion and exclusion criteria, and summarizing data. The papers selected here will be revisited in Sect. 5 in a comparative evaluation involving Care Ami.

2.1 Finding Keywords

This research investigates the online-based patient navigation systems that can improve the experience of patients during their healthcare journey and is not limited to lung cancer. Through the iterative exploration of papers, important keywords used for querying scientific databases were found to be: virtual patient navigation, web-based, patient advocate, healthcare, and interactive. We used common technical and medical databases in this review: Scopus (which covers IEEE Xplore, ACM Digital Library, Springer, Elsevier, and others), Web of Science, Medline (Ovid), ProQuest, and Google Scholar. Google's regular search engine was also used to find information about commercial systems.

2.2 Searching Queries

The abstract query we used is: ("patient navigat*" OR "patient advocate" OR "healthcare advocate" OR "healthcare navigat*") AND ("virtual" OR "web-based" OR "interactive"). This abstract query was tailored to the specific syntax and limitations of each search engine. Furthermore, Google Scholar was searched based on titles only, Medline (Ovid) was searched using abstracts only, and the other databases were searched using abstracts and titles. No time limit was enforced.

2.3   Gathering and Filtering Papers

The query resulted in 99 unique scientific papers. Many irrelevant papers were quickly removed based on titles and abstracts through exclusion criteria: papers unrelated to patient navigation in healthcare (many were about robotics for surgery), applications for healthcare providers only (instead of patients), posters found during the search, papers for which full text is not attainable and PN systems that were professional or peer-based (not virtual). The 6 remaining papers were reviewed again by going through their introduction, results, methods, and conclusions in detail. This step further reduced the number of relevant papers to 4 scientific papers and 3 commercial systems.

An additional backward chaining step was used, which consisted in looking at the references of the 3 scientific papers (plus a survey paper) for including additional relevant systems. As a result, we found another virtual PN systems, the Gabby System [16] that was added, for a total of 8 papers.

2.4   Summarizing Data

The selected papers are shown in Table 1. They include the scientific papers as well as the commercial systems related to virtual patient navigation.

Table 1. Summary of related virtual patient navigation systems

Article code	System name	Search engine	Year	Ref.
P1	Oncology Interactive Navigator (OIN)	Scopus	2013	[32]
P2	Lupus Interactive Navigator (LIN)	Scopus	2016	[37]
P3	A web-based portal to improve patient navigation	ProQuest	2014	[23]
P4	Accenture patient navigation application	Google	2013	[24]
P5	Patient navigator by MobileCare247	Google	~2012	[36]
P6	Gabby system – Virtual patient advocate	Reference	2013	[16]
P7	Project RED – Virtual patient advocate	Google Scholar	2009	[3, 25, 26]
P8	Diagnostic Assessment Program – Electronic Pathway Solution (DAP-EPS)	Google	2011	[6]

Articles P1, P2, P3, P6, and P7 are the virtual patient navigation systems that were found in the databases or through their references. Articles P4, P5, and P8 are commercial systems. Although P3 and P5 are not exactly online systems for patients, they target human patient navigators who can further guide the patients through their healthcare journey.

3 Application Architecture

This section summarizes the goals and requirements of the Care Ami application, discusses important technology choices, and gives an overview of the resulting architecture.

3.1 Goals and Requirements

The primary goals of the application are to:

(G1) Improve the patient experience, reduce uncertainty, and reduce fears of not being taken care of/about.
(G2) Improve interactions between patients and nurses/physicians.
(G3) Provide a generalizable solution as a clinical care support tool in various contexts (beyond lung cancer assessment).

With regards to the above goals, several requirements (Table 2) were identified by discussing needs and features of existing systems during meetings with physicians, nurses, information technology personnel, patients, a social worker, and patients' family members.

Table 2. Care Ami application requirements and their contributions to goals

R#	Requirements	Sub-requirements	Goals
R1	Provide information about the diagnosis and healthcare providers [17]	(1-1) List major lung cancer symptoms	G1
		(1-2) Provide information about the diagnostic plan	G1
		(1-3) Provide information about the medical staff involved in the patient's management	G2
R2	Support patient engagement [22]	(2-1) Provide different features for patients to document their medications, symptoms, and questions	G2
R3	Provide a follow-up plan	(3-1) Provide the description of each stage of treatment	G1, G2
		(3-2) Provide a visual indication of a patient's current stage of treatment	G1, G2

(*continued*)

Table 2. (*continued*)

R#	Requirements	Sub-requirements	Goals
		(3-3) Provide a calendar that contains information about the tests and appointments of the patient and the exact time and date of the appointment/test in addition to a description of the test that will be taken	G1, G2
		(3-4) Provide a mechanism to import the calendar content to personal calendars	G1, G2
		(3-5) Provide nurses and clerks with the means to revise and update the content of the calendar	G1, G2
		(3-6) Send an email notification to the patient when an appointment is booked	G1, G2
		(3-7) Send a reminder email two days before each test or appointment	G1, G2
R4	Enforce role-based access [40]	(4-1) Provide an editable profile for each user	G3
		(4-2) Provide each user the relevant type of access, view, and features	G3
		(4-3) Provide permissions to patient users to cancel their account at any time	G3
R5	Create a peer support group [44]	(5-1) Provide a private peer network of other patients being diagnosed, to help them interact with and support each other	G1
		(5-2) Provide the contact information of reliable lung cancer support communities	G1
R6	Display maps integrated with appointments [42]	(6-1) Provide a map of the hospital floor where the test or appointment will be held, with an indication of the room	G1
		(6-2) Provide hospital parking information	G1
		(6-3) Provide information about how to get to the hospital using public transportation	G1
R7	Provide information about a healthy lifestyle [41]	(7-1) Provide reliable informative and videos about how to maintain a healthy lifestyle during the patient's journey	G1, G2
		(7-2) Provide information about smoking cessation and health information units that can help patients quit smoking.	G1
R8	Support official languages [8]	(8-1) Provide information in English and French	G1
R9	Support mobile devices	(9-1) Support Android and Apple mobile phones and tablets	G1
R10	Support other types of disease processes in the future	(10-1) Support multiple sites, one per disease	G3
		(10-2) Support sharing of relevant information and privileges between sites	G3

Five different categories of users were also identified for this application: patients and their family members, hospital clerks, nurses and physicians, site administrators (e.g., for lung cancer), and super administrators (for the computing infrastructure). Each class of users has its own set of read/write access privileges. In addition to goal G3 about reuse/generality, several concerns and policies related to security, privacy, usability, performance, and maintainability were noted and have influenced our implementation.

3.2 Technology Decisions

In order to meet the mobile device support requirement (R10 in Table 2), several multi-platform technologies were evaluated, including:

1. Aurelia [1], a JavaScript-based client side framework for mobile and web applications.
2. Xamarin™ [45], a C#-based mobile application programming language.
3. MEAN [35], a JavaScript-based stack combining MongoDB, Node.js, Express, and AngularJS.

However, the need for role-based access (R4) and for a general application that would support diseases other than lung cancer (R10) led us to conclude that we were essentially designing a *Content Management Systems* (CMS). A CMS is "a software package that provides some level of automation for the tasks required to effectively manage content" [2]. It was hence decided to move away from basic technologies such as Aurelia, Xamarin, and MEAN, in favor of a CMS-based solution.

Among popular CMS solutions such as WordPress and Joomla! [10], *Drupal* [11], a feature-rich and community-supported free solution, has been chosen in order to be compatible with TOH and the University of Ottawa, since both institutions use Drupal for their web-based content management and could provide proper maintenance and technical support after deployment of the Care Ami application.

3.3 Architecture

Figure 2 shows Care Ami's multi-tier architecture, including the main user roles and the key components of the application.

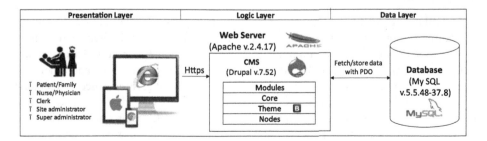

Fig. 2. Architecture of the Care Ami application

In the presentation layer, patients (and their family members), nurses/physicians, clerks, site administrators, and super administrators are users who can sign-in to and access the application via a web browser running on a computer, tablet, or phone.

In the logic layer, a web server (Apache Web Server v.2.4.17 in our case) interacts with web browsers via secure Https communication. This server also hosts the CMS component (Drupal v.7.52). Drupal itself has four categories of components:

- *Modules*: As Drupal itself is implemented with the PHP scripting language, modules are packages written in PHP that can be used to provide functionalities in a Drupal server. Core modules are installed on Drupal by default whereas external modules are installed manually. Several existing external modules were installed, configured, and adapted for the implementation of the Care Ami application, for example a Calendar Module, designed for helping patients track their appointments, and a Content Translation Module to allow the content of the web pages to be translated into other languages.
- *Core*: Basic libraries, modules, and features of the Drupal CMS, which are crucial to design and maintain the web site.
- *Theme*: The visual style of the application. The base theme selected for this application is the Bootstrap framework (v.7.x-3.8) [4]. This framework is one of the leading front-end frameworks for designing web applications and websites. The responsive nature of this framework makes web pages and menus adjust automatically to the sizes of phone, tablet, and desktop screens.
- *Nodes*: All content types of the Drupal 7 CMS such as articles and basic pages are stored as nodes.

In the data layer, a database management system (MySQL V5.5.48-37.8 here) is used to manage and store user information, content, and administrative information. PHP Data Objects (PDO) are used as a communication means between Drupal and the database.

4 *Care Ami* Virtual Patient Navigator

This section highlights some of the main features of the Care Ami application.

4.1 Role-Based Access Control

Care Ami uses Drupal to manage different roles (patient/family, clerk, nurse/physician, site administrator, super administrator) where each role can have different permissions according to the view/modify requirements. The super administrator has full access to the Drupal infrastructure and can also add and modify its different modules and other features, whereas a site administrator has full access to one site (e.g., lung cancer) except for health-related content (e.g., patient's information). The clerk can add, view, and modify patient users and calendar events only whereas the nurse/physician can also view the patient's health information. Patients can document their health information (symptoms, medications, etc.), view their calendar events, and modify/delete their accounts.

4.2 Record My Symptoms, My Medications, and My Questions

Three features (Record My Symptoms, Record My Medications, and My Questions) are available to patients to document their personal health information so they can remember it correctly during appointments and share it (read only) with nurses and physicians, even remotely. Only a patient can update his/her personal information.

In Record My Symptoms (Fig. 3), a patient can record the symptoms he/she had during the process of diagnosis development (diagnosis takes about three weeks in the case of lung cancer assessment). This feature allows the patient to fill a form that includes the date, symptoms that can be selected from a list, and precautions taken by the patient. The list of documented symptoms of that patient is displayed at the top of the page in a tabular format.

The Record My Medication feature is very similar in nature and behavior. Patients can keep track of their medications and dosage instructions, the reason for taking these medications, the prescriber's name, when medications are taken, side effects, and advices for side effect relief (similar to the information recorded in the paper-based passport, see bottom-left of Fig. 1).

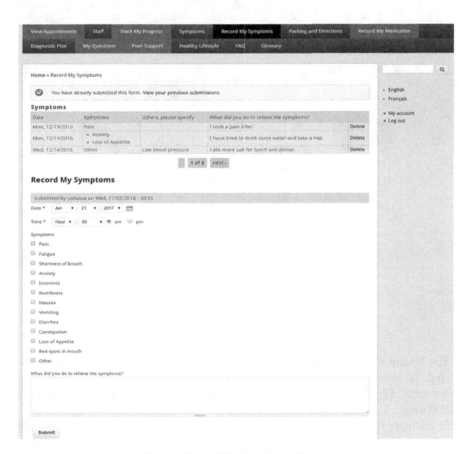

Fig. 3. Record My Symptoms feature

The My Questions feature follows the same pattern. This feature simply enables documenting possible questions that patient wants to ask during consults with physicians or during discussions with nurses over the phone (so patients do not forget what to ask in case they are sick or under medication). Answers can then be recorded if needed.

4.3   Appointments

The appointments feature relies on Drupal's external calendar module, which provides an integrated framework for creating and managing appointments. This feature gives the authorized person the ability to create new patient appointments, to reschedule, edit, or delete an existing appointment. This feature is also very helpful for the patients by offering a bird's eye view of all their appointments. The appointments can be viewed on a monthly, weekly, or daily basis, as shown in Fig. 4.

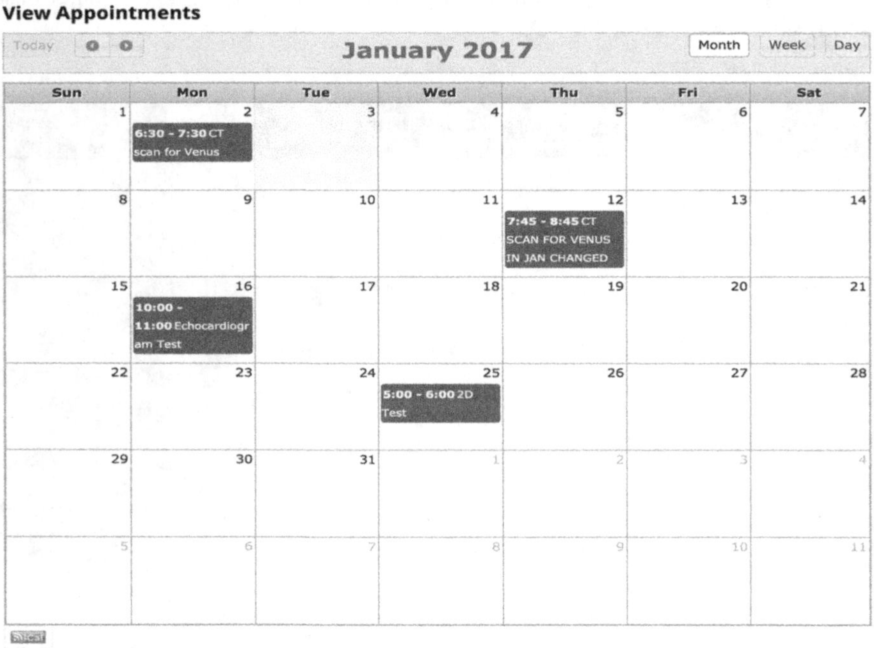

View Appointments

	Sun	Mon	Tue	Wed	Thu	Fri	Sat
	1	2	3	4	5	6	7
		6:30 - 7:30 CT scan for Venus					
	8	9	10	11	12	13	14
					7:45 - 8:45 CT SCAN FOR VENUS IN JAN CHANGED		
	15	16	17	18	19	20	21
		10:00 - 11:00 Echocardiogram Test					
	22	23	24	25	26	27	28
				5:00 - 6:00 2D Test			
	29	30	31	1	2	3	4
	5	6	7	8	9	10	11

January 2017 — Month / Week / Day

Fig. 4. Patient's appointment feature

The feature enables sending a notification email when an appointment is created, updated, or deleted. Also, a reminder email is sent two days prior to the actual appointment. The feature also provides easy integration with iCal and Outlook Calendar (Google Calendar is yet to be supported).

In addition, the appointments feature provides all the essential information related to each appointment, as shown in Fig. 5. The information includes the appointment's time, location, and the associated building map. In the case of a consult, the feature

Appointment Date/Time: Monday, January 16, 2017 -
10:00 to 11:00

2D Echocardiogram

Test Name: 2D Echocardiogram
Test Description:
An echocardiogram is a special ultrasound examination of the heart that provides your doctor with live pictures of your heart to evaluate the anatomy and function of the heart muscle, chambers, and valves. It is the same technology that is used to look at unborn babies in a pregnant woman. It is a painless examination that takes approximately 30 to 45 minutes to perform. A specially trained technologist called a sonographer will attach electrodes to your chest so that we may record your heart's rhythm. You will be asked to remove your clothing from the waist up and change into a hospital gown. You will be asked to lie down on your left side on the exam table. The lights will be dimmed during the examination. The sonographer will put gel on an ultrasound transducer which will be applied to your chest to look at your heart. The recorded pictures will be analyzed later by a cardiologist who will send a report to your physician. If parts of your heart muscle are not well seen, you may be given an intravenous injection of a medication called Definity which will allow us to see your heart better and increase the accuracy of the test.
Test Instructions: No preparation necessary.
Room Name: Module R
Location:

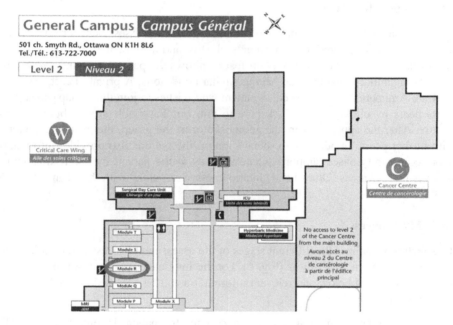

Fig. 5. Appointment details with map and highlighted target location

provides the physician's name (and a link to his/her web page) whereas in the case of a diagnostic test, the feature describes the test as well as any needed preparation.

The appointments feature is very beneficial to patients as they have a single and up to date source of information concerning their appointments, useful information (nature, location, time, map, instructions, physician, etc.), and the possibility to integrate the appointments with personal calendars on desktops and mobile devices. The automatic reminders and the ability to easily avoid appointment clashes also helps the nurses and clerks with scheduling.

4.4   Maps

Zoomable and printable floor maps (Fig. 5) are associated with every appointment description, in order to guide patients to the exact location and floor where their appointment is going to take place. TOH buildings are particularly difficult to navigate, so this feature helps patients reduce their anxiety and uncertainty levels.

Links to the appropriate Google Maps Indoor [18] locations are also provided (which enable the user to navigate through the individual floors of a building via Google Maps), but at this time the room locations are not specifiable as navigation destinations because Google is not yet in possession of that information.

4.5   Support for Patients

Care Ami facilitates social support to patients undergoing assessment for lung cancer. Support is usually offered to help patients identify and achieve their personal goals as part of their journey. The Peer Support feature allows the patient to connect with other patients in similar situations and having similar conditions. A private Facebook group for Care Ami patients was created. A patient who wishes to join that group can connect to its peers by clicking the "Click here to join our Facebook group" button on the feature. After the approval from the administrator of the group, the patient can interact with his/her peers. In addition to social support, the feature also provides information about community-based supportive care services to the patient by listing trustworthy services in local areas (Ottawa and Ontario in our case) along with their contact details.

4.6   My Progress

This feature visualizes the different stages of the assessment process and highlights the stage where patient currently is (Fig. 6). For the lung cancer assessment process these stages are outlined below and relevant information can be accessed by clicking on the corresponding stage label:

1. **Initial Referral:** This refers to the stage when the patient is referred to the TOH, usually by family physician or another TOH physician.
2. **Contact Phone Call:** This is a stage when the patient is contacted by TOH for the first time. The patient might then be asked to provide certain reports for a review process. The patient could be offered a Care Ami account at that stage (or later).
3. **Consult Review:** The reports submitted by the patients or referring physician are reviewed by the specialists. Depending on the results of this review, the patient might be asked to submit additional information, or she/he might be scheduled for a visit to the cancer clinic at TOH for additional tests and assessments (it is called a "navigation day").
4. **Specialized Testing/Navigation Day:** This is the first time the patient visits the hospital. On this day, she/he is scheduled to undergo a series of tests. The intention here is to complete all the required tests and registration-related formalities on that day.

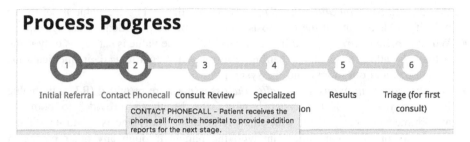

Fig. 6. Progress bar for patient along the assessment process

5. **Results:** This stage refers to the day when tests' results become available. These results are then analyzed and, depending on the outcome, the patient might be asked to undergo additional tests or she/he might be referred for a specialist consult.
6. **Triage** (for the first consult): This is a final stage for Care Ami, the patient is referred to a specialized service of TOH.

This feature helps the patient understand where she/he is in the diagnostic process, what came before, and what future stages are. This also helps physicians and nurses avoid having to explain these steps to the patient at each encounter. We also plan on using online videos to better explain and illustrate these stages in the future.

4.7 Healthy Lifestyle

This feature provides advice on how to adhere to a healthy lifestyle, especially in the context of the disease under assessment (lung cancer in our case). Proper lifestyle choices have positive impact on disease management, even if disease is chronic and cannot be cured [9]. The Healthy Lifestyle feature provides trusted information and helpful tips about the diet and daily exercises relevant to the patients (potentially) with lung cancer. This information aims to help patients better manage their health during the assessment and treatment processes, and also afterward. Additionally, as smoking is the main cause of the lung cancer [38], this feature introduces different smoking cessation programs and provides information about relevant support programs.

5 Evaluation

This section provides a brief comparison of Care Ami with the related work identified through the literature review, together with a discussion of the limitations.

5.1 Comparison with Related Work

In this section, we assess the different systems identified in Table 1 and compare them with Care Ami. The comparison criteria correspond to the high-level requirements from Table 2 (R1–R10), plus one more criterion related to validation:

- Whether *information about the diagnosis* is provided (R1) – the value is set to *yes* only if the details about the diagnosis or treatment are provided by the system.
- Whether *patients are engaged* in the system (R2) – the value is set to yes only if the patient is allowed to input her/his information (regarding their medications, symptoms, and questions) into the system.
- Whether *follow-up plans during/after the assessment* are provided (R3) – the value is set to *yes* only if the system enables the healthcare provider to book an appointment for the patient, with email reminders. The value is set to +/− if the healthcare provider can follow up with the patient through any other means of communication.
- Whether *role-based access* is supported (R4) – the value is set to *yes* only if the system enables the healthcare provider to book an appointment for the patient, with email reminders. The value is set to +/− if the healthcare provider can follow up with the patient through any other means of communication.
- Whether *peer support* is provided (R5) – the value is set to *yes* only if the system ensures that information can be read/written only by specific roles.
- Whether *maps* are displayed (R6) – the value is set to *yes* only if maps (e.g., Google Maps or static/bitmap/PDF maps) to buildings and rooms are integrated into the system. The value is set to +/− if only textual directions to reach the healthcare providers are provided.
- Whether *healthy lifestyle information during/after the treatment* is provided (R7) – the value is set to *yes* only if the system provides information regarding incorporation of healthy habits into a patient's life.
- Whether the interface supports *multiple languages* (R8) – the value is set to *yes* only if the system supports more than one language.
- Whether *mobile devices* are supported (R9) – the value is set to *yes* only if the system supports mobile apps or mobile web browsers.
- Whether *multiple types of diseases* are supported (R10) – the value is set to *yes* only if the system supports more than one disease, +/− if only the infrastructure to do so is there, and *no* otherwise.
- *Validation* of the application – the value is set to *yes* if there is some validation regarding the implementation and usefulness of the system, +/− if there is an implementation only, and *no* otherwise.

Table 3 summarizes the comparison of Care Ami with other relevant systems against the above criteria. In articles P3 and P4, human patient navigators use tools for providing healthcare navigation to the patients. All the other systems have as common objective a focus on patients by providing them with high-quality and reliable information about diagnosis/treatment processes.

None of the systems meets all requirements, although in all fairness many of these systems may not have had all of our requirements in their scope and may have had to satisfy other unknown requirements. However, Care Ami scores well on most of them. In terms of supporting multiple types of diseases (R9), Care Ami, being based on Drupal, has most of the infrastructure in place to do so, but this remains to be demonstrated. The Care Ami application was implemented and demonstrated to stakeholders with success, but it is yet to be deployed and validated formally at the

Table 3. Comparison with related work

Article	Information provided about diagnosis	Patient engagement	Follow-up plan	Role-based access	Peer support network	Map display	Healthy lifestyle	Multi-language	Support mobile devices	Multiple types of diseases	Validation
P1	Yes	No	No	Yes	Yes	No	Yes	No	Yes	Yes	Yes
P2	Yes	No	No	Yes	Yes	No	Yes	No	Yes	No	Yes
P3	No	No	No	Yes	No	+/−	No	Yes	Yes	No	Yes
P4	No	Yes	Yes	No	No	+/−	No	No	Yes	No	No
P5	Yes	Yes	Yes	Yes	Yes	No	Yes	No	Yes	No	No
P6	Yes	Yes	+/−	No	No	No	Yes	No	Yes	No	Yes
P7	Yes	Yes	+/−	No	No	No	Yes	Yes	No	No	Yes
P8	Yes	Yes	Yes	Yes	No	+/−	Yes	Yes	Yes	Yes	Yes
Care Ami	**Yes**	**Yes**	**Yes**	**Yes**	**Yes**	**Yes**	**Yes**	**Yes**	**Yes**	**+/−**	**+/−**

hospital. The closest competitor to Care Ami at this point (P8 in Table 3) is the DAP-EPS system developed by Cancer Care Ontario [6]. DAP-EPS does support two types of cancer assessment processes and has been deployed. However, maps to rooms are not provided, and peer support is unavailable. DAP-EPS was also not deployed at TOH in part because of the required high level of integration with existing health information systems (e.g., to report test results while ensuring privacy).

5.2   Limitations

Although Care Ami scores better than the other, its implementation and assessment has a number of limitations:

- Care Ami was demonstrated to multiple stakeholders and feedback was very positive and encouraging. However, the application has not been deployed or formally assessed in everyday use.
- There are still security and privacy issues to be solved, especially in terms of compliance to the hospital policies regarding patient data, and in terms of relying on external services (such as Facebook) for peer support.
- Care Ami is not yet integrated with the hospital's information systems, hence patient accounts and appointments need to be created manually, even if relevant information exists elsewhere.
- Our assessment of related work is solely based on the literature review and not on experiments where these systems were used. In addition, related systems may have feature important to their context but not to ours.

6   Conclusions and Future Work

While being assessed for lung cancer, many patients suffer from a fear of not being properly informed and are uncertain about what information to trust and what to do next. Virtual PN systems can improve the overall experience of such patients by addressing these fears and guiding patients throughout their care journey.

This paper contributes the requirements, architecture, and a CMS-based implementation of a virtual PN application called Care Ami, which supports patients undergoing lung cancer assessment in an Ontario hospital. This application provides many patient-oriented features that go beyond the existing paper-based solutions, including: dynamic appointment updates with e-mail reminders, navigation maps, personal health information that can be shared with nurses and physicians, status information along the assessment process, peer support, and a wealth of reliable online information (including videos) on medical conditions, on tests, on healthcare lifestyle tips, and on the hospital itself and its healthcare providers (hence contributing positively to goal G1). Care Ami has also the potential of improving the experience of nurses and physicians as they can have access to a patient's symptoms and medications when a patient contacts/meets them and they can likely save efforts setting and confirming appointments (hence helping satisfy goal G2). Physicians will also likely have more productive consults with patients as the former will spend less time explaining basic concepts and treatments covered by the application or discussing unreliable sources of health information.

Although Care Ami satisfies most of the identified requirements and goes beyond related virtual PN systems discovered during our literature survey, the limitations we identified in the previous section lead to many future work items. In the short term, we plan to extend Care Ami by integrating Google Maps Indoor, so patients can be told how to navigate (in real-time, on their phones/tablets) inside the hospital buildings. We also need to solve the security and privacy issues that currently prevent deployment and formal usability/usefulness studies. On the long term, there is a need to generalize the application for other types of cancer and other diseases (to better satisfy goal G3). We also consider exploring the suitability of similar application in non-cancer contexts such as supporting management of high-risk multiple pregnancies, where interactions with patients normally span over multiple months (instead of 3 weeks, as is the case with Care Ami) and where context-based decision-making needs to be supported.

Acknowledgements. This work was supported in part by the funding from the Telfer Health Transformation Exchange (THTex) at the Telfer School of Management, University of Ottawa. We are also thankful to Carl Maisonneuve for useful discussions about the TOH platforms, and to Jacques Sincennes for his help with the infrastructure.

References

1. Aurelia. http://aurelia.io. Accessed 5 Jan 2017
2. Barker, D.: Web Content Management: Systems, Features, and Best Practices. O'Reilly Media, Sebastopol (2016)
3. Berkowitz, R.E., Fang, Z., Helfand, B.K., Jones, R.N., Schreiber, R., Paasche-Orlow, M.K.: Project ReEngineered Discharge (RED) lowers hospital readmissions of patients discharged from a skilled nursing facility. J. Am. Med. Directors Assoc. **14**(10), 736–740 (2013). doi:10.1016/j.jamda.2013.03.004
4. Bootstrap. http://getbootstrap.com/. Accessed 21 Jan 2017
5. Campbell, C., Craig, J., Eggert, J., Bailey-Dorton, C.: Implementing and measuring the impact of patient navigation at a comprehensive community cancer centre. Oncol. Nurs. Forum **37**(1), 61–68 (2010). doi:10.1188/10.ONF.61-68

6. Cancer Care Ontario: Diagnostic Assessment Program – Electronic Pathway Solution (dap-eps). https://patient.dap-eps.ca. Accessed 2 Jan 2017
7. Cancer Care Ontario: Ontario Cancer Statistics (2016). https://www.cancercare.on.ca/common/pages/UserFile.aspx?fileId=360956. Accessed 2 Jan 2017
8. Cashen, M.S., Dykes, P., Gerber, B.: eHealth technology and internet resources – barriers for vulnerable populations. J. Cardiovasc. Nurs. **19**(3), 209–214 (2004)
9. Chiuve, S.E., McCullough, M.L., Sacks, F.M., Rimm, E.B.: Healthy lifestyle factors in the primary prevention of coronary heart disease among men. Circulation **114**(2), 160–167 (2006). doi:10.1161/CIRCULATIONAHA.106.621417
10. CMS Matrix. http://www.cmsmatrix.org/. Accessed 21 Jan 2017
11. Drupal™. https://www.drupal.org/. Accessed 2 Jan 2017
12. Eng, E., Parker, E., Harlan, C.: Lay health advisor intervention strategies: a continuum from natural helping to paraprofessional helping. Health Educ. Behav. **24**(4), 413–417 (1997). doi:10.1177/109019819702400402
13. Freeman, H.P.: Patient navigation – a community centered approach to reducing cancer mortality. J. Cancer Educ. **21**(1 Suppl.), S11–S14 (2006). doi:10.1207/s15430154jce2101s_4
14. Fung-Kee-Fung, M., Maziak, D.E., et al.: Lung cancer diagnosis transformation: aligning the people, processes, and technology sides of the learning system. J. Clin. Oncol. **34**(Suppl. 7S; abstr 50) (2016). http://meetinglibrary.asco.org/content/160997-181
15. Gabitova, G., Burke, N.J.: Improving healthcare empowerment through breast cancer patient navigation: a mixed methods evaluation in a safety-net setting. BMC Health Serv. Res. **14**, 407 (2014). doi:10.1186/1472-6963-14-407
16. Gardiner, P., Hempstead, M.B., et al.: Reaching women through health information technology: the gabby preconception care system. Am. J. Health Promot. **27**(3 Suppl.), eS11–eS20 (2013). doi:10.4278/ajhp.1200113-QUAN-18
17. Ghaddar, S.F., Valerio, M.A., Garcia, C.M., Hansen, L.: Adolescent health literacy – the importance of credible sources for online health information. J. Sch. Health **82**(1), 28–36 (2012). doi:10.1111/j.1746-1561.2011.00664.x
18. Google inc.: Google Maps Indoor. https://www.google.ca/maps/about/partners/indoormaps/. Accessed 21 Jan 2017
19. Haase, K.R., Loiselle, C.G.: Oncology team members' perceptions of a virtual navigational tool for cancer patients. Int. J. Med. Inform. **81**(6), 395–403 (2012). doi:10.1016/j.ijmedinf.2011.11.001
20. Haase, K.R., Strohschein, F., Lee, V., Loiselle, C.G.: The promise of virtual navigation in cancer care: insights from patients and healthcare providers. Can. Oncol. Nurs. J. **26**(3), 238–245 (2016)
21. Hevner, A.R., March, A.T., Park, J., Ram, S.: Design science in information systems research. MIS Q. **28**(1), 75–105 (2004)
22. Hibbard, J.H., Greene, J.: What the evidence shows about patient activation – better health outcomes and care experience; fewer data on costs. Health Aff. (Millwood) **32**(2), 207–214 (2013). doi:10.1377/hlthaff.2012.1061
23. Highfield, L., Hanks, J.: Interactive web-based portals to improve patient navigation and connect patients with primary care and speciality services in underserved communities. Perspect. Health Inf. Manag. **11**(Spring), 1e (2014)
24. Horowitz, B.T.: Accenture Crafts Prototype Mobile App to Guide Patients to Care. eWeek (2013). http://bit.ly/2iYNgaR
25. Jack, B., Bickmore, T.: The Re-Engineered Hospital Discharge Program to Decrease Rehospitalization. CareManagement **16**, 12–15 (2010)
26. Jack, B., Bickmore, T., et al.: Virtual Patient Advocate to Reduce Ambulatory Adverse Drug Events. The Agency for Healthcare Research and Quality (AHRQ) (2011)

27. Jandorf, J., Cooperman, J.L., et al.: Implementation of culturally targeted patient navigation system for screening colonoscopy in a direct referral system. Health Educ. Res. **28**(5), 803–815 (2013). doi:10.1093/her/cyt003

28. Katz, M.L., Young, G.S., et al.: Barriers reported among the patients with breasts and cervical abnormalities in the patient navigation research program – impact on timely care. Women's Health Issues **24**(1), e155–e162 (2014). doi:10.1016/j.whi.2013.10.010

29. Kent, S.M., Yellowlees, P.: The technology-enabled patient advocate: a valuable emerging healthcare partner. Telemed. J. E Health **21**(12), 1030–1037 (2015)

30. Kitchenham, B., Brereton, O.P., et al.: Systematic literature reviews in software engineering – a systematic literature review. Inf. Softw. Technol. **51**(1), 7–15 (2009). doi:10.1016/j.infsof.2008.09.009

31. Lee, Y.J., Kim, J.H., et al.: Lung cancer in never smokers: change of a mindset in the molecular era. Lung Cancer **72**(1), 9–15 (2011). doi:10.1016/j.lungcan.2010.12.013

32. Loiselle, C.G., Peters, O., Haase, K.R., Girouard, L., Korner, A., Wiljer, D., Fitch, M.: Virtual navigation in colorectal cancer and melanoma: an exploration of patient's view. Support. Care Cancer **21**(8), 2289–2296 (2013). doi:10.1007/s00520-013-1771-1

33. Loiselle, C.G.: Virtual Navigation in Cancer: A Pilot Study. Canadian Partnership Against Cancer, Toronto (2010)

34. Lorhan, S., Dennis, D., van der Westhuizen, M., Hodgson, S., Berrang, T., Daudt, H.: The experience of people with lung cancer with a volunteer-based lay navigation intervention at an outpatient cancer center. Patient Educ. Couns. **96**(2), 237–248 (2014). doi:10.1016/j.pec.2014.05.002

35. MEAN. http://mean.io/. Accessed 5 Jan 2017

36. Mobilecare247 inc.: Patient Navigator. http://mobilecare247.com/services/patient-navigator/. Accessed 2 Jan 2017

37. Neville, C., Da Costa, D., et al.: Development of the lupus interactive navigator as an empowering web-based ehealth tool to facilitate lupus management: Users perspectives on usability and acceptability. JMIR Res. Protoc. **5**(2), e44 (2014). doi:10.2196/resprot.4219

38. Pesch, B., Kendzia, B., et al.: Cigarette smoking and lung cancer – relative risk estimates for the major histological types from a pooled analysis of case-control studies. Int. J. Cancer **131**(5), 1210–1219 (2012). doi:10.1002/ijc.27339

39. Post, D.M., McAlearney, A.S., Young, G.S., Krok-Schoen, J.L., Plascak, J.J., Paskett, E.D.: Effects of patient navigation on patient satisfaction outcomes. J. Canc. Educ. **30**(4), 728–735 (2015). doi:10.1007/s13187-014-0772-1

40. Rhodes, A., Caelli, W.: A review paper role based access control. Information Security Research Centre (2000)

41. Shahab, L., McEwen, A.: Online support for smoking cessation – a systematic review of the literature. Addiction **104**(11), 1792–1804 (2009). doi:10.1111/j.1360-0443.2009.02710.x

42. Talha, M., Sneha, R., Eunji, I.: Importance of patient-centered signage and navigation guide in an orthopedic and plastics clinic. BMJ Qual. Improv. Rep. **5**(1) (2016). doi:10.1136/bmjquality.u209473.w3887

43. The Ottawa Hospital: Patient Passport, P1024 ENGLISH (REV 11/2015). http://ottawahospital.libguides.com/ld.php?content_id=19954598. Accessed 2 Jan 2017

44. Vorderstrasse, A., Lewinski, A., Melkus, G.D., Johnson, C.: Social support for diabetes self-management via ehealth interventions. Curr. Diab. Rep. **16**(7), 56 (2016). doi:10.1007/s11892-016-0756-0

45. Xamarin™. https://www.xamarin.com. Accessed 5 Jan 2017

Responsiveness to Persuasive Strategies at the Workplace: A Case Study

Humu-Haida Selassie$^{(\boxtimes)}$, Kiemute Oyibo, and Julita Vassileva

University of Saskatchewan, Saskatoon, Canada
{haida.selassie, kiemute.oyibo}@usask.ca,
jiv@cs.usask.ca

Abstract. Persuasive technology capitalizes on the use of technology and the art of persuasion to change the behaviors and attitudes of people without the use of coercion. They have been used at workplaces to achieve positive outcomes like increase in employee motivation, engagement and productivity. While a number of researchers have investigated the effectiveness of Cialdini's principles of persuasion, little or no research has been conducted in the context of work environments. In many workplaces, it is important that employees provide detailed records of their activities for easy tracking of an organization's day-to-day activities and future historical reference. However, research has shown that some employees find it difficult to comply. In an attempt to address this problem, we carried out a pilot study among 20 healthcare Applied Behavior Analysis(ABA) frontline employees, working with autistic patients. The study is aimed at investigating how effective Cialdini's principles of persuasion are in motivating employees to record details about the sessions they have with patients. A Two-Way Mixed ANOVA analysis showed that ABA frontline employees are most susceptible to Commitment and Reciprocity, followed by Authority, and least susceptible to Consensus and Scarcity. These results suggest that designers of gamified persuasive systems tailored to healthcare ABA frontline staff should focus on implementing Commitment, Reciprocity and Authority as persuasive strategies aimed at motivating them in engaging in sufficient and quality data entry.

Keywords: Persuasive technology · Workplace · Persuasive strategy · Cialdini's persuasive principles

1 Introduction

Persuasive technology (PT) and gamification have been making headways in the workplace over the past few years. BJ Fogg [1], the pioneer of PT, defined persuasive technology as any interactive computing system designed to change people's attitudes and behaviors. So far, both PT and gamification have helped organizations to increase their employee productivity, retention, engagement, as well as reduce workplace issues caused by gradual changes in employee demographics [2]. Previous literature identifies a continuous increase in the number of distrustful employees through generations, with the level of distrustfulness of each generation being less encouraging than the previous [3]. A recent survey conducted by Gallup [4] on employee engagement rate in 2016

© Springer International Publishing AG 2017
E. Aïmeur et al. (Eds.): MCETECH 2017, LNBIP 289, pp. 273–284, 2017.
DOI: 10.1007/978-3-319-59041-7_17

showed that 65.9% of workers in the US are disengaged [4]. Employees, who are engaged and attached to their jobs emotionally, have been found to be more productive [4, 5]. Therefore, the main goal of implementing PT and gamification at workplaces is to increase employee engagement by leveraging the motivating power of these persuasive technologies.

Moreover, video games, mostly perceived to be banal and meaningless, have been used to promote positive habits by leveraging some of the game elements and features that appeal to the core drives of players. The term "gamification" is defined as the use of game design elements in non-game contexts [6]. Gamification is a type of persuasive technology that is gaining momentum at workplaces because managers have begun to see the opportunities in tapping into the sources of intrinsic motivation stemming from games to engage employees without paying them more money. Top companies, like Google, T-Mobile, Ford, NetApp, Allied Global, and Sun Life Financial, have incorporated gamification into their workplaces and witnessed encouraging results as reported by the website gamification company, BunchBall [7]. For example, in 2013, T-Mobile contracted BunchBall to implement game elements within their employee collaboration platform to increase productivity in service levels. This resulted in a 96% increase in participation, 583% increase in contributions, and a 783% increase in responses. Also, there was a 31% increase in customer satisfaction scores and 40% improvement in deflection, which caused a reduction in support costs [8].

While persuasive technology and gamification have recorded considerable success in their implementation, research has also shown that implementing the wrong persuasive strategies could lead to undesirable results like boycott of the persuasive or gamified system or an adverse behavioral change [9–11]. The most common way of curbing this problem has been to tailor persuasive strategies to individuals or groups. Most often, personalization in workplace gamified persuasive systems has been enabled with self-expression, which allows players to customize their profiles. However, individuals are motivated by different things and the "one-size-fits-all" approach of choosing persuasive strategies for groups or individuals, despite bringing improvements on average, may be actually demotivational to particular individuals or groups [10]. This calls for tailoring motivating factors (example persuasive strategies) to individuals or groups. The variances in the receptivity to different persuasive strategies which are impacted by factors like culture, age, gender, caused us to explore the susceptibility of employees to Cialdini's persuasive principles. So far, there is little to no literature on the susceptibility of workplace employees (ABA frontline staff) to Cialdini's persuasive principles and the role workplace factors play in employees' susceptibility to these persuasive principles.

Specifically, we targeted the workplace of Autism Spectrum Disorder (ASD) frontline care workers who have adopted the Applied Behavior Analysis (ABA) approach to behavior change in ASD patients. ABA is data-driven; detailed data on each therapy session is necessary to draw informed conclusions on the progress of a patient, make decisions on how to design or modify the patient's program, as well as keep parents and guardians informed about their ward's progress. It is therefore critical for frontline care workers to record high quality and detailed information about each session. ABA workplaces often have high rates of frontline care workers' turnover, due to burnout, despite being offered training to gain experience by the companies that hire them [12]. The high turnover rate is undesirable for ASD patients as routine and repetitive behavior is a part of their life. Trying to keep everything in order helps ASD patients to reduce the fear they experience due to the chaos they perceive to be happening around them all the time [13]. Persuasive technology and gamification could help engage ABA frontline workers in recording detailed and high-quality data, and possibly, reduce the employee turnover, thus improving the therapy chances of success and the wellbeing of ASD patients.

In this paper, we present the findings from a study targeted at tailoring persuasive strategies to ABA frontline staff to increase engagement in their responsibilities, especially with regard to recording quality data during ABA sessions. Persuasive strategies, which employees are susceptible to, will be integrated into an already existing software application, which is currently being used to record ABA data and manage autistic patients. It is hoped that the implementation of effective persuasive strategies in the system has the potential of persuading employees to provide adequate data, which is of high quality. While the small scale of our study did not allow us to draw conclusions about personalization to individuals, we identified the level of effectiveness of various persuasive strategies on the group of ABA employees. Also, while we could not generalize the differences in susceptibility to these persuasive strategies based on employment status, our study contributes essential discoveries regarding the susceptibility of ABA frontline staff to Cialdini's persuasive principles.

In summary, our findings show that ABA employees are most susceptible to Commitment and Reciprocity followed by Authority. However, ABA employees are least susceptible to Consensus and Scarcity as persuasive strategies. Our recommendation is for persuasive system designers to focus more on persuasive elements that support Commitment, Reciprocity and Authority when implementing persuasive technologies at ABA workplaces.

2 Background and Related Work

There is a substantial number of persuasive strategies and principles proposed by researchers, for example Cialdini's six principles of persuasion [14], Fogg's 42 persuasive strategies [15] and the 40 persuasive strategies proposed by Kukkonen et al. [16]. Kaptein et al. [17] were among the first to study the individual differences in susceptibility to persuasion (i.e., persuadability) in the design of persuasive technologies. Based on previous findings, they argued that tailoring persuasive systems to individuals based on their susceptibility to various persuasive strategies is key to increasing their effectiveness [9, 17]. The first attempt by Kaptein et al. [17] to measure persuadability involved using a 12-item questionnaire with two questions for each of the six Cialdini persuasive principles. Kaptein et al. [9] later developed and validated a 7-point 26-item scale to explicitly measure people's susceptibility to each of the persuasive principles identified by Cialdini [18]. These principles are briefly explained.

- **Authority:** People are likely to perform a task if it is suggested by a person who is an expert in a subject area or an individual with a high title and/or wielding some form of power. Deference to authority stems from systematic socialization practices where people are made to believe that obeying people in authority is a morally upright practice [14].
- **Consensus:** Some individuals are likely to perform a task if all other people in their social group are performing it. Such individuals practice imitation learning in which they observe the actions of others and the consequences before making a decision to act same [14].
- **Commitment and Consistency:** People innately have the tendency to act in ways that are consistent with stands they have taken. This principle works because being committed and consistent is viewed as a highly-admired value by society [14].
- **Scarcity:** People are likely to opt for something which is in limited supply or availability. This principle is heightened when an item becomes scarce and when there is competition for such an item [14].
- **Liking:** People are inclined to perform a task if it is suggested by a person they know and like. Likeness is influenced by factors like attractiveness, similarity, increased familiarity, and praise [14].
- **Reciprocity:** People will probably perform a task if it is suggested by someone they feel they owe a favor. The rule for reciprocation is that you repay in kind when a favor is done to you. This creates a sense of obligation and fosters the development of lasting relationships. The most common tactic used in reciprocation is to give something and ask for something else in return [14].

To understand the power of psychological processes that drive behavior change, Foster et al. [19] leveraged Facebook to build an application, Step Matron, which provided a competitive context for step counts read by a pedometer. The authors used leaderboards as a persuasive strategy to motivate employees. Lehrer and Vasudev [20] also developed a web-based social network to help shape employees' attitudes and behaviors towards sustainability at the workplace. In these works, the choice of persuasive strategies were not based on empirical evidence. Also, Makanawala et al. [21] implemented gamification in a system for customer service personnel by creating what they called a player's persona, which included attributes such as name, gender, birthday, relationship status, industry, job goals, and pain-points. However, the authors did not explain how the data for the persona were gathered (perhaps the users customized their personas themselves by filling a form), and how the data were used to personalize the game elements. The only type of personalization they addressed is the one that made use of self-expression (user profiles).

People are motivated by different needs and desires and this happens to be the biggest challenge of meaningful and effective gamification and persuasive technology, even at the workplace [19]. The workplace brings together employees who can be very different in terms of factors like cultural background, age, technological skills, social attitudes, personality and psychological traits. Although the above implementations were reported to be successful, there was no empirical support for why those persuasive strategies were adopted. Thus, the persuasive strategies employed in these systems were not based on persuasive strategies that the employees involved were more influenced by. We believe that this could lead to undesirable outcomes, and result in adverse behavior change after a period of time [9–11]. One way this challenge is tackled is to tailor persuasive strategies to targeted individuals or user groups. Tailoring persuasive strategies to individuals or user groups also increases the efficacy of the implementation of persuasive technology and gamification as susceptibility is influenced by certain factors depending on the target group in question. For example, Orji [11, 22] found that individuals respond differently to Cialdini's persuasive strategies and susceptibility could be influenced by factors like gender and culture [11, 22]. However, no study has explored the impact of employment status on susceptibility of employees to Cialdini's persuasive principles and the role employment status plays. Employment status has been shown by previous literature to have a major impact on employees' attitudes towards organizational characteristics and job satisfaction [22]. This informed the decision to carry out a study to investigate the susceptibility of ABA frontline employees to Cialdini's persuasive strategies and the impact of employment status in their susceptibility. The end goal is to implement persuasive and game elements (integrated into an existing ABA therapy application) that support the most influential persuasive strategies among ABA employees.

3   Method

In this section, we discuss the measurement instrument used for the study, the participants' demographics, and the data analysis that was performed on the collected data.

3.1   Measurement Instrument

The online survey was approved by the University of Saskatchewan research ethics board and administered through a web-based survey tool called Fluid Surveys. The survey was made of three sections. In Sect. 1, participants were asked to read a consent form describing the reason for the study and only continue with the study if they agreed to the terms in the consent form. Section 2 contained items from Kaptein et al.'s [9] Susceptibility to Persuasive Strategies Scale adapted to measure five of Cialdini's six principles of persuasion. During the research design, the "Liking" principle was omitted because interviews with the ABA managers suggested that they did not want to use "likeness" as a form of influence at their workplace. The possibility of employing a peer-review system to measure the quality of data recorded during ABA therapy sessions raised concerns they were uncomfortable with. For example, reviewing an otherwise poorly recorded data just because of a feeling of likeness towards a colleague. Participants were asked their level of agreement to some questions (23 items) on a 7-point Likert scale, ranging from 1 ("Completely Disagree") to 7 ("Completely Agree"). Some of the items in the scale are presented in Table 1. Section 3 asked participants to answer some questions relating to demographics, such as age, employment status and gender.

Table 1. Sample items from Kaptein et al.'s susceptibility to persuasive strategies scale [9]

Commitment
- *Once I have committed to something, I will surely do it*
- *Whenever I commit to an appointment, I always follow through*

Reciprocity
- *When a family member does me a favor, I am very inclined to return this favor*
- *When I receive a gift, I feel obliged to return a gift*

Authority
- *I am more likely to do something if told, than when asked*
- *I always obey directions from my superiors*

Scarcity
- *I believe scarce products are more valuable than common products*
- *Products that are hard to get represent a special value*

Consensus
- *It is important to me to fit in*
- *I often rely on other people to know what I should do*

3.2   Participants

Participants were recruited from ABA providers in Edmonton, Canada, who used an online system for tracking sessions with ASD patients. This system was developed by a local software company. This target group was chosen because they were currently using the online system. The ultimate goal of the study was to integrate/implement effective persuasive strategies in the system in order to motivate employees to enter adequate and quality data into the system. An organization-wide email was sent to employees inviting them to take part in the survey. A total of 42 participants clicked on the link to visit the survey. Out of these responses, 12 were incomplete so they were discarded. Further, 10 other responses were excluded because they came from managers. Finally, our analysis was based on 20 responses only from ABA frontline staff, our target employee group. Participants were also given the chance to enter a draw to win one of ten $20 gift cards.

3.3   Data Analysis

To establish internal validity and reliability of the data collected, we performed a Cronbach's alpha test. The data was proven to be reliable with a Cronbach's alpha value greater than 0.8. The mean score of each of the persuasive strategies measured was calculated and then tests were performed to ensure the data satisfied all the conditions necessary to perform a Two-Way Mixed ANOVA using persuasive principle as a within-subjects factor and employment status as a between-subjects factor. Our data passed all the conditions to perform a repeated measures ANOVA including the Mauchly's Test of Sphericity ($\chi 2$ (9) = 4.929, p = 0.84). The responses were normally distributed across the various cells of the study design as indicated by a Shapiro-Wilk test for normality: Reciprocity (p = 0.51), Scarcity (p = 0.57), Consensus (0.87),

Competition (0.63), and Authority (p = 0.85). Also, there were no outliers as indicated by the inspection of a box plot. Finally, there was homogeneity of variances, which was assessed by Levene's Test of Homogeneity of Variances (p > 0.05).

4 Results

The results of the study are presented in this section. First, we present the demographics of the participants and the results of the Two-Way Mixed ANOVA analysis of susceptibility of ABA frontline employees to the measured persuasive strategies.

4.1 Participants' Demographics

A total of twenty (20) valid participants took part in the study. They consisted of two (2) males and 18 females. All participants were between the ages of 16–44 years old. Fourteen (14) participants fall between the ages of 16–34 years old and five (5) participants were between the ages of 35–44 years old, while one participant preferred not to provide his/her age. These age ranges were adopted from a previous study based on generational differences in personality traits [3]. We explored the presence of generational differences in susceptibility to Cialdini's persuasive principles. However, there were no statistically significant differences. Moreover, 50% of the participants were gamers and the other 50% were non-gamers. Finally, regarding employment status, fifteen (15) participants were fulltime and five (5) participants were part-time employees.

4.2 General Persuasive Principles Susceptibility

A Two-Way Mixed ANOVA showed that strategy had a main effect on employees' persuadability by Cialdini's persuasive principles (F (4, 72) = 9.78, p < 0.0001). This means that there were significant differences in the degree of persuadability of employees by the various Cialdini's persuasive principles investigated. A posthoc pairwise comparison test showed that Commitment (M = 5.82, SE = 0.17) and Reciprocity (M = 5.20, SD = 0.22) had the strongest effect and there was no statistically significant difference between them (p > 0.05). Authority (M = 4.80, SE = 0.26) was the next most influential persuasive strategy. On the other hand, ABA employees were least susceptible to Scarcity (M = 4.52, SE = 0.24) and Consensus (M = 4.31, SE = 0.27). There was no statistically significant difference between the susceptibilities to Scarcity and Consensus (p > 0.05). However, the susceptibility to Commitment was significantly higher than the susceptibilities to Scarcity (p < 0.01), Consensus (p < 0.001) and Authority (p < 0.05). In addition, the susceptibility to Reciprocity was higher than the susceptibilities to Scarcity, Consensus and Authority, and these differences were statistically significant (p < 0.05) (see Fig. 1). There was a statistically significant interaction between persuasive strategy and employment status on employees' level of persuadability (F (4, 72) = 3.294, p < 0.05, $\eta2 = 0.15$). There was a statistically significant difference in the levels of susceptibility to Scarcity between part-time and full-time employees (F (1, 18) = 4.84, p < 0.05, partial $\eta2 = 0.212$).

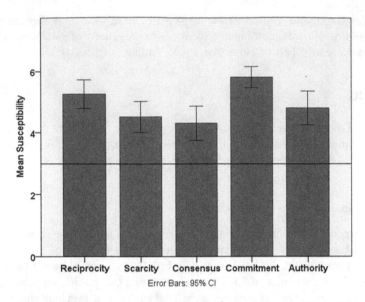

Fig. 1. A bar graph of the overall mean employees' susceptibility to Cialdini's persuasive strategies

Also, there was a statistically significant difference in the levels of susceptibility to Consensus between part-time and full-time employees (F $(1, 18) = 4.59$, $p < 0.05$, partial $\eta2 = 0.20$). Full-time employees were more persuadable by Scarcity and Consensus than part-time employees (see Table 2).

Table 2. Susceptibility of full time and part time ABA employees to scarcity and consensus. M = Mean Susceptibility; SE = Standard Error

Persuasive principle	Level of susceptibility
Scarcity	Fulltime (M = 4.80, SE = 0.24)
	Part-time (M = 3.68, SE = 0.53)
Consensus	Fulltime (M = 4.60, SE = 0.28)
	Part-time (M = 3.40, SE = 0.53)

5   Discussion

This study was carried out to explore the persuadability of ABA employees by Cialdini's principles of persuasion. The results show that ABA frontline staff are more persuadable by the Commitment and Reciprocity principles. These results replicate a prior finding by Orji et al. [11]. In her study among a general population (in a non-workplace setting), she found that Commitment and Reciprocity had the strongest persuasive effect on individuals with different cultures. However, in our study Consensus and Scarcity turned out to be the least persuasive, which differs from the result of Orji, who found only Scarcity to be the least persuadable. However, both results are similar in that they both found Scarcity as least persuasive.

5.1   Tailoring Persuasive Strategies to ABA Frontline Staff

We found Commitment, Reciprocity and Authority as the most persuasive Cialdini's principles among ABA employees. These principles have been reported in previous literature to be very important to organizational success, so it was not surprising to see them as the strongest persuasive principles in our study [24–26]. Software applications for the entry of data on and management of autistic patients can leverage all three principles as persuasive strategies to motivate front-line staff to enter both sufficient and high-quality data on their patients. A possible explanation for the relatively high level of employees' susceptibility to Commitment is that employees' commitment is very important in a patient-care type of workplace, and people drawn to this job are characterized with a high level of commitment and appreciate seeing it in others. Research has shown there is strong correlation between employee commitment, on one hand, and organizational performance and organizational turnover, on the other hand [24]. This also ties in with the concept of reciprocity in the workplace, where employees are paid salary, and, in return, render service to their employers by being committed to the job. In addition, reciprocity among employees is also key to organizational success, especially in the ABA type of workplace, where the job performance, in this case attending to an autistic patient at a given time and place, may require employees standing in for each other in situations where an employee is absent. Also, research has shown that there is a strong link between reciprocity in employees' behavior and the organization's productivity [25]. Further, Authority (i.e., the passing of instructions from higher management staff to frontline staff through supervisory staff, who enforce them) may be key to the success and profitability of an organization [26]. Usually, in organizations, obeying authority in the form of accomplishing assigned tasks and duties may translate, in the long run, into higher rewards like bonuses and promotions for the subordinate staff. Thus, for ABA employees, Authority as a persuasive principle turns out to be the next strongest persuasive strategy, following Commitment and Reciprocity. On the other hand, the low susceptibility of the ABA frontline workers to the Consensus principle could be explained by the age group of employees. The composition of this type of employees is mainly young adults (usually hired from colleges) ranging from the ages of 16-34 (75% of the sample). Young adults are usually independent-minded; as such, they tend to do things on their own as opposed to imitating what others do [3].

5.2   Design Implications

The design implication of these results is the implementation of persuasive or game elements that support Commitment, Reciprocity and Authority among ABA employees. Commitment can be implemented in the application used for the ABA therapy sessions by allowing employees to set goals on not just the quantity of data they collect in a certain period, but also a commitment to recording quality data. Allowing users to set their own goals creates a feeling of autonomy and raises the chances of sticking to such goals. In addition to this, system-generated goals can be suggested to users to choose from, especially when they are goals users will probably not think of. It is important that these system-generated goals are not imposed on users. Providing users, a list of goal suggestions gives them an idea on the variety of goals they can commit to and complete. This also gives them complete autonomy as to whether to choose these goals or not, giving them a sense of autonomy. Autonomy has been shown by research to facilitate intrinsic motivation as well as the internalization of target behaviors (data entry in this case) [27].

Reciprocity can also be implemented using a reward mechanism. Employees can be awarded virtual or real medals/badges, achievement certificates and points in exchange for executing tasks like recording high-quality data. Rewards can also serve as a way to affirm employees' competence, which also facilitates intrinsic motivation and internalization [27]. In cases where the reward mechanism implemented uses points, an economic market design which allows employees to exchange their points for real-life items can be incorporated. Employees can also be given a chance to enter draws with specific number of points. This system gives every employee a chance to win gifts and also adds an element of surprise and uncertainty, which has been shown by previous research to increase enjoyment and engagement in activities [28, 29].

The implementation of triggers based on these persuasive strategies may also be an effective way in engaging employees. For example, to persuade ABA frontline employees using a textual trigger based on Authority, a notification like this could be sent at the start of a therapy session: *"Did you know ABA specialists require quality data to be able to design successful and effective ABA programs for therapy sessions?"* Tailored persuasive messages, such as this, have been proven to be effective in prior studies. For example, Kaptein et al. [9] found that text messages that are personalized to individuals, based on the persuasive strategies they are most susceptible to, resulted in a considerable decrease in their snacking consumption.

6 Limitations and Future Work

The limitation of this study is that it is based on a self-report and a limited sample. However, given the limited research on this topic in the workplace domain, our findings will serve as a basis for more elaborate research in the workplace in the future. Although our study found significant differences in persuadability between fulltime and part-time employees, as presented in Table 2, it was not discussed due to the small sample size of our study. Consequently, as part of future work, we intend to use a larger sample size as well as extend our study to other work environments. Finally, we intend to consider other interaction factors that influence workplace dynamics such as employment status, culture, gender, and age/generational gaps.

7 Conclusion

We presented the level of susceptibility of ABA employees to Cialdini's principles of persuasion. Similar to previous study [22], we found that ABA employees are most susceptible to Commitment and Reciprocity, followed by Authority, and least susceptible to Scarcity and Consensus. These findings will provide designers of persuasive technology in the workplace environment in general, and ABA organization in particular, with insight into developing more effective and efficient persuasive applications. Although we could not generalize the differences in susceptibility to these persuasive strategies based on employment status, our study contributes useful findings regarding the susceptibility of ABA frontline staff to Cialdini's principles of persuasion.

References

1. Fogg, B.J.: Persuasive Technology: Using Computers to Change What We Think and Do. Morgan Kaufmann Publishers, San Francisco (2003)
2. Oprescu, F., Jones, C., Katsikitis, M.: I Play at Work-ten principles for transforming work processes through gamification. Front. Psychol. **5**, 1–5 (2014)
3. Wong, M., Gardiner, E., Lang, W., Coulon, L.: Generational differences in personality and motivation Do they exist and what are the implications for the workplace? J. Manag. Psychol. **23**, 878–890 (2008)
4. Gallup Inc: U.S. Employee Engagement Reaches New High in March, Gallup. http://www.gallup.com/poll/190622/employee-engagement-reaches-new-high-march.aspx
5. Kumar, J.: Gamification at work: designing engaging business software. In: Marcus, A. (ed.) DUXU 2013. LNCS, vol. 8013, pp. 528–537. Springer, Heidelberg (2013). doi:10.1007/978-3-642-39241-2_58
6. Deterding, S., Dixon, D., Khaled, R., Nacke, L.: From game design elements to gamefulness: defining gamification. In: Proceedings of the 15th international academic MindTrek conference: Envisioning future media environments, pp. 9–15, (2011). ACM
7. Gamification Success Stories, Bunchball. http://www.bunchball.com/customers/gamification-success-stories
8. BunchBall: T-Mobile Success Story, Bunchball. http://www.bunchball.com/customers/t-mobile-success-story
9. Kaptein, M., De Ruyter, B., Markopoulos, P., Aarts, E.: Adaptive persuasive systems: a study of tailored persuasive text messages to reduce snacking. ACM Trans. Interact. Intell. Syst. **2**, 1–25 (2012)
10. Orji, R.: Design for behaviour change: a model-driven approach for tailoring persuasive technologies (2014)
11. Orji, R.: Persuasion and Culture: Individualism-Collectivism and Susceptibility To Influence Strategies. CEUR Workshop Proceedings, vol. 1582, pp. 30–39 (2016)
12. I Love ABA!: ABA Staff Training. http://www.iloveaba.com/2013/10/aba-staff-training.html
13. Howlin, P.: Autism and Asperger Syndrome: Preparing for Adulthood (2004). http://books.google.com/books?id=Y5V_AgAAQBAJ&pgis=1
14. Cialdini, R.B.: Influence: Science and Practice. Pearson Education, Boston (2009)
15. Fogg, B.: A behavior model for persuasive design. In: Proceedings of the 4th International Conference on Persuasive Technology - Persuasive 2009, p. 1. ACM (2009)
16. Oinas-Kukkonen, H., Harjumaa, M.: Persuasive systems design: key issues, process model, and system features. Commun. Assoc. Inf. Syst. **24**, 485–500 (2009)
17. Kaptein, M., Lacroix, J., Saini, P.: Individual differences in persuadability in the health promotion domain. In: Ploug, T., Hasle, P., Oinas-Kukkonen, H. (eds.) PERSUASIVE 2010. LNCS, vol. 6137, pp. 94–105. Springer, Heidelberg (2010). doi:10.1007/978-3-642-13226-1_11

18. Cialdini, R.B.: Harnessing the science of persuasion. (cover story). Harv. Bus. Rev. **79**, 72–79 (2001)
19. Foster, D., Linehan, C., Lawson, S.: Motivating physical activity at work: using persuasive social media extensions for simple mobile devices. CEUR Workshop Proceedings, vol. 690, pp. 11–14 (2010)
20. Lehrer, D., Vasudev, J.: Evaluating a social media application for sustainability in the workplace. In: CHI 2011 Extended Abstract Human Factors Computing Systems, pp. 2161–2166 (2011)
21. Makanawala, P., Godara, J., Goldwasser, E., Le, H.: Applying gamification in customer service application to improve agents's efficiency and satisfaction. In: Design, User Experience and Usability: Health, Learning, Playing, Cultural, and Cross-Cultural User Experience, NA, pp. 548–557 (2013)
22. Orji, R., Mandryk, R.L., Vassileva, J.: Gender, age, and responsiveness to Cialdini's persuasion strategies. In: MacTavish, T., Basapur, S. (eds.) PERSUASIVE 2015. LNCS, vol. 9072, pp. 147–159. Springer, Cham (2015). doi:10.1007/978-3-319-20306-5_14
23. Eberhardt, B.J., Shani, A.B.: The effects of full-time versus part-time employment status on attitudes toward specific organizational characteristics and overall job satisfaction. Acad. Manag. J. **27**, 893–900 (1984)
24. Irefin, P., Mechanic, M.: Effect of employee commitment on organizational performance in coca cola nigeria limited maiduguri. IOSR J. Humanit. Soc. Sci. (IOSR-JHSS), **3**(3), 33–41 (2014)
25. Barr, A., Serneels, P.: Reciprocity in the workplace. Exp. Econ. **12**, 99–112 (2009)
26. Coase, R.H.: The nature of the firm. Economica **4**, 386–405 (1937)
27. Ryan, R., Deci, E.: Self-determination theory and the facilitation of intrinsic motivation. Am. Psychol. **55**, 68–78 (2000)
28. Klimmt, C., Rizzo, A., Vorderer, P., Koch, J., Fischer, T.: Experimental evidence for suspense as determinant of video game enjoyment. Cyberpsychol. Behav. **12**, 29–31 (2009)
29. Langer, R., Hancock, M., Scott, S.D.: Suspenseful design: engaging emotionally with complex applications through compelling narratives. In: Conference Proceedings - 2014 IEEE Games, Media, Entertainment Conference, IEEE GEM 2014 (2015)

E-Payment Plan: A Conditional Multi-payment Scheme Based on User Personalization and Plan Agreement

Ghada El Haddad[1(✉)], Hicham Hage[2], and Esma Aïmeur[1]

[1] Department of Computer Science and Operations Research,
University of Montreal, Montreal, Canada
{elhaddag, aimeur}@iro.umontreal.ca
[2] Computer Science Department, Notre Dame University,
Zouk Mosbeh, Lebanon
hhage@ndu.edu.lb

Abstract. In the past two decades, the development of payment solutions has significantly changed the way online retail businesses are conducted and enlarged the scope of numerous payment technologies offered in the market. Despite the multitude of payment solutions, card-based systems are still the most prevalent. While secure, card-based systems still lack privacy protection, user control and supervision. In this paper, we propose a new e-payment framework relying on card-based payment systems, with the aggregation of virtual credit cards and a personalized conditional E-Payment Plan defined by the cardholder. In our framework, the cardholder's privacy is ensured with the use of Virtual Credit Cards. Moreover, with the E-Payment Plan Service Manager (E-PPSM), our proposed framework brings considerable improvements to the shopping practice. Through this service, cardholders can efficiently control and supervise their online purchases. The proposed framework thus ensures three considerable concentrations: personalization, control, and supervision applicable in multi-purchase checkouts, which are, in addition to privacy protection, our main contributions.

Keywords: E-payment · Payment plan · Card payment · Payment framework · E-commerce · Card-based systems · Credit card · Personalization · Multi-payment

1 Introduction

In recent years, the growth of the Internet has provided the e-commerce domain with a highly efficient and effective online environment. E-commerce has become an important business field for trading, distributing and selling products between organizations, among organizations and consumers, and even between consumers. A report released in 2014 by Statistics Canada shows that Canadian companies sold over $136 billion in goods and services over the Internet in 2013, up from $122 billion a year earlier.[1] Payment frameworks therefore appeared in the market to support online

---

[1] http://www.statcan.gc.ca/daily-quotidien/140611/dq140611a-eng.htm consulted on 05/June/2016.

© Springer International Publishing AG 2017
E. Aïmeur et al. (Eds.): MCETECH 2017, LNBIP 289, pp. 285–299, 2017.
DOI: 10.1007/978-3-319-59041-7_18

transactions by offering different methods of payment such as card-based systems (credit/debit cards), cash on delivery, e-wallets and bank transfers. Card-based systems will be our focus in this article.

Card-based payment systems are founded on traditional two-party business models with a customer (cardholder) and a merchant (product/service provider) [1]. The payment methods in such systems represent a particular form of e-commerce, typically referred to as Card Not Present (CNP) transactions. This implies that customers enter their card details on the payment page of a merchant's website. Existing research addresses card-based payment frameworks in terms of security [2] without any real focus and consideration for simultaneous user privacy protection, payment control and supervision.

Indeed, despite their security, card-based systems are still far from privacy, control and supervision. Specifically, these systems do not provide a payment environment that prevents the seller or an attacker from misusing the cardholder's information [3]. The merchant can still control which data fields are used to authorize the payment even if he cannot physically verify that the customer actually has the debit or credit card. As a result, the transactions exchanged with the merchant usually include customers' sensitive financial and non-financial information. Financial information refers to payment details such as credit card number, expiry date and card verification value. Non-financial information relates to the products being purchased (such as price or product type). Both types of information can be intercepted by anyone and require a lot of control before and after the transaction. Further, safeguarding the data might not prevent any unauthorized access.

In addition to the lack of privacy, card-based systems do not allow users to manage their online transactions. Generally, when performing multiple purchases customers must provide their card information at checkout for every purchase. This information is then passed on to various parties who further process it before authorizing or rejecting the payment request. Each of the aforementioned parties has a different responsibility. Hence, the payment process with card-based systems does not include the following properties: user personalization, control of purchases/checkouts, and management of payments with respect to multi-purchase scenarios.

To better highlight these issues, consider the following scenario: In a retail company, a chief executive officer (CEO) wants to provide several credit cards for his employees to make online purchases. He must decide on the line of credit for each card and provide instructions regarding online purchase conditions, such as selected merchants, type of purchases, price range, expenditure, etc. The CEO then receives statements of account, has to verify each payment and match it with the corresponding purchase item, and ensure it is in line with his instructions before settling the invoices. Besides this daunting task, the CEO cannot specify which merchants are allowed, expense limits or characteristics of the products purchased online. Note that this scenario can be easily extended to other cases, including parents providing credit cards to their children.

Current card-based payment systems have limitations to enforce these features and are thus still behind in terms of privacy protection, control and supervision in a multi-purchase scenario.

In this work, we propose and design a new e-payment framework based on the work of Ruiz-Martínez *et al.* [4], which provides a general approach founded on a set of generic components to help with the design of different payment frameworks for negotiation and choice of the payment protocol. We modify the framework and improve it, adding new layers to provide privacy and support: user personalization, data protection, purchase control and payment supervision with respect to multi-purchase scenarios and conditional payment.

Section 2 of this paper provides an overview of e-payments along with all their challenges. Section 3 describes our e-payment framework and highlights its different layers/components. Section 4 provides a detailed discussion about the procedures within a complete scenario of application. Section 5 analyzes the framework's properties, i.e., our main contributions, and finally Sect. 6 concludes the paper.

2 Background and Related Work

For a number of decades, the payment market denoted a rapid growth due to the increase of e-payment systems. Many payment solutions have been deployed; e-cash, prepaid cards, credit cards, and debit cards are widely used in e-commerce environments. The security issues in payment frameworks have been investigated extensively. However, ensuring a secure payment does not guarantee privacy protection. The open nature of e-commerce payment systems renders them susceptible to several critical threats and attacks due to the presence of malicious participants. Customer privacy thus becomes a concern in payment frameworks [5].

In this context, E-cash payment systems raise the degree of privacy protection to such a level that even the police are unable to associate the payee with the payer, just as with cash payments in the physical world [6]. Yet, the adoption of e-cash has mostly been a series of failed initiatives [7]. Conversely, e-payments using credit and debit cards have been growing over the years, and analysts agree that this will be the case for the next few years, as highlighted by the United Nations Conference on Trade and Development (UNCTAD) in their report[2] titled "UNCTAD B2C E-COMMERCE INDEX 2016."

In the sub-selection of credit card payments, considerable innovations have appeared in e-commerce to integrate this method into payment frameworks. Large companies, such as *PayPal* and *Google Wallet,* have expanded their efforts to create and provide payment solutions. Payment solutions were also introduced to mobile environments by *Apple Pay* [8]. In their integration with card business, these companies have brought service improvements to the marketplace and appeared as payment providers with a role of mediating online payments between merchants and buyers. In other words, they act as intermediaries between suppliers and their customers who buy and then pay for goods and services. However, they essentially gain insight into transactions as they process personal information—credit card number, expiry date, customer name—or any other information, i.e., address, card limits, shopping data.

---

[2] http://unctad.org/en/PublicationsLibrary/tn_unctad_ict4d07_en.pdf consulted on 05/June/2016.

Conceptually, intermediaries' participation has an impact on customer privacy since they are in a position to access sensitive payment details that can be used to build a detailed profile of customer shopping habits [9]. Cardholders are asked to provide a lot more sensitive information in an online transaction, and merchants get to retain the information on their data servers for as long as they wish and consider additional investments in trust-generating tactics [10]. Thus, such exposure of personal and financial data over the Internet gives rise to a number of relevant privacy challenges that must be addressed [11, 12], in addition to the lack of personalization and flexibility in card-based payment systems.

There have been some attempts to provide anonymous payment systems by integrating virtual credit card mechanisms [13], in an effort to mitigate the loss in card theft. Initially, virtual credit card accounts are derived from a user's existing physical credit card account. Another approach with regard to privacy was creating an e-payment scheme that guaranteed authenticity while keeping the customer's sensitive details secret from the respective parties involved in the online transaction [1]. However, relatively little was done to payment frameworks that enabled credit card payments and protected customers' information, while still being configurable and manageable.

In this respect, our proposed framework attempts to provide a card-based system, configurable and manageable that also protects customer privacy.

3   Conditional Anonymous Multi-payment Framework

This section provides a detailed description of our proposed payment framework (illustrated in Fig. 1).

The proposed framework is detailed in layers that are represented in a conceptual way to reflect all the elements that a payment framework should include to support our new approach. The various layers are grouped into two fundamental parts: the *Cardholder Space* and the *E-Payment Plan Service Manager (E-PPSM)*.

Note that *Transport/Security Mechanisms* represents a communication layer sensitive information can be exchanged. In this layer, it is primordial to choose a protocol that guarantees a secure exchange of information, such as the TLS Protocol [14].

3.1   The Cardholder Space

The *Cardholder Space* reflects two components that are fundamental to supporting our proposed payment framework in a card-based system: the *Credit Card* and the *Credit Card Payment System (CCPS)*. Another significant component is represented in the *Virtual Credit Card (VCC) Generation* layer, which provides a privacy-preserving e-payment scheme that guarantees authenticity while preserving the cardholder's sensitive details. In this layer, the *VCC*, *Personalization* and *Private/Public Conditions* are the three leading components, which we will explain in detail.

Credit Card. The *Credit Card* component contains the basic credit card information known by the cardholder and the issuing bank. Unlike the traditional card-based

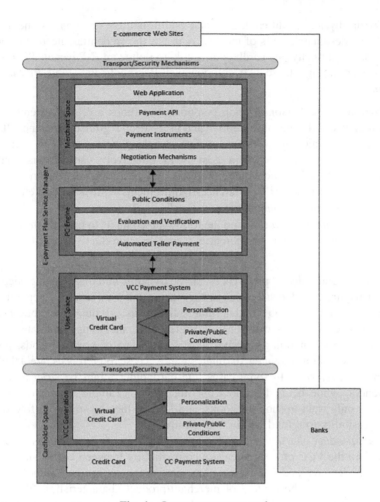

Fig. 1. Our payment protocol

payment system, in our payment framework, the cardholder's sensitive details are not revealed to the merchant, effectively preventing any potential misuse or data leaks.

Credit Card Payment System. In general, this component handles the transfer of funds between the payer and payee. The payment amount is debited from the cardholder's issuing bank and deposited into the merchant's account at the acquiring bank. In our payment framework, the payment process settlement does not require the disclosure of any personal information about the cardholder. A functionality for multi-payment process is required to support multi-purchases.

Virtual Credit Card Generation. The *VCC Generation* layer represents the main component in our proposed framework. It generates the necessary details for registration, identification and authentication of users who perform online transactions in addition to their *E-Payment Plans*. Through this layer, cardholders can create a *VCC* linked to their physical credit card, designate additional users and assign them a *VCC*. Moreover, the designated users of the *VCC* can get the credentials needed to perform transactions. Additionally, the cardholder is able to define an *E-Payment Plan* for each *VCC*–user pair through these two components: *Personalization* and *Private/Public Conditions*.

Personalization. The *Personalization* component outlines a primary element in our proposed framework that enables intuitive and user-specific guided assistance. It can be described as any action that restricts online shopping done by *VCC* users to the cardholder's preferences. The main goal is to effectively use various contextual information to personalize merchants, products and payments and ensure their compatibility with the cardholder's preferences/requirements. Our approach encompasses two main parts: *Context Management* and *Feedback/Reviews*.

The *Context Management* relies on the following contexts to provide the cardholder with personalized content: preferences, merchant/product characteristics and environment.

- *Preferences*: Cardholders' preferences can be dynamic and might change depending on their required products/services or the designated *VCC* user. In general, search mechanisms retrieve web content that satisfies users' objectives but not their preferences. Cardholders can generate preferences, including parameters such as payment method, shopping websites, cost limits, type of goods, brands, purchase and delivery conditions, area of interest, etc. These preferences are labelled as *required* or *preferred*. In some cases, the cardholder might be strict about some preferences, while being flexible with others. For example, the cardholder may specify "I only want to shop for books, and I prefer they be sold with free shipping and a possibility to refund within one month."
- *Merchant/product characteristics*: Incorporate the merchant/product/service information into the *VCC* process to ensure compatibility between online shopping and credit card features and constraints. Any preference set by the cardholder can be evaluated based on the context of merchant/product characteristics. For example: The payment would be rejected if a merchant required payments in a currency other than the one requested by the cardholder.
- *Environment*: Provides cardholders with services that fit their current context, such as location, time, type of business and assigned responsibilities. The objective of integrating the environment context into the *VCC* is twofold: select products that fit a certain context and ensure that card payments are properly accomplished depending on specific environment conditions.

In the *Feedback/Reviews*, cardholders can provide comments after making their purchase to indicate their level of satisfaction of the service/product selected. The contents of such information can be populated to be shown for *VCC* users in order to improve their shopping experience.

Private/Public Conditions. The *Private/Public Conditions* component is an additional element in the *VCC* and in the process of the *VCC Generation*.

- *Private conditions*: Any single information considered as private to the card issuer or cardholder himself such as personal information (full name, age, sex, address and email) or payment details (account number, card expiry date, billing information). This information is not revealed to the merchant or even the *VCC* user. Therefore, our proposed framework conserves the property of cardholder anonymity during the shopping transaction.
- *Public conditions*: Any single information considered as public and that can be revealed to other parties without jeopardizing the cardholder's privacy. The *VCC* includes parameters that can be known by the *VCC* user such as *VCC* limit, *VCC* expiry date and current *VCC* balance. Suppose P is a public condition, it can be represented as follows: (*Pn, Tn, Vn*) where *Pn* is the number of the condition, *Tn* is the content, and *Vn* is the type of condition once published outside the cardholder space with two possible values (0,1). The content of these values can be populated, for instance, in the *Private/Public Conditions,* one of the components of the *VCC* layer included in the *E-PPSM Space* described in the next section.

3.2   The E-Payment Plan Service Manager

The *E-PPSM* is composed of three parts: the *Merchant Space,* the *Payment Conditional Engine (PC Engine) Space* and the *User Space.*

Merchant Space. The *Web Application* layer represents the web page where the checkout information is displayed. Through this page, consumers can pay for products they want to purchase. Two fundamental aspects should be present: identification/authentication and trust. Several mechanisms are available for identification and authentication, including: X.509 certificates, Mozilla Persona,[3]WebID.[4] As for trust, there have been several efforts made to determine how trustworthy a website is. For example, TRUSTe[5] uses directories of certifying identities.

The *Payment Web API* layer is in charge of defining an Application Programming Interface (*API*) that allows for the development of various processes. These processes are related to the use of different payment instruments that help the customer manage their payments in a uniform and well-established way through the merchant website. They include negotiating a payment instrument, making a payment and getting a receipt.

The *Payment Instruments* layer is defined to support a variety of payment instruments. In general, the payment system provides a solution to reduce the risk of fraud and enhance security and user anonymity. In this work, the payment system considers the *VCC* as a payment solution.

The *Negotiation Mechanisms* layer is responsible for the agreement between the customer as payer and the merchant as payee. The layer supports different issues related to the transaction such as the payment instrument and, optionally, the price or any other

---

[3] https://developer.mozilla.org/en-US/Persona consulted on 27/Sep/2016.

[4] https://www.w3.org/2005/Incubator/webid/spec/ consulted on 27/Sep/2016.

[5] https://www.truste.com/privacy-certification-standards/ consulted on 27/Sep/2016

payment conditions. To facilitate the purchase procedure, the major goal is to build negotiation interchanges based on consumers' preferences and thereby allow them to select the system that works better for them [15]. The process can also be performed by human computer negotiating agents [16].

Payment Conditional Engine. In the *E-PPSM*, the *Payment Conditional Engine (PC Engine)* includes the main core tasks to preserve user privacy and conditional multi-merchant purchases. The engine includes three components: *Public Conditions*, *Evaluation and Verification*, and *Automated Teller Payment*.

- The *Public Conditions* layer is based on the extension of the different criteria that are used to access e-products and populated by the merchants. To define these conditions, a set of logical expressions can be configured with various parameters. For instance, suppose a database D contains data records contributed by a set of *n* merchants about *m* items. Each item could represent in reality a service or product included in the purchase transaction. Each record in dataset D is a tuple (*rID; mID; pID; attrP*), where *rID* is the record ID, *mID* corresponds to the merchant who contributed this record, *pID* is the item which the record is about, and *attrP* holds the public conditions populated by the merchant. In reality, various information can be customized in a set of attributes that are related to the item characteristics (price, type or quality) or merchant qualifications (classification, rating or credibility).
- The *Evaluation and Verification* layer is essential and one of the most important components. It performs the comparison and verification between the *VCC* user's public conditions and the merchant's public condition. Specifically, this element enables the vendors to specify different conditions, and the payment engine will match them with the *Private/Public Conditions* specified by the user.
- The *Automated Teller Payment* layer supports the feature of multi-merchant processing. It is important to point out that if the designed payment framework does not consider this layer, the user performs different purchase transactions, and each transaction belongs to a merchant. Through this layer, the consumer performs the payment using the *VCC* for multiple purchases and for different merchants. As long as the *Automated Teller Payment* is authorized by the *Evaluation and Verification* layer, it can get the payment information and start the payment procedure for the registered consumer. It acts as an involved entity in non-repudiation services, as the originator sending messages to multiple recipients, and as recipient of messages.

User Space. The *VCC Payment System* layer is the cornerstone for the support of the message generated by the *Automated Teller Payment*. Within this message, the payment information can be included and used to launch the transaction. The messages regarding the payment should be exchanged by means of a payment protocol supporting the payment by virtual card number. In this paper, we assume that the protocols and the exchanging authorization transactions will provide enough message confidentiality, authenticity and integrity such that the security of an exchange is never disputed [17]. Additionally, it is important to guarantee a user's identity in a transaction. Through this layer, a request is sent to authenticate the issuer of the message based on the *VCC* information located in the *VCC* layer.

The *VCC* layer represents the component responsible for the *VCC* information; it is in charge of hiding the real cardholder's identity and safeguarding his or her information. The *VCC* user is authenticated in this layer using a high-security authentication (e.g., a three-factor authentication scheme which combines biometrics, a password and a secure element such as smart card [5]).

Similarly to the *VCC Generation* component in the *Cardholder Space* (refer to Sect. 3.1), this layer provides *Personalization* and *Private/Public Conditions*.

- The *Personalization* component helps *VCC* users to model an *E-payment Plan* depending directly on their intentions and current circumstances. The automation of such tasks is highly dependent on the user's personal context. Moreover, this component ensures that the context is in line with the cardholder's personalization and preferences, specified during the *VCC Generation*. The *E-Payment Plan* can include: a set of preferred websites based on the nature of the user's personal goals, a set of keywords that describe the user's interest, and the desired products the user expects to retrieve. Additionally, this component holds all the previous *E-payment Plans* mediated by the user and brings a considerable benefit to the *E-PPSM* partition.
- The *Private/Public Conditions* component represents a supplementary element in the *VCC* layer. This component improves the user's experience through the automation of repetitive and ordinary tasks to fulfill goals and contextual information. As stated earlier, the *Private/Public Conditions* in the *Cardholder Space* will be populate in this layer. Suppose (*Pn, Tn, Vn*) is the public condition. The value of *Vn* will designate the type of the condition. In case the *Vn* = '1', the *Pn* can be published and considered as a public condition, otherwise *Pn* is reserved as a private condition.

The next section will further detail our e-payment framework, explain the procedures and provide the flow of information with a scenario of application.

4 Procedures of Scenario Application

Consider a cardholder who has already acquired a credit card. The issuing bank provides him with a solution to get virtual cards. We can also suppose that the cardholder has a list of users he wants to provide with virtual cards. In our e-payment framework, the process of information can be split into two flows.

The first flow, illustrated in Fig. 2, starts from the validation of the credit card until the readiness of the *VCC* and the *E-Payment Plan* for future use. The steps involved are related to the components embedded in the *VCC Generation* and *User Space* layers (excluding the *VCC Payment System* component) described earlier. For simplicity, only the operations performed from the user's point of view are included, whereas the different operations that the card issuer performs to generate a credit card and *VCC* are omitted.

The second flow, illustrated in Fig. 3, features an online purchase transaction with multiple merchants. It includes different functions related to the *PC Engine* and *Merchant* layers in addition to the *VCC Payment System* component.

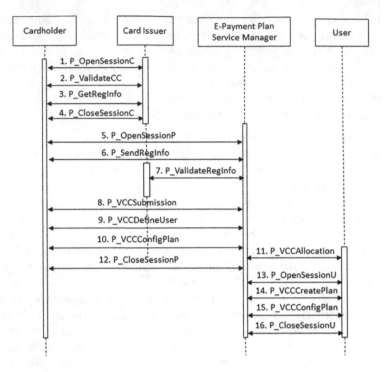

Fig. 2. VCC and E-Payment Plan configuration

The process would be as follows: The cardholder performs two actions: opens a session with the issuing bank using his credentials (step 1 in Fig. 2) and validates his credit card (step 2 in Fig. 2). After proof of validation, the cardholder sends a request to register for a new *E-Payment Plan* (step 3 in Fig. 2). Once the cardholder is authenticated, the issuing bank returns to him the necessary *VCC* registration information to be deployed within the *E-PPSM*. After finalizing the validation and registration, the cardholder closes the session (step 4 in Fig. 2).

Afterwards, the cardholder initiates a secure session with the *E-PPSM* (step 5 in Fig. 2). When the corresponding function is invoked, the cardholder can register (step 6 in Fig. 2) using the registration information previously acquired from the issuing bank. For the first time, the *E-PPSM* provides the user with a new *E-Payment Plan*.

The *Issuer* and the *E-PPSM* exchange the identification information (step 7 in Fig. 2). The issuing bank adds a set of entities to the user profile: (*E_IdInf, E_PayPlan, TimeStamp, StatEvent*) where *E_IdInf* is the identification information provided by the issuing bank, *E_PayPlan* is the *E-payment plan* supplemented by the *E-PPSM*, *TimeStamp* is the date/time of the event, *StatEvent* represents the status of the event. Initially, the status is "pending." When the cardholder validates the *E-Payment Plan*, the status is changed to "validated," otherwise it cannot be deployed.

Following the *VCC Generation*, cards are submitted to the *E-PPSM* (step 8 in Fig. 2). The cardholder defines a list of users (step 9 in Fig. 2) and configures his

E-Payment Plan with a set of *Private/Public Conditions* (step 10 in Fig. 2), i.e., list of designated merchants, limited prices, brands, type of purchases, range of time. As a result, the functions return a message indicating whether the *VCC* is configured successfully or not. Once configured properly, the *VCC* is created with a status of "unassigned" to indicate that the *VCC* can now be allocated to a registered user. In fact, a *VCC* user must be registered to access the services offered by the *E-PPSM*. The allocation process starts (step 11 in Fig. 2), and the status of the *VCC* is updated to "allocated," which signifies it cannot be allocated to another user, and the Service Manager returns a confirmation message to the cardholder. Finally, the cardholder can close his session (step 12 in Fig. 2).

Subsequently, the allocated *VCC* user starts the process of the *VCC* configuration. He opens a secure session (step 13 in Fig. 2). Once authenticated by the service, he proceeds to create an *E-Payment Plan* (step 14 in Fig. 2) and configures it with a set of *Private/Public Conditions* (step 15 in Fig. 2). In addition to these steps, the *E-PPSM* validates all inputs and considers the user *E-Payment Plan* as a sub-plan in the cardholder's plan, keeping in mind the possibility of personalizing it at the user's discretion. Subject to the result of the validation, the *E-PPSM* accepts or denies the new *E-Payment Plan*. When finished, the *VCC* user can end the session (step 16 in Fig. 2).

Prior to the payment, the *E-PPSM* can invoke different functions to manage the process or to query information regarding the purchases: e.g., searching for the product, initiating a session with the merchant, negotiating prices and offers, concluding the payment and preparing the order details (steps 1, 2, 3, 4 and 5 in Fig. 3). These functions can be invoked at any moment, repeated for the next purchase and before the execution of the *E-payment Plan*.

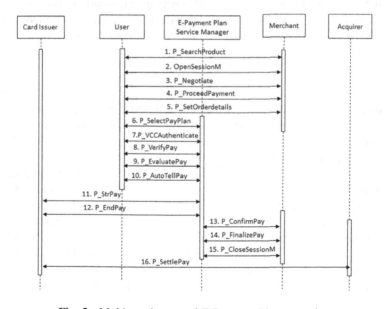

Fig. 3. Multi-purchases and E-Payment Plan execution

When the user completes all purchases and proceeds to checkout, that page would usually include the merchant's name, the order details and the final amount to be paid. As a result, all purchases will be grouped on one page where the user can go through a series of steps, for example: checking the order details and deciding to withdraw, add or keep items. Finally, the user may decide to proceed with the final payment, so he initiates the next step to invoke the selection of the *E-Payment Plan* (step 6 in Fig. 3). According to the plan's role, three actions happen: authenticate the user, identify the allocated *VCC* and validate the payment details (step 7, 8 and 9 in Fig. 3). The next state (step 10 in Fig. 3) processes the message received which contains the checkout details. The message should be without errors for payment initiation (step 11 in Fig. 3), otherwise the operation is rejected. In this step, the two parties send/receive the necessary information for authorization and validity. The *Card Issuer* sends back an approval or denial message to the *E-PPSM*. By the end, the session is closed (step 12 in Fig. 3).

Afterwards, the *E-PPSM* sends the status to the merchant (step 13 in Fig. 3), who can update the order status in their own server and send it back to confirm the result (step 14 in Fig. 3). Finally, the end of the process is indicated by the end of session (step 15 in Fig. 3).

After reviewing the whole process, the next section provides a detailed analysis of the main properties of our proposed framework.

5 Framework Analysis

Our payment framework is namely a design that supports the card payments. Moreover, it includes provisions for *privacy protection, conditional e-payment*, cardholder's *control* and *supervision* for purchases and payments simultaneously. These are the improvements we have made to the payment process, in addition to the availability of *multi-purchases*. The following paragraphs provide an analysis of the main properties.

5.1 Privacy

The cardholder's *privacy* is one of our major concerns in the proposed e-payment framework. Access to the exchanged card's sensitive information is restricted to the *Issuer* and the *Cardholder*. The *Issuer* is the single entity who can validate the card's information and provide the *VCC* information to be allocated to the users. We suppose that the *Credit Card Issuer* is a trustworthy entity. A corresponding factor dealing with privacy is the *Credit Card Payment System (CCPS)*. It helps preserve the cardholder's sensitive details. Both components in the *VCC Generation, Personalization* and *Private/Public Conditions* are configured by the cardholder. Thus, personal or shopping information is not revealed to any third party. Additionally, the *Payment Conditional Engine (PC Engine)* includes the main core tasks to preserve cardholder's *privacy* and compile the payment transaction without revealing any sensitive information such as card number, card expiry date, verification code.

5.2   Control

In 1916, Henri Fayol formulated one of the first definitions of control as it pertains to management: "*Control* consists of verifying whether everything occurs in conformity with the plan adopted, the instructions issued, and principles established..."[6] With this in mind, our e-payment framework attributes the *Control* factor to the cardholder. The *VCC* is based on a set of *Private/Public Conditions* specified first by the cardholder, and then by the *VCC* user. The *Payment Conditional Engine (PC Engine)* ensures that these conditions are met through the intermediate *Evaluation and Verification* layer and their harmonization with merchants' public conditions. Such conditions help cardholders gain the control of their purchases.

5.3   Supervision

The *Supervision* property brings a lot of improvement to the shopping experience. Specifically, it provides an effective tool for cardholders to be able to supervise their credit card expenses. Note that the *VCC* part includes a personalization setting. The *VCC* user is able to perform transactions within the restrictions indicated in cardholder's preferences, within a defined context with the possibility of giving feedback or reviews. These components, along with the *Control* property described earlier, lead us to the establishment of a payment architecture that facilitates supervision for the cardholder.

5.4   Multi-purchases

Ensuring the *multi-purchases* in a healthy, safe and efficient e-payment system is essential for e-commerce to continue to flourish. Most payment protocols have some limitations to support multiple credit card at the same time and in one checkout page [18]. However, in our proposed framework the cardholder can generate multiple *VCCs* linked to different credit cards that may belong to same or different card issuers. Additionally, as stated in the flow, the *VCC* user is able to select different products or services from different merchants, add them to one shopping cart and launch the *E-Payment Plan*, which will take care of the payment process through the *Automated Teller Payment* layer satisfying the multi-purchases scenarios.

5.5   Conditional Payments

The last property in our analysis is the *Conditional Payment* feature. As described in the payment flow, a payment cannot be made unless all conditions are satisfied. In a

---

[6] https://www.boundless.com/management/textbooks/boundless-management-textbook/introduction-to-management-1/principles-of-management-17/fulfilling-the-controlling-function-115-3962/ consulted on 16/Jan/2017

traditional payment scenario, a number of conditions can be defined such as credit card limit and expiry date. In our e-payment framework, additional user specified conditions can be set based on the *Private/Public Conditions* layer defined in the *VCC* components.

6 Conclusions and Future Work

Secure online payment services have been extensively investigated in card-based systems. Nevertheless, the main concern of existing solutions is security, whereas privacy protection, control and supervision are barely addressed. In this article, we present a new e-payment framework that, in addition to security, is primarily aimed at protecting consumers' privacy, while providing control and flexibility, by integrating the *E-Payment Plan* and the *VCC*.

First, this combination ensures privacy protection. With online purchases, the user needs to provide payment-related information at various moments. In our proposed framework, there is no need to include any sensitive card details that could be stolen. Second, personalization is ensured in our proposed framework, providing an easier/more flexible shopping experience. Cardholders are able to define a set of private and public conditions in their *E-Payment Plan*. Finally, cardholders get an effective solution where they can control and supervise their credit card expenses, leading to a great extent of other properties like multi-purchase scenarios and conditional payments. As a result, the contribution in our work is to provide a holistic approach that integrates, in addition to security, personalization, control, and supervision into online credit card payments while still ensuring cardholder privacy.

Moreover, we analyze the different components required in our proposed payment framework, its functionality, and the different solutions that are available for its development. All three identified workspaces—cardholder, *E-PPSM* and merchant—have an influence on the shopping scenario. We present an example illustrating the whole workflow and interaction between the various components. In addition, we outline each element's characteristics, derive its role and explain how it is integrated into the whole process.

As a future work, an analysis should be conducted to assess cardholder privacy in terms of secrecy and determine how to mitigate privacy risks when arranging the private and public conditions in the *E-Payment Plan*. Additionally, a comprehensive evaluation should be elaborated to show the security and feasibility of the proposed framework and how to incorporate it into a merchant's site.

References

1. Ashrafi, M.Z., Ng, S.K.: Privacy-preserving e-payments using one-time payment details. Comput. Stand. Interfaces **31**, 321–328 (2009)
2. S.S.E.T. LLC, SET Secure Electronic Transaction Specification, Book 1: Business Description. Version, vol. 1 (2002)

3. Dixon, C.J., Pinckney, T.: Indicating website reputations during website manipulation of user information. Google Patents (2013)
4. Ruiz-Martínez, A., Reverte, Ó.C., Gómez-Skarmeta, A.F.: Payment frameworks for the purchase of electronic products and services. Comput. Stand. Interfaces **34**, 80–92 (2012)
5. Vu, K.-P. L., Proctor, R.W.: User Privacy Concerns for E-Commerce (2016)
6. Cellary, W., Rykowski, J.: Challenges of smart industries–privacy and payment in Visible versus unseen internet. Gov. Inf. Q. (2015)
7. Ruiz-Martínez, A.: Towards a web payment framework: state-of-the-art and challenges. Electron. Commer. Res. Appl. **14**, 345–350 (2015)
8. Gray, J.M.: How apple pay coincides with the consumer financial protection act: will apple become a regulated entity. J. High Tech. L. **16**, 170 (2015)
9. Preibusch, S., Peetz, T., Acar, G., Berendt, B.: Purchase details leaked to PayPal. In: Böhme, R., Okamoto, T. (eds.) FC 2015. LNCS, vol. 8975, pp. 217–226. Springer, Heidelberg (2015). doi:10.1007/978-3-662-47854-7_13
10. Bansal, G., Zahedi, F.M., Gefen, D.: Do context and personality matter? Trust and privacy concerns in disclosing private information online. Inf. Manag. **53**, 1–21 (2016)
11. Carminati, B., Ferrari, E., Tran, N.H.: Trustworthy and effective person-to-person payments over multi-hop MANETs. J. Netw. Comput. Appl. **60**, 1–18 (2016)
12. Pascual-Miguel, F.J., Agudo-Peregrina, Á.F., Chaparro-Peláez, J.: Influences of gender and product type on online purchasing. J. Bus. Res. **68**, 1550–1556 (2015)
13. Luo, J.N., Yang, M.H., Huang, S.-Y.: An unlinkable anonymous payment scheme based on near field communication. Comput. Electr. Eng. **49**, 198–206 (2016)
14. Turner, S.: Transport Layer Security. IEEE Internet Comput. **18**, 60–63 (2014)
15. Mu, N., Rui, L., Guo, S., Qiu, X.: Generalized lagrange based resource negotiation mechanism in MANETs. In: 10th International Conference on Network and Service Management (CNSM) and Workshop, pp. 218–223 (2014)
16. Cao, M., Luo, X., Luo, X.R., Dai, X.: Automated negotiation for e-commerce decision making: a goal deliberated agent architecture for multi-strategy selection. Decis. Support Syst. **73**, 1–14 (2015)
17. Gommans, L., Vollbrecht, J., Gommans-de Bruijn, B., de Laat, C.: The service provider group framework: a framework for arranging trust and power to facilitate authorization of network services. Future Gener. Comput. Syst. **45**, 176–192 (2015)
18. Sureshkumar, V., Anitha, R., Rajamanickam, N., Amin, R.: A lightweight two-gateway based payment protocol ensuring accountability and unlinkable anonymity with dynamic identity. Comput. Electr. Eng. (2016)

Reflex-SMAS, a Complex Adaptive System: An Empirical Evaluation

Hicham Assoudi[(✉)] and Hakim Lounis[(✉)]

Université du Québec à Montréal (UQAM), Montréal, Canada
assoudi.hicham@courrier.uqam.ca, hakim.lounis@uqam.ca

Abstract. Despite the profusion of approaches that were proposed to deal with the problem of the Automatic Schema Matching, yet the challenges and difficulties caused by the complexity and uncertainty characterizing both the process and the outcome of Schema Matching motivated us to investigate how bio-inspired emerging paradigm can help with understanding, managing, and ultimately overcoming those challenges.

In this paper, we explain how we approached Schema Matching as a Complex Adaptive System (CAS) and how we modeled it using the approach of Agent-Based Modeling and Simulation (ABMS) giving birth to a new tool (prototype) for schema matching called Reflex-SMAS.

This prototype was submitted to a set of experiments which aimed to demonstrate the viability of our approach to two main aspects: (i) effectiveness (increasing the quality of the found matchings) and (ii) efficiency (reducing the effort required for this efficiency). The results, came to demonstrate the viability of our approach, both in terms of effectiveness or that of efficiency.

Keywords: Schema matching · Complex adaptive systems · Agent-Based Modeling and Simulation

1 Introduction

Schema Matching and Mapping are an important task for many applications, such as data integration, data warehousing and e-commerce. Schema matching process aims at finding a pairing of elements (or groups of elements) from the source schema and elements of the target schema such that pairs are likely to be semantically related [2, 3].

Schema matching existing approaches rely largely on human interactions, either for the matching results validation, during the post-matching phase, or for the matching process optimization, during the pre-matching phase. Although this human involvement in the automatic matching process could be considered as acceptable in a lot of matching scenarios, nevertheless it should be kept to a minimum, or even avoided, when dealing with high dynamic environments (i.e. semantic web, web services composition, agents communication, etc.) [1]. Thus, the existing approaches are not suited for all the matching contexts due to their intrinsic limitations. We can summarize those limitations as follows:

© Springer International Publishing AG 2017
E. Aïmeur et al. (Eds.): MCETECH 2017, LNBIP 289, pp. 300–318, 2017.
DOI: 10.1007/978-3-319-59041-7_19

- Lack of autonomy to the extent that the user involvement is still needed for the results validation and analysis and also for matching process configuration and optimization (tuning) to improve the matching result quality (reduce uncertainty)
- Lack of adaptation in sense that the optimization task of the matching tool should be repeated and adapted manually for every new matching scenario

Accordingly, uncertainty and the complexity remain as open questions in the field of Schema Matching. Thus, we were motivated to investigate other prospects that have not yet been applied on it, with a view to try to answer the following general question:

How can we, with the help of a generic approach, better manage complexity and uncertainty inherent to the automatic matching process in general and in the context of dynamic environments (minimal involvement of the human expert)?

More specifically, we asked the followings questions: (i) how can we model the complexity of the matching process to help reduce uncertainty? (ii) How can we provide the matching process of autonomy and adaptation properties with the aim to make the matching process able to adapt to each matching scenario (self-optimize)? (iii) What would be the theoretical orientation that may be adequate to respond to the above questions?

The central idea of our work, is to consider the process of matching as a Complex Adaptive System (CAS) and model it using the approach of Agent-Based Modeling and Simulation (ABMS). The aim being the exploitation of the intrinsic properties of the agent-based models, such as emergence, stochasticity, and self-organization, to help provide answers to better manage complexity and uncertainty of Schema Matching.

We proposed a conceptual model for a multi-agent simulation for schema matching called SMAS (Schema Matching as Multi-Agents Simulation). The implementation of this conceptual model has given birth to a new prototype for schema matching (Reflex-SMAS).

Our prototype Reflex-SMAS was submitted to a set of experiments which aimed to demonstrate the viability of our approach to two main aspects: (i) effectiveness (increasing the quality of the found matchings) and (ii) efficiency (reducing the effort required for this efficiency). The results, came to demonstrate the viability of our approach, both in terms of effectiveness or that of efficiency.

The empirical evaluation results, as we are going to show in this paper, were very satisfactory for both effectiveness (correct matching results found) and efficiency (no optimization needed to get good result from our tool).

We are confident, after this empirical evaluation, to announce the birth of a new tool, namely Reflex-SMAS which is representing a significant paradigm-shift, in the field of automatic Schema matching. In fact, to the best of our knowledge, never the automatic Schema Matching problem has been addressed by adopting systemic thinking (holistic approach), or has been considered as a CAS and modeled using ABMS modeling approach.

2 Schema Matching

Many algorithms and approaches were proposed to deal with the problem of schema matching and mapping [1, 4–15]. Although the existing schema matching tools comprise a significant step towards fulfilling the vision of automated schema matching, it has become obvious that the user must accept a degree of imperfection in this process. A prime reason for this is the enormous ambiguity and heterogeneity of schema element names (descriptions). Thus, it could be unrealistic to expect a matching process to identify the correct matchings for any possible element in a schema [16, 17].

A comprehensive literature review, of the existing matching tools and approaches, allowed us to identify the most important factors impacting, in our opinion, the schema matching process. Moreover, some causal relationships, between those different factors, participating to the schema matching difficulties and challenges, were found. As shown in the diagram below, the factors impacting the Schema Matching are:

- Heterogeneity: In general, the task of matching involves semantics (understanding the context) to have complete certainty about the quality of the result. The main challenge in all cases of automatic matching is to decide the right match. This is a very difficult task mainly because of the heterogeneity of the data.
- Uncertainty: The cause for this uncertainty lies mainly in the ambiguity and heterogeneity, both syntactic and semantic, that often characterize the Schema Elements to match.
- Optimization: the uncertainty about the matching results implies the optimization of the process to improve the matching quality. Testing different combinations (e.g. different Similarity Measures, Aggregate Functions, Matching Selection Strategies). Each step of the matching process involves choosing between multiple strategies which leads to a combinatorial explosion (complexity).
- Complexity: Matching process optimization generates complexity because of the search space (combinatorial explosion). In addition, changing matching scenarios exacerbates this complexity to the extent the result of the optimization often becomes obsolete with changing scenarios.

One of the commonalities between all existing approaches is the thinking behind these approaches namely reductionism (as opposed to holism). The reductionist thinking, although very common and efficient thinking approach, is behind the characteristics that are, in our view, the root causes that prevent the automatic matching schemes to cope fully with the challenges and difficulties (Fig. 1).

Reductionism, as opposed holism, (systemic) is a philosophical concept that refers both to the way of thinking solutions as well as to their modeling methodology (analytical). Reductionism advocates reducing system complexity or phenomenon to their basic elements which would then be easier to understand and study [18]. This reductionist approach, despite its high efficacy in several areas, shows, however, its limits for certain subjects. In fact, for explaining certain phenomena or solving certain problems, the approach consisting of reducing or abstracting the reality to a linearization of simple relationships of causes and effects between a complex system underling fundamental components, could appears as a highly limiting and simplifying approach.

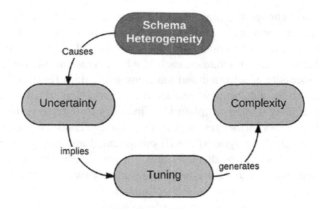

Fig. 1. Schema Matching impacting factors causality diagram

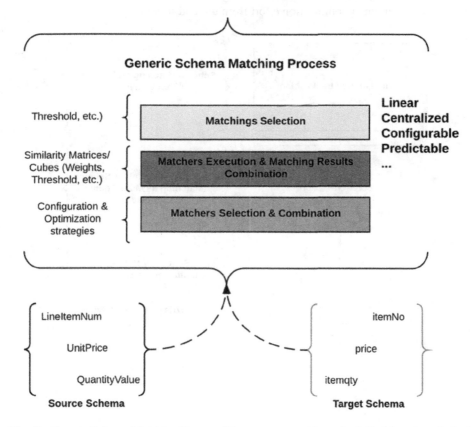

Fig. 2. Generic Schema Matching Process (Linear process with an Analytical-based resolution)

With regard to Schema matching, it seems clear, as it can be shown in the figure below, that all current approaches follow the reductionist thinking. They abstract the Matching process to a linear function with a set of inputs and outputs. This function can be decomposed into a series of modules, each of which is responsible for the running of a stage of the process (e.g. selection and matching execution) (Fig. 2).

Some fundamental and intrinsic characteristics, common to all current Schema Matching systems, may partially explain their inability to overcome the limitation of the complexity and other challenges such as uncertainty. Those characteristics can be declined as following: these systems are (i) complicated and not complex, (ii) linear (analytical, deterministic and predictable) and not non-linear, (iii) centralized rather than decentralized (parallelism and emerging solutions) (iv) and finally configurable and not adaptable (self-configuration, self-optimization).

The need to explore new approaches in order to make systemic and holistic responses to the problems of matching leads us to raise the question: how can we have a matching solution that could give us high-quality matching results, for different matching scenarios and this with a minimal optimization effort from the end-user? (Fig. 3).

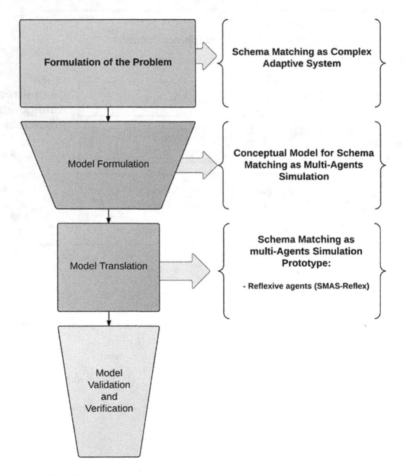

Fig. 3. Methodological approach for Schema Matching as CAS

Our premise is that a good part of the answer may come from the theory of CAS where modeling the complexity of adaptation and evolution of the systems is at the heart of this theory. Having a schema matching approach that can face and overcome the challenges facing the existing schema matching tools requires, in our view, a paradigm shift, placing the notions of adaptation, evolution and self-organization at its center. We strongly believe that CAS, which were used to explain some biological, social and economic phenomena, can be the basis of a programming paradigm for schema matching tools. Our methodological approach, as depicted in the figure above, for validating our central hypothesis is based the empirical validation of a prototype called Reflex-SMAS.

3 Schema Matching as Complex Adaptive System

As part of our research we investigated the use of the theory of CAS (systemic thinking), in order to try to find an innovative response to challenges (i.e. complexity, uncertainty) that the conventional approaches for schema matching are still facing.

We think that the CAS could bring us the adaptation capability to the realm of schema matching tools (self-configuration and self-optimization), which should relieve the user from the complexity and effort resulting from configuring and optimizing the automatic schema matching systems.

Our conceptual model for schema matching, based on the theory of complexity, sees the schema matching process as a complex adaptive system (Fig. 4).

In this model, each schema element of the schemas to match (source or target schema) is modeled as an autonomous agent, belonging to a population (source or target schema population). Each agent behaviors and interaction, at the micro level, with the other agents in the opposite population and with its environment, brings out at the macro level, a self-organized system which represents the global solution to matching problem (i.e. relationships between schemas elements). In other words, the resolution of the matching problem goes through individual effort deployed by each agent, locally, throughout the simulation to find the best match in the opposite population.

We think that many intrinsic properties of our model, derived from the ABMS modeling approach, can contribute efficiently to the increase of the matching quality and thus the decrease of the matching uncertainty:

- Emergence: The emergence of the macro solution (schema matching) from local behaviors, rules and interactions between agents (micro solutions).
- Self-organization: The cooperation of source and target schema elements (represented as agents) to reach a consensus about their best matching.
- Stochasticity (randomness): The randomness on which the model is based gives the ability to perform statistical analysis on the outcome of multiple simulations (meta-simulation) for the same matching scenario.

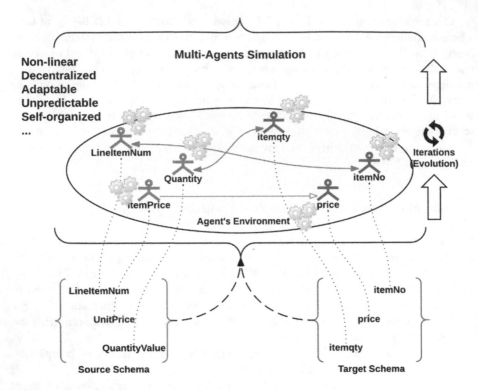

Fig. 4. Schema Matching as Multi-Agents Simulation (non-linear process with emergence-based resolution)

3.1 Schema Matching as Agent-Based Simulation (SMAS)

Briefly, our idea is to model the Schema Matching process as interactions, within a self-organized environment, between agents called "Schema Attribute Agent". In the rest of the paper we are going to refer to the "Schema Element Agent" simply as agent. Each schema element is modeled as an agent belonging to one of two populations: source or target schema group. Furthermore, the schema matching process is modeled as the interaction between the two populations of agents.

The figure bellow illustrates how the schema source and target elements are represented as two sets of agents in a simulation environment (Fig. 5).

In our model the internal architecture of the agents is Rule-based (reflexive agent). The agents have as a main goal to find the best matching agent within the other group of agents. The foundation of the rules governing the agent's behaviors is stochasticity (randomness). In fact, a certain degree of randomness is present in each step executed by each agent during the simulation.

Below are the steps executed during each tick of the simulation run:

1. Calculation of the name similarity: each agent calculates the similarity between its name and all other agent names (in the other group) and identify the best match

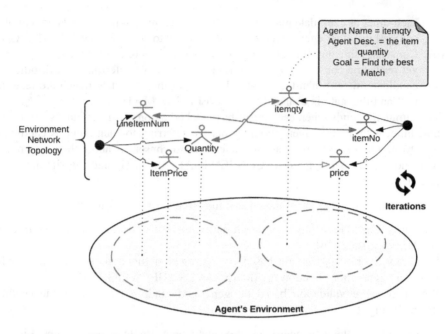

Fig. 5. Schema Element modeled as simulation agents

based on the best name similarity score. For each similarity calculation a similarity measure is selected randomly from a similarity measures list. The score should be greater than a random TREASHOLD (generated random threshold value within interval).

2. Calculation of the Comment Similarity: each agent calculates the similarity between its comment and all other agent comments (in the other group) and identify the best match based on the best comment similarity score. Again, for each similarity calculation a similarity measure is selected randomly from a similarity measures list. The score should be greater than a random TREASHOLD (generated random threshold value within interval).

3. Compare the best matches: If the best match for name and the best match for comment are converging to the same Agent (in the other group) then the agent identify it as the candidate match and update its status from "UNDEFI-NED_MATCH" to "CANDIDATE_MATCH". An aggregation calculation is done between name similarity score and comment similarity score of the candidate match. The aggregation function is selected randomly from an aggregation function list (MAX, AVERAGE, WEIGHTED). If the new aggregated score is greater than a random TREASHOLD (generated random threshold value within interval) and is better that the one obtained previously the object CandidateMatchingAttribute is updated with the new scores (name and comment).

4. Check for Consensus:
   (a) Consensus watching: watch for other agents candidate match update in order to check if a consensus was reached with another agent (both agents are referring to

each-other as candidate match). If so then the agent coalition is updated with the name of the other agent and the state is changed to "CONSENSUAL_MATCH"

  (b) Consensus timeout: If after a certain number of ticks (e.g. 250) the agent has not yet reached a consensus with another agent (both are referring to each-other as candidate match) then the agent beliefs about the candidate match are reset to null and the state is changed to "UNDEFINED_MATCH"

5. The simulation ends when each agent has reached a consensus, about its candidate matching, with another agent (both agents are referring to each-other as candidate match). In other words, if all agents have reached consensus about their matchings then their status is changed to "CONSENSUAL_MATCH" and the simulation is ended.

The main random elements influencing the simulation are as follows:

- Similarity Calculation based on a similarity measures selected randomly from a similarity measures list.
- Similarity Scores aggregation based on aggregation functions selected randomly from an aggregation function list (MAX, AVERAGE, WEIGHTED).
- Similarity score validation based on generated random threshold value (within interval) (Fig. 6).

The state of the agent changes to the next state per a simple transition rules (Fig. 7).

As opposed to deterministic solutions for schema matching, all the existing matching solutions, the nondeterministic and stochastic nature of our agent-based simulation increases the confidence in the quality of the matching results. Despite the fact, that the agent's behaviors are based on randomness (e.g. during the similarity calculation), our model can often produce the right matchings at the end of each simulation run.

The main key-features of our conceptual model could be summarized as follow:

- Stochastic Linguistic Matching: Similarity Calculation based on a similarity measures selected randomly from a similarity measures list. Similarity Scores aggregation based on aggregation functions selected randomly from an aggregation function list (MAX, AVERAGE, WEIGHTED). Similarity score validation based on generated random threshold value (within interval) (Fig. 8).
- Consensual Matching Selection: To form a valid pairing/correspondence the two agents (form opposite populations: source and target schemas) should refer to each other as candidate match (in the same time: tick) (Fig. 9).
- Meta-Simulations and Statistical Analysis: Performing statistical analysis on multiple simulation runs data is a good way to improve the confidence in the matching result obtained from our model (Fig. 10).

We believe that the conceptualization and the modeling of schema matching as multi-agent simulation will allow the design of a system exhibiting the following characteristics: (i) an easy to understand system, composed of simple reflexive "agents" interacting according to simple rules, and also (ii) an effective and efficient system, capable of autonomously changing over time, to adapt, and self-organize in order to make emerge a solution for any given matching scenario.

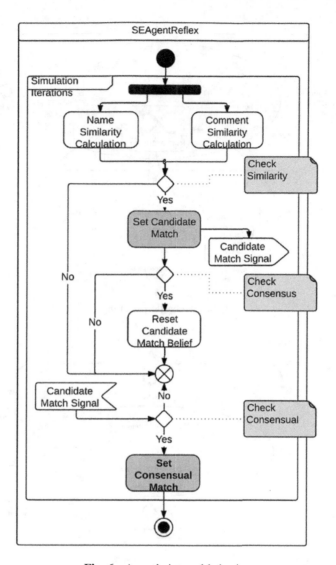

Fig. 6. Agent's internal behavior

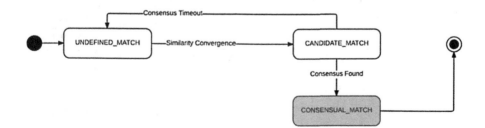

Fig. 7. Transition between states

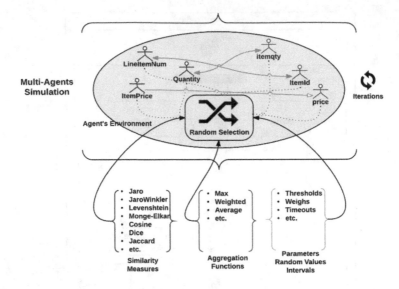

Fig. 8. Stochastic matching

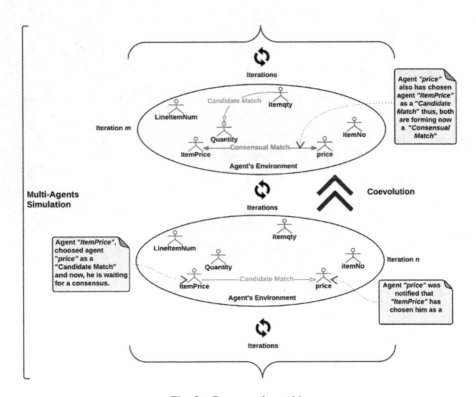

Fig. 9. Consensual matching

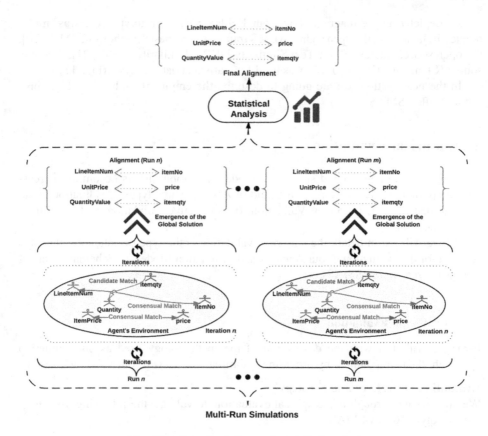

Fig. 10. Meta-simulation and statistical analysis

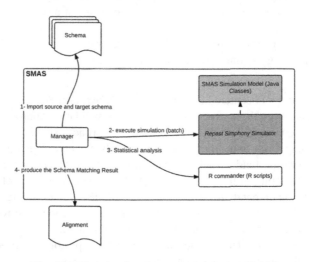

Fig. 11. High-level architecture for Reflex-SMAS

As depicted in the diagram above, our Relflex-SMAS prototype core was implemented in Java using the open source ABMS framework Repast Simphony (2.1) [19, 20], the open source framework for Text Similarity DKPro Similarity (2.1.0) [21], the open source R language (R 3.1.0) [22] was used for statistical data analysis (Fig. 11).

In the next section, we are going to describe the empirical evaluation of the prototype Reflex-SMAS.

4   Empirical Evaluation

The validation of agent-based simulation models is a topic that is becoming increasingly important in the literature on the field of ABMS. Three types of validation could be identified [23]: (i) Empirical Validation, (ii) Predictive Validation, and (iii) Structural Validation.

As we will see in detail, the empirical validation is the type of validation that was adopted for the evaluation of our Agent-based Simulation Model for Schema Matching (i.e. prototype Reflex-SMAS).

4.1   Prototype Evaluation

First, we will start with the description of the methodology used as our validation approach, then we continue by providing a summarized view of our validation results.

Evaluation Objectives and Strategy

We are seeking, through this empirical evaluation, to validate the following aspects of our prototype Reflex-SMAS:

- That our solution is, indeed, an effective and efficient automatic schema matching system, capable of autonomously changing behaviors and evolving over time, to adapt, and to self-organize and thus make the solution for any matching scenario to emerge.
- That our solution is easy to understand and therefore could display a high degree of maintainability (e.g. adding new matchers).

The proof strategy is centered around conducting experiments and then collecting and analyzing data from these experiments. Thus, the validation approach that we have adopted could be considered as a hybrid validation approach combining two validation approaches coming from two different fields, namely Schema Matching and ABMS. On one hand, from the field of Schema Matching, we are leveraging a popular evaluation method consisting of the comparison of results with those expected by the user [24], and on the other hand, from the field of ABMS, we are using the Empirical Validation [23] which is mainly based on the comparison among the results obtained from the model and what we can observe in the real system.

Thus, the strategy adopted for the validation of our prototype (implementing our multi-agent simulation model for schema matching) consists of:

- defining different synthetic matching scenarios (three matching scenarios namely "Person", "Order" and "Travel") with different sizes and different level of lexical heterogeneity, so we can evaluate the prototype matching performance in different situations (adaptation);
- conducting experiments, compiling results and evaluating the matching performance by comparing, for those three matching scenarios, the matching results (matchings) obtained from our prototype Reflex-SMAS with the results expected by the user.

In the first matching scenarios "Person" we need to match two schemas with small size (i.e. six elements) showing a medium lexical heterogeneity level (Fig. 12).

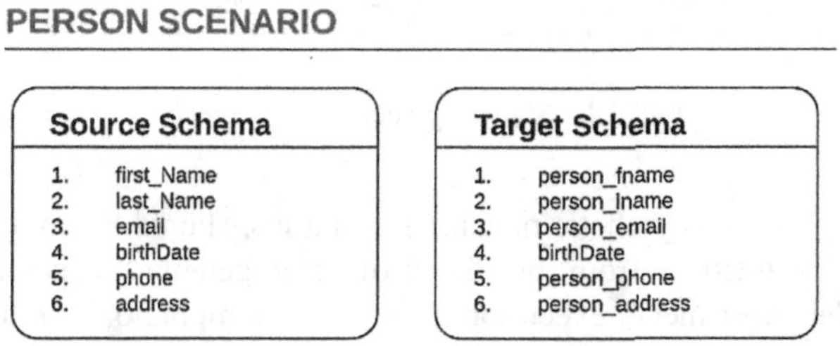

PERSON SCENARIO

Source Schema		Target Schema	
1.	first_Name	1.	person_fname
2.	last_Name	2.	person_lname
3.	email	3.	person_email
4.	birthDate	4.	birthDate
5.	phone	5.	person_phone
6.	address	6.	person_address

Fig. 12. Matching scenario "Person"

The second matching scenarios "Order" is composed of schemas with medium size with a high lexical heterogeneity level (Fig. 13).

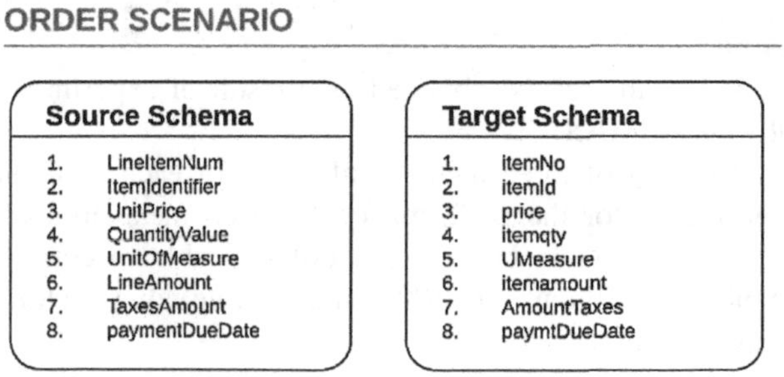

ORDER SCENARIO

Source Schema		Target Schema	
1.	LineItemNum	1.	ItemNo
2.	ItemIdentifier	2.	itemId
3.	UnitPrice	3.	price
4.	QuantityValue	4.	itemqty
5.	UnitOfMeasure	5.	UMeasure
6.	LineAmount	6.	itemamount
7.	TaxesAmount	7.	AmountTaxes
8.	paymentDueDate	8.	paymtDueDate

Fig. 13. Matching scenario "Order"

The schemas in the last matching scenarios "Travel" have a relatively big size with a low lexical heterogeneity level (Fig. 14).

In order to assess the relevance and level of difficulty that can represent those synthetic matching scenarios (i.e. "Person", "Order" and "Travel"), we decided to evaluate them, first, using the well-known matching tool COMA [25–27]. Since, the COMA tool was not able to resolve all the all expected matches for those scenarios, we

TRAVEL SCENARIO

Source Schema	
1.	departure
2.	Destination
3.	DepartDate
4.	RetDate
5.	FlightNumber
6.	BookClass
7.	Meal
8.	Duration
9.	Distance
10.	Airport
11.	Baggage
12.	Reservation
13.	Price
14.	SeatMap
15.	TicketNum

Target Schema	
1.	departureCity
2.	DestinationCity
3.	DepartureDate
4.	ReturnDate
5.	FlightNo
6.	BookingClass
7.	MealService
8.	JourneyDuration
9.	JourneyDistance
10.	SameAirportInd
11.	BaggageAllowance
12.	AirReservation
13.	PricingOverview
14.	SeatMapDetails
15.	TicketNumber

Fig. 14. Matching scenario "Travel"

can say that the proposed synthetic matching scenarios, should be enough challenging scenarios for our validation (from their level of heterogeneity perspective).

Regarding the experiments execution and results compilation, we have decided to run series of three meta-simulations for each scenario (each meta-simulation includes 10 simulations).

The final matching result is based on a statistical analysis of each meta-simulation outcome. In other word, the matching result is based on the calculation of the frequency of occurrence of a found match on the ten simulations composing the meta-simulation. Furthermore, executing for each scenario the meta-simulations three times, is a choice that have been made to help with the assessment of the experiment repeatability.

Experiment Results
This section summarizes the results obtained as a result of experiments conducted to evaluate the tool Reflex-SMAS.

After executing the set of three meta-simulations for each matching scenario we have compiled the results for the performance for each meta-simulation for all scenarios. As indicated in the table below, our tool was able to correctly find all the expected correspondence by the user (a 100% success rate) after each meta-simulation, and for each scenario (Table 1).

Now, if we compare the results of our Reflex-SMAS prototype with COMA tool results, we can clearly notice that our tool outperformed the COMA tool in all the syntactic matching scenarios. The table below shows the compared result for Reflex-SMAS vs. COMA (Table 2).

The figure below shows a comparison of the performance obtained for scenarios "Person", "Order" and "Travel" with our prototype compared to those obtained with the COMA tool (Fig. 15).

In order to challenge the "perfect" results obtained with our tool Reflex-SMAS for the synthetic matching scenarios, we were curious to know to what extent the performance obtained at the meta-simulations, may be impacted by a reduction in the

Table 1. Reflex-SMAS experiment combined results

Scenario	M.S.[a]	M. to F.[b]	C.M.F.[c]	% C.M.F.[d]
Person	1	6	6	100%
Person	2	6	6	100%
Person	3	6	6	100%
Order	1	8	8	100%
Order	2	8	8	100%
Order	3	8	8	100%
Travel	1	15	15	100%
Travel	2	15	15	100%
Travel	3	15	15	100%

[a] Meta-Simulation.
[b] Matchings to Find.
[c] Correct Matchings Found.
[d] % Correct Matchings Found.

Table 2. Reflex-SMAS vs. COMA experiment combined results

Scenario	M. to F.	Reflex-SMAS C.M.F.	% C.M.F.	COMA C.M.F.	% C.M.F.
Person	6	6	100%	5	83%
Order	8	8	100%	6	75%
Travel	15	15	100%	13	87%

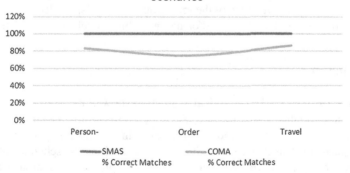

Fig. 15. Comparative result between Reflex-SMAS and COMA

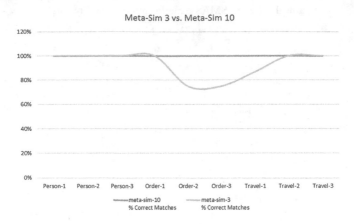

Fig. 16. Meta-simulation with 3 vs. 10 individual simulations

number of individual simulations composing a meta-simulation. So, we decided to conduct further experimentation, reducing, this time, the number of individual simulations of a meta-simulation from ten simulations to only three simulations (Fig. 16).

As we can notice in the figure above, the performance obtained in the experiment with the meta-simulations composed of three individual simulations instead of ten, has dropped for the scenarios "Order" and "Travel". Which means that our matching tool Reflex-SMAS was not able to properly find all the expected matchings during some of the meta-simulations for those two scenarios (due to the high level of heterogeneity of the scenario "Order" and the big size of the scenario "Travel"). Unquestionably, we can conclude that the number of individual simulations, composing the meta-simulation is an important factor to ensure good matching performance (better quantification of the uncertainty regarding the outcome of the matching process) especially when it comes to scenarios involving large schemas and/or having a high level of heterogeneity.

5   Conclusion

Our prototype (Reflex-SMAS) empirical evaluation showed us clearly its capability of providing a high-quality result for different schema matching scenarios without any optimization or tuning from the end-user (the experiments results could be considered as very satisfactory). Thus, we can conclude that approaching the schema matching as a CAS and modeling it as ABMS is viable and very promising approach that could greatly help to overcome the problems of uncertainty and complexity in the field of schema matching.

As future work, we are planning to enhance the conceptual model of our prototype to tackle challenges such as complex schema ($n{:}m$ cardinalities) by exploiting other Similarity Measures such as Structural Similarities (schemas structures).

References

1. Rahm, E., Bernstein, P.A.: A survey of approaches to automatic schema matching. VLDB J. **10**(4), 334–350 (2001)
2. Bohannon, P., Elnahrawy, E., Fan, W., Flaster, M.: Putting context into schema matching. In: Proceedings of the 32nd International Conference on Very Large Data Bases, pp. 307–318 (2006)
3. Cross, V.: Uncertainty in the automation of ontology matching. In: Fourth International Symposium on Uncertainty Modeling and Analysis, ISUMA 2003, pp. 135–140 (2003)
4. Madhavan, J., Bernstein, P.A., Rahm, E.: Generic schema matching with cupid. VLDB **1**, 49–58 (2001)
5. Villanyi, B., Martinek, P., Szamos, A.: Voting based fuzzy linguistic matching. In: 2014 IEEE 15th International Symposium on Computational Intelligence and Informatics (CINTI), pp. 27–32 (2014)
6. Duchateau, F., Bellahsene, Z.: Designing a benchmark for the assessment of schema matching tools. Open J. Databases OJDB **1**(1), 3–25 (2014)
7. Zhang, C.J., Chen, L., Jagadish, H.V., Cao, C.C.: Reducing uncertainty of schema matching via crowdsourcing. Proc. VLDB Endow. **6**(9), 757–768 (2013)
8. Viet, H.N.Q., Luong, H.X., Miklos, Z., Aberer, K., Quan, T.T.: A MAS negotiation support tool for schema matching. In: The Twelfth International Conference on Autonomous Agents and Multiagent Systems (2013)
9. Shvaiko, P., Euzenat, J.: Ontology matching: state of the art and future challenges. IEEE Trans. Knowl. Data Eng. **25**(1), 158–176 (2013)
10. Peukert, E.: Process-based schema matching: from manual design to adaptive process construction (2013)
11. Peukert, E., Eberius, J., Rahm, E.: A self-configuring schema matching system. In: 2012 IEEE 28th International Conference on Data Engineering (ICDE), pp. 306–317 (2012)
12. Nian-Feng, W., Xing-Chun, D.: Uncertain schema matching based on interval fuzzy similarities. Int. J. Adv. Comput. Technol. **4**(1) (2012)
13. Ngo, D., Bellahsene, Z.: YAM++: a multi-strategy based approach for ontology matching task. In: Teije, A., et al. (eds.) EKAW 2012. LNCS, vol. 7603, pp. 421–425. Springer, Heidelberg (2012). doi:10.1007/978-3-642-33876-2_38
14. Gong, J., Cheng, R., Cheung, D.W.: Efficient management of uncertainty in XML schema matching. VLDB J. — Int. J. Very Large Data Bases **21**(3), 385–409 (2012)
15. Sarma, A.D., Dong, X.L., Halevy, A.Y.: Uncertainty in data integration and dataspace support platforms. In: Bellahsene, Z., Bonifati, A., Rahm, E. (eds.) Schema Matching and Mapping. Data-Centric Systems and Applications, pp. 75–108. Springer, Heidelberg (2011)
16. Gal, A.: Managing uncertainty in schema matching with Top-K schema mappings. In: Spaccapietra, S., Aberer, K., Cudré-Mauroux, P. (eds.) Journal on Data Semantics VI. LNCS, vol. 4090, pp. 90–114. Springer, Heidelberg (2006). doi:10.1007/11803034_5
17. Gal, A.: Uncertain schema matching. Synth. Lect. Data Manag. **3**(1), 1–97 (2011)
18. Fortin, R.: Comprendre la complexité: introduction à La Méthode d'Edgar Morin. Presses Université Laval (2005)
19. North, M.J., Tatara, E., Collier, N.T., Ozik, J.: Visual agent-based model development with repast simphony, Technical report, Argonne National Laboratory (2007)
20. North, M.J.: R and Repast Simphony (2010)
21. Bär, D., Zesch, T., Gurevych, I.: DKPro similarity: an open source framework for text similarity. In: Proceedings of the 51st Annual Meeting of the Association for Computational Linguistics: System Demonstrations, pp. 121–126 (2013)

22. R.C. Team, R: A language and environment for statistical computing. R Foundation for Statistical Computing, Vienna, Austria (2012). Open Access Available https://cran.r-project.org (2011)
23. Remondino, M., Correndo, G.: Mabs validation through repeated execution and data mining analisys. Int. J. Simul. Syst. Sci. Technol. 7(6) (2006)
24. Bellahsene, Z., Bonifati, A., Duchateau, F., Velegrakis, Y.: On evaluating schema matching and mapping. In: Bellahsene, Z., Bonifati, A., Rahm, E. (eds.) Schema Matching and Mapping. Data-Centric Systems and Applications, pp. 253–291. Springer, Heidelberg (2011)
25. Do, H.-H., Rahm, E.: COMA: a system for flexible combination of schema matching approaches. In: Proceedings of the 28th International Conference on Very Large Data Bases, pp. 610–621 (2002)
26. Aumueller, D., Do, H.-H., Massmann, S., Rahm, E.: Schema and ontology matching with COMA++. In: Proceedings of the 2005 ACM SIGMOD International Conference on Management of Data, pp. 906–908 (2005)
27. Massmann, S., Raunich, S., Aumüller, D., Arnold, P., Rahm, E.: Evolution of the COMA match system. In: Proceedings of the International Semantic Web Conference, pp. 49–60 (2011)

Author Index

Printed in the United States
By Bookmasters